Four Wise Men

Four Wise Men

The Lives and Teachings of
Confucius, the Buddha, Jesus, and Muhammad

Mark W. Muesse

CASCADE *Books* · Eugene, Oregon

FOUR WISE MEN
The Lives and Teachings of Confucius, the Buddha, Jesus, and Muhammad

Cascade Books
An Imprint of Wipf and Stock Publishers
199 W. 8th Ave., Suite 3
Eugene, OR 97401

www.wipfandstock.com

PAPERBACK ISBN: 978-1-4982-3222-7
HARDCOVER ISBN: 978-1-4982-3224-1
EBOOK ISBN: 978-1-4982-3223-4

Cataloguing-in-Publication data:

Names: Muesse, Mark W.

Title: Four wise men : the lives and teachings of Confucius, the Buddha, Jesus, and Muhammad / Mark W. Muesse.

Description: Eugene, OR: Cascade Books, 2017. | Includes bibliographical references.

Identifiers: ISBN: 978-1-4982-3222-7 (paperback) | 978-1-4982-3224-1 (hardback) | 978-1-4982-3223-4 (ebook)

Subjects: LCSH: Confucius. | Buddha. | Jesus Christ—Teachings. | Muḥammad, Prophet, –632.

Classification: BL41 M72 2017 (print) | BL41 (ebook)

Manufactured in the U.S.A.   JANUARY 11, 2017

In Honor of Four Wise Women

Ariyana Prabashwari Muesse
Dhammika Swarnamali Muesse
Lemma Mills Muesse
Prabashwari Wijerathne Pathirage

"Choose someone whose way of life as well as words, and whose very face as mirroring the character that lies behind it, have won your approval. Be always pointing him out to yourself either as your guardian or as your model. There is a need, in my view, for someone as a standard against which our characters can measure themselves. Without a ruler to do it against you won't make crooked straight."

SENECA

Contents

Acknowledgments

I am deeply grateful to the many colleagues, friends, and family members whose assistance and support have enabled me to bring this book into being. Professors Patrick Gray, John Kaltner, Han Li, Michael Drompp, and Steve McKenzie—all of whom are my colleagues at Rhodes College—and Nancy Eskridge, Director of Content Development at The Great Courses, generously provided me with thoughtful conversation and suggestions as the manuscript was taking shape. Maddie Carwile and Philip Culbertson furnished invaluable editorial scrutiny. I acknowledge the contributions of my students, too numerous to name, who demonstrated their enthusiasm and insight in the several seminars on Confucius, Buddha, Jesus, and Muhammad that I have facilitated at Rhodes College. A special note of appreciation to Suhail Mirza in London and Wasim Rock in Nazareth, Israel, who have been students from afar and who have become special friends. I thank those whose gift of friendship has sustained me in the years since this project first began. Among them, I am especially appreciative of my dear friends Pat Shade, Joel Chapman, Manoj Jain, David Peacock, Bill Walker, Bill Howell, Steve Haynes, Lu Ivory, Bob Scott, and Hal Bishop. And, as always, I am most grateful for the love of my family: my parents, Billy and Lemma Muesse; my wife, Dhammi; and our daughter, Ariyana. These last three, along with Dhammi's mother, Prabashwari Wijerathne Pathirage, are the four wise women to whom this book is dedicated.

A Note on Translations and Transliterations

This study relies heavily on primary texts that were originally written in languages other than English. Fortunately, most of these texts have been ably translated. In several cases, such as the *Analects* of Confucius, the New Testament, and the Qur'an, a great number of excellent translations, in fact, are widely available to English readers. In as much as possible, I have used these translations in my analysis. Often, I quote from several different translations of a single text in order to utilize the version that seems most accurate or apt. Because of this reliance on a variety of translations, there may be slight differences in the transliterations and diacritics of particular words (e.g., K'ung and Kong or Qur'an and Koran). When I am not quoting from a particular translation, I have employed the standard current transliteration system (e.g., the Pinyin rather than Wade-Giles for Chinese). For the sake of simplicity, I have omitted the use of most diacritical markings in the transliterations. Occasionally, I made my own renditions of the primary sources for stylistic or, less frequently, substantive reasons. Throughout the exposition, I have indicated when the rendering is my own.

Introduction

In 1978, astrophysicist Michael H. Hart published a provocative book that ranked the one hundred people who had most influenced world history. Hart's book, titled simply *The 100*, argued that the five most influential persons who ever lived were the Prophet Muhammad, Sir Isaac Newton, Jesus of Nazareth, the Buddha, and Confucius—in that order.[1] The book's appearance caused quite a stir, especially among folk who thought their particular hero was not rated highly enough or did not make the list at all. Much of the controversy was due to the failure of many to understand the author's intention. Hart was not trying to evaluate and rank the *best* persons who had ever lived. He was merely making judgments about the *impact* on history of prominent individuals. Certainly he had a point. While we might quibble about the order, any list of, say, a dozen persons who have most affected the course of human events would surely include Muhammad, Jesus, the Buddha, and Confucius.

While the historical influence of these four can hardly be doubted, what prompts this study is not simply an interest in history, although that fact alone certainly merits comparative investigation. My fascination with this quartet of sages derives from another concern, the same interest that led me to the study of religion and philosophy in the first place: the desire to know how to live life well. After over thirty years of studying the world's religious and philosophical traditions, I am convinced that these four figures represent some of our finest teachers of the art of living. There are others whom I might rank with Confucius, the Buddha, Jesus, and Muhammad, but no one who excels them. By their lives they have inspired me—and obviously countless others—with their dedication to living deeply and thoughtfully and with the courage they mustered in the face of adversity.

Because of their dual significance—as persons who decidedly shaped history and as teachers who offered compelling visions of how to live—this book addresses both historical and philosophical interests. We will talk

1. Hart, *The 100*.

about who these men were and what they said but also about the import of their lives and teachings for us today.

The approach to our study is simple, but it requires a bit of explanation and some justification. The overall structure is twofold. We will first study each figure separately, as an individual situated in his own time and place. Then, after considering each person independently, we will turn to a comparative study of their lives and their teachings.

The study of the four as individuals follows a chronological order. We begin with the most ancient figure, Confucius, followed by the Buddha, then Jesus, and finally Muhammad. This sequence implies nothing other than the passage of time. I am not suggesting any kind of philosophical, moral, or religious advancement or regression; we are merely considering these persons in the order in which they lived. Although there are occasional references to preceding chapters throughout the book, it is not essential that these four figures be studied in the order presented here. One might easily begin with Muhammad and end with Confucius.

To introduce each man, I will sketch out the historical and cultural framework that informed his life and worldview. In each case, we will see that he was born into an ancient culture in the midst of great changes. We will examine the nature of the cultural turbulence of his day to provide the essential details for understanding each man in greater context.

The study of his historical situation will be the background against which we will recount the major events in the life of each teacher. We will first examine the nature of the source materials for our biographical sketches and discuss some of the problems in obtaining a historically accurate picture of each of our sages. I will explain where the most recent scholarship draws the line between fact and legend in the accounts of their lives; often, there is considerable disagreement among scholars as to where that line should be drawn. As our discussion of their lives unfolds, we will begin to notice some remarkable similarities amid the obvious differences. We will observe how all four are reported to have had a royal or aristocratic lineage and yet were unable or unwilling to take advantage of the benefits of that heritage. We will note the accounts of unusual circumstances surrounding the conception and birth of each of the four and see some atypical features in their families of origin. In the life of each we will explore the pivotal moments of transformation in which some new insight is realized or new revelation received. Our biographical sketches then close with discussions of their later years and their deaths. Along the way, we will try to get a sense of the personal qualities and attributes that made these individuals who they were.

Outlining the life history of each figure will provide the framework for examining the essential components of his teachings and practices. In studying the wisdom these sages offered, we will be interested in a set of common questions. First, we will ask: How did each of the four understand the nature of the world and ultimate reality? This question puts us in the realm of what Western philosophy calls metaphysics. Metaphysics is that aspect of human thinking that reflects upon the fundamental character and qualities of reality in its broadest sense. Whenever we wonder about the origin of the universe or whether there is something deeper or something more to the world than the way it appears, we are entering the realm of metaphysics. Metaphysics tends to be a highly abstract way of thinking, since it tries to grasp the nature of reality in its entirety. Within this category, we will examine the way each of our subjects thought about the nature of the divine and the ultimate powers governing the world.

The next questions of our set pertain to what theologians and philosophers call anthropology. Anthropology in the philosophical sense should be distinguished from the academic discipline that also goes by that name. While the discipline of anthropology tends to focus on specific human groups, philosophical and theological anthropology is interested in understanding the nature of humanity in a more universal way. It wants to know whether or not there is such a thing as human nature and what the character of this nature might be. Philosophical anthropology investigates the distinctive qualities of being human and reflects on the meaning and purpose, if any, of human existence. As we study our four sages, we will look carefully at what each of them said—or assumed—about the nature of humanity. We will ask: What did he think about existence and the attributes of the self and of society? How did he envision the final fulfillment of humanity and human individuals? How did he understand the relationship between human beings and the rest of the world, including the ultimate reality?

Exploring the metaphysical and anthropological aspects of the teachings of each sage will clear the ground for discussing and understanding the moral principles each advocated. Here we enter the branch of philosophy and theology known as ethics. We will ask: How did each of the four think we should treat our fellow humans and other beings? What was the basis for his ethical views? Did he see proper human behavior as rooted in the will of a god or in the structure of the cosmos itself? Or did he think that morality was simply a social convention invented by human beings to facilitate our survival as a species but without any connection to a transcendent reality? These are the questions that will take center stage when we consider the ethical dimension of the teachings of the four.

Our final area of interest is spiritual discipline. When we move into this aspect of the sages' teachings, the central question that will occupy our attention is: What activities did each teacher encourage as a means of attaining full humanity and relating to the ultimate or fundamental reality? Within this category, we will explore the place of such things as ceremony and pilgrimage, feasting and fasting, and prayer and meditation in cultivating the life of the spirit. Confucius, the Buddha, Jesus, and Muhammad did not become the persons they were merely because they were endowed with certain gifts of understanding and insight. They all practiced specific regimens that enabled them to refine their innate talents and to deepen their wisdom and compassion for the world. Those of us who study and write about such persons often neglect the role of spiritual practices in their teachings, preferring instead to focus attention on their ideas and beliefs. I hope to counterbalance that tendency by placing special emphasis on the practical disciplines they observed. I contend that by stressing spiritual practice, we are being more faithful to the lives and teachings of our four subjects, each of whom made *acting* a certain way as important as—if not more important than—*believing* a certain way.

To conclude the study of each figure as an individual, we will examine the reverberations of his life in its immediate context and in world history. The principal focus of investigation now turns to the development of the traditions with which he is associated and to the way his life and teachings were interpreted in the years subsequent to his death. Our study of each figure therefore begins in history with an examination of his cultural context, and returns to history with a consideration of how his life affected that context and the world at large.

Before we move on to discuss the comparative feature of this course, let me comment briefly on how I have structured the consideration of each teacher. First, I have separated the study of each man's life from the study of his teachings. I am not very happy about doing this. What troubles me about this division is the fact that in a very important sense, each man's life *was* his teaching. To modify a phrase from Marshall McLuhan, the man was the message.[2] The Hasidic tradition of Judaism relates the story of the famous rabbi Leib Saras (1730-1796), who had just returned from a visit to *his* rabbi and was asked by family and friends what words of Torah he had learned. Rebbe Saras replied, "I did not go to my teacher to hear his words of Torah; I went to see how he ties his shoelaces."[3] All good teachers know they teach as much by example as by the words they utter.

2. McLuhan, *Understanding Media*.
3. Kurzweil, *On the Road with Rabbi Steinsaltz*, 143.

This was especially true for the individuals we study here. Confucius was the exemplar of the kind of person he taught others to be. His protégés gained as much from observing him act as they did from listening to him talk. The Buddha not only spoke about the path to *nibbana*, or nirvana, as it is better known; he walked that way himself, and others could see the fruits of *nibbana* in his very life. The apostle Paul, perhaps the most important interpreter of Jesus, never once cited one of Jesus's parables or sayings; Paul was almost exclusively concerned with the crucified and resurrected Jesus, as if to suggest that in those events of his life the real significance of Jesus was revealed. Aishah, one of the wives of the Prophet Muhammad, was once asked about the personal qualities of her husband, and she replied, "His character was the Qur'an."[4]

These observations all indicate that the lives of these four were inextricably connected to their teachings, yet I have structured these chapters in such a way that puts their lives and teachings asunder. How do I justify this? The reason is simple: to make things clearer. Later in the book, we will compare and contrast the patterns of their lives and the content of their teachings, and it will be much easier to do that once we have teased out the points of comparison as carefully and clearly as possible. We need always to bear in mind, however, that this analytical separation is an artificial one, created for the sake of helping us to see how the lives and teachings of these four both parallel and diverge. Fortunately, the fact that we cannot ever completely and neatly divide their lives and teachings will constantly remind us of the artificiality of this division.

The way we shall study the teachings is by means of another contrivance. Confucius did not sit down with his students and say, "Today, students, I'll be discussing my metaphysical position and my understanding of ultimate reality." Jesus did not gather his disciples by the Sea of Galilee and give them a lecture on his anthropological views of the nature and destiny of human beings. It might have made things easier for twenty-first-century scholars if they *had* taught that way, but I suspect they were not terribly concerned about packaging their ideas for the benefit of twenty-first-century scholars. These sages taught with yarns and parables, aphorisms and proverbs, and of course with their very lives. They were not academic philosophers and theologians, and for that we can all be grateful!

Obviously, none of our four teachers would have presented their ideas in the way we will study them here. But again, the rubrics we use are for the sake of clarity and to facilitate our comparative interests towards the end of the book. Someone else writing about these four—or any one

4. Al-Adab Al-Mufrad, Hadith 308, http://sunnah.com/urn/2203080/.

of them—might use a different set of categories to present their ideas. The framework I have suggested provides the best way I know to keep the material clearly organized, but it is not the only way. My discussions will certainly be colored by those aspects of the lives and teachings of the four that I find important and interesting. I will choose to highlight certain things and deemphasize others. For better or worse, there will be much of my own thinking involved in this study. Yet the same would be true of *any* presentation of their lives and thought. No one escapes this fact of interpretation. Please consider me as only one voice in vast chorus of interpretations seeking to understand the lives and teachings of these great sages. I encourage you, therefore, to read the interpretations of others and, more importantly, to read the words of these sages for yourself and form your own opinions about their views.

We should also note that the categories we will use—metaphysics and ultimate reality, anthropology, ethics, spiritual practices—do not all occupy the same place or play the same role in the teachings of these four. While Confucius, the Buddha, Jesus, and Muhammad all had things to say that fit under each of these rubrics, they did not all assign equal importance to each area. For instance, Confucius was far more concerned with ethical matters than he was with the question of ultimate reality. Jesus did not speak as much about spiritual exercises as he did about his god and appropriate human behavior. Furthermore, these categories will not always appear as discrete subjects in our analysis. In some cases, for instance, metaphysics and anthropology necessarily converge, as when the human being is regarded as a part of the ultimate reality. For some of the sages, ethics is an essential component of their spirituality. These categories are thus a kind of typology that seems nice and neat in theory but is not always as well-ordered when we begin the work of analyzing the actual teachings.

One final comment on methodology: Often, these four are regarded as the founders of four of the major world religions. For the purposes of this study, it is important that we try not to think of them too much in this light. None of these figures thought his mission in life was to establish a new religion; in some senses, in fact, each of them understood themselves as calling their contemporaries to return to ancient truths. Describing Confucius, the Buddha, Jesus, and Muhammad as religious "founders" may distort our understanding of the way they thought of their own lives and might expose them to judgments better reserved for those who call themselves their followers. Let us not make the mistake of evaluating any one of our four sages on the basis of what we think of the religion that developed in his wake. It is not intellectually responsible to impute uncritically to Jesus the views of Christians or to hold Muhammad accountable for all actions carried out in the name of Islam.

It is also important to remember that these figures are often associated with religions *other* than the one they ostensibly founded. The Buddha, for instance, may have spent a significant part of his life as what we today would call a Hindu, although that label would not have been available to him during his lifetime. He would not have identified himself as either a Hindu or a Buddhist. Furthermore, the Buddha is *still* associated with Hinduism, as many Hindus regard him as a manifestation of the god Vishnu, and he even played a small but fascinating role in Christian history, as we shall see when we study the Buddha's legacy to the world. And although Jesus is frequently called the founder of Christianity, Jesus was not a Christian. He was born a Jew and remained a Jew all his life. If this were a text on the founders of the world religions, I would probably name the apostle Paul the founder of Christianity, not Jesus. Christianity is the religion *about* Jesus, but it was not the religion *of* Jesus. Moreover, Jesus is a major figure in Islam. He is embraced by Islam as a *muslim*, that is, one who submits to the will of Allah, and as a great prophet to the world, second only to Muhammad himself.[5]

Let us therefore refrain from thinking of these four primarily as representatives or founders of four major religions. We will consider them first and foremost as individual teachers in their unique historical and cultural settings, and only secondarily in relation to the very complex realities that became the religions with which they are commonly associated.

The final part of this study will offer us the opportunity to reflect on Confucius, the Buddha, Jesus, and Muhammad from a comparative perspective and to discern ways in which their examples and teachings can continue to nourish the human spirit. One part of our analysis will be devoted to comparing the patterns of their personal lives. Although they were unique individuals separated by time and place, certain features of their biographies are surprisingly similar. I have already mentioned that they each lived at a time of cultural upheaval and that each could lay claim to an aristocratic heritage. We will also see some other unexpected commonalities, such as the fact that each survived at least one assassination attempt. Another section will compare their teachings and practices. We will ask: Were these sages actually saying the same thing, as many today would like to believe? While I think the answer to that question is basically no, at least on one essential point they do seem to agree, which is the conviction that self-centeredness thwarts human happiness and well-being. To counteract selfishness, they all taught methods for cultivating humility and compassion

5. For more analysis of these issues, see Muesse, "Crossing Boundaries."

for others. In the final part of the book, we will try to garner enduring lessons from these four and apply them to the world today.

One might contend that trying to compare these four figures is like comparing apples and oranges. Each was a unique individual and his significance for his followers was and is equally unique. In the minds of Christians, Jesus is the savior, the second person of the Trinity, the divine in human form. Some Christians might think, therefore, that he should not be placed on the same level as the other three—or any other human being. For Buddhists, the Buddha was indeed a human, like Jesus and the others, but by attaining Buddhahood, he transcended even the gods and so rose to a rank not only beyond the human but also beyond the divine. Muhammad, for Muslims, was one in a long line of over one hundred thousand prophets who presented Allah's will to humanity. But Muhammad was, nonetheless, different from all others; he was god's *final* messenger, the "seal of the prophets." His message was the *final* revelation, Allah's ultimate communication to the world. That fact sets him apart from all other humans, including the other prophets like Jesus.

On what basis, then, can we compare these four? In a sense, trying to compare them really *is* like comparing apples and oranges (and pears and bananas, to extend the metaphor a bit to fit our discussion). But the fact is, you actually *can* compare apples, oranges, pears, and bananas. After all, they are all edible fruit, contain seeds, and grow on trees. Although different in many ways, apples and oranges do share some bases for comparison, and so do Confucius, Buddha, Jesus, and Muhammad. For instance, they were all human beings—even though some of them were subject to claims of divinity or something greater—and they were all teachers of wisdom and compassion. On these points I think everyone will agree, including those who want to press further to claim a particular uniqueness for one or another sage. And so it is on this basis that we will take up our study. We do not deny that Jesus was the messiah for his followers, or that the Buddha excelled the common lot of humanity according to Buddhists. But the focus of our study will be their human lives and their vocations as teachers of wisdom and compassion.

When we discuss Confucius, Buddha, Jesus, and Muhammad, we are not merely speaking of historical figures like Napoleon or Marie Curie or even Michael Hart's number-two figure, Isaac Newton. For billions of persons around the world, one or more of these four is a *sacred* figure, which puts him in a different category altogether. In this work, I will strive to be sensitive to these sentiments. Accordingly, we will not attempt to rank these four in relation to one another. Although we will compare and contrast these individuals with each other, we will do so to gain deeper insight into their lives and teachings, not to rate them. I will do my best to treat all four with an even hand and show no favoritism to one over the others.

1

CONFUCIUS

Confucius's China

By the time Confucius was born in the sixth century BCE, China was already an ancient civilization. China was also an *anguished* civilization, in desperate need of renewal. Confucius was acutely aware of both facts. China's antiquity and its political and social problems informed Confucius's personal life profoundly, as well as the insights that ultimately shaped his philosophical vision and spiritual practice. Understanding his life and teachings thus requires a good grasp of China as it was 2,500 years ago, at least to the degree that our historical sources will allow. Because written documents from this time are rather scarce, the fine details of this sketch may at times recede into indistinctness, rendering an image that leaves much to the imagination, not unlike an old Chinese ink drawing. This image will be the background against which we will brush in our portrait of Confucius himself.

What Do We Mean by "China"?

Today we refer to the immediate world of Confucius as "China," but this was not a word that he would have known. It is rather ironic that the man who is renowned as perhaps the greatest Chinese of all time could not have identified himself as "Chinese." The term "China" is a word of Sanskritic and Persian origin, most likely based on the name Qin, one of the many ruling dynasties of East Asia. Since the Qin Dynasty did not come to power until the third century BCE, long after the death of Confucius, he would not have thought of himself as living in a country called China.

Confucius and his contemporaries would have referred to their civilization by many names, including *huaxia*—a word that could be translated as the Grand Florescence or Illustrious Blossoming. As this translation implies, the term *huaxia* suggests a cultural rather than a geographical or political identity. Instead of thinking of themselves as subjects of a kingdom or inhabitants of a terrestrial location, the ancient Chinese primarily identified themselves as participants in a specific way of life, a way they regarded as more refined than others. They considered those outside of *huaxia* culture to be "barbarian." These "barbarians" may have been ethnically indistinguishable from the "Chinese" and may have even lived within the geographical region we would call "China," but their style of life was different from that of *huaxia*. Since the difference between Chinese and barbarian was cultural and not ethnic or racial, barbarians could become "civilized"—that is, become Chinese—simply by adopting the distinguishing marks of *huaxia* culture, such as wearing particular clothing, eating certain kinds of food, and most important, practicing Chinese etiquette. We know today that the *huaxia* culture of Confucius's time was itself an amalgam of many different and distinct regional cultures that gradually influenced one another to form the grand florescence that Confucius and later Chinese considered to be a single culture and the primary identifier of the "Chinese" people.

Another word that denotes this sense of cultural rather than ethnic identity is *zhongguo*,[1] a term meaning the "central kingdom." As the name intimates, those who belonged to the central kingdom regarded themselves as the center of civilization, not unlike the way Bostonians sometimes to refer to their city as the "Hub of the Universe."[2] But *zhongguo* also had a more literal sense. By the time of Confucius, the ruling dynasty of this region— the Zhou Dynasty—governed from a kingdom surrounded by numerous vassal states that owed allegiance to the Zhou family. The central kingdom was indeed in the middle of things.

Throughout its long history, the geopolitical contours of *huaxia* culture have changed greatly.[3] For much of its past, Chinese culture was centered in the Yellow River Valley, located in the northeastern quadrant of the area occupied by the present-day People's Republic of China. In the last four

---

1. The term *zhongguo* first appeared in the *Shujing* (*The Classic of History*) in the sixth century BCE.

2. The phrase "Hub of the Universe" was coined by Oliver Wendell Holmes. The hub is more precisely located at Filene's in downtown Boston.

3. See http://en.wikipedia.org/wiki/Image:Territories_of_Dynasties_in_China.gif/ to see how these contours have changed.

millennia, the external boundaries of China have expanded, contracted, and assumed an array of shapes; its internal divisions, likewise, have changed in many different ways.

Why the Past Mattered

When Confucius reflected on his cultural identity, he thought not only of his immediate era but the whole of its past as well. For Confucius, the past was profoundly significant and simply could not be separated from the present. His view of the world embraced the ancient as well as the contemporary. In a sense that modern Westerners might find difficult to grasp, the past was still alive for the Chinese. One can observe this characteristic in ancestor reverence, a fundamental religious practice that runs throughout Chinese history. In ancestor worship, the dead are treated as still existent and significant in everyday life. Ancestors must not be neglected by their descendants, who must attend to them with food and gifts and seek their advice on important matters. The veneration of ancestors symbolizes the way past and present interrelate in Chinese thought.

As moderns, we often take a cavalier attitude toward the past, in part because we frequently judge our own era as more advanced than that of bygone ages. As Henry Ford so bluntly put it, "History is more or less bunk."[4] Such a quip about the past would have appalled Confucius. In fact, he would have considered that judgment itself to be both a symptom and a *cause* of the sorry state of the world. For Confucius, forgetting the past did not condemn us to repeat it, as the philosopher George Santayana famously said,[5] but rather dooms us to moral and spiritual decline. A true conservative, Confucius *longed* to repeat the past—or at least one outstanding part of it.

His orientation to the past is one thing that sets Confucius apart from the Buddha, Jesus, and Muhammad. While these other three were not necessarily inattentive to the past, the focus of their teachings took different temporal trajectories. The Buddha, as we shall see, grounded his spirituality in the present moment, even to the extent that some of his later interpreters regarded him as denying the reality of the past and the future altogether. Jesus and Muhammad, on the other hand, placed a great emphasis on the future. Jesus proclaimed the coming of new divine order, and Muhammad regarded the approaching day of requital as the final moment of reckoning for believers and unbelievers alike. Only in Confucius do we find a teacher

4. Ford, *Chicago Tribune*, May 25, 1916.

5. "Those who cannot remember the past are condemned to repeat it" (Santayana, *Life of Reason*).

whose fundamental spiritual practice involved taking the past as the guide to, and the standard for, living in present. "If by keeping the old warm one can provide understanding of the new," he told his followers, "one is fit to be a teacher."[6]

The Legendary History of China

The past for which Confucius pined was the early society of the Yellow River Valley. Dating to at least the fifth millennium BCE, the Yellow River culture was old enough and sophisticated enough for it to be considered in modern times as one of "cradles of civilization." The evidence disclosed by archaeologists suggests that by the end of the Neolithic period, the citizens of this area were practicing elaborate burials and other rituals and had established social hierarchies regulated by patrilineal descent. Both ritual performance and social stratification were extremely important elements throughout later Chinese history, and both figured prominently in the life and teachings of Confucius. Sometime after 2,000 BCE, the citizens of the ancient Yellow River culture had mastered the use of bronze and developed the rudiments of a writing system.

By tradition, the Chinese remember this ancient past in a slightly different manner than just described. To be sure, Chinese tradition, like modern historiography, regarded this predynastic period as the time in which the basic features of civilization were established, including agriculture, carpentry, religious rituals, government, and writing. But the traditional legends also recall this era as an age when wise and benevolent monarchs ruled the land. Stories mention numerous philosopher-kings who were pious individuals reigning with only the welfare of the people at heart. Of special note were Yao, Shun, and Yu, the last three of a group called the Five Emperors. From the perspective of modern historiography, these figures were either altogether fictional or greatly exaggerated representations of actual rulers. Be that as it may, these three were often invoked as models of moral kingship, an ideal image against which lesser rulers were compared when times were bad. The last of these great sage-emperors—Yu—is traditionally considered the founder of China's first dynasty, the Xia. But just as the historicity of these great kings is in doubt, so too the historicity of the Xia Dynasty is debated. This time in China's past is in that area of our sketch where the details become fuzzy and ultimately vanish.

---

6. Dawson, trans., *Analects* 2:11 (p. 7).

The Shang Dynasty

As we enter the next era of Chinese history, details slowly begin to come into greater clarity. This period is known as the Shang Dynasty, the earliest epoch that has been amply verified as historical. The Shang probably began sometime in the sixteenth or fifteenth century BCE in the Yellow River Valley. For many years, most scholars thought that the Shang Dynasty was part of the mythic prehistory of China, simply because there was no tangible evidence from the Shang period.

A little more than a century ago, however, the discovery of a curiosity first known as "dragon bones" changed that. These dragon bones, which actually turned out to be tortoise shells and bovine shoulder blades, not only proved the historicity of the Shang Dynasty but also revealed a good deal about the religious and political practices of the time. Inscribed on these shells and bones in an archaic script were all manner of questions inquiring about such things as the best time to plant a crop, the meaning of a dream, whether or not a particular ancestor was pleased with a sacrificial gift, and when to leave for a journey or to set out on a military expedition. Modern scholars determined that after they were inscribed, the shells or bones were heated, which caused them to crack. The resulting patterns were then interpreted as providing answers to the questions posed. There is no doubt that these animal artifacts were used for the practice of divining—the art of consulting the spirit world to gain knowledge that could not otherwise be available to human beings. The fact that over one hundred thousand such fragments of bone and shell have been recovered indicates that divination was an extremely important part of this early period in China and that it was used for both religious and political purposes.

The questions etched into these fragments are what provide us with the greatest insight into the Shang period. From them we learn that the Shang was an agrarian culture whose members revered the dead and ritually offered them sacrifices of food and wine. We know that the king played an especially important role in these rituals, and his success in pleasing the ancestors and keeping harmony with the spirit world was essential to the welfare of the kingdom. We also learn that Shang armies fought frequent wars with neighboring realms and with nomads from the inner Asian steppes. These facts are significant for our purposes because they bear greatly on our understanding of Confucius, who had much to say about respect for ancestors and family members, about the king's role in effecting the happiness of his subjects, about war and peace, and about the importance of ritual. Confucius's concern with these subjects put him in a long-standing Chinese tradition.

The Early Zhou Dynasty

Scholars are not absolutely sure when the Shang Dynasty began, but they have a fairly precise idea of when it ended. In or around the year 1045 BCE, the Shang rulers were conquered and deposed by the rulers of a neighboring realm, thus initiating the next epoch in Chinese history, the Zhou Dynasty. This dynasty ruled, at least in name, for some eight hundred years, until it was supplanted by the Qin Dynasty in 221 BCE.

The founder of the Zhou Dynasty is traditionally considered to be King Wen, who was known as the "Cultured King" and who was also credited with contributing to a very important book of divination called the *Yijing*, or *The Book of Changes*. King Wen had been a feudal lord who was imprisoned by the last Shang king. When his son, later known as King Wu (the "Martial King"), overthrew Shang rule, he freed his father from imprisonment and bestowed on him the honorary title "king," although King Wu himself was the actual ruler. But shortly after the conquest, King Wu died, leaving the throne to his thirteen-year-old son. Fortunately for the nascent dynasty, King Wu's younger brother Dan stepped in to act as regent for the teenage sovereign. Although he might have attempted to gain the monarchy for himself, Dan, who is usually known by his title, the Duke of Zhou, chose instead to serve as the power behind the throne. These figures in the early history of the Zhou Dynasty—especially the duke—came to be regarded as the paragons of leadership and moral behavior by later Chinese, including Confucius. Confucius's admiration of Dan was so deep that he reports having frequent dreams about the duke. Undoubtedly part of Confucius's veneration of the Duke of Zhou derived from the sage's own aspiration to high office as an advisor to royalty.

The duke's reputation as a moral exemplar was shaped by what cynics might regard as a public relations campaign to legitimize the Zhou conquest of the Shang. Most scholars believe that the duke essentially invented the theory of *tianming*, the mandate of heaven. According to this concept, the ruler governed with divine sanction *as long as* he was virtuous. If a ruler became corrupt or inept, heaven withdrew its mandate and the ruler's reign was no longer morally legitimate. On the basis of this doctrine, opposing and even deposing the king could be morally justified—and wresting power from the Shang rulers, of course, was exactly what the Zhou family had done. The Zhou people claimed that the Shang kings had neglected their commitment to virtue—and there probably was some merit to that allegation—and that consequently heaven's mandate had passed to the Zhou. From that point on, the theory of the mandate of heaven came to assume a critical role throughout Chinese history, up until the twentieth century.

Those who would govern China had to invoke this doctrine to demonstrate their legitimacy as rulers.

Despite the high esteem in which later Chinese held the early Zhou rulers, the Zhou reign was not as culturally advanced as the Shang Dynasty it replaced. Zhou culture lacked a writing system and skill in bronzework, but it soon acquired these practices. The Zhou rulers also adopted many of the Shang's religious observances. The Zhou kings even gave a parcel of land to the remaining Shang family members so that they could continue to worship and sacrifice to their ancestors. The Zhou rulers themselves probably worshiped the Shang ancestors, although they had ousted their descendants!

The Later Zhou Dynasty

Despite the adoption of Shang ways and the claim to govern by virtue of moral superiority, the Zhou period was not an altogether happy time in Chinese history. Even though it lasted eight hundred years and was China's longest dynasty, serious rifts began to appear just a few centuries after its establishment. In the year 771 BCE, the Zhou king was murdered by an invading alliance of Chinese and barbarians, and the capital had to be moved further eastward. This easterly move marked a division between what is known as the Western Zhou and Eastern Zhou periods. The Eastern Zhou, which lasted about 550 years, was further divided into two eras known as the Spring and Autumn Period and the Period of Warring States.

The Spring and Autumn age obtained its designation from a book titled *The Spring and Autumn Annals*, a chronicle that was traditionally—but probably incorrectly—attributed to Confucius. During this era, the power of the Zhou Dynasty declined significantly, destabilizing the entire region. Many smaller kingdoms that had been subject to the Zhou rulers saw this weakening as a chance to assert their independence. As these vassal states began to vie with one another to succeed the ancient dynasty, violence and lawlessness ran rampant. Political power became more localized and invested in so-called hegemons, who were essentially warlords powerful enough to dominate weaker rivals. Might, rather than virtue, now came to be seen as the hallmark of the ruler. This political flux engendered rapid social changes as well. The old nobility began to lose privileges based on birth, creating a new class of persons who were of noble descent yet who were increasingly required to prove themselves by talent and hard work. Confucius was born into this new social rank.

The political situation had greatly deteriorated when the Period of Warring States began. This era, which lasted from 403 to 221 BCE, was characterized by extensive fighting among the many principalities that had once been loyal to the Zhou kingdom. By now, the nature of war itself had begun to change. Chariot warfare conducted by aristocrats was being replaced by a mounted cavalry and an infantry composed mainly of conscripted peasants armed with crossbows and weapons of iron. Military leadership was increasingly allotted to individuals who could prove their skill and expertise rather than automatically given to the nobles simply by virtue of their pedigree.

The pace of social and political changes continued to accelerate during the Warring States period. Government bureaucracy increased. New offices were created and filled by appointed administrators to regulate a population growing as a result of advances in agriculture and industry. As the old aristocracy gave way to a meritocracy, the peasantry began to have new opportunities—symbolized, for instance, by the emergence of a large class of peasants who were landowners. All of these changes were facilitated by the use of currency rather than barter as a means of exchange.

Interestingly, these latter years of Zhou Dynasty were also known as the Period of One Hundred Schools of Thought, because they were an immensely creative time philosophically and religiously. Although it is a poetic exaggeration, this alternative name indicates that this age of political and social disruption was a stimulus to innovative thought and lively debate among rival viewpoints. Clearly, the commotion created by the many changes rocking ancient China prompted the intellectuals to address the pressing issues of the day.

For the thinkers of Confucius's time, the most urgent problems were social and ethical in nature. Essentially, debate centered on the question of human harmony: What does it take for people to get along with one another? Many thinkers weighed in on this issue with proposals of various kinds. Although the matter is of a practical nature, it necessarily involved deeper questions and assumptions about the fundamental character of reality, the basic qualities of human beings, and the purposes for which human life is intended.

Confucianism was one of these schools of thought contributing to this lively philosophical conversation. China's other great indigenous philosophy, Daoism, was another. We do not know for certain how many different schools there were, but there were at least a half dozen prominent contenders. In terms of influence and longevity, Confucianism and Daoism have been the most successful, even though they provided perspectives that often seemed at odds with one another.

Becoming a Sage

As we noted earlier, the name China probably derived from Qin, a dynasty that postdated the life of Confucius. Although the Qin emperors ruled for only fifteen years, they unified China and established it as an imperial power. But they had no use for Confucius and his philosophy. During this dynasty, his teaching fell into disfavor because his views were at odds with the highly authoritarian philosophy of the Qin government. The Confucian school was officially and vigorously suppressed; Confucian texts were burned, and hundreds of Confucian scholars were stoned to death or buried alive.

In the long history of Chinese culture, however, this episode was clearly and simply a blip, an aberration. Soon after the brief reign of the Qin rulers, Confucius and his way of thought were restored to a place of privilege in the Chinese world. Eventually, the man himself would be regarded as a demigod by many, and temples would be dedicated to his spirit and sacrifices made in his honor. After surviving the efforts of the Qin Dynasty to eradicate his teachings, Confucius became the fountainhead of virtually all aspects of Chinese life. Historian Annping Chin says in her biography, "Until the mid-twentieth century, China was so inseparable from the idea of Confucius that her scheme of government and society, her concept of self and human relationships, and her construct of culture and history all seemed to have originated from his mind alone."[7] Confucius has even been credited with inventing the popular game of Mahjongg. An even more exalted accolade was offered by Mencius (Mengzi), the brilliant philosopher who lived almost two centuries after the sage: "Ever since man came into this world," said Mencius, "there has never been one greater than Confucius."[8] To judge solely by his humble beginnings and the course of most of his life, such high acclaim would hardly seem expected. For most of his seventy-odd years, Confucius was a virtual unknown.

Who was this man who garnered such high praise from people like Mencius, and what made his philosophy such a menace to people like the Qin emperors?

Confucius and Kongzi

Just as this man would not have identified himself as Chinese, he would not have identified himself as *Confucius*. That was neither his given name nor the name by which the Chinese have known him, at least not until rather

7. Chin, *Authentic Confucius*, 2.
8. Lau, trans., *Mencius* 2a.2 (p. 80).

recently. Throughout the history of China, he has been called Kongzi, or Master Kong. Kong was his family name. His personal, or taboo, name was Qiu, and his courtesy, or social, name was Zhongni.[9] As is still common in many parts of Asia, it was often considered disrespectful to use someone's personal name, and so a social name or nickname was used for public purposes. The name Confucius did not come into existence until the seventeenth century, when European Jesuit missionaries in China Latinized his honorific title, K'ung-fu-tzu, which essentially means "Mister K'ung."[10] And Confucius is the name that has stuck, even for scholars who are quite aware of its imprecision.

The Sources for the Historical Confucius

We cannot say much about the life of Confucius with historical dependability. This is true about lives of the Buddha and Jesus as well. In the case of Muhammad, the historical reliability of sources is also an issue, but much less so than with the other three. As we take up the life story of each of these individuals, we will discuss the matter of their historicity as real persons and the problems scholars have in gaining a clear picture of who they were and what they actually did and said. The problem of historicity as it pertains to Confucius illustrates many of the issues we encounter when we try to gain access to individuals from the ancient world by modern historiographical methods.

In the instance of Confucius, we have no documents written during his lifetime on which to base our portrait of him as a person. The same can be said of the Buddha, Jesus, and Muhammad. Nor do we have any writings from their own hands. None of them committed their teachings to the written word, or if they did, no evidence of it remains. All four lived in cultures in which the spoken word was supreme, and writing was mainly reserved for legal and political matters. Literacy rates were very low. At the time of Jesus, for example, only around 5 percent of the population of Judea could read and write. It is not clear whether the Buddha and Jesus were literate, but it is almost certain that Confucius was and that Muhammad was not. If Confucius were literate, the absence of his own writings might be due to his conviction that the words of the ancient sages were more important that anything *he* had to say. In any event, all of our primary sources come from followers and others who were reporting their memories or the memories

---

9. Chin, *Authentic Confucius*, 2.

10. Italian Jesuit priest Matteo Ricci is traditionally credited with this coinage.

of others. No doubt many of them were even inventing "memories," so to speak, consistent with their idea of who the individual was.

Sima Qian's Biography

The first biography of Confucius probably contained both authentic and invented memories. It was written by Sima Qian (ca. 145–85 BCE), a court historian of the Han Dynasty, around the year 100 BCE, four hundred years after the sage's death. Sima Qian wrote under the new regime that arose after the Qin Dynasty came to a close. Under the Han, China had become a Confucian state. Sima Qian's biography of Confucius, which appears in a work known as the *Shiji*, or *Records of the Grand Historian*, must therefore be regarded with a healthy dose of suspicion, since it recounts the life of an individual who lived four centuries earlier and since it would have served the interests of the state to make Confucius seem larger than life. Nevertheless, this early biography is useful to help us understand how the example of Confucius was understood by many Chinese, even if that portrayal does not precisely correspond to the historical Confucius.

The Analects

Despite the value of Sima Qian's biography, the best source for glimpsing the man Confucius is the *Analects*, the text known in Chinese as the *Lunyu*, a work that most scholars believe bears the imprint of his own thinking, if not some of his very words. Yet the *Analects* is by no means a biography—or even a narrative. Rather, it is a collection of aphorisms, conversations, and anecdotes related to the sage's life, most of which are attributed to Confucius himself. It is evident to critical scholars, though, that the text was written and compiled by his disciples after his death and that it probably took shape over the span of many generations.

The sayings and vignettes comprising the *Analects* are often very brief and sometimes rather cryptic, a fact that has helped shape the popular image of Confucius in the West as an old man uttering jewels of wisdom, as well as perplexing and sometimes irrelevant opinions. Not only are many of the pieces in the *Analects* obscure in themselves, but they do not seem to be compiled according to any organizing principle. One translator of the *Analects* describes its arrangement as "slapdash."[11] Furthermore, as a source for understanding Confucius's life, it is woefully incomplete. There is much

11. Raymond Dawson's term.

about Confucius that the *Analects* does not consider important to report. Where there were gaps, later sources usually filled them in with imaginative stories that seemed congruous with the image of Confucius that emerges in the *Analects*. Despite its shortcomings, though, the *Analects* at least possesses the virtue of portraying Confucius as an ordinary person rather than the demigod he was later taken to be.

Compounding these interpretive difficulties is the fact that there is no consensus among modern historians about how much of the *Analects* is historically reliable. Almost everyone agrees that much of the text reflects the perspectives and words of his followers, some of whom may have been removed from him by many generations. Subtle—and sometimes glaring—contradictions within parts of the text itself suggest that many hands were involved in its composition.[12] Of twenty relatively short chapters, only the first half of the book is generally regarded as reflecting the thought and words of Confucius himself, but even here there is no universal agreement. Some say only chapters 3–9 contain words that Confucius *may* have actually spoken. Two scholars have recently argued that only a single section of chapter 4 is authentic.[13] Still another has gone so far as to claim that Confucius was not a historical figure at all, but an invented character who personified the values of the Chinese elite.[14] Since almost all scholars believe a similar thing about Laozi, the reputed founder of Daoism, the idea that Confucius was fictional is plausible, but the argument has not yet convinced the majority of researchers.

Most Confucius scholars believe there was an authentic historical person who at least inspired the school of thought associated with his name. For the last two millennia, virtually all readers of the *Analects* have assumed that all parts of the *Analects* derive from a real person named Confucius or Kongzi. For our purposes, we will not spend more time on these matters, even though they are part of a lively conversation among academics. We will

---

12. Benjamin I. Schwartz cautions against making too much of these apparent inconsistencies: "While textual criticism based on rigorous philological and historic analysis is crucial, and while the later sections [of the *Analects*] do contain late materials, the type of textual criticism that is based on considerations of alleged logical inconsistencies and incompatibilities of thought must be viewed with great suspicion . . . While none of us comes to such an enterprise without deep-laid assumptions about necessary logical relations and compatibilities, we should at least hold before ourselves the constant injunction to mistrust all our unexamined preconceptions on these matters when dealing with comparative thought." Schwartz, *World of Thought in Ancient China*, 61.

13. Brooks and Brooks, trans., *Original Analects*.

14. Jensen, *Manufacturing Confucianism*.

take Confucius to be a historical person (as most believe he was) and rely mainly on the *Analects* as the chief source for our investigation.

But even though the *Analects* is our best source for constructing a picture of Confucius, it is hardly an ideal work for biographical purposes. Although it is marked by the mind of Confucius—or at least someone known to history by that name—and probably contains some of the sage's actual words, it is not a contemporaneous writing, and it is very fragmentary. Trying to sketch a literary portrait of Confucius from the *Analects* is somewhat akin to the way paleontologists try to understand how a prehistoric animal looked and lived based on a few fossil fragments. This does not doom the project from the outset, but it certainly advises caution in pressing our claims with too much conviction.

Dating Confucius's Life

So with the bits and pieces available to us, let us begin our sketch. At each point along the way, we will note when we are on firm historical ground and when we are moving into the legendary and mythical areas.

Chinese tradition suggests that Confucius was born around the year 551 BCE, during the Spring and Autumn Period, in the province of Lu, one of the several small principalities that began to compete with one another as the Eastern Zhou Dynasty started its slow decline. The same sources indicate that he died in 479 BCE. That would mean the sage lived seventy-two or seventy-three years. Of course, as we will also discover in the case of the Buddha, the traditional dates for Confucius are not accepted by everyone. There is good reason to be suspicious of the exactness of these traditional dates, since the sage lived during a time when the births and deaths of individuals were not recorded with great precision. Recently, some Confucius scholars have made the case that he lived closer to the end of the Zhou Dynasty, around the time of the Warring States period.[15] But in the absence of compelling evidence to the contrary, I suggest we simply stay with the time-honored dates.

Heritage and Parentage

Although the *Analects* says nothing about this, the historian Sima Qian claims that Confucius's lineage extends back to the royal family of the state of Song, one of the principalities of the early Zhou Dynasty. The members of

---

15. E.g., Brooks and Brooks, trans., *Original Analects.*

this noble family were appointed to conduct rituals dedicated to the Shang ancestors. There is no real evidence that Confucius was actually the descendant of such a family, but the theme of royal figures charged with maintaining ritual observances fits the image of Confucius perfectly, as we shall later see. In fact, this ancestral claim fits him almost *too* perfectly, which is one reason this heritage may be doubtful. As mentioned earlier, our four sages were all accorded aristocratic or royal heritage by later writers, although in each and every case the sage was unable or refused to enjoy the life of worldly privilege afforded by his noble descent.

Sima Qian goes on to flesh out the story of Confucius's ancestry. Confucius's great-grandfather had fled the state of Song, which was in political turmoil, and moved to the state of Lu, somewhere near the present town of Qufu, in southeastern Shandong province. Following the migration, however, the family fell on hard times and became impoverished, a state from which it never recovered. It was here that Confucius was born. Lu had been established five centuries earlier by one of the sons of the Duke of Zhou, the great regent who became the model of an ideal person for Confucius. Because of its connection to the duke, Confucius took pride in claiming Lu as his home province.

The story of Confucius's birth, as reported by Sima, is interesting in terms of our comparisons with the other three figures in our study, although the tale lacks independent corroboration. Apparently, Confucius's father, Shu-liang, was a very old man, and his mother a mere girl in her teens when Confucius was conceived. It is not clear if their relationship constituted a legal marriage. Shu-liang already had nine daughters by his chief wife and a crippled son by a concubine. Perhaps as he approached death he wanted a healthy male heir and so divorced his wife, or perhaps she had died. Sima Qian does say that Confucius was conceived while his parents were "making love in the field" (*yehe*), a reference that might suggest an illicit union because it does not occur under the auspices of a formal ritual. At least one scholar thinks this reference might also suggest a divine conception.[16] After this unconventional consummation, his parents' went to *Ni Qiu* (Mount Ni), a sacred mountain, to pray for a child, and when Confucius was born months later, they considered him to be the answer to their prayers. It is interesting to observe that Confucius's personal name was *Qiu*, the same Chinese word for "hill," and that Kong, his family name, can be used as an expression of gratitude for answered prayers. We cannot know if there is any historical validity to this story. It may have been invented by Sima as a clever wordplay on Confucius's Chinese names. What we want to observe at this

16. Chin, *Authentic Confucius*, 224–25.

juncture is simply the theme of an unusual conception that has become part of the life-story of Confucius as it has been accepted for over two thousand years.

Young Man Kong

About his youth we know almost nothing with historical assurance. His father probably died early in his life, around the age of three, leaving him to be raised by his young mother. She too died when he was only twenty-three. The *Analects* reports that Confucius and his mother endured a poverty-stricken life. As a young man, he had to accept lowly jobs such as keeping accounts and caring for livestock. Later in life he tells his disciples that he was "skilled in many menial things,"[17] not out of desire but out of necessity. Sima tells us that as a boy he enjoyed pretending to officiate at mock rituals. Confucius seemed to delight in arranging ritual vases on sacrificial altars, or so the story goes. Again, this anecdote fits the later Confucius almost too perfectly, but it may bear some authenticity. One final note on his early life concerns his physical appearance. Tradition says he was born with a concavity on the crown of his head and was uncommonly tall for an ancient Chinese, reaching well over six feet at adulthood. He must have cut a striking figure indeed.

Despite his modest beginning—or perhaps because of it—Confucius was an eager and dedicated student. He says in one of the famous passages from the *Analects*, "At fifteen, I set my heart on learning,"[18] and this love of learning stayed with him for his entire life. He later described this dedication as one of his distinctive qualities: "In a community of ten households there will certainly be someone as loyal and trustworthy as I am, but not someone so fond of learning as I am."[19] With no wealth or prestige, Confucius was nonetheless entitled to an education by virtue of his social standing. His ancestry placed him in the growing new class called the *shi*, or the common gentleman, situated between the declining nobility and the common peasantry. This emerging social rank comprised members of formerly aristocratic families whose success in life now depended on their own talents and determination rather than on mere birth. We do not know exactly how Confucius was educated, but it is safe to assume that he was schooled in all or most of the so-called Six Arts of ancient China: ritual, music, archery, charioteering, calligraphy, and mathematics. It is almost certain that

17. Lau, trans., *Analects* 9.6 (p. 97).
18. Dawson, trans., *Analects* 2.4 (p. 6).
19. Ibid., *Analects* 5.28 (p. 19).

he mastered at least ritual and music, because these two skills figured so prominently in his own philosophy and teaching.[20] As we shall see later, Confucius believed that ritual and music had important moral dimensions; performing ceremonies and listening to proper music served to make one a better person. Indeed, becoming a better person was what Confucius thought education was all about.

Confucius not only *loved* learning; he seems to have discovered a key aspect about the process of learning. The *Analects* quotes him as saying, "When I study, I do not get bored; in teaching others I do not grow weary."[21] Confucius is not simply telling us about one of his inborn character traits, as if not getting bored were in his nature. I think he is talking about a skill that is an essential ingredient in learning. The twentieth-century American composer John Cage once wrote, "If something is boring after two minutes, try it for four. If still boring, try it for eight, sixteen, thirty-two, and so on. Eventually one discovers that it's not boring at all but very interesting."[22] Cage's remark suggests that boredom is not generated by anything outside oneself. The experience of boredom is really about the state of our own minds rather than about the thing we are reading or watching or listening to. "When people are bored," said philosopher Eric Hoffer, "it is primarily with their own selves that they are bored."[23] Cage believed that with the proper frame of mind, anything could be interesting and that without it, anything could be boring. Confucius was aware of the importance of this quality in the art of learning. We might call this quality mindfulness—or simply paying attention. Thus, he expected his students to share his love of learning and to practice the discipline of paying attention.

> The Master said, "I will not open the door for a mind that is not already striving to understand, nor will I provide words to a tongue that is not already struggling to speak. If I hold up one corner of a problem, and the student cannot come back to me with the other three, I will not attempt to instruct him again."[24]

Or to use the words of another august teacher, Confucius refused to cast his pearls before swine.[25]

---

20. Some traditions indicate that Confucius studied ritual with the Daoist Master Lao Dan, music with Chang Hong, and the lute with Master Xiang.

21. Dawson, trans., *Analects* 7.1 (p. 24).

22. Cage, *Silence*, 93.

23. Hoffer, *True Believer*, 52.

24. Slingerland, trans., *Analects* 7.8 (p. 66).

25. Matt 7:6.

Marriage and Family

To add some finishing touches to our sketch of young man Confucius, let us briefly mention what takes him to the threshold of maturity: his marriage. We do know that he was married, although we know next to nothing about his wife, Qi Quan. The pair married in their late teens and had a son and a daughter together. The son predeceased Confucius. We do not know what Confucius was like as a father or husband, but there are suggestions in the early literature that his marriage ended in divorce. It is unfortunate that we have such sparse information about his family life, because familial relationships were an important aspect of Confucian ethics. In fact, Confucius viewed the political domain as the family writ large, and he derived many of his precepts for governance from what he understood to be appropriate for family life.

A Gentleman and a Scholar

Confucius lived a meager existence as a young man, taking what he considered to be humble jobs to support himself and his family. What distinguished him from others in similar circumstances was his dedication to learning. From the time of his adolescence and marriage until his appointment as the minister of crime, Confucius was principally occupied with the study of the classic texts and traditions of *huaxia* culture. On the basis of what he learned by examining the past, Confucius pondered the decline of Chinese culture and developed his vision of what it would take to return China to the glory days of the Zhou and earlier dynasties. By his late twenties, he was recognized as an authority on history, ritual, and music, and served as an occasional ceremonial consultant to several rulers and aristocratic families in Lu and the adjacent states. In his thirties, he founded a private school to teach the classics to a wide range of male students, from the sons of the nobility to those brought up in modest conditions, as he had been. Some of his followers had even been criminals. He only required that his students be zealous learners like himself. Confucius was one of the first in Chinese history to offer such instruction to the members of lower classes, who were now beginning to regard education as the best way to improve their prospects in life. What Confucius was able to provide to them was training in gentlemanly conduct, or how to comport themselves so that they might serve the state and hence their fellow humans. Almost all of his disciples wanted a career in government, and it was to that end that they sought the services of Master Kong.

Minister of Crime

It was not until around 500 BCE, when he was nearing the age of fifty, that Confucius is named in the records of Chinese history as a state official. His first appointment was as deputy minister of public works; shortly thereafter he was selected as the minister of crime. In this capacity, Confucius had opportunities to appear before the ruling court and confer with more powerful ministers of state. His tenure in the position was fairly unremarkable for the most part, although his later admirers go a bit over the top in describing his accomplishments. Xunzi, one his early interpreters, and Sima Qian both claimed that almost immediately after Confucius assumed office, a new wave of morality swept through the province, driven almost solely by his reputation. Shepherds stopped bloating their sheep with water before taking them to market, horse and cattle dealers no longer tried to swindle their buyers, husbands forced out their adulterous wives, and outsiders were made to feel welcome. If we are to believe reports such as these, we would have to accept that within just months of his appointment, Confucius had restored social harmony where there had been rampant discord for generations.

While such stories are surely exaggerations, they nonetheless highlight two important matters, one pertaining to Confucius's philosophy and the other to his personality. Concerning the first, Confucius believed that the pursuit of virtue by leaders—whether of the state or of the family—had salutary ramifications throughout the collective body. Virtuous leaders inspire virtuous behavior in their subordinates, thus stabilizing and harmonizing society. This belief would be quite consistent with the legends suggesting that when Confucius assumed office the world became a much better place. These accounts also say something about Confucius's personal qualities. Obviously, the stories are intended to relate that Confucius was the kind of person whose example and power of virtue could bring about such wholesome changes.

This is precisely the image of Confucius that emerges in the *Analects*. Piecing together his aphorisms and the impressions of his disciples, the sage emerges as the paragon of wisdom, compassion, and humility. One summary of his personal character describes him as "absolutely free from four things: free from conjecture [and unnecessary speculation], free from arbitrariness, free from obstinacy, free from egoism."[26] Freedom from egoism—in other words, humility—seems to be the quality that most impressed his contemporaries. They remarked upon it in a variety of ways. It was evident even in his physical carriage and demeanor: The *Analects* reports that

---

26. Huang, trans., *Analects* 9.4 (p. 101).

"on going through the outer gates to his lord's court, he drew himself in, as though the entrance was too small to admit him."[27] He "was genial and yet strict, imposing and yet not intimidating, courteous and yet at ease."[28] According to one of his closest followers, Zigong, the master was gentle, benevolent, respectful, frugal, and deferential.[29] Other disciples described him as "rather unassuming" and as someone who "seemed as if he were an inarticulate person."[30] Yet at court he always spoke eloquently, with caution, carefully choosing his words. There seemed to have been not a shred of pretense in him. He never claimed to be a special individual or to possess any great knowledge. "As for sageness and humaneness," he said, "how dare I claim them?"[31] He did not consider himself to be the ideal person that others took him to be. To the contrary, he appeared to be more focused on correcting his deficiencies than displaying his assets. The *Analects* quotes him as saying, "Virtue uncultivated, learning undiscussed, the inability to move toward righteousness after hearing it, and the inability to correct my imperfections—these are my anxieties."[32] He advised his followers: "When you come across an inferior person, turn inwards and examine yourself."[33] They confirmed that "when he made a mistake, he was not afraid to correct it."[34]

Confucius was also a person capable of great empathy for others, particularly for those who were suffering. "On seeing a man in mourning, even an intimate friend, he always changed his countenance."[35] If he "dined beside a bereaved person, he never ate his fill."[36] His empathy for others evoked in him a keen attention to the gestures of respect and courtesy: "When the Master saw a man in mourning, or one wearing an official hat and suit, or a blind man—when he saw one, even a younger person, he always rose; when he passed one, he always quickened his pace,"[37] which was regarded as a sign of respect. When there were state ceremonies honoring the elderly, he would

27. Lau, trans., *Analects* 10.4 (p. 101).

28. Dawson, trans., *Analects* 7.38 (p. 27).

29. Huang, trans., *Analects* 1.10 (p. 49).

30. Dawson, trans., *Analects* 10.1 (p. 35).

31. Huang, trans., *Analects* 7.33 (p. 94).

32. Ibid., *Analects* 7.3 (p. 87).

33. Dawson, trans., *Analects* 4.17 (p. 14).

34. Huang, trans., *Analects* 1.8 (p. 48).

35. Ibid., *Analects* 10.19 (p. 114).

36. Ibid., *Analects* 7.9 (p. 88).

37. Ibid., *Analects* 9.10 (p. 103).

not leave until all the senior guests had left.[38] Yet, despite his concern with personal decorum and conduct, Confucius was never stiff or pompous.[39]

These images and memories signify the way Confucius appeared to his close followers and to others and probably have some basis in the historical Confucius. The details may be debatable, and perhaps occasionally altogether wrong, but the early literary images of Confucius cannot have been wholly disconnected from the person he was. Confucius appears in the *Analects* as a wise, compassionate, and modest individual because he was in fact that kind of person.

That is what led his biographers to make such high claims about his term as a government official. In all likelihood, Confucius's achievements as minister of crime in Lu were much more modest than his later biographers thought, but they were not insignificant. He is credited with negotiating an important agreement with the neighboring state of Qi that resulted in the return of previously stolen lands to the kingdom of Lu. This diplomatic victory was impressive because Confucius was able to succeed using his powers of moral persuasion where several military expeditions had failed. The appeal to virtue and rehabilitation was always a first resort for Confucius, and the use of violence and punishment was always an inferior final solution.

That preference, however, did not mean that Confucius was a pacifist or a proponent of absolute nonviolence. Although there are clear similarities in their teachings on virtue and expediency, Confucius was no Gandhi. As minister of crime, Master Kong was directly responsible for the deaths of several individuals. One incident occurred during the very negotiation celebration at Qi, where Confucius ordered the execution of a troupe of singers and dancers who had been sent to entertain the Duke of Lu. Confucius justified the order by saying the entertainers had "made a mockery" of the dignity of their ruler.[40] Presumably, Confucius found their spectacle "lewd" and "vulgar," and hence contrary to the rites of propriety. This was by no means the only occasion on which Confucius voiced his objections to what he considered rude entertainments.

Nor was it the only time he sent someone to his death. During his appointment as minister of crime, he ordered the execution of one Shaozheng Mao, a man well known in Lu and respected by many as a teacher of virtue. Shaozheng had violated no laws of the state, yet Confucius condemned him for what amounted to moral pretense and subversion, believing he constituted a threat to the social fabric by stealthily teaching dangerous

38. Ibid., *Analects* 10.7 (p. 112).
39. Ibid., *Analects* 7.4 (p. 87).
40. Chin, *Authentic Confucius*, 38, citing Sima Qian.

ideas under the guise of integrity. The charges were not unlike those lev-
eled against Socrates and Jesus, which of course resulted in their executions.
The condemnation of Shaozheng scandalized many of Confucius's own disciples, some of whom thought he was trying to eliminate a rival teacher. Yet,
Confucius never regretted his decision. His later interpreters were at pains
to reconcile his action with his teachings on benevolence and the sacredness
of human life.[41] In Xunzi's spin centuries later, the episode portrays Confucius as a man of "keen discernment," to use one of the sage's own terms,
capable of extraordinary penetration of the depths of personal character.
No one else could see it, but Confucius recognized Shaozheng as a wolf in
sheep's clothing, and hence deserving the ultimate penalty.[42]

Confucius's career as minister of crime was not long-lived. Within four
or five years of his appointment, he unexpectedly left the position—and the
province of Lu—to seek another ruler to serve in another state. The reasons
for his departure are not clear and have long been the subject of scholarly
speculation. Characteristically, the *Analects* is obscure on this matter, offering only this terse statement:

> When the Duke of Qi presented a group of singing girls, Jihuan-
> zi, the prime minister of Lu, accepted them and there was no
> court for the next three days. Confucius left.[43]

His interpreters, of course, felt compelled to elaborate on this incident to
help explain an otherwise baffling event. Most regarded the exodus as a
protest: Confucius refused to work for a government that was vulnerable
to morally corrupting influences from outside officials. And then there are
those entertainers again! We're not sure if Confucius objected to their music
or sexually provocative behavior or both. In any event, it was the prime
minister's fascination with the singing girls that left Confucius disconcerted.
Mencius adds another element to the story, indicating that in spite of the
prime minister's impropriety, Confucius decided to give the ruler another

41. See especially Wang and Xunzi, *Xunzi Jijie*, ch. 28, 341–42.

42. These executions trouble me and do not fit the image I have of Confucius, or
perhaps the image I want to have of him. I prefer to think of Confucius as a believer
in the redeemability of everyone, regardless of the depth of their depravity. Even if
Shaozheng were as wicked as Confucius thought, I would like to think that somehow
a sage like Confucius could have put him on the straight path. But perhaps this is too
much to ask for, even from Confucius, who never professed to be perfect—or even to
be a sage. He lived in desperate times, and his actions need to be viewed in that context.
Capital executions and brutal military violence were standard practices of the day. Perhaps there is some comfort in knowing that Confucius exercised this power sparingly
and with considerable forethought and conviction.

43. *Analects* 18.4, my rendering.

chance. When Confucius was not offered a sliver of the sacrificial meat at a state ritual a short time later, he quietly stood up and left. Some commentators suggested that the ceremonial blunder was part of a conspiracy cooked up by those in the kingdom intent on halting Confucius's campaign to restore virtue to the government. Mencius wants us to understand that Confucius was not *personally* offended by the slight but that the omission confirmed that the Lu rulers were not serious about observing traditional ritual and hence not serious about promoting moral reform. Confucius had no choice but to leave. To stay would be to squander his talents, which could be of genuine use elsewhere.

Itinerant Counselor

So Confucius upped and left. Along with an entourage of protégés, he became an itinerant political consultant. He wandered from kingdom to kingdom for over a dozen years, seeking opportunities to put his ideas into practice as well as to continue to learn. But he could never find a job that suited him, and in many cases he consented to serve rulers who were far less worthy than those he had left in Lu. Some of them, like Duke Ling of Wei, frankly admitted that they were more interested in military conquest and sexual exploits than in taking seriously what Confucius had to offer. Apparently, the rulers of these kingdoms were simply not prepared to receive Confucius's advice on how to govern on the basis of virtue and ritual observance. After a while in one location, he and his followers would pack up and move along on foot to seek better horizons. He must have covered over a thousand miles in his years abroad, and he sought residence in at least four other kingdoms.

The journeys between states were arduous. On one occasion, Confucius and his company almost starved to death after their provisions were depleted in the wilderness. We are not certain how they were able to survive the ordeal, but they did, and the experience provided some good material for later writers to highlight the finer aspects of Confucian thought. The *Analects* reports that after they ran out of food, Confucius's disciple Zilu approached the master with considerable resentment and asked sarcastically, "So the superior person is also susceptible to adversity?" To which Confucius responded, "The noble one rests at ease in adversity; the petty person when faced with adversity is reduced to recklessness."[44] Confucius's retort sounds remarkably similar to his near contemporary, the Buddha, who also had much to say about the characteristics of the noble one and his or her

44. *Analects* 15.2, my rendering.

capacity to face the sufferings of life with equanimity. Both the Buddha and Confucius indicate that nobility does not imply avoidance of adversity but rather meeting it with an inner resolve and serenity. Furthermore, Confucius goes on to challenge his disciple's assumption that the pursuit of virtue necessarily results in some tangible or worldly reward. Shortly after Zilu left, according to Sima Qian, Zigong arrives and tells Confucius, "Your way is too demanding. The world is unable to attain it. Why don't you make it a bit easier?"[45] Confucius responded:

> A good farmer can work as hard as he can but does not always reap a harvest. A fine artisan can produce wonderful craftsmanship but is not always appreciated. A gentleman can be cultivating a [superior] way for himself; he can outline and summarize what he has learned, and gather all the strands and sort them into [interlocking] principles. Yet people will not always accept what he can teach them. Now it seems you are not pursuing [learning and] self-understanding. Rather, you seek to have your ideas gain acceptance. Your goal is not far enough![46]

Confucius, the Buddha, Jesus, and Muhammad all had to contend with someone trying to persuade them to modify their teachings to make their precepts more palatable and popular. All had to face rejection by others and a sense of failing to accomplish their goals.[47] The response of each teacher was to locate the criteria for success in something other than popular acceptance and applause. For Confucius, success was to be measured by the depth of self-understanding and personal refinement, qualities that could be attained regardless of circumstance or public acclaim.

During his journeys, Confucius not only confronted death by starvation but also was twice the object of attempted murder. In one case, the would-be assassins mistook him for someone else; in the second, the minister of the army of the state of Song, Huan Tui, chopped down a tree in an effort to crush Confucius while he was performing a ritual. This was no case of mistaken identity, but we are not told of the army minister's motivations. In both instances, Confucius responded by recalling his sense of divine mission: "Heaven is author of the virtue that is in me. What can Huan T'ui do to me?"[48] By now—in his midsixties—Confucius had become convinced that his work in the world had been sanctioned by the highest realities and

45. *Shiji* 47:1930-32, paraphrased from Chin, *Authentic Confucius*, 107.

46. *Shiji* 47:1930-32, quoted in Chin, *Authentic Confucius*, 107-8.

47. In his famous parable of the sower, Jesus suggested that the teachers of unconventional wisdom are lucky if they bear fruit a quarter of the time (Matt 13:1-23; Mark 4:1-20; Luke 8:1-15).

48. Lau, trans., *Analects* 7.23 (p. 89). See also *Analects* 9.5.

that imprimatur secured the worth of his vision and the significance of his mission. The Buddha, Jesus, and Muhammad also survived assassination attempts, and, like Confucius, remained undeterred by them. Each had discovered a source of courage rooted in a truth beyond the triumphs and failures of their individual lives.

"The First of Teachers"[49]

Fourteen years on the road seems to have nourished Confucius's courage and confidence. Certainly, it took a good measure of fortitude for him to leave the state of Lu in the first place and strike out on his own after finally landing a job he had long sought; but it is also fair to say that these years of itinerancy were important in maturing Confucius's thought and the personal qualities that made him so attractive to many. Opening to the unfamiliar and the unexpected often strips away the inessential and discloses hidden parts of ourselves. Whatever agents of transformation were in play during his wanderings, at the end of his exile Confucius was sufficiently at home in his own skin to return to Lu.

His homecoming was probably prompted by an invitation from the government of Lu. He arrived home in 484 BCE, enjoying an even greater reputation than he had when he left. There was no lack of young men interested in apprenticing themselves to him. In part, his new status was due to the professional success of some of his older protégés who had left years earlier and proven themselves in the government bureaucracies. By now, Confucius was in his midsixties and no longer so keen to be intimately and actively involved in politics. Nor were the rulers of Lu really so eager to accept his advice, despite the enticements to bring him home. In his later years, he occasionally consulted with kings and counselors but increasingly turned his energies towards educating his young followers.

Tradition tells us that in these years he also devoted himself to editing the texts that became classics in later Confucianism, including the *Book of Songs*, the *Spring and Autumn Annals*, and the *Yijing* (*Classic of Changes*), the much revered book of divination. These claims are doubtful, though, and may only reflect the later tradition's image of the man as a dedicated scholar doing what scholars do. Be that as it may, it is clear that during this period, his zeal for learning and teaching had not diminished in the least. The *Analects* records his incisive mind still at work, prodding his disciples to think for themselves and practice the hard, straight way that had become his hallmark.

49. *Xianshi.*

In this way—learning and teaching, constantly striving for self-improvement—Confucius occupied himself until the end of his days. Although less absorbed with the realm of politics, he never withdrew completely from society to become a recluse, as did other notable sages of his day. A man of the world throughout his life, he remained so up until his death. He died in 479 BCE, says tradition, and was buried in the time-honored manner by his followers, who then entered a three-year mourning period, the traditional pattern observed following the death of a parent.

We noted at the beginning of our study that some recent scholars have argued that Confucius was only a fictional character conjured up by later Confucians, just as Laozi was an invention of Daoist philosophers. If that were true, the fact hardly matters. "Confucius"—whether that name applies to a fictional character or an actual individual—was a superb embodiment of the Confucian worldview. In the final analysis, it was the *image* of Confucius—as portrayed in the *Analects* and the other sources—that succeeding generations of Chinese held up as their model of ideal humanity and not the historical Confucius, who may have been more or less consistent with the literary portrait of him. As we turn our attention to the teachings of Confucius, we will never be far removed from the life of the one who, according to Chinese tradition, embodied virtue more than any other.

Heaven and Earth

Confucius would probably be surprised to find us engaged in a study of his thought, since he did not consider himself a great thinker. He was far more comfortable calling himself a "learner." He once told his followers: "I used to go without food all day, without sleep all night, [in order] to think. No use, better to learn."[50] He refused to claim originality for his ideas. "The Master said: I transmit rather than innovate. I trust in and love the ancient ways."[51] Like many others through history, Confucius believed in a bygone golden age. He shared with other Chinese the belief that this brilliant period extended from the earliest dynasties down to founding of the Zhou, some five hundred years before his time. They regarded these halcyon days as a time in which virtuous rulers governed virtuous subjects, and high culture flourished. Much of the lore about this age, as we have seen, was mythical. Yet Confucius took this belief seriously. His study of the past had convinced him that the China of his day was in turmoil precisely because its leaders had neglected the traditions and values of these earlier eras. What was

50. *Analects* 15.31, in Graham, *Disputers*, 11.
51. Slingerland, trans., *Analects* 7.1, (p. 64).

desperately needed was to return China to its foundations, to the pristine practices and values on which it had been established. Discerning lessons from the past and implementing them in the present was necessary, he thought, to restore social harmony and well-being. Confucius would certainly have applauded our efforts to learn from our wise forebears, but he may have urged us to look past him to the sages of an even earlier time.

Needless to say, we shall disregard that suggestion. Notwithstanding his self-assessment, Confucius's interpretation of the past and his particular way of applying the received tradition to his own time attest to a keen intellect matched with a compassionate heart. One of his twentieth-century interpreters writes: "When I began to read Confucius I found him to be a prosaic and parochial moralizer . . . Later, I found him a thinker with profound insight and with an imaginative vision of man equal in its grandeur to any I know. He tells us things not being said elsewhere . . . He has a new lesson to teach."[52] That is high praise to give to someone who considered himself only a conduit of tradition.

Sources and Approach

As with the study of Confucius's life, our investigation into his philosophy and spirituality relies principally on the *Analects*. It is hard to overestimate the importance of this small text for understanding not only Confucius but the last 2,500 years of Chinese history as well. As one recent translator put it, "if a single book can be upheld as the common code of a whole people, it is perhaps . . . *The Analects of Confucius*."[53]

With little more than this single brief text to grasp, comprehending the Confucian worldview might seem fairly easy, but that assumption would be wrong. Understanding Confucian philosophy through the *Analects* is not simple. The book is not easy to read. As we noted earlier, it can appear to be little more than a disjointed collection of proverbs and pieces of conversation. To present Confucius's ideas and practices in a more accessible way, we will use a structure by which we can discuss the salient themes in his sayings. Of course, it is highly unlikely that Confucius himself would have presented his thought in this way. His style of teaching was much more informal, allowing specific situations to provide the occasion for a particular lesson, which was usually imparted in an exchange with his students. Since we do not have the opportunity for such casual conversations here, we will have to settle for this rather un-Confucian approach to Confucius.

52. Fingarette, *Secular as Sacred*, vii.
53. Huang, trans., *Analects*, 4.

The framework that we use was outlined in the introduction. We begin by discussing the basic features and assumptions of Confucian thought: the metaphysics of his worldview. Under this rubric, we explore what Confucius thought about the nature of reality, particularly the divine and its relationship to the human. Then we examine the anthropological and ethical dimensions of the sage's philosophy, his ideas about how we should act as individuals and as a society, and conclude with a discussion of the disciplines of Confucian spirituality.

Confucian Metaphysics

Among our four figures, Confucius is the one who seems to have said the least about metaphysics; he was far more loquacious about human behavior than he was about the basic structure of reality. He shared with the Buddha a reticence about the world of gods and spirits, but even the Buddha was more forthcoming about his understanding of the nature and character of reality. Like the Buddha, Confucius never denied the existence of spiritual beings, but neither did he make the belief in them central to his view. In the *Analects*, a student recalled—with only slight exaggeration—that the Master did not speak of "mysteries, violence, rebellions, and gods."[54]

The marginal role of gods in the thought of Confucius and the Buddha has led many Western observers to argue that their worldviews are better characterized as philosophies than religions. I have some sympathies with that argument, but ultimately it is based on unnecessarily narrow definitions of religion. As we shall see, both Confucius and the Buddha practiced and taught specific spiritual disciplines and held particular realities as sacred, both of which are elements that characterize religious worldviews. Although divine beings do not figure prominently in the thought of Confucius and the Buddha, we are justified in describing their thinking and practice as *both* philosophical *and* religious. When we reach the comparative portion of our study, we will have occasion to discuss these issues in further detail. For now, we need only observe the reluctance of Confucius to speak of the gods and spirits, as well as noting his general hesitancy to make metaphysical assertions.

But hesitancy does not mean silence. Scattered throughout the *Analects* are references to the principal metaphysical concepts of ancient China. Although Confucius did not speculate or speak much about the world of gods and spirits, he clearly thought that acknowledging the divine in certain ways was essential to human welfare.

54. *Analects* 7.21, my rendering.

The Harmony of Heaven and Earth

Like all Chinese of his day, Confucius accepted the ancient belief that reality comprised two worlds: the realm of heaven and the realm of earth. Heaven, or *tian*, was the domain of gods, spirits (*shen*), and ancestors; earth, or *di*, was the sphere of humans and nature. One of the Chinese terms for the universe or cosmos was *tiandi*, a simple compound of both words.[55] As this linguistic combination suggests, heaven and earth could not be thought of apart from one another. They formed a holistic and symbiotic unity. Each one depended on the other. The Western concept of the absolute transcendence of god, as exemplified in Søren Kierkegaard's famous claim that there is an "infinite qualitative difference"[56] between god and humanity, was utterly foreign to the Chinese way of thinking. Heaven and earth were permeable realms, and there was an intimate connection between them. The many gods and spirits of the universe were thought to be immediately available to human beings, and hence they could be consulted by means of divination and could even enter and possess individuals.

Due to the interdependence of heaven and earth, the well-being of everyone and everything in them rested on their harmonious relationship. Preserving this harmony was one of the king's principal functions. The *Commentary of Zuo,* one of the earliest narratives of Chinese history, states that the ruler's primary responsibility was "pacifying the multitude of spirits and putting in harmony the myriad of people," and if this was not done, "the spirits will be incensed against him and the people will revolt."[57] Accordingly, the king was charged with performing the appropriate rituals and sacrifices to curry the favor of the divine figures whose good graces were essential to the well-being of the state and its citizens.

The Denizens of Heaven

The idea of heaven in Chinese philosophy and religion meant more than just the dwelling place of the divine beings, although it certainly included that. Originally, *tian* simply meant "sky," but over the centuries from the Shang Dynasty down to Confucius's time, the idea of heaven accumulated a rich variety of meanings. During the Shang, *tian* appears to have been a generic term for the heavenly realm. The people of the Shang imagined this divine world as a heavenly court that paralleled the royal court on earth. As

55. 天地, literally "heaven and earth."

56. Kierkegaard, *Concluding Unscientific Postscript.*

57. Quoted in Fung Yu-lan, *History of Chinese Philosophy,* 1:25.

the earthly king governed through a bureaucracy of nobles, counselors, and various other ministers of state, so the high god ruled heaven with his spiritual minions and assistants. The Shang people called the high god "Shang Di," the Supreme Emperor or the Supreme Ancestor. Although he was never depicted by physical representations, Shang Di was imagined to preside over a court that included many lesser divinities, or *shen*, that controlled, or at least influenced, the powers of the natural and human worlds. These were the gods and spirits the Chinese turned to for help in matters of agriculture, hunting, military campaigns, health, and longevity. The high god would not be bothered with these trivial, mundane concerns. Unlike Shang Di, the lower gods were not universal and did not have broad powers; most were decidedly local, such as the town or village gods whose power extended only as far as the city limits, like the jurisdiction of a municipal magistrate.

In addition to the divine hierarchy, heaven was also home to ancestors and ghosts.[58] The ancestors—who were not sharply distinguished from the gods—were the deceased individuals who now existed in the spirit world. Ghosts (*gui*) were the spirits of the dead who had suffered an unfortunate or tragic death. They often caused misfortune to the living, particularly those who were involved in their deaths. The ancestors, on the other hand, were generally benevolent. Throughout Chinese history, the ancestors have been seen as having a continuing interest in the welfare of their earthly families. They were to be consulted on important family matters, and they needed to be honored with sacrifices and gifts. They were also believed to mediate with the higher gods, especially if they were ancestors of a powerful family such as that of the king. Confucius did not say much about the ancestors, although he thought it was necessary to revere them in ritual. He did, however, have much to say about venerating the members of one's family who were still alive, especially one's parents. The virtue of filial piety, indeed, was a cornerstone of his entire ethical outlook.

Between Spirits and Humans

The relationships between the ancient Chinese and their gods were formal and rather businesslike. The human interest in gods was delimited by what the gods could do. We find no evidence to suggest that individuals sought friendships or close personal relationships with the gods of the sort we shall see in the life of Jesus.

---

58. Belief in ancestors is widespread throughout the world's religions. American Indian, African, Polynesian, and Asian believers have all revered ancestors.

A collection titled the *Sayings of the State* reflects on China's golden age and remarks on the relationship between divine beings and humans. In those days, according to this commentary,

> the people, having their duties differentiated from those of the spirits, were *respectful and not unduly familiar*. Therefore the spirits conferred prosperous harvest upon them and the people offered things up out of gratitude. Natural calamities did not arrive, and there was an inexhaustible supply of what would be useful.[59]

An intimate relationship between an individual and a god would have been regarded as encroaching upon the dignity of the divine and a threat to the proper order of things. A human being would no more try to buddy up to a god than a peasant would try to strike up a friendship with the emperor.

For their part, the gods were also reserved in their involvements with humans. In the earliest part of Chinese history, the gods were not even concerned with the moral behavior of human beings. These gods did not give commandments or grant favors on the basis of how well humans treated each other, and the ancient Chinese did not interpret disasters or other misfortunes as the gods' retribution for immoral behavior. The divine-human relationship was simply a quid pro quo arrangement. In exchange for agreeable sacrifices and tribute, the gods would assist humans with commonplace things such as producing an abundant crop, gaining victory over one's enemies, healing illness, and living a long life with many descendants. This sacred economy bound together the divine and human worlds.

Theological Developments

The image of a polytheistic heavenly court that prevailed during the Shang Dynasty persisted into and throughout the Zhou era, even as other theological developments were taking place. During the Zhou Dynasty, the idea of heaven became more ambiguous and acquired richer meanings than it had in previous periods. Unlike the Shang, the Zhou people considered *tian* a *personal* deity, that is, a divine being conceptualized in anthropomorphic terms, as Shang Di had been. In fact, the people of Zhou initially used the names Shang Di and *tian* interchangeably to refer to the highest god. Over time, however, the name *tian* came to be used with much greater frequency and was viewed as less anthropomorphic and more impersonal than Shang

59. *Kuo Yü*, quoted in Fung Yu-lan, *History of Chinese Philosophy*, 1:23 (italics added).

Di. By impersonal, I mean that *tian* assumed the character of an overarching principle or force, somewhat akin to the way Westerners might think of fate. By the time of Confucius, *tian* could mean both a supreme being conceived in personal terms and an impersonal, ultimate principle or power, although the latter meaning predominated.

The crucial difference between the Zhou and the Shang concepts of the divine powers was not the question of personality but of morality. As we have just observed, the Shang gods had little interest in how human beings behaved toward each other and did not make moral character a condition for granting favors. As long as the sacrifices were pleasing, the gods really could not care less whether you were a nice person. During the Zhou era, however, *tian* acquired a moral dimension. It is not completely clear just how far *tian*'s moral interests initially extended, but it was evident that heaven had an interest in who the ruler was and how he treated his subjects. At the very beginning of the Zhou Dynasty, we recall, the concept of the mandate of heaven entered the Chinese lexicon, specifying that the ruler must govern morally in order for his reign to be legitimate. By the Spring and Autumn Period, the Chinese believed the will of heaven concerned not only the ruler but everyone.

Interestingly, this attribution of moral preferences to the divine world was part of a larger process occurring in many of the major centers of civilization during the first century BCE. During this period, which is known as the Axial Age (800-200 BCE), metaphysical conceptions such as god, rebirth, and the afterlife came to be closely associated with moral human behavior. In ancient Iran, for example, the prophet Zoroaster taught that the individual's personal destiny in the life to come was predicated on whether or not one identified with the supreme god, whose fundamental quality was absolute goodness. In ancient India, the belief in rebirth was connected to the principle of karma, which meant that one's status in the next life was determined by his or her moral actions in present existence. Today, because we live on this side of the Axial Age, we usually take the moral character of ultimate reality for granted. Yet the moral quality now usually assumed in concepts of god has not always been a part of the way humans have thought about the divine.

This overview of the evolving idea of heaven has revealed a rich variety of theological conceptions circulating in ancient China at the time of Confucius. The ultimate reality could have been understood as a kind of polytheism, with a supreme being in charge of a retinue of lesser gods and spirits. It could have been thought of as a virtual monotheism, if one focused exclusively on *tian* as an anthropomorphized entity. Or the ultimate reality might have been regarded as a rather abstract, impersonal force or cosmic principle, to which the gods, ancestors, humanity, and nature were subject. Further complicating these concepts was the issue of morality—whether the ultimate reality was considered basically moral or amoral. Let us now turn to see how Confucius appropriated this rich tradition in his philosophy.

Confucius's Appropriation of Chinese Metaphysics

During the Enlightenment period in Western history (ca. 1620-1790 CE), when the teachings of Confucius became more widely known among scholars, many intellectuals saw Confucius as a fellow rationalist who had articulated a sophisticated ethical system without the burden of belief in god.[60] Weary of the animosity generated by centuries of religious sectarianism, these Western thinkers wanted to develop a wholly secular, rational ethic, devoid of reference to the divine. They were able to point to certain passages in the *Analects* that suggested an agnosticism or theological skepticism on the part of Confucius. The most prominent of these passages was one in which a disciple asked the sage about wisdom. The Master replied, "To apply oneself to the duties of humanity and, while revering the spirits and gods, *to keep away from them*—this may be called wisdom."[61] Many interpreters of Confucius from the Enlightenment into the twenty-first century construed this statement as evidence that he was at least agnostic, if not an outright atheist. Why else would Confucius counsel the wise to stay away from the gods? But this reading of the *Analects* neglects the formal, reserved way the Chinese have historically related to their gods and spirits. Confucius was merely encouraging the ancient practice of respecting the dignity of the divine. To advocate maintaining one's distance from the gods is nowhere near the same as professing agnosticism. Yet, there is no denying that Confucius said very little about the gods and spirits, and the role that they played in his worldview was only tangential. What we shall discover in our study is that Confucius considered the formal rituals associated with revering the gods to be intrinsically beneficial to human flourishing. When he promoted ritual veneration of the deities, he did so not to benefit the gods, but to evoke specific qualities in human beings.

While understanding the gods and spirits had a very peripheral function in his thinking, the concept of heaven was clearly central, although he was still fairly reserved on that topic. When Confucius spoke of heaven, he occasionally seemed close to thinking of it as a supreme anthropomorphic

---

60. Western fans of Confucius include Voltaire, Diderot, Leibnitz, and Wolff.

61. *Analects* 6.22, my rendering and italics.

being, as when he claimed that heaven ordained his teachings,[62] or when he exclaimed, "The only one who understands me is perhaps Heaven!"[63] Still, the impersonal sense of *tian* overwhelmingly dominated Confucius's sayings. One of his students remembered that Confucius had said, "Life and death are the decree of Heaven; riches and reputation depend on Heaven."[64] In this aphorism, Confucius seemed to understand heaven as a kind of impersonal fate, to which humans and spirits are all subject. The gods, therefore, were not the ultimate or highest reality. In this sense, the Enlightenment interpreters of Confucius were correct, for he did not base his worldview on a god or the gods—at least not as divine beings are ordinarily understood in the West. Yet to regard Confucius's philosophy as completely devoid of a transcendent dimension is simply not true to Confucius.

Confucius understood heaven as a dynamic, creative reality that gave and supported life on earth. It was the source of all things and of the processes of change.[65] Although he sometimes thought of heaven as a kind of fate, it would be a mistake to think that Confucius was fatalistic, believing that *everything* that happens is inevitable or predestined. Confucius certainly thought, for example, that it was possible for human beings to resist the will of heaven. In his view, heaven had certain powers, such as determining the span of one's existence, yet it did not have *absolute* power.

Confucius was unambiguous, though, in his belief that heaven was moral and wanted human beings to be good. On this point, Confucius stood firmly with the view of *tian* emergent in the Zhou Dynasty. Heaven's will for human beings was disclosed not by revealed commandments but in the lives and teachings of the virtuous sages of old, and now—he believed—in his own teaching.[66] Furthermore, Confucius thought that heaven not only *wanted* human goodness but had also endowed human beings with a nature that makes it possible for us to cultivate this goodness in ourselves. In this sense, Confucius believed humans could work as collaborators with heaven, in a creative process of realizing our potential goodness and thereby fulfilling our purpose as human beings.

62. Dawson, trans., *Analects* 7.23 (p. 26).

63. Huang, trans., *Analects* 14.35 (p. 148).

64. *Analects* 12.5, my rendering.

65. *Analects* 17.19.

66. The Master said: "I wish to give up speaking." Zigong said: "But Sir, if you do not speak, what shall your students pass on to others?" The Master said: "What does Heaven say? Yet the four seasons come and go and a hundred things are born and grow. What does Heaven say?" (*Analects* 17.18, my rendering).

Doing unto Others

Heaven was an important part of Confucius's understanding of the world, yet he had relatively little to say about it. As we shall see, Confucius's understanding of human beings helps illuminate why he did not feel compelled to make heaven the subject of lengthy discourse.

A clue lies in an anecdote from the *Analects*. As the story goes, a student approached Confucius to ask how to serve the gods and the ancestors. The Master responded: "You are not able even to serve your fellow humans. How can you ask about the gods and spirits?" When the student went on to ask about death, the Master said, "You do not understand even life. How can you understand death?"[67] As this exchange confirms, Confucius believed that attending to the concerns of *this* world took precedence over understanding the world beyond. But the story does not suggest that Confucius was *only* concerned with this world. What it indicates is that attending to the concerns of earth is a *prerequisite* for comprehending heaven. We must begin with the things nearest to hand before we approach the things farther away. He told his protégés, "I learned lower things and perceive higher things."[68] Another translator renders the passage this way: "In my studies, I start from below and get through to what is up above."[69] By devoting himself to understanding human affairs, Confucius came to know heaven and believed others would as well.

Many of his early Western interpreters failed to grasp this important aspect of Confucius's philosophy, and consequently they were unable to appreciate the sacred dimension in his thought. For Confucius, the ultimate reality is manifested through the most ordinary things; the higher is revealed through the lower; what is above comes through what is below; the transcendent saturates the immanent. Accordingly, Confucius recognized the sacred through humanity and saw humanity as sacred. To better appreciate the connection between the sacred and the human, let us explore Confucius's rather complex views about human character and relationships.

Human Nature

In spite of the deeply troubled times in which he lived, Confucius had the audacity to believe that human beings were perfectible. Every person, he thought, has the capacity to become a sage (*sheng ren*), an individual of

---

67. Lau, trans., *Analects* 11.12 (p. 107).
68. Huang, trans., *Analects* 14.35 (p. 148).
69. Lau, trans., *Analects* 14.35 (p. 125).

great compassion and wisdom.[70] That was an astounding conviction when one considers that not much in Confucius's world could be invoked as evidence to support that belief. During the Spring and Autumn Period, one might have been more inclined to conclude that people were no good and utterly unable to reform themselves. Confucius's faith in human possibility, however, was based not on what he *saw* in the China of his day, but on his *study* of great sages of the past and his own self-awareness.

The focus of Confucius's understanding of human character was less on the way that human beings *are* and more on the way he believed we *could be*. Just as he was not explicit about his metaphysical views, so Confucius was also less than explicit about what he thought of human nature. His disciple Zigong once complained, "The Master's cultural accomplishments—we get to hear about them, but the Master's ideas on human nature and the way of Heaven—we hardly get to hear them."[71] But the sage did say enough to indicate that he believed that all persons shared a common nature. "By nature," he said, "people are close to one another; through practice, they drift far apart."[72] This maxim, by the way, was quoted and affirmed by UNESCO, the United Nations Educational, Scientific, and Cultural Organization, in its 1950 statement titled "The Race Question."[73] That document, which was drawn up largely in response to Nazi racial ideology, maintained that all human beings are fundamentally united as members of the same species, and that putative racial differences are social fictions, not biological realities. Confucius would have agreed. Even the people known to the Chinese as barbarians were not considered different by nature; they could always become civilized by the adoption of Chinese mores.

Confucius thought human beings come into the world with the same raw material, but the ways we are socialized and conditioned, and the choices we make as individuals, shape that basic substance into divergent forms. Confucius did not offer an assessment or an analysis of our basic stuff. He did not say whether he considered human nature good or evil, but he clearly thought that it could be fashioned in good or evil ways. Humans are malleable creatures; our natures are such that we can become good, evil, and anything in-between. We could say that Confucius viewed humans as unfinished beings whose life-work was to bring ourselves to completion.

70. As Mencius later put it, "Everyone may become a Yao or Shun [the highly revered moral rulers of China's past]" (Lau, trans., *Mencius*, 6b.2).

71. Huang, trans., *Analects* 5.13 (p. 75).

72. Ibid., *Analects* 17.2 (p. 163). The UNESCO quotation was slightly different: "Men's natures are alike; it is their habits that carry them far apart."

73. http://unesdoc.unesco.org/images/0012/001282/128291eo.pdf.

Although human character can be molded in any number of ways, for Confucius there was only one way worthy of pursuit: perfect goodness. The Master thought that not only was perfect goodness within the realm of human possibility; it was the will of heaven that we pursue it. The aspiration for moral excellence is, therefore, embedded in the fabric of the universe; moral goodness lies latent in our human nature and in the urging of heaven itself. For Confucius, to become morally perfect was to attain human fulfillment. Perfect goodness functioned in Confucius's philosophy the way that nirvana functioned in the Buddha's teaching—as the person's ultimate completion. We become fully human when we live the most moral life we are capable of achieving.

Because perfection was the ideal, the Master helped his followers envision this objective and prescribed specific methods to achieve it. Since humans have a great responsibility to cultivate their moral character, we must be very careful about how we shape it. It is not surprising that for this reason Confucius directed his contemporaries to look to China's legendary sages as worthy models. In the ancient sages persons aspiring to moral perfection have both a vision of the destination and a map for the journey.

Humaneness

Throughout the *Analects*, Confucius refers to a wide array of characteristics he thought were part of the makeup of the morally perfect individual. All told, he must have mentioned nearly two dozen such traits, including respectfulness, refinement, deference, simplicity, and sincerity.

The most important among all of them was *ren*, or humaneness or humanity. Yet despite its centrality in Confucian thought, the *Analects* never fully explains the concept of *ren*. Confucius apparently regarded this quality as rather mysterious—perhaps even magical. Fortunately, Confucius did say enough for us to form an impressionistic sense of *ren*. A good place to begin is with the way the word is written in Chinese. In its ordinary sense, *ren* simply means person, and the Chinese character is two strokes that suggest the image of a human being: 人. As a technical term in Confucius's philosophy, *ren* is written by adding the number two to the basic character for person: 仁.[74] This addition turns "human" into "humaneness" and implies that *ren* is a trait manifested in interpersonal relationships. Some of the alternative English translations of *ren*, such as "kindness," "benevolence," "goodness," and "compassion" help highlight the relational dimension of this concept. The word "noble" is also apt because *ren* suggests the quality of an exalted

74. In this character, "person" (人) is simplified to 亻.

character.[75] Perhaps "noble humaneness" or "uncommon kindness" helps get us closer to Confucius's meaning.

Although the concept did not originate with him, Confucius was the first to make *ren* central to his philosophy. He understood *ren* to be the wellspring of all the virtues of the perfect person. To embody this quality in full measure was to attain perfect goodness. Rather than offer a clear and systematic description, Confucius referred to it obliquely by offering examples of persons who manifested it in their lives. Because he taught about it this way, it is not clear whether Confucius thought that *ren* was innate to human nature or an acquired characteristic. Either way, *ren* was a virtue to which one had to aspire, and human beings were endowed by heaven with the capacity to cultivate and nurture it to full expression.

Reciprocity

One of the clearest expressions of his understanding of humaneness came in a version of the Golden Rule: "What you do not wish for yourself, do not impose on others."[76] For Confucius, this principle was based on *shu*, or reciprocity.[77] Reciprocity is a way of judging what others may want or not want. The Master said:

> The humane person, wanting to establish himself, helps others establish themselves, and wanting to be successful, helps others to be successful. Taking one's own feelings as a guide may be called the method of humaneness.[78]

Simply by using our own likes and dislikes as clues, we may imagine what others desire or seek to avoid. We might call this practice empathy; the Buddha called it "seeing others as like yourself."[79]

The principle of reciprocity, of course, is only the first step on the way to full humaneness. Not only must we develop a basic sense of what others want and do not want; we must also train ourselves to act on that knowledge in a compassionate way. Confucius thought the truly noble person actively promotes the success of others and celebrates their accomplishments. Those

75. A. C. Graham also prefers this translation. See Graham, *Disputers*, 19.

76. Huang, trans., *Analects* 12.2 (p. 125) and 15.24, (p. 156).

77. Ibid., *Analects* 15.24. Some refer to this Confucian formulation as the "Silver Rule." The great rabbi Hillel the Elder (c.110 BCE—10 CE) also formulated the ethical principle this way (*BT Shabbat* 31a).

78. *Analects* 6.30, my rendering.

79. *Dhammapada* 10.1, my rendering.

of us who have not yet fully realized the virtue of humaneness may, if we are truthful with ourselves, recognize that we often fall short of that standard. Not only do we find it difficult to wish for the success of others, but we often take positive delight in their failures. Confucius believed that such *Schadenfreude* was a major obstacle to realizing our full humanity, and surmounting it required great effort. Indeed, the very difficulty of such an accomplishment is part of the reason the word *noble* is so pertinent in discussing the virtue of humaneness. The full expression of *ren* is accomplished only through great discipline.

Love of Parents, Love of Others

Confucius also used the language of love to help his followers understand humaneness. For one student, he summarized this virtue by saying "It is to love others."[80] But simply translating *ren* as "love" has many problems, not the least of which is the way love is so closely associated with romance in the Western world. To connect *ren* and the English word *love* might be misleading if we do not understand the full context of Confucian teachings. The sage did not believe that the humane person would—or even *should*—love everyone equally. He thought that we should love those closest to us more than those farther away. Those who have assisted us the most are the ones most deserving of our love. Since our parents have given us the priceless gift of life, we are obligated to love and care for them most.[81] The debt we owe them, in fact, is beyond measure and can never really be repaid. The only proper response is reverential love.

By affirming the priority of love of one's parents and family, Confucius stayed faithful to Chinese tradition. An old proverb declared that filial piety (*xiao*), the love and veneration of parents, is the first of the virtues. In conversations with his protégés, Confucius offered examples of filial behavior. To the traditional duties of the filial child—to feed parents when they are alive, mourn them when they die, and sacrifice to them when the mourning period ends—Confucius added other precepts that went beyond conventional expectations and encouraged the cultivation of noble humaneness. For example, he urged his students to be gentle if they ever found it

80. Dawson, trans., *Analects* 12.2 (p. 47).

81. A classic poem from the *Book of Songs* poignantly described this sense of indebtedness to parents: "Oh father, you begat me! / Oh mother you nourished me! / You supported and nourished me, / You raised me and provided for me,/You looked after me and sheltered me, / In your comings and goings, / You [always] bore me in your arms. / The kindness I would repay / Is boundless as the Heavens!" (*Shijing* "Odes" in Legge, trans., *Chinese Classics*, 4:352).

necessary to correct their parents. If parents resist respectful remonstration, the child must continue to be reverential and express no disobedience or resentment.[82] One must always be patient with one's parents, no matter what.

Confucius thought that filiality was not only the most natural form of love; he also believed it was the very basis of *all* forms of loving. He said, "The noble person is concerned with the root; and if the root is firmly planted the Way grows. Filial piety and fraternal duty—surely these are the roots of humaneness."[83] Family life, Confucius might say, is the classroom where we learn to love. Being a good son or daughter is the foundation for being a good person. If we cannot learn to love our parents, who have given us so much, how can we even hope to love others?

Although love for others begins in the family, it does not stop there. Love of family is the root, not the whole tree. From parents, the person of noble humanity next extends love to the members of his or her immediate family, then to the larger family and to friends, to the village, the province, and on to the whole world, all with decreasing intensity. Confucius did not suggest that we love *only* those near to us; but we should love those far away less than those close by. Confucius's form of "graded love" stands in tension with the more universal forms of compassion and love espoused by the Buddha and Jesus. It was also at odds with a school of thought known as Mohism, established by Chinese philosopher Mozi. Mohism, however, was ultimately rejected by the ancient Chinese, who overwhelmingly concurred with the Confucian belief that love of family is the foundation of social stability.

Saints and the Junzi

Noble humaneness, based on the principle of reciprocity and nourished by filial piety, was the essential ingredient of the virtuous life, the life well-lived. But it was not the only component of a life of superior character. As we observed, Confucius discussed more than a few virtues throughout his teachings. Often he spoke of these other characteristics and aspirations in the context of explaining a particular ideal type. Although they were abstractions rather than historical individuals, these ideal persons functioned as saints do in other traditions, providing worthy models for imitation. Indeed, education in ancient China was largely a matter of training in emulation as much as acquiring knowledge from books.

---

82. *Analects* 4.18.
83. *Analects* 1.2, my rendering.

For Confucius, there were several such ideal models. The highest ideal was the sage. The sage represented the complete fulfillment of human potential, the person in whom humaneness has been perfected. Although he believed that anyone was capable of becoming one, Confucius also admitted that he had never actually met a sage and had given up hope of ever doing so.[84] He even disavowed the title of sage for himself. Confucius also mentioned the ideals of the "good man"[85] and the "complete man,"[86] and these were often associated with particular stations in society. By casting these terms as male, we are simply repeating the way Confucius thought about them; clearly he prized patriarchal values in the family and the society, and when he discussed these ideals he plainly had men in mind. But in terms of the virtues that constitute these saintly persons, there is nothing intrinsically male or female about them.

We should bear this point in mind as we examine the ideal type he stressed above all others: the *junzi*, usually translated as the "gentleman" or "superior man." The *junzi* was not the highest ideal, but it was the ideal for those destined for a political career, as were most of Confucius's students. Sometimes, *junzi* is translated as "scholar-official" in recognition of its association with government work. "Gentleman" is probably a better rendering if we bear in mind that is not to be taken as a generic term for all men. For Confucius, a gentleman was a specific kind of person, someone who, among other things, was courteous and honorable, as in the expression "a gentleman's agreement." A *junzi* was someone who had attained a noble character and superior status by hard work and self-cultivation. Confucius distinguished the *junzi* from the "small" or "petty" man. The small person, in contrast to the gentleman, was self-centered, narrow-thinking, materialistic, and undisciplined.

Based on his study of earlier Chinese culture, Confucius maintained that there were certain qualities or traits that were hallmarks of the gentleman. Humaneness, generosity, reciprocity, and filiality were fundamental, of course. But there were others. The gentleman was not only compassionate, but wise. By wisdom, Confucius meant that one knew what was right and what was wrong; one was a good judge of character and possessed self-knowledge. He told his followers, "If you understand it, say you understand it. If you do not understand it, say you do not understand it. This is wisdom."[87] The quality of wisdom also meant that one thought for oneself

---

84. *Analects* 7.26.

85. *shan ren.*

86. *cheng ren.*

87. Huang, trans., *Analects* 2.17 (p. 55).

and made independent judgments. A gentleman did not blindly follow others or show partiality: "The Master said: The gentleman, in his attitude toward all under heaven, neither favors anyone nor disfavors anyone. He keeps close to whoever is righteous."[88]

Just as the gentleman displayed impartiality in his dealings with others, he practiced equanimity with respect to all circumstances of his life. Confucius greatly admired one of his protégés for the way he was able to live in near poverty without ever complaining or allowing his situation to dictate his disposition. The disciple lived in a small hut and had only a bowl of rice to eat and a ladle of water to drink each day. Yet such wretched conditions never ruined his happiness. For Confucius, matters such as living circumstances, wealth, and fame were determined by heaven, not by the individual. We have no control over these situations, but we can choose to respond to those circumstances with dignity and nobility.

The quality of equanimity pertained also to the opinions of others. In the very first passage of the *Analects*, Confucius defined this quality according to his usual high standards: "not to be resentful at others' failure to appreciate one—surely that is to be a true gentleman."[89] In the same section he took this trait to near the saintly level: "it is not the failure of others to appreciate your abilities that should trouble you, but rather your failure to appreciate theirs."[90] To develop such an attitude obviously entails a radical reorientation of the way most of us experience life. Yet, if we can imagine such a possibility, consider the sense of freedom one would have without having to be so self-absorbed. No wonder Confucius characterized the gentleman as "self-assured and relaxed."[91]

The Road is Long

As we observed, some his followers found this path a hard one to walk. Discussing the Confucian way with another disciple,

> Master Zeng said, "A Gentleman must be strong and resolute, for his burden is heavy and the road is long. He takes benevolence as his burden. Is that not heavy? Only with death does the road come to an end. Is that not long?[92]

88. Ibid., *Analects* 4.10 (p. 68).
89. Dawson, trans., *Analects* 1.1 (p. 3).
90. Lau, trans., *Analects* 1.16, (p. 62).
91. Slingerland, trans., *Analects* 7.37 (p. 77).
92. Lau, trans., *Analects* 8.7 (p. 93).

The discipline of striving for goodness is a lifelong process, and in the end it may not be attained. A gatekeeper who had heard of the reputation of Confucius asked one of the sage's disciples: "Is that the [Kong] who keeps working towards a goal the realization of which he knows to be hopeless?"[93] With no assurance of reward or success, Confucius did ensure that those who took the path of cultivating goodness did so for its own sake and not for any other reason. Confucius said, "The man of humanity places hard work before reward. This may be called humanity."[94] The responsibility for this task lay, of course, with the individual person. The road was long and difficult, but worth the effort. As we shall see, taking the hard way was beneficial to oneself and to society at large.

How to Rule a Kingdom

Confucius, the Buddha, Jesus, and Muhammad all had different relationships with the political dimension of human experience, and each had a different outlook on its importance in the grand of scheme of things. Of the four, only the Buddha was born into the ruling class. He was groomed to become head of state, but an epiphany as a young man suddenly convinced him to renounce his right to rule and instead to pursue a life of greater significance than he thought politics could offer. In his teachings, the Buddha had relatively little to say about political affairs, because the pursuit of human fulfillment was an individual quest that could be achieved irrespective of the political situation. Like the Buddha, Jesus seemed to attach little significance to matters of human governance; he preached about a new order centered in the divine that would overcome and supplant human rule, and he made a point of breaking conventional social regulations to dramatize his message. Ultimately, that proclamation led to his being charged with sedition, for which he was tried and executed.

In the Prophet Muhammad's early life, he apparently cared little about government, for there was little government to speak of in ancient Arabia; but he had a keen interest in the principles of fairness and justice, as did Jesus. As the Muslim community grew, Muhammad necessarily had to attend to political concerns, and he eventually assumed the civic and military leadership of the Arabian city of Madinah. Many of the revelations he received were centrally concerned with matters of politics, law, and governance. Confucius's thought was not based on revelation, and he never had the same leadership responsibilities as the Prophet did, but his conviction about the

93. Ibid., *Analects* 14.38, (p. 130).
94. Huang, trans., *Analects* 6.22 (p. 84).

importance of the political dimension may have exceeded even that of Muhammad. Politics probably mattered more to Confucius than to any of the other three. From his early adulthood until the end of his life, Confucius thought about, taught about, and trained his protégés in the art of governing. Although he aspired to hold a major office to implement his ideas on governance, he was unable to gain such a position. Yet despite what he considered the failure of his political career, almost all of his students sought him as a teacher to help them secure positions as government officials.

There is no wonder why Confucius devoted so much attention to political matters. In the late Zhou period, governance was the main issue of the day. The dynasty's early political and social stability had dissolved as the smaller kingdoms that had once been loyal to the Zhou commenced fighting among themselves for supreme power. The escalating warfare took its toll domestically as rulers increasingly became more interested in self-aggrandizement than in tending to the needs of their subjects. The suffering was massive.

Legalism

Confucius was only one of many Chinese philosophers in the latter half of the first millennium BCE to offer opinions on how to address this dire situation. One school of thought, which came to prominence in the Qin Dynasty, sought to make the ruler's authority absolute. The School of Law, or Legalism as it came to be called, argued that the head of state must maintain an aura of power and mystery to command the obedience of the people. The ruler was charged with keeping order within the kingdom to further the interests of the state. He was to maintain stability by promulgating clear and explicit laws that were to be enforced swiftly and surely. Punishments had to be severe to serve as deterrents to further misconduct. Legalism was the ancient Chinese version of a political philosophy manifested throughout history in a variety of forms and championed by the likes of Machiavelli and Mao Zedong. In essence, this approach regards the interests of the state as paramount and protects those interests by instilling fear in the hearts of those who are perceived to threaten them. It relies on violence and the threat of violence to motivate people to obey the law.

Daoism

Another contemporary school encouraged a political tack that was the opposite of Legalism. Daoism contended that overregulation and governmental heavy-handedness, along with the self-centeredness of the ruling class, was the real source of China's malaise. According to the *Daodejing*, the classic text of this tradition,

> The people are hungry because those above eat up too much in taxes;
> This why the people are hungry.
> The people are difficult to govern because those above engage in action;
> This is why the people are difficult to govern.
> People look upon death lightly because those above are obsessed with their own lives;
> This is why the people look upon death lightly.
> Those who do not strive to live are more worthy than those who cherish life.[95]

Since the suffering of the masses was rooted in the rulers' greed and callous disregard for others, the Daoist philosophers contended that those at the top of the social hierarchy were obliged to curtail their extravagance and live simply. "When it comes to serving Heaven or ruling the people," said the *Daodejing*, "there is no virtue as good as frugality."[96] The early Daoists believed that the world would be an infinitely better place if the rulers would simply stay out of other people's lives.

Confucian political philosophy shared some aspects with Legalism and Daoism but differed from them in several important ways. Like the Daoists, Confucius believed the solution to China's problems lay in the rulers' pursuit of the virtuous life. But Confucius had a different idea about how virtue was to be cultivated. The Daoists thought virtue came naturally by following the way (*dao*) of nature; Confucius believed virtue had to be nurtured with ritual and decorum. Confucius shared Legalism's appreciation for order and hierarchy, especially when compared to Daoism's more anarchistic predilections. But he greatly disdained legislation and the use of fear as a tactic to enforce social harmony. Confucius also had a different understanding of the purpose of government. The Legalists subordinated the interests of persons to that of the state; individuals were expected to serve the state. The Daoists regarded government as a necessary evil and looked forward to the day when governments as such could be eliminated altogether because everyone lived in accord with the way of nature.

95. Ivanhoe, trans., *Daodejing*, 78.
96. *Daodejing*, ch. 59, my rendering.

Rule by Virtue

In distinction to both schools, Confucius believed governments should exist to promote the moral well-being of all citizens. That view of politics derived directly from his anthropological perspective. Since the purpose of human existence is to manifest our humaneness to the fullest, governments ought to facilitate progress toward that end. Confucius had no desire to abolish government or to intensify its power by making the state an end in itself. He never advocated changing the basic structure of the way China was ruled. The idea of a democracy or a republic was completely alien to his mind. He fully accepted the notion that countries had to be administered by trained and qualified specialists—trained and qualified not in economics or jurisprudence or military science but in humaneness and the rituals that nurture it. He imagined a kingdom governed by a sovereign who was a sage and officials who were gentlemen. To the ruler of a kingdom adjoining the state of Lu, Confucius once said: "Good government consists in the ruler being a ruler, the minister being a minister, the father being a father, and the son being a son."[97] Not only does this statement underscore Confucius's belief in the necessity of clearly established hierarchies, but it also highlights his conviction that each individual had to live up to the role to which he or she has been assigned by heaven. A prince had to be a prince; that is to say, a prince had to take his responsibility seriously and discharge it to the best of his ability. Perhaps that sounds trite. But remember, Confucius lived at time when these responsibilities were *not* being accepted by those who were charged with them. For Confucius, taking these responsibilities seriously meant keeping paramount the welfare of the people and suppressing the temptation to seek personal gain through one's office. What a revolutionary idea!

These sage-kings and gentleman-officials would rule their subjects primarily through instruction and example rather than legislation and enforcement. In general, Confucius was suspicious of laws. The Chinese never believed that laws were handed down by a god, like Yahweh giving the Ten Commandments to Moses, or Muhammad receiving revelations from the angel Gabriel. The ancient Chinese always saw the regulations governing society as human products, subject to human flaws. Confucius was particularly sensitive to the potential deficiency of human legal systems. He did not think laws could be written to cover every conceivable situation. He preferred to allow morally qualified persons to judge what is right or wrong in particular cases. He was also fearful that the production of laws would

97. *Analects* 12.11, my rendering.

increase litigation, and he longed for the day when litigation would not be necessary.[98] But most important, Confucius resisted rule by law because it did not appeal to the better part of our natures. If laws work to maintain order in society, he thought, it is because people fear the repercussions of breaking them. And fear is not a good basis for establishing social harmony or personal well-being. Fear eats up the soul.

> The Master said: "If you govern them with decrees and regulate them with punishments, the people will evade them but will have no sense of conscience. If you govern them with virtue and regulate them with rituals, they will have a sense of conscience and will flock to you."[99]

Virtue, rather than law, was the Confucian ideal. Only virtue can evoke what is best in persons and allow society to flourish.

But what did Confucius mean by ruling with virtue? In part, it meant for the ruler and the ruling class to be moral examples for their subjects. It meant that the rulers would instruct their citizens on moral conduct through schools and the promotion of study. But most of all, rule by virtue consisted in a force generated by a virtuous superior that would arouse virtuous conduct in subordinates. To grasp this fascinating idea, we need to understand the Chinese concept of virtue.

The Power of Virtue

The word *virtue* is the usual English translation for the Chinese term *de*. The Daoist classic, the *Daodejing*, is often rendered as the "Classic (*jing*) of the Way (*dao*) and the Power (*de*)." That translation gets us a little closer to the ancient Chinese understanding of *de*. Not only was *de* thought to be a quality or an aspiration, as suggested by the word *virtue*; it was also regarded as a force or power, as suggested by the title of the Daoist classic. Those who sought to live virtuous lives, and who consistently performed acts of kindness and generosity, accumulated within themselves a powerful moral presence or charisma. Virtuous power was generated by an individual's inner disposition or attitude. That moral energy dwelling within the person of high virtue could mysteriously—almost magically and effortlessly—transform others in wholesome ways. Those who benefited from or witnessed the acts of virtuous persons were believed to feel a deep indebtedness and

---

98. Dawson, trans., *Analects* 12.13 (p. 46): "what is surely necessary is to bring it about that there is no litigation."

99. Huang, trans., *Analects* 2.3 (p. 52) I have slightly edited the Huang translation.

would want to respond in like manner. The Chinese called this desire *bao*, the natural wish to respond to a kindness with kindness. Thus, virtuous acts encourage virtue in others. Recall some of the legends about Confucius's appointment to the office of minister of crime and how almost immediately there was a sudden outbreak of morality throughout the state of Lu. Those stories illustrated the charismatic force of virtue as understood by the ancient Chinese.

This conception helps us to see why moral self-cultivation was essential to the ruler and his ministers. The mysterious power of virtuous rulers could do what laws and police could not: to make others *want* to do what was right. Confucius knew very well that it was impractical and ultimately counterproductive to have the police stationed at every street corner to make sure the populace behaved. The power of virtue, on the other hand, is less obvious but far more effective. "The gentleman's moral character is wind," Confucius said in a metaphor that became famous in Chinese literature, "and the small man's moral character is grass. When the wind blows, the grass must surely bend."[100] The power of transformative virtue was so great that the use of physical force would become unnecessary. In advising a magistrate, the Master said: "If one's character is rectified, then things will get done without orders being issued; but if one's character is not rectified, then although orders are issued they are not followed."[101] A hundred years of moral rule, he predicted, could completely eliminate killing within a realm.

The Role of the People

The Confucian view of society suggests a rather passive role for the masses. The ordinary people were to be influenced and guided but not consulted about matters of state. Confucius believed in a government "for the people" but not "by the people." Yet, it was essential that rulers enjoy the confidence of their subjects. The Master said: "If the people do not trust you, you have nothing to stand on."[102] In the early Zhou, rulers could count on the trust of the governed by invoking the mandate of heaven. But in the days of Confucius, such a claim would hold little water if not supported by the ruler's moral character: the governor had to earn the confidence of the governed. Without that basic faith, the ruler could not exert the moral suasion vital to good governance.

---

100. *Analects* 12.19, my rendering.
101. Dawson, trans., *Analects* 13.6 (p. 50).
102. Huang, trans., *Analects* 12.7 (p. 127).

But the role of the ordinary folk was more than simply being the passive recipients of the power of virtue, streaming down from on high. Commoners were also expected to participate in the well-being of society by living virtuous lives. When someone asked Confucius why he was not involved in government, he indicated that one could serve the purpose of government without holding an office. He said:

> Just by being a dutiful son and an honorable brother, a man can influence government. By following virtue a man is, in fact, taking part in government.[103]

The Chinese have long regarded society as a great extended family, with the ruler as *paterfamilias* and the people as his children. Appropriate behavior in society followed the same patterns and values of life in the family. I doubt that Confucius believed that everyone could follow his path to complete goodness. Even his highly motivated protégés found it hard going at times. But practicing filiality—the love and respect for one's parents—was well within everyone's ability and strengthened not only the family but the world at large.

Thus, the direction of moral charisma was not only from the top down. Confucius believed that social superiors could be influenced by their subordinates, just as children could positively influence their parents. This is one reason why he encouraged his followers to take government positions, where they would be situated to influence the lower classes as well as the ruler and his court. For Confucius, the personal moral character of all citizens reverberates throughout a society. The goodness of the individual makes a real difference in the world.

Li

If the most important component for ruling a kingdom was the ruler's personal moral character, then the next ingredient was the practice of ritual. Proper observance of ritual, Confucius thought, was absolutely essential to the welfare of the state. He said, "If a ruler understands the rites at the altars of Heaven and Earth and comprehends the meaning of the ancestral sacrifices, then ruling his kingdom would be as easy as looking at the palm of his hand."[104]

103. *Analects* 2.21, my rendering.

104. *Analects* 19.6, paraphrased from Legge and Ford, trans., *Teachings of Confucius*, 404.

The importance placed on ritual in governance may strike many modern persons as a bit odd. The secularized contemporary world has a hard time appreciating the role of ceremony in traditional cultures and might especially find it difficult to grasp its function in matters of state. But as moderns, we have not completely lost touch with the value of state rituals. We still inaugurate our leaders and conduct state funerals when they die. Visiting dignitaries are welcomed by ceremonies and honored with formal state dinners. The signings of treaties are conducted under ceremonial auspices. But these occasions are mere vestiges of times when ritual was far more central to the lives of individuals and societies. In the Han Dynasty, the Chinese government even had a board of rites, which functioned alongside the boards of revenue, war, and public works. Imagine a secretary of ceremony in the cabinet of the president of the United States!

Ritual, or *li* to use the indigenous term, had always been important in Chinese government, but Confucius gave it new significance. In the Shang and early Zhou Dynasties, emperors sacrificed to the gods and ancestors and employed divination to maintain harmony between heaven and earth. Ritual was understood primarily as the performance of these acts. Simply going through the prescribed motions was sufficient to make the ritual do what it was intended to do. Nearer the time of Confucius, however, the idea of *li* came to include the sense of reverence and sincerity on the part of the ritual's participants. The sacrifice had to be enacted in the proper spirit, lest it be ineffective and displeasing to the gods and ancestors it intended to honor. Confucius took this concern with the interior dimension of ceremony a step further by connecting it with the quality of humaneness. As we learned earlier, for Confucius, ritual was an act performed not primarily to please divine beings but to shape the moral character of the participants and observers. I suspect that even if Confucius did not truly believe in gods and spirits, he would have still thought that sacrifices and rituals were immensely beneficial activities.

Furthermore, Confucius expanded the meaning of *li* to include not only what we ordinarily think of as ceremony, such as sacrifices and state funerals, but also the ritualized forms of everyday behavior—what we would call manners and etiquette. When we study the spiritual disciplines of Confucianism, we will have an opportunity to discuss *li* in this sense. But first, let us explore how Confucius understood *li* as public ritual rather than private conduct.

The ceremonies performed on state occasions were elaborate events that required extensive study before they could be performed. These rituals often required many persons to be directly involved with the ceremony. There were not only the specialists who conducted the rites but also musicians, dancers, and actors who performed for the pleasure of the audience, which consisted of both human and divine beings. The opening and closing ceremonies of the 2008 Summer Olympics in Beijing disclosed the traditional Chinese love of pageantry as well as the colossal forethought and coordination required for such grand occasions. Of course, the state rituals of ancient China were nowhere near the magnitude of the Olympic ceremonies; but both the ancient state rituals and this modern instance were informed by the same seriousness and attention to detail.

Unlike the rituals at the Beijing Olympics—but very much like the Games in ancient Greece—the gods were invited to attend the state functions of ancient China. They were offered food, but humans were also allowed to partake. The offerings were usually animals publicly sacrificed for the occasion and cooked or burnt whole. The most common victims were oxen, pigs, and sheep. A ritual that included one of each species was especially pleasing to the gods. Sometimes the spirits were offered gifts of silk and jade or rice and millet. But more important than the gifts themselves was the reverential and gracious attitude with which they were offered. According to the *Book of Songs*, the spirits rewarded with a long life those who sacrificed with the correct frame of mind.

There were many aspects to the rituals that Confucius saw as evoking and refining the sense of humaneness. The study required to perform the ritual served as a form of discipline and self-restraint and provided knowledge about the meaning of the ritual itself, which Confucius believed embodied the mysteries of heaven. Beyond this mystical dimension, the rituals had more mundane elements that contributed to moral development. They induced certain emotions and moods, such as reverence, gratitude, and humility. They promoted a spirit of cooperation among people and instilled a sense of the importance of subordinating personal needs and desires to the social endeavor. Rituals required concentration and attention to detail. They created a sense of the interconnectedness between humanity and divinity, providing a reminder that one was part of a vast web of interdependent relationships involving heaven, earth, and humanity.

Confucius was confident that returning to the serious practice of the ancient rites would restore harmony among the people more surely than the enactment and enforcement of laws. By simply attending to their ancient charge to perform state rituals, and conducting these rituals with sincerity and the proper frame of mind, the rulers would effect a great change among the people. The past would be honored and the spirits of all persons would be lifted. Life would be good.

What a Sage Does

Confucius thought that becoming a sage was within the grasp of everyone. But he never said it would be easy. The path was long and hard, and there was no guarantee that one who aspired would in fact become a sage or even a gentleman. Confucius could not even promise there would be happiness at the end of the long road. At most, those on the way—or the rare individual who reached the destination—could enjoy the satisfaction of knowing that they had lifted themselves above the common lot and pursued the purpose for which humanity had been intended. Confucius knew the way was difficult and had to be traversed one step at a time. There were no shortcuts to humaneness.

Up to this point in our study, we have concentrated on the conceptual dimensions of Confucius's philosophy—his ideas about heaven and virtue and politics. That focus should not obscure the fact that he intended his teachings to be implemented and practiced, not merely pondered and evaluated. As we shall do for each of the other figures, we turn now to give consideration to the aspect of his teaching I have categorized as spiritual discipline. Under this rubric we include those exercises and activities that these teachers promoted as ways of nudging their followers closer to what they considered human fulfillment, however that might be understood. Each of our four wise men regarded these practical disciplines as essential to their teachings. These practices were not optional activities for those interested in extra credit but were the very means by which each teacher sought to share his vision with others. In a very meaningful sense, therefore, we cannot completely appreciate what any one of them taught until we have actually taken the path he set forth and walked it to the end.

My choice of metaphor is deliberate. Confucius, the Buddha, Jesus, and Muhammad each referred to his spiritual practice as "the way" or "the path." Muhammad spoke of Islam as the "straight path"; Jesus called himself "the way and the truth and the life," and one of early Christianity's names for itself was simply "the way"; the Buddha established the "noble path" to nirvana; and Confucius urged people to follow the way, or *dao*, of heaven. Each teacher believed taking his path required commitment and discipline.

Discipline is a rather ambiguous term. We often associate the word with punishment. It hardly needs to be said, but that is not the sense in which we are using it here, although spiritual disciplines, like punishments, can sometimes be hard to bear. Spiritual disciplines can also serve a corrective or rehabilitative function, like some punishments. But unlike punishment—at least usually—spiritual disciplines are *voluntarily* undertaken. It is that voluntary aspect that can make spiritual discipline such a demanding, even grueling, experience. Discipline of the spirit means nothing if it is not willed for oneself. No one can force another to become enlightened or to seek perfect goodness. The motivation has to come from within, and that impetus is often very hard to muster, especially when there are so many diversions along the way.

The nature of the spiritual path, furthermore, is such that one is destined to fail before one succeeds. Failure, in fact, is essential to following any spiritual path. Confucius may have wanted people to attain perfect goodness, but they could only do so by failing to be perfect. Failure is required because the real strength of spirit is achieved when one has to find the gumption to get on the straight path yet again. The path of spiritual discipline may seem linear, but in reality it is a long process of starting over again and again and again. A lyric from the Mevlevi order of Sufism beautifully expresses this dynamic of discipline:

> Come, come, come again,
>
> Whoever you may be,
>
> A believer, an unbeliever, an infidel. Come.
>
> Ours is not the door of desperation.
>
> Even if you have broken your vows a hundred times,
>
> Come, come again.[105]

The repetitive quality of starting over, of breaking vows and renewing them, is one of the reasons spiritual disciplines are called exercises and practices in some traditions. It is the practice that perfects. It is the continuous reaffirmation of the vows that makes the spirit strong.

The Confucian Disciplines

The disciplines that Confucius recommended can perhaps be best understood when we first consider the impediments that prevent us from arriving at the goal of the virtuous life. At the top of the list would be self-centeredness or hubris, the tendency to believe and act as if one were the central item of reality. Not only did Confucius think that believing oneself to be at the center of everything was a mistaken notion; he thought that it carried destructive consequences for others and for oneself. The Buddha, Jesus, and Muhammad all said similar things. For Confucius, the problem with hubris was simple. If humaneness is a virtue manifested in interpersonal relationships, it is difficult to bring that quality to expression if one discounts the

---

105. Attributed to Jalal ad-Din Muhammad Rumi but not attested: my version.

significance of another. Self-importance is the catalyst for ingratitude, arrogance, insincerity, dishonesty, anger, and a multitude of other defilements. Our list of obstructions to humaneness might also include ignorance—failing to know enough or to have sufficient self-awareness to act wisely in particular situations. Ignorance might cause us to act rashly, to resort to violence, to speak an unkind word, or to neglect the humanity that connects us to one another. Confucius might single out ignorance of the past as a particular impediment to the virtuous life. How can we act virtuously when there are no contemporary models on which to base our behavior? Only in the past were there such worthy paragons.

The practices of Confucian spirituality functioned to disable these obstacles and to train individuals in more wholesome ways. Some of the practices were quite basic and common to a variety of spiritual paths; we will begin with those. Others were more specific to the Confucian approach and relate to his deep appreciation of the value of ritual for regulating human life. As far as we know, Master Kong never provided his apprentices with a step-by-step program for attaining moral perfection. But certain themes recur throughout the *Analects*, and it is upon those that we will focus our attention.

The fundamental practices endorsed by Confucius, and many other great teachers throughout history, come as no surprise. They are basic to all forms of self-discipline. We might simply call them exercises in restraining desires; Confucius called them "subduing oneself."[106] If an overweening self is a key barrier to humaneness, then merely keeping the self in check goes a long way toward allowing us to practice virtue. Confucius admonished his students to live simply, without ostentation or luxury, as he himself did. He said, "A gentleman seeks neither a full belly nor a comfortable home. He is quick in action but cautious in speech."[107] Not only was Confucius aware that pursuing wealth was no avenue to happiness or satisfaction, but he also believed that possessing more than was necessary deadened the spirit. On the other hand, China's sages have never really cared for the intense asceticism that one finds in the history of Indian religions and parts of Christianity, and Confucius was certainly among them. You will not find Confucius telling his protégés to wear hair shirts or to flagellate themselves. But he did think that a *little* discomfort was a good thing. A touch of asceticism was necessary to keep the mind attentive to itself and sensitive to the wider world, for both self- and other-awareness were vital to the way of virtue.

106. Dawson, trans., *Analects* 12.1 (p. 44).
107. Lau, trans., *Analects* 1.14 (p. 61).

Introspective Self-Awareness

Self-awareness was cultivated through moments of introspection. Master Kong called these periods of reflection "quiet-sitting," "abiding in reverence," and "rectifying the mind." The purpose of such times was not to commune with the divine or experience extraordinary states of consciousness. More than anything, Confucius viewed these times of serenity as opportunities for critical self-examination. There was nothing exotic about the practice at all. It simply afforded the aspiring noble person time to remove himself or herself from the din and distractions of daily life to attend to self-improvement. Quiet-sitting allowed the sage-in-training to look objectively, with ruthless honesty, at his or her own character and make changes as necessary. "When the gentleman makes a mistake," Confucius said on many occasions, "he is not afraid to correct it."[108] Confucius's own habit of self-examination and the humility it required to undertake were among his most admirable traits. He told others, "When you see a noble person, think of equaling him; when you see an unworthy person, examine yourself inwardly."[109]

Quiet-sitting contributed to the development of other characteristics of the noble one. It refined the faculty that Confucius called "keen discernment," by forestalling reflexive actions. When a student asked about "keen discernment," Confucius said, "When slanders that seep under the skin and grievances that cause pain do not drive you to an immediate response, you may be said to have keen discernment."[110] No doubt introspective moments also gave a clearer understanding of one's limitations and abilities, the basis of what he called wisdom. The sage said, "If you understand it, say you understand it. If you do not understand it, say you do not understand it. This is wisdom."[111] Introspection fine-tuned one's listening and speaking skills. It sharpened the proficiency to listen to others with an open mind, free from preconceived opinions, and it facilitated discretion in speech. Without the self-awareness nurtured in introspection, thought Confucius, one is not fit to serve in government.

Attention to Mundane Details

We observed on several occasions that Confucian philosophy was decidedly oriented toward life in this world. Confucius never seemed to express a clear

108 Huang, trans., *Analects* 1.8 (p. 48).

109. *Analects* 4.17, my rendering.

110. *Analects* 12.6, in Chin, *Authentic Confucius*, 131.

111. Huang, trans., *Analects* 2.17 (p. 55).

opinion about what he thought of the afterlife. In the depth of his heart, he may have believed in or hoped for, or perhaps even denied, a form of continued existence after death. But he certainly did not make that belief part of his teachings. Partly as a consequence of his this-worldly emphasis, Confucius gave paramount significance to the matters of ordinary existence. Where other great teachers may have called for a radical disregard for the things of this world, Confucius urged a radical engagement with them. But he did not do so to promote a kind of Epicurean enjoyment of what life had to offer. Rather, he viewed everyday experience, including the most mundane things, with an eye to seeing their moral and spiritual significance. For Confucius, the commonplace details of life could become the signifiers of heaven. Such things as clothing, food, and even posture were matters of great importance. The *Analects* reports that Confucius gave much attention to wearing the appropriate robes for each occasion, eating meats with the right condiments, and ensuring that the mat on which he sat was properly aligned. All that fuss about the daily routine may strike us as rather wearisome and pointless. But to Confucius, attending to these everyday matters gave expression to one's respect for the social fabric and helped foster a greater awareness of the sacred dimension within all things.

Decorum

As someone sensitive to the sacred aspect of the mundane world and to the transformative effects of ceremony, it should not surprise us that Confucius thought the whole of life ought to be conducted as a grand ritual. In an innovative move, Confucius extended the ancient role of *li* in Chinese statecraft and religion to include all aspects of human relationships. His perspective on life as a sacred rite was vital to his view of the world and was one of his major contributions to world religion and philosophy. The essence of this ideal was the belief that in all interpersonal relationships, human beings ought to comport themselves with the same poise and decorum appropriate to a sacred ceremony. According to the *Book of Songs*, the spirits admired rituals that were conducted in a spirit of sincerity, close attention to detail, humility, respectfulness, and generosity.[112] These were precisely the qualities Confucius valued in everyday life. Properly conducted state rituals and personal rites of passage such as marriages and funerals were the special areas where these qualities were cultivated and expressed. But in the everyday world, these qualities were formed and manifested in proper etiquette and manners.

112. Waley, trans., *Book of Songs*, 209.

Confucius was especially aware of the capacity of everyday etiquette to give shape to our potential for humaneness, thus evoking the best of what is in the human heart. The principle underlying this belief is fairly easy to understand. To observe good manners means to act in a clearly prescribed way that is considerate of the feelings of others, and—this is the important part—*to do so whether you feel like it or not.* So you really didn't care much for the gift you received for your birthday. Your feelings notwithstanding, you know the mannerly thing to do is to express appreciation anyway. Fortunately, the words and gestures have already been formulated for you by society. "Thanks, I always wanted one of these," you say, followed by a nice thank-you note a few days later. Your benefactor is happy, and you feel good knowing you have done the right thing by preserving the harmony between you. And who knows, you might really learn to like the gift—or maybe you won't. It doesn't really matter. What matters is that you express appreciation for another person's generosity. The simple expression of gratitude edges you a little bit closer to actually feeling it. You don't have to like the gift to be grateful for it.[113]

Confucius thought that continual practice of mannerly acts could engender sincere feelings in the one who performs them. You may not feel particularly humble, but after several thousand bows and prostrations, feelings of genuine humility begin to surface. Humans are habitual creatures, and so repetitious actions can do amazing things to transform the character. As Will Durant says in expounding Aristotle's philosophy, "We are what we repeatedly do. Excellence is not an act, but a habit."[114] As character is shaped by behavior, the performance of humane acts becomes natural and spontaneous. It loses the artificial quality that may have attended it at first. For Confucius, this dialectical relationship between the external act and the internal disposition is the key to understanding how both ritual and decorum can make us more humane.

Music and Poetry

A sophisticated enjoyment of music, poetry, and dance was also an important dimension of Confucian spirituality. Like the practices of ritual, decorum, and introspection, so also the cultured arts have the capacity to awaken and refine moral sensitivities. For Confucius, in fact, the principal value of these fine arts was moral rather than aesthetic. Music, poetry, and dance were of course important aspects of the rituals Confucius valued so

---

113. See *Analects* 10.16 for an example from Confucius's life.

114. Durant, *Story of Philosophy*, 98.

highly, but he thought that they could be important quite apart from the ceremonial context.

Confucius was especially fond of music. The *Analects* quotes him as saying, "One is inspired by poetry, strengthened by rituals, and perfected by music."[115] His followers noted that he loved to sing, and often did so with them. He also played the *qin*, a stringed instrument somewhat like a zither, to accompany the singing. Late in life, he learned to play the stone chimes. The songs he sang were usually from the classic *Book of Songs*, from which we have quoted several times. An especially fine piece of music well performed could send him into a state of ecstasy. Once, while visiting the province of Qi, Confucius heard "The Succession," a composition often played at state ceremonies. A student reported that for three months afterwards, Confucius did not notice the taste of meat. Unfortunately, we have no record of the melodies Confucius and his contemporaries may have heard, but archaeologists have recently uncovered some examples of the instruments on which they were played.

The *Analects* does not really give us enough information to know exactly what it was about music that appealed to Confucius or what precisely he thought refined the moral sense. There are passages that indicate that the lyrics to the songs he enjoyed expressed high ethical sentiments. But there must have been more than just the words that were significant, otherwise he would have been content simply with poetry. A bit of reflection on the nature of music might help us understand the sage's infatuation with it. We are all aware of how particular forms of music can express and arouse specific moods and feelings. Certain moods, such as reverence and pensiveness, would have been especially appropriate for encouraging humaneness. The powerful effect of music on the human spirit has been noticed throughout history. Muslim physicians in the Middle Ages, for example, used music to treat patients who had been diagnosed with mental illnesses. We can also imagine how musical harmonies would have reminded Confucius of the ideal of harmony between heaven and earth, ruler and subject, husband and wife. A perfectly performed musical piece, especially fitting the occasion and involving the coordination of dozens of musicians and singers each playing his or her allotted role would have been the consummate metaphor for his vision of the virtuous society. But even more than suggesting the ideal of a harmonious society, music can assist in making the ideal a reality. Anyone who has ever taken part in collective singing or listening to a concert understands the sense of unity and fellow-feeling that such an

---

115. *Analects* 8.8, my rendering.

experience can produce. For some, the point might be illustrated with a single word: Woodstock.

Just as he thought music, poetry, and dance had the potential for elevating the human spirit, Confucius believed they could also debase and disrupt humanity. He seems to have been especially concerned about the way music and dance could incite lust. He was particularly annoyed by the music from the province of Zheng. "Banish the music of Zheng," he said. "The music of Zheng is licentious."[116] The ruler of Zheng, it seems, had a liking for music and parties that Confucius found offensive. This ruler was reported to have enjoyed late-night drinking festivals in a large garden in which he had a pond filled with wine and invited men and women to cavort naked into the wee hours of the morning, all to the accompaniment of music. Confucius would not have cared much for Woodstock.

Confucius also had firm opinions about dancing. Like music and poetry, he appreciated the potential of dance to embody and stimulate harmony and reverence. But he was also concerned with the possibility that dance, like music, could be used in nefarious ways. Recall the two episodes from Confucius's life involving dancers, both of which illustrated that he considered dance serious business. In the first, he ordered the execution of a troupe whose performance he found to be lewd and disrespectful to the dignity of the ruler. In the second, he resigned political office when the prime minister of Lu became enamored with dancing girls sent as a gift from a neighboring state.

Given the great power of poetry, music, and dance to affect the moods and dispositions of the heart, Confucius believed it was morally necessary to apply thoughtful control over the kinds of entertainment one attends. In a more general sense, he was concerned about the choices we make about our environments that might have an impact on our character. That concern extended to the people with whom we are friends. He recommended that those aspiring to be gentlemen should not enter the domain of someone who continually acted in an immoral way. The gentleman, he said, "draws near to those who possess the Way in order to be set straight by them."[117]

Confucian spirituality was nothing if not comprehensive. It involved disciplined attention to all aspects of life, from the interiority of thoughts and feelings to the exteriority of actions and deeds. It moved throughout the sacred and the secular and diminished the distinction between them. It gave place to the worship of the spirits and to the folding of clothes. It concerned the person as individual and the individual within a nexus of relationships.

---

116. *Analects* 15.11, my rendering.

117 Slingerland, *Analects* 1.14, (p. 6).

It sought to bring humanity to completion and harmony between heaven and earth.

Confucius and Confucianism

In life, Confucius enjoyed modest renown at best; in death, however, his reputation flourished and his influence far exceeded anything he could have possibly expected. After Confucius died, his ideas and practices were kept alive and developed by his immediate protégés, many of whom went on to start their own schools and become teachers in their own right. These disciples began the process of preserving the Confucian legacy for future generations and disseminating his teachings throughout China. We turn now to a brief examination of how that legacy fared in Chinese history. We will discuss the initial compilation and interpretation of his ideas, their influence in Chinese politics and education, and the gradual development of religious practices centered on the sage himself.

As we intimated in our discussion of the *Analects*, preserving the memory and teachings of Confucius was not a simple matter of writing down what he had said and done. His students naturally had somewhat different recollections of his life and teachings and different senses about what his words and actions meant. It was extremely easy to mesh one's own beliefs and ideas with what one thought the Master had said. There was nothing necessarily sinister or deliberate about that process. All of us sometimes attribute to someone we greatly admire the ideals or values that we ourselves hold. Certainly, those very human tendencies came into play as the sage's students compiled the text of his sayings over a period of several generations. This of course is why much of Confucian scholarship is devoted to trying to extricate the authentic sayings of Confucius from the words and ideas of others. The difficulty of the task is symbolized by the glaring lack of scholarly consensus about what is genuine and what is not.

But even if Confucius had authored a book of his own, explaining his philosophy carefully and systematically, his ideas would still be subject to diverse interpretations. Nowhere is this point more clearly seen than in the divergent interpretations of two of the most important early Confucian philosophers, Mencius and Xunzi. Mencius and Xunxi came to what appear to be diametrically opposite positions about the nature of human beings. Exploring the substance of their debate will help us appreciate the way the teachings of Confucius, the Buddha, Jesus, and Muhammad can be subject to such a range of understandings that often lead to sectarian divisions among their followers. This exploration will also open us to a different level of thinking about Confucius himself. The question at stake is an ancient one: Is human nature basically evil or basically good? With Confucius as their guide, Mencius and Xunzi came down on opposite sides of the issue.

Mencius

Most scholars consider Mencius (372-289 BCE) to be the most important Confucian thinker next to Confucius himself. He is the only other philosopher besides Confucius to whom scholars refer by a Latinized name. In Chinese, he is known as Mengzi, or Master Meng. Mencius was born eighteen miles from Confucius's hometown of Qufu about a century after the death of the sage. Tradition claims that Mencius was a protégé of Confucius's grandson. Mencius was the first Confucian thinker of any real significance after Confucius, and as such, his understanding of the master's thought became immensely influential in subsequent history. The relationship of Mencius to Confucius can be compared to that between Paul and Jesus. Paul was one of the first major interpreters of Jesus's life, and later Christians tend to see Jesus through the eyes of Paul. Likewise, many read the teachings of Confucius through the perspective of Mencius.

Mencius was concerned with all dimensions of Confucian philosophy and religion, but one area seems to have interested him more than any other: the basic makeup of human beings. Confucius, as we recall, thought that all persons shared a common nature by birth, but through upbringing and education they were molded in different ways: some became good and others wicked. I suggested that Confucius thought of humans as "unfinished" beings who required socialization and self-cultivation to be complete. What Confucius did not say was whether or not he thought human beings were naturally good or bad. His reticence on this topic probably related to his aversion to speculative issues and to the practical orientation of his teachings. And it was simply not a question that philosophers of his day were asking.

But Mencius was working in a different intellectual environment from Confucius. For the most part, Confucius did not try to defend his position against rival points of view. The *Analects* essentially presents his teachings as assertions rather than systematic arguments. Confucius did not feel compelled to provide a rational case for his ideas. Mencius, on the other hand, *did* feel obliged to respond to the questions and criticisms of other thinkers who were trying to advance their own philosophies. He was committed to the way of virtue espoused by Confucius but was aware that the sage had not fully elaborated his perspective on many matters. Because he genuinely believed the Confucian way offered the best hope for China in an age on the brink of despair, he attempted to provide the comprehensive development and argumentation that Confucius's aphoristic teachings lacked. In the Period of the Warring States, when Mencius lived, one of the prominent points of discussion was the moral nature of human beings. The issue was not merely theoretical. Whatever position one might take could have important consequences for addressing the questions of governance and human harmony. If humans were by nature evil, for example, then it might be prudent for the government to curtail that inclination by any means necessary, including force or the threat of violence. This in fact was the position of the school known as Legalism.

Mencius, however, maintained that human nature was innately good. He argued his case by means of a thought experiment:

> Suppose someone suddenly saw a child about to fall into a well: anyone in such a situation would have a feeling of alarm and compassion—not because one sought to get in good with the child's parents, not because one wanted fame among one's neighbors and friends, and not because one would dislike the sound of the child's cries.[118]

Mencius does not argue that everyone would be *moved* to save the child, only that each person would experience a surge of fellow-feeling. That spontaneous reaction was the evidence, Mencius thought, of basic human goodness. Whether or not one acted on that impulse would be another matter. His argument seems to be specifically directed to challenge the position of another philosopher, Yang Zhu, who argued that all human actions are driven solely by self-interest. With his example, Mencius tries to show that at least *some* actions can be motivated by involuntary, selfless urges.

Mencius goes on to claim that such altruistic impulses are the defining quality of human beings:

> From this we can see that if one is without the feeling of compassion, one is not human. If one is without the feeling of disdain, one is not human. If one is without the feeling of deference, one is not human. If one is without the feeling of approval and disapproval, one is not human.[119]

In short, Mencius locates the roots of the principal Confucian virtues in human nature. We come into the world with these basic qualities.

118. Van Norden, trans., *Mengzi*, book 2A6.3 (p. 46).
119. Ibid., book 2A6.4 (p. 46).

Yet, if human nature is fundamentally compassionate, how does Mencius explain the fact that compassion does not appear to be the prevailing characteristic of human existence? Mencius, after all, lived during a particularly brutal period in China's history. How can he account for that brutality and simultaneously argue that persons are essentially good? This was the same question that vexed the Christian theologian Augustine, who developed his theory of original sin to account for the discrepancy. The answer Mencius provided was different from Augustine's. The origin of human wickedness was not a primordial fall from god's good graces, as Augustine suggested, but the failure fully to foster and strengthen basic human goodness. Mencius compares innate virtue to seedlings rooted in the fertile soil of human nature:

> The feeling of compassion is the sprout of benevolence [that is, *ren*, or noble humanness]. The feeling of disdain is the sprout of righteousness. The feeling of deference is the sprout of propriety. The feeling of approval or disapproval is the sprout of wisdom.[120]

Failing to care for and nurture these tender seedlings causes them to wither and die. In other words, persons are not naturally evil, but they become evil when their upbringing and education neglect moral cultivation or deliberately thwart it. Mencius offers a story that provides an allegory of his understanding of human nature:

> The trees of Ox Mountain were once beautiful. But because it bordered on a large state, hatchets and axes besieged it. Could it remain verdant? Due to the respite it got during the day or night, and the moisture of the rain and dew, there were sprouts and shoots growing there. But oxen and sheep came and grazed on them. Hence, it was as if it were barren. Seeing it barren, people believed that there had never been any timber there.[121]

According to this analogy, the prevalence of evil in the world does not disprove innate human goodness. Human wickedness only illustrates our failure to care for and develop the fragile qualities of our basic goodness.

Like Confucius, Mencius believed that education and domestic nurturance were the keys to cultivating virtue. The practice of filial piety and the parental love for the child were essential for an individual to realize his or her potential for kindness. Mencius also envisioned a prominent role for government in this endeavor. Like Confucius, he believed the ruler should govern by virtue rather than by law. Because of our deep innate goodness,

---

120. Ibid., book 2A6.5 (pp. 46–47).
121. Ibid., book 6A8.1 (pp. 151–52).

human beings are more responsive to displays of goodness than to demonstrations of force or the threat of punishment. It was essential, he thought, for rulers to provide outstanding models of virtuous character, which their subjects would then aspire to emulate. This idea was based on the Chinese concept of *de*, the belief that the accumulation of virtue has the power to awaken virtue in others.

Mencius also helped clarify some of the religious elements implicit in Confucius's teaching. Confucius had indicated that he considered himself commissioned by heaven to teach the way of virtue; Mencius took that idea one step further to suggest that heaven has endowed *all* human beings with virtue. Mencius sees this endowment as a gift, and our proper response is to serve heaven by bringing our humane qualities to their fullness. Thus, following the way of heaven is the ultimate purpose of existence and the source of our deepest happiness. Mencius writes, "The ten thousand things are brought to completion by us. There is no greater delight than to turn toward oneself and discover Genuineness."[122] Perfecting our moral natures, thought Mencius, brings us into accord with the will of heaven and is the source of our greatest joy.

But not only does self-cultivation fulfill heaven's will for our lives; it also empowers humans to participate in the very transformation of the universe. In an early Confucian text titled *Centrality and Commonality*, we find this passage reflecting the Mencian viewpoint:

> Only that one in the world who is most perfectly [genuine] is able to give full development to his nature. Being able to give full development to his nature, he is able to give full development to the nature of other human beings and, being able to give full development to the nature of other human beings, he is able to give full development to the natures of other living things. Being able to give full development to the natures of other living beings, he can assist in the transforming and nourishing powers of Heaven and Earth; being able to assist in the transforming and nourishing powers of Heaven and Earth, he can form a triad with Heaven and Earth.[123]

The benefits of moral self-cultivation, thought Mencius, reverberate throughout the entire cosmos.

---

122. Ibid., book 7, A4.1–4.2 (p. 172).

123. De Bary and Bloom, *Sources of Chinese Tradition*, vol. 1, ch. 3, quoted in Adler, *Chinese Religious Traditions*, 41.

Xunzi

Working with the same Confucian teachings and in the same context of rigorous philosophical dialogue, Xunzi came to the opposite conclusion from Mencius and denied that humans were innately good. Xunzi lived most of his life in the third century,[124] and was probably born about the time Mencius died, so they never knew each other. But Xunzi knew of Mencius's work. Although they agreed on many other points about Confucian philosophy, they took what appear to be contrasting positions on the question of human nature. This difference in views was the first major divergence within Confucian ranks.

At first glance, Xunzi seems to claim that human beings are born evil, with a tendency toward what he called "waywardness," an inclination to act in self-serving and self-pleasing ways. Because of this predisposition, individuals can become selfish and society can gravitate towards anarchy. Xunzi, however, probably did not intend to suggest that humans are evil to the core, but that they have essentially *non*moral natures. The tendency toward waywardness is simply an outgrowth of the basic drive of self-preservation, but fundamentally people are not naturally inclined towards moral or immoral behavior. In view of this basic moral neutrality, it is essential that persons receive deliberate and careful training in the cultivation of good behavior. Domestic nurturance and education are therefore vital to instilling morality and shaping amoral nature into human benevolence. Like Confucius and Mencius, Xunzi considered rituals and social etiquette to be the principal ways of fostering benevolence. But unlike Mencius and perhaps Confucius himself, Xunzi did not think of rituals and manners as expressions of human nature. Instead, he regarded them as artificial constructs designed by the ancient sages to benefit people living in society. Furthermore, unlike Mencius and Confucius, Xunzi did not believe that heaven *willed* for humans to be moral. For him, heaven was merely the natural world, which had no moral preferences whatsoever. Thus, for Xunzi, the way was not mandated in heaven but in human societies that deemed morality as being essential to their survival and well-being.

Although Mencius and Xunzi held different understandings about the nature of the divine and the human, the practical components of their teachings were in accord. Like the sage who inspired them, both philosophers valued moral education that emphasized the study of tradition and ritual. With such training, both thought that human beings were morally perfectible. The major difference between them seems to be in the way they

---

124. ca. 310–ca. 235 BCE.

conceptualized the operation of education. Mencius considered education to be akin to cultivating a field of wheat, and Xunzi thought of it like more throwing clay on a potter's wheel. To extrapolate a larger point from this analysis, perhaps we can say that conceptual differences about metaphysics and anthropology need not preclude agreement on practical and ethical matters.

The Dissemination of Confucianism

Confucius's protégés kept his memory alive not only by producing the *Analects* but also by opening their own schools. These academies produced generations of disciples who entered government service and helped spread the ideals of the Confucianism throughout the royal courts of China. As these new Confucians assumed official positions, the name of Master Kong became more widely known and attracted both respect and derision. As we observed with Mencius and Xunzi, as the Confucian way became more prominent, philosophers from other traditions felt free to offer criticisms. Sometimes their disagreements took the form of satire, as in the *Zhuangzi*, a great classic of the Daoist tradition. But even as the authors of the *Zhuangzi* mocked Confucius, they sometimes used his character to give voice to the Daoist perspective. In other words, the sage's reputation had grown to such an extent that other philosophers were using his good name to express their own points of view.

Qin Suppression

As the reputation of Confucius grew, so did opposition to his philosophy. During the Qin Dynasty, which succeeded the Zhou, that opposition became more than mere parody and academic disagreement. The Qin Dynasty came to power in 221 BCE when the state of Qin conquered the last of its rival kingdoms and unified China. The Qin rulers were not favorably disposed to the ideals of Confucianism; they embraced Legalism and its heavy-handed approach to governing, which partly explains their success in coming to power. The Legalists, as noted earlier, advocated the centralization of authority and the strict enforcement of the law. The Qin rulers outlawed all philosophical schools except Legalism. Many Confucian texts were destroyed, and well over a thousand Confucian scholars were tortured and killed.

Han Restoration

The Qin Dynasty lasted only fifteen years. It was succeeded by the Han Dynasty, which reigned about four hundred years, from 206 BCE to 220 CE. The Han rulers not only reinstituted Confucianism, but they made it the official state philosophy. By now there was an official canon of Confucian classics known as the Wu Jing, comprising five books, most of which we have already mentioned in the course of elaborating Confucius's life and teachings. They were the *Yijing*, the classic book of divination, the *Book of History*, the *Book of Songs*, the *Spring and Autumn Annals*, and the *Book of Rituals*. This collection formed the core curriculum for Chinese education and the basis for civil service exams for government officials from the mid-Han period until 1911, for just about two thousand years.

The Canonization of Confucius

Han rule was critical to the perpetuation of Confucian philosophy; it was also instrumental in establishing religious practices dedicated to the spirit of Confucius. In 195 BCE, Emperor Han Gaozu went to the tomb of Confucius in Qufu, where he offered sacrifices. This event was a key step in a gradual process whereby Confucius was given a succession of posthumous titles including "Duke," "Earl," "Venerable, Accomplished Sage," and "Emperor." His last official title was bestowed in 1906 when he was formally declared by imperial decree to be the "Co-Assessor with the deities of Heaven and Earth."[125]

As his rank steadily rose by official proclamation, temples were built in his honor. Appropriately, educational institutions were among the first to sponsor Confucian temples. In the fifth century CE,[126] the first state temple to Confucius was erected in South China. In the seventh century CE,[127] the Tang Dynasty mandated that schools in all provinces of China should have a Confucian temple. At these shrines, sacrifices were offered to the spirits of Confucius and many of his disciples. These offerings were part of the greater system of rituals conducted to honor and appease the other spirits and ancestors of the Chinese pantheon. But despite the efforts to give Confucius near-divine status, the cult of Confucius was never really popular among the vast majority of ordinary Chinese.

---

125. Hick, *Interpretation of Religion*, 257.

126. 454 CE.

127. 630 CE.

The Confucian way also developed in new directions when it had to face the challenges posed by Mahayana Buddhism, which was introduced to China in the Han Dynasty, and by Daoism, the other great indigenous Chinese tradition. During the Song Dynasty,[128] the scholar Zhu Xi[129] incorporated ideas from Buddhism and Daoism into his understanding of Confucianism. Zhu Xi's synthesis was largely ignored during his lifetime, but after his death his ideas became the new orthodox view of what Confucianism actually meant. Today, philosophers and historians believe that Zhu Xi developed a perspective significantly different from traditional Confucianism and hence call his philosophy Neo-Confucianism.

In much of the modern era, the reputation of Confucian philosophy steadily declined among the Chinese. Many intellectuals blamed what they considered the backwardness and conservativism of Confucianism for the tragic events in nineteenth-century China, including the Opium Wars with the British Empire. When the Communist Party came to power under the rule of Mao Zedong, Confucius and Confucianism were portrayed as quaint, backwards, and antirevolutionary.

Confucius's importance has grown and declined at various points in the last two thousand years, but on the whole he has received overwhelming admiration from the Chinese. His philosophy has been influential not only in China but in other countries with which the Chinese had significant contact, especially Korea, Japan, and Vietnam. Although Mao did much to eradicate Confucianism in China, in the post-Mao era Confucianism seems to enjoying renewed interest among Chinese and others around the world.

128. 960-1279 CE.
129. 1130-1200 CE.

2

THE BUDDHA

India in the Time of the Buddha

The life of the Buddha was almost contemporaneous with that of Confucius, yet they lived worlds apart. Siddhattha Gotama, the given name of the man who later earned the title the Buddha, was born in ancient India just before the death of Confucius. Although they were vastly different, India and China 2,500 years ago shared at least one thing: both were age-old cultures in the midst of great changes. But the Buddha's India was not disrupted by the kind of political turbulence that beleaguered ancient China; in fact, India was enjoying a period of relative political stability. It was, however, experiencing another kind of ferment—a profound transformation in thought. By the time Siddhattha Gotama was born, a slow but certain conceptual shift had been underway in India for several centuries. Just as the political situation in ancient China had prompted an outpouring of creative intellectual responses, the evolution of the Indian worldview likewise inspired a movement of impressive philosophical and spiritual innovation. Siddhattha Gotama was one of the many individuals who grappled with this transition that redefined the way Indians thought of themselves, their gods, and their world.

To set the Buddha's thought and practice in its historical context, we will investigate the nature of these changes and the new problems they created. Beginning with the earliest known inhabitants of the Indian subcontinent, we will trace the major cultural developments in this region up to the time of the Buddha, the middle of the first millennium BCE. We will pay special attention to the deepening anxiety about death and the transient nature of the world and to the mounting hopes for overcoming these fears. This outline will be the background for our later discussion of the Buddha. It will also serve as a brief primer on classical Hinduism, as the Buddha's life and teachings emerge out of the same context that gave the Hindu tradition its distinctive character.

The Indus Valley Civilization and the Aryans

Long before the birth of Siddhattha Gotama, India had been the home of a great civilization that was every bit as sophisticated as the culture that existed at the same time along the banks of the Yellow River. By 3000 BCE, or perhaps even earlier, a remarkable society had begun to develop along the valley flanking the Indus River in the area now occupied by northwestern India and Pakistan. We know little about this civilization apart from the archaeological remains that have been unearthed in the last 150 years. Its written language has never been deciphered, so we have no idea what its inhabitants called themselves. Today, it is simply known as the Indus Valley Civilization or the Harappan Culture, after one of its major cities. The archaeological artifacts from the Indus Valley Civilization indicate that its citizens lived a relatively peaceful life based on an agricultural economy and some trade, and that they prized order and stability. Their religious practices focused on rituals for ensuring the continuance of life on earth, much like the religion of the Shang Dynasty in China.

By 1500 BCE, however, this splendid civilization had nearly come to an end and a new people had begun to dominate the region. These newcomers were the Aryans, who had started to migrate into the area from central Asia by way of Iran.[1] The Aryans brought with them a decisively different religious and cultural outlook from that of the Indus Valley inhabitants. They worshiped different gods, practiced different rituals, and lived a seminomadic existence based on a pastoral economy. They also brought a vast oral tradition they called the Veda, borne by their native language, Sanskrit, and a stratified social arrangement known as the varna system. Both the Veda and the varna system became immensely important in the development of the Hindu tradition. The Veda, which the Aryans regarded as revealed sacred knowledge, eventually became the highest scriptural

---

1. Although most critical scholars believe the Aryans migrated *into* India, a small minority of researchers argues that the Aryans were indigenous to India and migrated from the subcontinent into Central Asia and other places. See Bryant, *Quest for the Origins of Vedic Culture.*

authority for Hinduism, while varna became the basis of the caste system. Varna was the Aryans' name for the social classes, of which there were four. The highest varna was the Brahmin, who were the priests and educators; next was the Kshatriya, the varna of warriors and nobility, followed by that of the Vaishya, the merchants and artisans. The lowest varna was the Shudra, the farmers and the manual laborers. Although the Buddha was a descendant of these Aryan migrants, he came to reject the validity of both the varna system and the Veda.

The Second Urbanization of India

By the time of the Buddha, the Aryans had occupied northern India for around a thousand years. They had begun to expand into northeastern India, into the region known as the Gangetic Plain, the area surrounding the Ganges River and its tributaries.[2] This was the area in which Gotama was born and spent his entire life. As they expanded eastward, the Aryans became more sedentary, establishing villages and towns and taking up farming and trade in addition to their traditional pursuits as pastoralists. With urbanization and a new economy, the Aryans began to enjoy material wealth as never before. At least a dozen small states governed by the warrior caste began to arise throughout the region.

As Aryan society evolved, traditional religious beliefs and practices, especially the rituals that had been the exclusive domain of the Brahmins, came under question. Accordingly, the power and prestige of the priests diminished somewhat, abetted by the rise of the middle varnas, particularly the warriors and merchants. This growing dissatisfaction with traditional religion, as well as an increasing restlessness among those with a philosophical bent of mind, was driven by several new ideas that were gaining widespread acceptance throughout the Gangetic Plain.

The Shift in Religious Paradigms

The new thoughts that disrupted Indian religion began to surface around 800 BCE, the beginning of the Axial Age, some three hundred years before the birth of Siddhattha Gotama. Near this time, small coteries of intellectuals in northeastern India began to think seriously about death and its aftermath in response to increasing anxiety about the ultimate human

---

2. Occupying the current Indian states of Bihar and Uttar Pradesh and southern Nepal.

destiny. To appreciate the importance of this emerging concern, we have to recognize that the Aryans and their Indus Valley predecessors were not especially troubled by death. To these more ancient inhabitants of India, death was more or less accepted as a fact of life—a sad event, to be sure, but nothing warranting great fear or terror. Religious practices were intended to help secure the goods of the world that could make life here and now more comfortable and more pleasurable. Not a whole lot of attention was given to what might lie beyond the cremation pyre. But that attitude began to change in the centuries just before the Buddha. Death was now a subject occupying some of the brightest minds of the age. The anxiety about death was prompted by the emerging sense of the self as an individual. In a fascinating tale from the *Upanishads*, the great collection of philosophical reflection from this era, a young Brahmin finds himself sent to the underworld, where he confronts Yama, the god of death.[3] There, in death's own home, the young priest, whose name is Nachiketas, boldly presses Yama to divulge the secrets of life after death. When Yama offers him a long life with many descendants and great wealth instead, Nachiketas refuses, declaring that with death looming over existence, the pleasures of the world were ultimately meaningless. What this story revealed was the new intensity with which questions about death were being discussed among thoughtful Aryans. Along with the questions, there was, of course, no shortage of answers.

Gradually, one view began to dominate all others and over several centuries gained wide acceptance among the Indian populace. The consensus view was that the individual's death would be followed by another birth, then another life and death, and another birth, and so on. In what came to be called Hinduism, this process was called the transmigration of the soul, or better, self, because it was conceptualized as a spiritual entity traveling from one body to another. This was a novel idea; the ancient Veda of the Aryans had suggested nothing like this in any clear fashion. Conjectures about how and why this series of deaths and births occurred varied widely. But over time, virtually everyone accepted that it *did* occur and that it was a highly *undesirable* situation. This apparently vicious cycle was called *samsara*, a word that meant "meandering," suggesting that the whole process was aimless and without meaning.

The idea of rebirth was yoked with another concept that made samsara a unique idea in the history of world religions—the concept of karma. The doctrine of karma imbued the Indian view of rebirth with an ethical element, just as Confucius had given the ancient practice of ritual moral significance.

3. Mascaró, trans., *Upanishads*, 55.

Karma was an ancient Aryan term that originally referred to the mechanism by which rituals were understood to operate. It later came to mean "action" in a more generic sense. In its fundamental meaning, then, karma was an act, and that included any *thought* or *word* as well as deed. Moreover, *karma* referred to the *consequences* of the act; hence, one might have said that a particular action generated or produced karma. Karmic acts, furthermore, could be either good or bad. In classical Hinduism, the quality of any karmic act was determined by whether or not it conformed to *dharma*, the duties incumbent on individual persons according to their caste and gender.

Hinduism did not embrace a universal ethic for all people at all times but thought that moral obligations were different for different kinds of people. It was the moral responsibility of members of the warrior caste, for example, to protect and defend their country, and the moral duty of priests to sacrifice on behalf of others. Fulfilling one's dharma was the way to produce positive karma; neglecting or violating dharma resulted in negative karma. The Buddha accepted the principle of karma (or *kamma*, as it is known in Pali), but he rejected the idea that its moral quality was contingent on one's caste and gender duties.[4]

The Buddha, however, did agree with the classical Hindu view on a very important point: that the consequences of karmic acts eventually returned to the agent. Simply stated, the one who acts reaps the good consequences of a good action and the negative consequences of an evil action. The return, or "ripening," of karma might not happen immediately; it might take a very long time for the consequences of an action to come back to the agent, but its return is inevitable. The good or bad events that occurred could be regarded as the result of the individual's actions performed in the past. One's so-called good or bad luck is not luck at all but simply the ripening of past karmas. The doctrine of karma means that the events of one's life

---

4. In our study, you will notice slight variations in the spelling of certain Indian words. For example, we have just used "karma" and "kamma." We will also use "dharma" in one context and then "dhamma" in another. That difference is deliberate and significant. *Dharma* is a Sanskrit term; *dhamma* is a word from Pali, a language closely related to Sanskrit. We will use Sanskrit terms to discuss Hindu concepts because Sanskrit is the classical language of Hinduism. But we will use Pali for Buddhist terms because Pali is the language of the earliest Buddhist writings. It is helpful to use these different languages because the words can have different meanings in their respective contexts. *Dharma* and *dhamma* mean "truth" in both Hinduism and Buddhism, but they carry significantly different senses of what constitutes truth. This shift between Sanskrit and Pali accounts for other differences, such as Siddhattha Gotama rather than the better-known Sanskrit name Siddhartha Gautama; "sutta" rather than "sutra"; "bodhisatta" rather than "bodhisattva."

are not predetermined by fate or a god. For better or worse, human beings have determined their own destinies.

The doctrine of karma significantly altered the conception of rebirth. Since it is not evident that one always reaps the consequences of one's actions in *this* life—after all, the wicked often prosper, while the good often suffer—ancient Indian thought extended the possibilities for karma's return into future lives. One's karma could come to fruition at rebirth or later in the next life. Thus, the performance of good karmic acts conditioned a favorable rebirth; evil karmic acts, by the same token, led an unfavorable rebirth. Obviously, the expressions "favorable" and "unfavorable" imply a standard for making these value judgments. A favorable rebirth was one that raised one's place on the hierarchy of being; an unfavorable rebirth lowered one's status. This hierarchy of being ranged from the divine realm of the gods to the human stratum, with its own ranking system based on caste, down to the animal, plant, and mineral levels. Potentially, one might be reborn at any place on this hierarchy, but it was always self-generated karma that governed the process and dictated where one was reborn.

When the idea of rebirth acquired its ethical dimension, a new outlook on life began to color the Indians' view of the world. From the samsaric perspective, existence now had but one valid objective: to achieve freedom from the endless cycle of death and rebirth. The world of samsara had its pleasures and satisfactions, to be sure, but from the perspective of an eternal parade of lives and deaths, the world was a wearisome place, laden with pain and grief. Even the best sort of life was permeated with anxiety and suffering and would ultimately end at the charnel ground. Sooner or later, one would realize that complete freedom from samsara was really the only thing worth seeking. The Hindus called this *moksha*, absolute and unconditional liberation. The Buddha called it *nibbana*, or *nirvana*, the Sanskrit term more familiar to Westerners.

Attaining release from samsara could not be accomplished merely by generating good karma. Even if one were the finest person possible, performing only good deeds, it would not be sufficient to break free from samsara's everlasting grind. Positive karmic acts might temporarily take one to the apex of the chain of being. But eventually, one's store of good karma would be depleted, and one would at last face another death and rebirth. As long as one produced karma of any kind—good or bad—one was bound to the wheel of samsara. Seeking a favorable rebirth could thus only be a short-term goal. In the long run, rebirth itself would have to be brought to an end.

The Renunciation Movement

As this new understanding of human nature and destiny gained wide acceptance throughout northern India, it provoked a vast movement of individuals who decided to forsake their connections with the world to seek
final liberation from samsara. They gave up their homes and possessions,
their families and jobs, because they considered nothing as important as
moksha. Men and women of all ages and castes joined this movement, but
persons from the middle castes were especially drawn to it. They were called
samanas, or "strivers," to indicate their dedication to practicing religious
austerities in pursuit of emancipation from rebirth. The samanas were a
common sight in the emerging villages and towns of the Gangetic Plain, and
ordinary people frequently sought their advice and teachings. These samanas often experimented with an immense array of disciplines and doctrines
to seek a way to their goal. Many wandered about northern India searching
out new teachers and new spiritual techniques. Some isolated themselves
in caves or deep within the forest. They all lived in self-imposed poverty,
frequently owning only a bowl for begging food. Some had even renounced
clothing. Although the individuals in this movement varied greatly in their
chosen paths and disciplines, they were united by a single ambition: to find
relief from the anguish of samsara. They were so dedicated to this cause
that they were willing to give up the pleasures and comforts of the world to
achieve it. Even more, they believed renouncing the world was *essential* to
that purpose.

Some of these ascetics declared they had indeed discovered the path
leading away from samsara. Although we have no records of many teachings, we know a considerable amount about a few of them. The most prominent among the early teachings became the *Upanishads*, the philosophical
anthology mentioned earlier, which was later designated as one of the sacred
scriptures of Hinduism. A brief exploration of Upanishadic perspectives will
be helpful before we turn to examine the teachings of the Buddha. Because
of the prominence of this philosophy, many of the Buddha's teachings were
developed in direct response to the Upanishadic outlook.

The Upanishadic Philosophy

The *Upanishads* was a fairly diverse collection of philosophical treatises and
parables written over a period of several centuries. But most of the writings
it contained concerned three fundamental matters: the nature of the self or
soul, the nature of ultimate reality, and the relationship between them. The

Upanishads offered several points of view on each of these issues, but it is possible to describe a consensus perspective.

We will begin with the self. The concept of *atman*, or self, had been a part of the Aryans' religion before they migrated into India. But in the Vedic tradition, this ancient concept was not clearly defined or well developed. There seemed to be little agreement about the origin of the self, where it went upon death, or what exactly it was. At most, the Veda understood the self as a vague entity that animates life and keeps the body from being a mere corpse. By the age of the samanas, though, a more definite idea about the *atman* had come into view. According to this perspective, the self was an eternal entity residing in, but separate from, the body. The authors of the *Upanishads* asserted that the self was not created and never came into being at a particular time. It simply had always been. Furthermore, since it was not subject to birth, it could never die.[5] The *atman* was immortal, beyond birth and death. While it is true that the self transmigrated, it was only the body that was born and died. The *atman*, which the *Upanishads* identified as the true self, the real self that underlies all appearances, was imperceptible, beyond description, and distinguished from not only the body but the mind as well.

Just as the sages of the *Upanishads* sought to comprehend the nature of the self, they also tried to grasp the ultimate reality, which they called *brahman*. Again, the authors did not wholly agree about *brahman*, but certain themes recurred, thus having a profound influence on subsequent Hinduism. Among the most prevalent was the idea that *brahman* was a single, indivisible reality that could not be adequately explained or comprehended by ordinary means. Although *brahman* was the deepest reality underlying all things, it was unavailable to the five senses. It encompassed the whole of the universe yet transcended it. It embraced both good *and* evil, and yet was beyond them. Later Hindu thinkers would suggest that although *brahman* was formless, it could be partially known through the images of the many gods and goddesses of the Hindu pantheon. *Brahman* itself transcended all the gods and yet empowered them.

In their search for overcoming samsara, many Indian ascetics came to a startling conclusion that led them to believe that their quest of moksha might indeed have come to an end. In the later *Upanishads*, the sages expressed their conviction that the self and the ultimate reality known as *brahman* were in fact identical: one and the same. The majority of these sages did not simply declare that the self was a *part* of *brahman*; *brahman*, after all, was indivisible. Rather, they suggested that *atman* and *brahman*

---

5. Mascaró, trans., "Katha Upanishad," 59.

were two names for the same reality. The true self *was* ultimate reality. *Brahman/atman* was the only reality there was.

The samanas now understood the source of human anguish on the wheel of samsara as a consequence of ignorance, a complete misunderstanding about the true nature of the self and reality. The failure to apprehend reality correctly encouraged the belief that the self is an individual entity, separate from *brahman*, separate from the rest of reality. This delusion is what caused persons to act in a self-obsessed manner, leading to the production of the karma that chained one to samsara. Believing oneself to be an entity separate from all else bred the desire and hatred that led to the anguish of samsara and ultimately caused the fear of death. The only way out of this morass was to realize completely the identity of the *atman* and the deepest reality. That realization came only at the end of a long road of intense spiritual discipline.

These were the essential features of the intellectual religious world into which Siddhattha Gotama was born. There were, of course, many subtleties and diverse viewpoints composing this world. But this broad sketch will suffice to portray the social and religious environment of his life. He lived at time of spiritual and religious questioning, when traditions were being re-evaluated, and the basic questions of existence—What are we deep down? Where do we come from? Where are we going? What is the fundamental character of reality?—were receiving exhilarating new answers. To this conversation the man later called the Buddha would add his own distinctive voice.

Siddhattha Gotama

The story of the Buddha is surely one of the great narratives in human history. A child born to the king and queen of an ancient realm in the foothills of the Himalayas, Siddhattha Gotama was brought up with every possible advantage. He was uncommonly handsome, a formidable athlete, and blessed with a brilliant mind. As heir apparent, he was entitled to a career that would bring him great power and fame. Loved by all, he was surrounded by dear friends who sought to fulfill his every whim. His own heart was filled with compassion for all living things. But heeding a warning by his court astrologers, the king took extreme measures to shield his son from any form of suffering or distress. The soothsayers had told King Suddhodana that the prince was so softhearted that he might renounce his right to rule and seek to become a holy man if any unpleasantness were to upset his sensitive constitution. Responding to their advice, the father made sure that his son wore only the finest silks, ate the most delectable food, and was constantly entertained by the best musicians and dancers. At sixteen, the prince married a ravishing princess, with whom he had a son. He and his young wife lived in three palaces, one each for the summer, winter, and rainy seasons. His excursions outside these palaces were carefully arranged by his father to guarantee that Prince Siddhattha would not encounter anyone or anything that might shatter his rose-colored view of the world.

It is hard to imagine what more could be added to this portrait to make his life seem any richer. Most people would be delighted to have just *one* of these things: good looks, physical prowess, great intelligence, devoted friends, political power and wealth, three luxurious homes, public adoration, and youth. Siddhattha Gotama had them *all*.

Yet despite his father's ministrations, the young man slipped away from his confinement and caught a glimpse of the world as it was when it was not prettified for his benefit. In short order, the prince saw for the first time (we are told) a sick person, an old person, and a corpse. Then he encountered another strange spectacle, one of the samanas of his time who had renounced the world and wandered about it with only a begging bowl in hand. With virtually nothing to call his own and amid a world of disease, decay, and death, the samana wore a happy and serene countenance. Deeply disturbed by the suffering he saw—and yet heartened by the sunny face of the holy man—Siddhattha Gotama decided he too must give up the life he knew and seek real happiness beyond the sham created by turning a blind eye to the world. On a warm summer night, he kissed his sleeping wife and child goodbye, and as the full moon lit his path, the twenty-nine-year-old Gotama walked away from all he had and gave it up forever.

There are not many stories like this one. The more popular narrative is one in which the individual starts out with little or nothing and, through prodigious effort or good fortune, attains some measure of success. Americans, especially, love such stories. We adore Abraham Lincoln, Andrew Carnegie, Rocky Balboa, Seabiscuit, and Cinderella. We're not so accustomed to the tale in which the hero starts out with everything imaginable and deliberately forsakes it. None of our other three teachers have even a remotely similar biography. Confucius, Jesus, and Muhammad all started out with little and accomplished their feats *in spite of* their humble beginnings. Only the Buddha began with everything and chose to give it all up. His is a riches-to-rags story.

The tale of the Buddha was so compelling that early Christians even adopted it, and it became wildly popular in the Middle Ages. Before it was appropriated by the church, though, the story received a good baptism. In the Christianized version, an Indian maharaja named King Abenner so despised the church that he began to persecute the Christians in his realm. Now, Christianity has a long history in India; tradition claims that Doubting Thomas, one of the twelve apostles, introduced the faith in South India several years after the resurrection of Jesus. When his son was born, the maharaja consulted the astrologers, who predicted that the prince, whose name was Josaphat, would grow up and become a Christian. Needless to say, the forecast alarmed the maharaja, and he went to great lengths to keep his son sheltered from outside influences, especially from anyone who might expose him to the teachings of Jesus. Yet one day, Josaphat ventured beyond his palace confines and confronted sickness, old age, and death, and met a Christian hermit by the name of Barlaam. Soon, the young man professed the Christian faith, and despite his father's unhappiness and pleas, Josaphat chose to remain a Christian. Eventually, the maharaja himself became a Christian and abdicated in favor of his son. In the end, Josaphat himself left the throne to become a desert recluse.[6]

There is no doubt that this Christian narrative is a retelling of the story of the early life of the Buddha. The name Josaphat has been traced back to "Bodhisatta," the Buddhist tradition's title for the Buddha before his enlightenment. The Eastern Orthodox Church still celebrates the feast day of Barlaam and Josaphat. In an odd way, the Buddha became a Christian saint.

If early Christians took the story of the Buddha and retold it to suit their purposes, is it possible that the Buddhists have done the same thing? Well, of course, and that is what very likely happened. But what parts of the Buddha's story, if any, are based on actual historical occurrences and what parts have been embellished for the sake of advancing the Buddhist worldview? Again, we face the issue we first met in our discussion of Confucius, and which we will meet again when we take up the other two teachers. And, again, the best way to tackle this matter is by first looking at the sources we have available for understanding the life of the Buddha.

The Sources

Like the Aryans who first migrated into India, their descendants who became followers of the Buddha preserved their sacred knowledge by oral means. The stories of the life and teachings of the Buddha did not appear in writing until several centuries after his death. The Buddha—like Confucius, Jesus, and Muhammad—left no writings in his own hand.

Nevertheless, according to Buddhist tradition, these texts accurately reflect the Buddha's own teachings both in spirit and letter. Three months

6. See McCracken, trans., *Barlaam and Josaphat*.

after the Buddha's death, five hundred of his senior students gathered in the town of Rajagaha on the Gangetic Plain of India to decide how best to preserve his teachings for future generations. At that time, so goes the tradition, the elder monk Ananda, who had served as the Buddha's personal attendant, was invited to recite to the assembly his recollection of the Buddha's many discourses. Ananda was reputed to have had an astounding memory. He began each of his recitations with the words, "Thus have I heard…," followed by a statement of the Buddha's location and audience and a verbatim account of what the Buddha taught. Another elder monk, Upali, recollected the rules of community discipline that the Buddha set out for his followers. After the recitations of both monks, their declamations were validated by all present. From that moment forward, the sangha—the community of monks and nuns—preserved the discourses and rules of discipline by memorization, and they often rehearsed them in community settings.

Because we have become so dependent on the written word, we moderns have a hard time believing that oral transmissions, especially of great length and over long stretches of time, could accurately maintain a body of knowledge. But such skepticism greatly underestimates the capacity of oral cultures to keep vast stores of information over time with little or no mutations. That ability is truly amazing, but it has been attested many times and in many places. In the case of the Buddhist material, the oral transmission was facilitated by numerous mnemonic devices such as numbered lists and the repetition of stock phrases, as well as by the awareness that the words held sacred significance.

The traditions of recited discourses and communal disciplines were finally committed to the written word sometime in the first century BCE, about four hundred years after the Buddha. They were written in the language of Pali, a vernacular closely related to the Sanskrit chanted by Brahmins during rituals and used for formal Hindu literature. Pali was very close to, but probably not identical with, the language the Buddha himself spoke, which most scholars believe to be a dialect called Old Maghadhi. Pali was developed specifically for the purpose of preserving the Buddha's teachings. The oral tradition that began at the first Buddhist Council in Rajagaha now exists in writing as the Pali Canon, which is probably our best resource for a historically reliable understanding of the Buddha's life. As a recent translator put it, "If your aim is to get as close to 'the Buddha's idiom' as possible, the Pali suttas are the logical starting point."[7] The Pali Canon is not the only collection of Buddhist scriptures, however. There is also a Chinese and a Tibetan canon, which replicate a great deal of the Pali material, but these

7. Wallis, trans., *Basic Teachings of the Buddha*, xxv.

also add other materials not found in the Pali. The Chinese and Tibetan versions were much later translations of Indian Buddhist texts. Furthermore, as Buddhism spread throughout Asia and diverged philosophically, new scriptures known as the Mahayana sutras were added to the collections of sacred literature. Unlike the Pali Canon, however, it is not possible to trace the Mahayana sutras back to the Buddha through a lineage of oral transmission, although these texts do claim an ancient provenance.

Because of its proximity to the Buddha's own time and dialect, we will rely mainly upon the Pali collection for discussing his life and teachings. As with the *Analects* of Confucius, we cannot be absolutely certain that these texts report historical fact; indeed, particular aspects of the Pali Canon, such as its accounts of past lives and the pantheon of gods, must be strictly excluded as verifiable facts according to modern historiographical principles. But there is good reason to believe that the Pali sources are *founded* on historical events and contain the substance of the Buddha's teachings and probably many of his actual words. The remarkable internal consistency of the canon has convinced many scholars that these scriptures originated as the work of a single mind.

The Pali Canon is large—much larger than the comparable sources we have for Confucius, Jesus, and Muhammad. The canon is split into three divisions, or "baskets." The first basket, called the Suttas, claims to be the record of elder Ananda's memorized discourses of the Buddha's teachings. The Suttas contain well over five thousand discourses. The second, called the Vinaya, purports to be based on Upali's recitation of communal regulations. The third, called the Abhidhamma, is a highly abstract and systematic presentation of the Buddha's philosophy. Although the early tradition asserts that the Abhidhamma dates back to the Buddha himself, this collection is almost certainly a later reworking of earlier material.

The Historical Buddha

To develop our portrait of the historical Buddha, we will be concerned almost exclusively with the Suttas. This basket of discourses is the one that presents the material most relevant to our interests, and it is the place where we find the greatest instances of the Buddha revealing his own life story. In sketching a portrait of the Buddha based on history, we are trying to set forth what we can reasonably know of the Buddha using the tools and principles of the historian's craft. I hasten to add that a historical image of the Buddha—or any of the other three figures—does not by any means exhaust his or their significance. Nor does such an image exhaust their histories. It merely states what can be said with some historical reliability. It does not—and cannot—report everything.

That said, let us begin. Up until a few years ago most scholars had set the date of the Buddha's birth on or near 563 BCE, based on a reckoning system from the Theravada, the oldest extant variety of Buddhism. That would have made the Buddha slightly older than Confucius. Today, most historians are inclined to place the Buddha's birth closer to the death of Confucius, somewhere near 490 BCE. No credible scholar, as far as I am aware, has ever argued that the Buddha never existed. The Buddhist tradition said that Siddhattha Gotama was born into the varna of the warriors and nobles in an area occupied by an Aryan clan known the Sakyas. There is no reason to doubt this claim. His hometown was called Kapilavatthu, which modern scholarship locates in present-day Nepal near its border with India. The tradition, however, names his birthplace as Lumbini, a tiny place about fifteen miles from Kapilavatthu. This tradition cannot be authenticated and is probably part of the legend of the unusual circumstances surrounding Siddhattha's birth.

The legend of his birth—of which there were several versions—clearly moves the narrative into the realm of the mythic. The basic account goes something like this: It begins not with the birth of Siddhattha 2,500 years ago but with the life of an individual named Sumedha, who lived untold eons ago in another world-system prior to the current one. Sumedha, a humble monk practicing spiritual austerities, was fortunate enough to meet the Buddha of that world, Dipamkara. Sumedha was so impressed with the compassionate demeanor of Dipamkara that he himself vowed to become a Buddha, one of those exceedingly rare individuals who attain the deepest understanding of reality by means of his own efforts. Through hard work over incalculable lifetimes, Monk Sumedha edged closer and closer to the realization of his vow. He was reborn in a vast array of forms in the animal, human, and divine realms. The stories of his many lifetimes—particularly those of his animal rebirths—comprise an extremely popular genre of Buddhist literature known as the Jataka Tales. The stories are a bit like Aesop's fables and serve to teach Buddhist values, particularly to children.

After so many lifetimes, the person who as Monk Sumedha had vowed to become a Buddha had acquired enough merit, or good karma, to be born as a god in Tusita, the heaven of the contented. This auspicious birth was to be his penultimate. He dwelled in the contented heaven for hundreds of thousands of years. When the time came for him to take rebirth, he surveyed the world and determined that the people of Jambudvipa, an ancient name for India, would be receptive to the message of a Buddha. According to tradition, a Buddha appears only when the teachings of the previous

Buddha have been forgotten and the world is amenable to hearing them again. Now was the time, and India was the place.

On the night he was conceived, the full moon shone in the clear sky and his mother, Queen Mahamaya, dreamt that a white elephant god touched her right side with a white lotus he carried in his trunk. The queen's pregnancy lasted for exactly ten lunar months. As her term neared the end, she felt a great longing to return to her native home. Along the way, she passed a pleasant grove near Lumbini and stopped to enjoy its beauty. As she reached up to touch the branch of a flowering sala tree, the Bodhisatta was born, while celestial beings looked on and auspicious stars shone in the heavens. According to the story, the child was born in full awareness, with the luminosity of the sun.[8] Immediately, he took seven steps and declared that he had been born for the benefit of the world and would never experience birth again. Seven days after giving birth to the Bodhisatta, Queen Mahamaya died, and she was reborn in the contented heaven, in recognition of the great merit she gained by bearing one destined for Buddhahood. After his mother's death, the prince was raised by her sister, Mahaprajapati, who was the king's second wife.

There is much about this story, of course, that excludes it from what the modern world considers historical. The discipline of history cannot verify or falsify claims about previous lives, celestial beings, and gods, and so would categorize most of this narrative as legendary or mythic. Modern historians even find it difficult to accept Siddhattha's royal status. On the basis of what we know from other sources about this region around the time of the Buddha, it is highly unlikely that he was born as a prince to a fabulously wealthy king and queen. At the time, the small states of the Gangetic Plain were governed by councils of elders, not autonomous monarchs. His father was probably a local chieftain or ranking member of the ruling council.

Little more about his early life can be established with confidence. The reports that he was a virtual prisoner of an overprotective father cannot be verified, and they were probably developed by the later tradition to highlight important features of the Buddha's philosophy. Interestingly, in the Pali Canon the Buddha did not say that his father tried to keep him confined and unsullied by the realities of life. He merely indicated that he was well-to-do and pampered by all the attention lavished on him. Looking back many years later, he described his youth to his followers:

> I was delicate, most delicate, supremely delicate. Lily pools were made for me at my father's house solely for my benefit. Blue lilies flowered in one, white lilies in another, red lilies in a third.

8. Conze, trans., *Buddhist Scriptures*, 34–36.

I used no sandalwood that was not from Benares. My turban,
tunic, lower garments and cloak were all made of Benares cloth.
A white sunshade was held over me day and night so that no
cold or heat or dust or grit or dew might inconvenience me . . .
I was entertained by minstrels with no men among them . . .
Though meals of broken rice with lentil soup are given to the
servants and retainers in other people's houses, in my father's
house white rice and meat was given to them.[9]

This account confirms the traditional view that Siddhattha grew up as a
privileged child, but it does not go so far as to claim that he had everything
imaginable and was hermetically sealed off from the world.

Later tradition seems to have added those embellishments. But those
embellishments serve an important purpose. Although they may not be
historically accurate, they are precise literary expressions of the Buddha's
teachings. The stories of the Bodhisatta's incredible wealth and his many talents and skills illustrate that the things almost all of us crave cannot possibly
give us the kind of satisfaction and happiness we really want. The man who
had them all discovered they were only an impediment to genuine freedom.
Similarly, the story of King Suddhodana's overprotectiveness can be read as
a cautionary tale about the dangers of ignorance. In short, refusing to face
the realities of life gets us nowhere. We can try to insulate ourselves from
the truths about living and dying, and live a comfortable existence as if the
rest of the world does not matter, but that is to accept a greatly attenuated
existence. The best in human nature comes to expression not in retreating
from life's sometimes tough realities, but in accepting them. As we shall see,
the Buddha came to believe that facing the truth, whatever it was, was the
only way to freedom. Sound trivial? The Buddha thought that all but a very
few courageous individuals lived their lives in a fog, preferring comfortable
illusions and fantasies even though they perpetuate suffering and anguish.
The truth about living and dying surrounds us and occasionally intrudes
into our lives. For a moment, we awaken to this truth, but just as quickly,
most of us hurry back to the warmth of our familiar fictions. Only a few take
a step outside and investigate. The Buddha was one.

The First and Second Great Awakenings

There is much about the traditional stories of the Buddha's life that cannot be verified by modern historical research. But two events were almost
certainly rooted in history. They may not have occurred exactly as described

9. *Anguttara Nikaya* 3.38, quoted in Ñāṇamoli, *Life of the Buddha*, 8.

by the Buddhist tradition, but I can see no way to dismiss them as complete fictions. The first took place when Siddhattha Gotama decided to leave the comforts of home at age twenty-nine and join the samana movement that had attracted so many other Indians of his era. The second occurred six years later as he sat under a tree, leading him to conclude he had discovered the way to end suffering and samsara. Without actual events grounding these two stories, the name Gotama would be unknown to the world, and there would be no religion known as Buddhism.

It is customary to refer to the first of these events as the Great Renunciation and the second as the Enlightenment, and these are perfectly acceptable names. For our purposes, however, let us refer to them as the First and Second Great Awakenings, designations we are actually taking from American religious history but using in a vastly different sense.

What many term the enlightenment was actually called the awakening by the Buddha. In fact, the title Buddha—and it is a title and not a name— literally means one who has awakened. This metaphor suggests that the pivotal experience of liberation is more a matter of coming to awareness than the acquisition of conceptual knowledge. Furthermore, it implies that those who have not yet "awakened" are living in a sleepy, dreamlike state. As it occurs, a dream seems real enough. Only when we awaken do we recognize that what we thought to be real was actually a fabrication of the mind. This was precisely the way the Buddha interpreted the human situation. All of us, excepting only rare, fully liberated persons, live in a self-generated fantasy, unable to distinguish reality from reverie.

I also want to use the metaphor of awakening to talk about the Great Renunciation, although it is not usually thought of in this light. My unconventional terminology underscores this event as a positive moment of insight and clarity, not as an impulse of revulsion or disgust, as perhaps suggested by the word renunciation. Using the same term, furthermore, connects the two experiences causally and qualitatively. Without the first awakening, there would have been no second. Without the second, we would have never known of the first. It is important to recognize that there was a process involved in the Buddha's transformation: his ultimate awakening was the result of years of preparation—or eons, if you accept the stories of his past lives. It did not occur simply as the effect of one night of really strenuous meditation. Of course, it might sound a little strange to speak of two awakenings. If he needed a second, was the first really an awakening? To me, it doesn't seem odd at all; in fact, it happens every day. My first awakening occurs when my alarm clock sounds in the morning and the second takes place when my second cup of coffee kicks in. Wakefulness can be a matter of degree. But the second awakening for the Buddha was as awake as you can get.

The First Awakening

The legends present the Buddha's first awakening in a highly dramatic form. We have already mentioned the basic elements of the story. The incredibly naïve and mollycoddled prince slips away from his gilded cage and is astonished to discover the world was not what he imagined. After seeing a sick person, an old person, a corpse, and a contented renunciant, he knew that he would have to leave behind the safety and security of home. The Buddhist tradition refers to this episode in the Bodhisatta's life as the Four Sights.

Interestingly, the Pali Canon presents this experience in a different way. According to these early texts, the Buddha said that his insight into the tough realities of life came not as the result of outwitting his father's protective measures but as the outcome of careful and deliberate reflection. Since it reveals the methodical nature of his thought and conveys the flavor of the discourses, let us quote his statement at length:

> While I had such power and good fortune, yet I thought: "When an untaught ordinary man, who is subject to ageing, not safe from ageing, sees another who is aged, he is shocked, humiliated and disgusted; for he forgets that he himself is no exception. But I too am subject to ageing, not safe from ageing, and so it cannot befit me to be shocked, humiliated and disgusted on seeing another who is aged." When I considered this, the vanity of youth left me entirely.
>
> I thought: "When an untaught ordinary man, who is subject to sickness, not safe from sickness, sees another who is sick, he is shocked, humiliated and disgusted; for he forgets that he himself is no exception. But I too am subject to sickness, not safe from sickness, and so it cannot befit me to be shocked, humiliated and disgusted on seeing another who is sick." When I considered this, the vanity of health left me entirely.
>
> I thought: "When an untaught ordinary man, who is subject to death, not safe from death, sees another who is dead, he is shocked, humiliated and disgusted; for he forgets that he himself is no exception. But I too am subject to death, not safe from death, and so it cannot befit me to be shocked, humiliated and

disgusted on seeing another who is dead." When I considered
this, the vanity of life left me entirely.[10]

The Pali account clearly lacks the drama of the later legend. But the report
in the Pali collection, for all its philosophical thoughtfulness, has the greater
ring of truth. It is hard to believe that Gotama could have lived three decades without ever having encountered sickness, old age, or death. Nobody
is *that* insulated from the world. Surely, it was no revelation to this young
man that people get sick, get old, and die, as the story of the Four Sights
would have us believe.

It matters little, of course, whether what occurred to Siddhattha happened outside the palace gates against his father's will or in the young man's
mind as he soberly reflected on the nature of existence. Undoubtedly, *something* serious happened to Siddhattha Gotama that prompted his exit from
a life of comfort and privilege. The real question is not *how* he came to leave
his familiar world but *why*. It is in answering this question that the Pali account may shed greater light than the more mythologized narratives.

According to the Pali passage, what happened to Siddhattha Gotama
around the age of twenty-nine was an awakening to the fact that there are
no exceptions to the rule of aging and death. Even as children and youth,
we know that people get sick, get old, and die. But at that tender age, our
knowledge is merely abstract and vague, and we don't really believe it will
happen to us. In the great Indian epic the *Mahabharata*, the wise and pious
Prince Yudhishthira was once confronted by a nature spirit who demanded
answers to a series of riddles, in a scene similar to Oedipus's encounter with
the sphinx. The spirit asked: "What is the greatest wonder in the world?"
Yudhishthira replied: "Every day, people see creatures die and depart to
Yama's abode. Yet, those who remain still seek to live forever. Truly, this is
the greatest wonder in the world."[11] The event that so profoundly disturbed
Siddhattha's life of ease was not coming to know that sickness, old age, and
death *existed*, but that they applied *to him* and to everyone he loved, *without
exemption*. Until we come face-to-face with this fact, we all will continue to
live sheltered lives, no matter how much experience we may have accumulated. You don't need to be locked up in a palace to be oblivious to this truth.
And you don't have to be a kid, either.

Coming to the awareness that the realities of life pertain to oneself
can be intensely disillusioning. I still remember the disbelief I felt when
I looked into the mirror around the age of twenty-nine or thirty and first

---

10. *Anguttara Nikaya* 3.38, quoted in Ñāṇamoli, *Life of the Buddha*, 9.

11. "The Enchanted Pool" in the *Mahabharata*; my paraphrase. See http://www.
mahabharataonline.com/rajaji/mahabharata_summary_43.php/.

noticed that I was aging. "Wait a minute; this is not supposed to be happening to *me!*" I spent months denying the evidence before my very eyes and then months afterwards trying to hide it. This was disillusionment in the best sense of the word—an experience of being stripped of illusion. My disillusionment meant having to let go of the pretense that I was special, different from everyone else. Something like this, I believe, happened to Siddhattha Gotama. Without a similar disillusionment, he would have had no second awakening, no insight while calmly sitting under a tree. The history of religions suggests that spiritual journeys often begin as the result of some disappointment or traumatic experience. Mahavira, the great hero of Jainism, set out on his path at age twenty-eight, when his parents died. Jesus inaugurated his prophetic activity at the death of his mentor, John the Baptizer. In Somerset Maugham's novel *The Razor's Edge*, Larry Darrell forsakes his plans for a conventional life, and leaves in search of spiritual adventure in India after he had witnessed the devastation of the First World War.[12] As Confucius succinctly put it, "No vexation, no enlightenment; no anxiety, no illumination."[13]

Unlike his final awakening, Gotama's first epiphany brought him not peace but restiveness. It was enough to cause him to walk away from his life of ease and comfort. He could have easily stayed within the walls of illusion. He could have done what most of us do when we glimpse our frailties and mortality: just forget about it. With the aid of alcohol and other drugs, cosmetics and surgeries, amusements and sports, mindless consumption and acquisitions, we try to stop thinking about what we know to be true. We do it so well that we are usually not even aware we are doing it. Perhaps this has been the approach of choice for most humans throughout history. Our species has devoted an incredible amount of creative energy to discovering new methods to hide the truth from ourselves.

Siddhattha might have, on the other hand, adopted a kind of philosophical resignation: let's eat, drink, and be merry, for tomorrow we die. This ancient philosophy was first articulated in *The Epic of Gilgamesh*. It differs from our ordinary perspective by virtue of awareness. Those who adopt this outlook do not *deny* death; they simply choose consciously to live by the principle of pleasure in the face of death. At its best, this philosophy seeks to maximize pleasure by making rational choices; it is not necessarily a mindless hedonism, which seeks pleasure at any cost.

But the Buddha chose neither of these possibilities, either of which would have permitted him to stay at home. His first awakening was too

12. Maugham, *Razor's Edge*.
13. Huang, trans., *Analects* 7.8 (p. 88).

deeply disturbing; returning to pleasure-seeking was just no longer an option. Siddhattha had awakened to the mystery of life. Like the young priest Nachiketas in the *Upanishads*, Gotama believed that the pleasures of life were meaningless with the Grim Reaper watching our every move. But leaving home—or "going forth into homelessness" as the Buddha called it—was also a risky venture. Gotama staked everything on the faintest of hopes. There was no guarantee that he would succeed at exchanging everything he already had for something better. What if there *was* nothing better? No doubt, many at the time thought that Siddhattha was crazy. Understandably, his father and mother tearfully pleaded with him to stay. He left anyway.

The Ascetic Years

The legends describe how he rode far away from his parents' house and exchanged his fine silks and jewelry for a patchwork robe of orange, the identifying color of the samanas. He cut off his long hair, picked up a begging bowl, and started to learn how to fend for himself as a wanderer in the world. He walked southward into the central areas of the Gangetic Plain where life in the new villages and towns was astir. He spent the rest of his days traveling throughout this region, never settling down for more than several months at a time.

His first order of business was to find a teacher to lead him to his objective, what he called "the supreme state of sublime peace."[14] He began his studies under the tutelage of Alara Kalama, a famed master of the spiritual disciplines known as yoga. The Buddha himself later reported that it did not take him long to learn everything Alara Kalama had to offer. Under his direction, Gotama was able to reach a level of meditative consciousness called the "sphere beyond materiality." But merely attaining a deep level of extraordinary consciousness was not what Gotama wanted. He found another renowned teacher, Uddaka Ramaputta, who taught him how to reach the sphere of "neither perception nor non-perception," but that was not "the supreme state of sublime peace" either. He continued to regard the yogic practices he learned as important, but could not accept that these were the highest attainments of spirituality, as his teachers had claimed. Gotama left Ramaputta and began to drift toward the central part of the Gangetic Plain, near a town called Uruvela. This time, five samanas who had been students of Ramaputta went with him as his disciples.

Gotama and his followers now intensified their efforts. To their meditative practices they added the extreme asceticism that many samanas

14. Ñāṇamoli, *Life of the Buddha*, 13.

observed. They would dwell in haunted shrines, what the Buddha described as "awe-inspiring abodes . . . which make the hair stand up"[15] to steel themselves against the "fear and dread" of being in such scary places, the ancient equivalent of spending the night in a haunted house. Considering the body a hindrance to the highest spiritual achievements, they systematically and deliberately tried to bring the flesh as close to death as possible. They fasted for long stretches of time; when they ate, it was only a handful of rice or lentils. They allowed their hair and beards to grow long and matted. Their bodies accumulated thick layers of dust because they had forsaken bathing. Years later, the Buddha would tell his followers that he began to resemble a skeleton covered in decaying flesh.[16] More than once, passersby mistook him for a corpse. Had he continued much longer down that path, their perception would not have been a mistake.

Fortunately, the ascetic realized the way of self-mortification would only end in death, with no compensating spiritual gains. "By this grueling penance," he said, "I have attained no distinction higher than this human state, worthy of the noble one's knowledge and vision."[17] The extreme practices of asceticism did not lead to "the supreme state of sublime peace." Just as he renounced his life of pleasure in Kapilavatthu, the samana Gotama now renounced his life of pain through religious austerities. He decided no longer to abuse his body in service to the spirit. He had tolerated as much pain as he thought anyone could take, and was not one whit better for it. He concluded that it would be necessary to look after the health of the body because the body would be required to sustain his continuing search for the sublime peace. Both denying the body's needs and indulging its appetites were errors, he decided. With this change of mind, he began to eat properly but moderately. Eventually his health returned. When his five disciples realized that he had abandoned the path of severe asceticism, they assumed he had lost his ambition to realize nibbana. They left him, just as he had left his teachers years before.

The Second Awakening

Having dismissed the way of worldly pleasures and the way of self-denial as both fruitless, the Bodhisatta was at a loss as to how to proceed. Having everything had not brought him the contentment he was seeking, and neither

15. *Majjhima Nikaya*, 4, in Ñāṇamoli, *Life of the Buddha*, 15.

16. "Mahasaccaka Sutta," 28, in Ñāṇamoli and Bodhi, trans., *Middle Length Discourses*, 339.

17. *Majjhima Nikaya*, 36, in Ñāṇamoli, *Life of the Buddha*, 21.

did having nothing. But he *had* attained the empty openness that often precedes creative thought, an achievement that should not be underestimated. It is not easy to reach this quality of mind. For Siddhattha Gotama, it took following to their bitter ends the way of wanting and acquiring and the way of aversion and denial for him to find this fertile openness.

It is amazing what the mind can toss up when it is not following its well-worn neuropathways. As he rested under a tree, the Bodhisatta recollected an old memory from childhood. He recalled sitting under a rose-apple tree as a mere boy, as his father was plowing a nearby field. He found the whole experience terribly uninteresting and, with nothing else to do, he started to pay close attention to his breathing. He remembered that attending to his breath as a child made him more acutely aware of his surroundings and dispelled his feelings of boredom and unrest. As he remembered the pleasant feelings of calm attentiveness, he pondered whether or not the path to nibbana might lie in this form of contemplation. The experience under the rose-apple tree had once sharpened his sense of awareness and brought him a tranquility that the years of strenuous asceticism had not. He decided to try this approach again.

Near the little town of Gaya, close to Uruvela, he found a congenial place. There, on the full-moon day of the month of Vesakha, he sat under a large peepul tree and vowed not to leave until he had attained complete awakening, even if it meant dying in the effort. The peepul tree later became known colloquially as the "Bodhi," or simply "Bo," tree, a term that means wisdom but more literally suggests wakefulness. It is interesting to observe how trees appeared at three of the most significant moments of the Buddha's life. He was born under a flowering sala tree as his mother reached for its branch; he attained awakening under the peepul tree; and he died, achieving final nibbana as he lay between two sala trees. It is also interesting to note the appearance of the full moon at these critical junctures. His birth, awakening, and final nibbana were all said to have occurred at the time of the full moon in Vesakha, which usually occurs during the Western months of April and May. Today, Vesak is the central holiday of the Buddhist world, and in some Buddhist countries, like Sri Lanka, every full-moon day is a holiday.

The story of the Buddha's second awakening is, of course, fleshed out in fascinating mythological detail by later tradition, but the Pali accounts of what happened are sparse. The later legends emphasize his heroic qualities as he resisted the onslaughts of his great nemesis, Mara, a demon-like figure whose chief objective was to keep Gotama from reaching his goal. As the Bodhisatta deepened his meditation through the course of the night, Mara tried to entice him with visions of lovely, seductive women. When the allure of sensual pleasure failed, Mara tried to frighten Gotama with images of hostile armies seeking to destroy him. That too was futile. Then Mara attempted to make Gotama feel doubtful about his capacity to accomplish something as lofty as nibbana. After trying everything in his arsenal, and failing each time, Mara finally acknowledged defeat.

Mara was quite a fascinating figure in Buddhist literature. He functioned like Satan in the New Testament stories of Jesus, not as much as a god of evil but as a tempter and a nuisance. Although mythically, Mara is depicted as a separate being, Buddhist psychology also suggests that Mara is that aspect of our personalities that tries to sabotage our own happiness. It is interesting that Mara does not appear in the story of the Buddha until the moment he decides to seek enlightenment, just as Satan only shows up to pester Jesus when the latter begins his proclamation about god's kingdom. As long as the Bodhisatta lived in ignorance of the world, Mara had no need to trouble him. When one sets off to live the noble life, the trials begin in earnest. Long after the Buddha defeated Mara in his quest for awakening, the later legends say, the two actually became good friends and sometimes commiserated over tea about the hardships of fulfilling the roles allotted to them.

Back to the seconding awakening: With the conquest of Mara, the Bodhisattva gained confidence that his goal was within reach. His mind was expanding as he gained deeper insights into the human condition. Just as the morning star appeared in the sky before dawn, he became aware of the fact that he had finally accomplished what he had to do. He had indeed lived up to his name: Siddhattha: "he who reaches the goal." But henceforth, he would no longer be known by that name but by the title he had earned: the Buddha.

The Buddha claimed that his final awakening gave him profound insight into the nature of reality as well as the assurance that he had attained "the supreme state of sublime peace" for which he had long searched. What the Buddha discovered during this night of insights was the basis for all that he subsequently taught. Of course, he had learned many of the components of his philosophy in other contexts, such as the ideas of samsara and karma and the form of concentration he stumbled upon as a boy during a moment of boredom. But at his final awakening, he gained something even deeper as well as the conviction of certainty. What he had first accepted as belief, he now knew as truth, as the result of what he called "direct knowledge"—that is, understanding gained and confirmed by immediate, personal experience.[18] "What had to be done has been done," he thought to himself as he recognized his achievement.

---

18. *Samyutta Nikaya*, 22.26, in ibid., 28.

Knowing the World

Epistemology

When he began to teach his vision of the world to others, he urged them not to accept it as true until they too had attained direct knowledge for themselves. This epistemology—that is, this approach to knowing—was especially important in the context within which the Buddha lived. The robust movement of samanas—the renunciants in search of liberation—and the urgency to address matters of ultimate concern had spawned a huge panoply of teachers, each of whom proclaimed his own "dhamma," or truth. Amid so many claims, spiritual seekers and laypeople alike were genuinely perplexed about whose teaching—if any—was true. When the Buddha appeared on the scene with *his* dhamma, audiences wanted to know not only what distinguished his teaching from that of all the others, but also *how* they could know that his was the real dhamma, as he claimed.

The Buddha offered them such a method. He told his listeners that the usual grounds on which most people accept something as true were insufficient for living the spiritual life. To one community, called the Kalamas, who had heard more than their share of spiritual teachers, he enumerated these inadequate reasons. He told the Kalamas that they should not accept anything simply because it was based on a claim of revelation, or because it was rooted in tradition or commonly repeated as fact, or because it came from scriptures, or because it conformed to logic and seemed rational, or because the teacher was competent and possessed a fine reputation.[19] These grounds were not enough, he thought, for a claim to pass muster as genuine knowledge.

Although we like to think differently about ourselves as modern people, most of what we accept as true is based on one or more of the grounds that the Buddha dismissed as insufficient. What we call knowledge usually comes from second- and thirdhand sources such as teachers, parents, friends, the news media, and the things we read. We all claim to "know" the earth is a sphere, but how many of us have actually investigated that assertion and proven it to ourselves? Most of us "know" that atoms exist, but few of us have taken the time to study the evidence supporting the atomic theory. We "know"—or maybe I should say, we believe—these things because we trust the persons or sources that inform us. Much of the time, this indirect knowledge gained through trust is fine—and even necessary. We simply don't have the time, energy, and skill to prove *everything* to ourselves,

19. "To the Kālāmas," *Anguttara Nikaya* 3.65 in Thera and Bodhi, trans., *Numerical Discourses*, 64–67.

and recognizing that limitation supports my point: most of what we consider "knowledge" in our everyday life is actually mediated to us by the faith we place in certain authorities.

The Buddha, however, discouraged faith in matters of ultimate importance. He wanted everyone to see the truth of his teachings for themselves and not to rely on his authority as a holy man or as a famous teacher or on what his followers said. Nor was it was enough for someone to consider his teaching true just because it seemed to make sense. He told the Kalamas:

> when you know *for yourselves* that these teachings are wholesome; that they are blameless; that they are praised by the wise; and that they, if undertaken and practiced, lead to benefit and happiness, then you should accept them and abide in them.[20]

Within this compact statement, the Buddha sets out the standards for accepting a spiritual teaching as true. To qualify as true, a doctrine or claim must be known by immediate experience. Mere belief, according to the Buddha, was not enough when it comes to matters of ultimate significance. Mark Twain was once asked if he believed in infant baptism. "Do I *believe* in it?" he said. "Hell, I've seen it!" Twain's play on the word *believe*, which reveals the ambiguous way the term is often used in the modern age, goes right to the heart of the matter for the Buddha. Belief is inferior to seeing for oneself. Indeed, beliefs without direct knowledge can actually be dangerous, as later tradition suggested in an anecdote about Mara, the tempter who tried to derail the Buddha's awakening. As the story goes,

> Mara . . . was traveling through the villages of India [one day] with his attendants. He saw a man doing walking meditation whose face was lit up with wonder. The man had just discovered something on the ground in front of him. Mara's attendants asked what that was and Mara replied, "A piece of truth." "Doesn't this bother you when someone finds a piece of the truth, O wicked one?" his attendants asked. "Not at all," Mara replied with a devilish smile. "Right after this they usually make a belief out of it."[21]

Mara knew what the Buddha knew: that belief was not the same as personal experience and that direct knowing was the only way to secure liberation.

Although the Buddha's criteria for judging what is true depended on personal experience, this judgment was not merely subjective. Claims to truth also had to be measured against the standards of other, wise individuals and had to bear wholesome fruit in practice. Thus, not only was the truth to be seen; it was to be embodied and lived out as well. The Buddha did his best to ensure that his dhamma was understood as a practical regimen leading to direct knowledge and not as a system of beliefs.

The Buddha's Metaphysics

The Buddha's teaching career lasted forty-five years, from a few weeks after his enlightenment at age thirty-five until his death at age eighty. During that long period, he instructed thousands of persons from all stations in life: men, women, and children of all castes, all occupations, and all levels of education and intellectual skill. As a masterful teacher, the Buddha was adept at addressing his audiences in a manner suited to their capacities to understand. For some, he spoke philosophy; for others, he gave object lessons or offered thought experiments based on ordinary life; for yet others, he taught by silence, simply refusing to answer questions put to him. To all, he presented his very life as the quintessence of his dhamma. "One who sees me," he said, "sees the dhamma."

Thus we have available to us a variety of ways to explore the Buddha's worldview. The best-known approach to his vision is the very cogent outline known as the Four Noble Truths, which we shall discuss later. But we will begin exploring his teachings by a different route. Our approach aligns the Buddha's dhamma with the outline of topics we are considering for the other three figures. As with Confucius, our first subject in the study of the Buddha's teaching is metaphysics, his understanding of the basic nature and structure of reality.

The Avyakata

To segue into that topic, and to bridge his metaphysics with our discussion of his epistemological views, we begin by noting the kinds of metaphysical issues that the Buddha intentionally *excluded* from consideration. Although he certainly made statements about the way the world is, he did not feel obliged to take positions on every possible question that might be raised about the nature of reality. For instance, he consistently refused to discuss questions about the temporal and spatial character of the world as a whole. Did the universe come into being at a particular moment in time and will it come to an end, or has it always existed and always will? Is the universe extended infinitely in space or is it finite? About such matters, the Buddha declined to comment. These and other disregarded metaphysical matters are known in the Buddhist tradition as the *Avyakata*, which is usually translated as the "things that are not revealed" but which more literally means the "things that create unnecessary speech."[22]

There has been a vigorous discussion about why the Buddha ignored these issues. Was it because he did not know the answers? Interestingly, he never said that. In fact, he often indicated that he knew a lot more than what he taught. Was it because answers to these questions were beyond the competence of language to articulate? That is quite possible, as the Buddha often found language inadequate to express his insights, which was one reason he insisted that his dhamma be personally realized. But his own explanation, which actually does not preclude these others, was rooted in practicality; knowing the answers to these kinds of questions, he said, was simply not relevant to the sole objective of his teaching: to end suffering. We can ask all sorts of questions about the world, and many of these are riveting questions. If god created the world, who created god? Or if god did not create the world, how did it come into existence? The Buddha thought that one does not need to know these things to attain human fulfillment and happiness. Dwelling on such questions merely distracts us from the immediate concerns of the here-and-now and, in its own way, contributes to our suffering. (Thinking about how god came into being, as I often did as a child, usually left me with a pounding headache!) Like Confucius, the Buddha admonished us to leave speculative issues alone.

The Gods and God

If the Buddha refused to answer questions about the world's creation, we might wonder what he thought about the gods, since creation is often associated with the divine. To be sure, the Buddha lived in a culture in which belief in creator gods (and gods of all types) was commonplace, and the Buddha never seemed to doubt their existence. He often spoke about the gods, and in the legends, as we noted earlier, he was even portrayed as having been a god in previous lives. The Buddha appeared to have accepted gods as part of a vast cosmos populated with all kinds of beings, including humans, animals, ghosts, and hell-beings. As in classical Hinduism, it was possible for beings to be reborn into another category depending on their karma. So a human being might become an animal, or a god might become a human in another life. Obviously, the gods of the Buddha's world were not the same as the supreme being worshiped by Jesus and Muhammad;

---

22. "Culamalunkya Sutta," from Ñāṇamoli and Bodhi, trans., *Middle Length Discourses*, 533-36.

these gods were extremely powerful and lived enormously long lives but were nonetheless limited by and subject to the same principles of karma and rebirth that governed the lives of all beings. Because the gods themselves were trapped in samsara, they too needed to take the path leading to nibbana. The ancient stories tell of the Buddha's journeys to the heavens to teach the divine beings his liberating dhamma. The gods therefore did not play a definitive role in the Buddha's teachings. They could help human beings in certain ways, but they could not help in the one thing that mattered most: attaining the supreme state of sublime peace. That was something each being—human and divine—had to discover for himself or herself.

Those were the gods. But what about god? Did the Buddha have a place for what many call god? If by god one means the monotheistic idea of a supreme being, the answer is clearly and emphatically no. Never once does the Buddha even hint that he accepted belief in such an entity. He told of the great gods known as Mahabrahmas who were very powerful but had an exaggerated sense of their own importance in the world. One of these great gods, Baka Brahma, was once reborn alone in one of the many heavenly realms[23] and assumed that he had caused his own existence and created his own realm, of which he was the sole supreme deity. But the Buddha simply maintained that such a claim was mistaken, arising out of a god's own conceit and limitations of knowledge. The implication of the Buddha's story is that he found monotheistic claims about a divine being with ultimacy, omnipotence, and singularity to be untenable.

But if the term god is used in a different sense to refer to an ultimate reality that transcends the anthropomorphic god of monotheism, then it might be possible to say that the Buddha embraced a functional analogue to the concept of god. On such a view, "god" must be taken to refer to an unconditioned or absolute reality, not a being or entity. This is not the dominant view of god in the Western religions, which clearly stresses the personal, human-like character of the divine. Yet there are places even within these Western traditions where ultimate reality is regarded in ways that transcend personal conceptions. The not-so-well-known Christian theologians such as Denys the Areopagite (also known as Pseudo-Dionysius) and Meister Eckhart are two examples of religious philosophers whose understanding of the divine effectively denied personality in favor of an ineffable absolute beyond the human ability to conceive.[24]

---

23. The idea of many heavens is also found in the Bible, e.g., 2 Cor 12:2-4.

24. See, for example, "Mystical Theology," 135-41; and Colledge and McGinn, trans., *Essential Sermons, Commentaries, Treatises, and Defense*, by Meister Eckhart.

If such is the understanding of god, then the analogue to god in the Buddha's worldview was nibbana. Nibbana demarcated an important distinction in the Buddha's metaphysical world between the unconditioned absolute and the conditioned world of samsaric existence. He sometimes spoke of these dimensions using the metaphor of a river. Nibbana was the farther shore and samsara the nearer shore. The Buddha regarded his dhamma as the means for crossing to the other side. Significantly, the Buddha said very little about nibbana, although it was clearly the aim of everything he taught. In this respect, nibbana was similar to Eckhart and Denys's god— inconceivably and unutterably absolute. Although the Buddha spoke rarely about the farther shore, he had much to say about the world of existence. He thought that understanding existence, the conditioned world, was essential to seeing the unconditioned, the nibbana.

The Three Marks of Existence

The Buddha summarized his understanding of existence in a simple three-part list that identified the salient characteristics of conditioned reality, or life as we know it. He called this statement the three marks of existence. The Buddha claimed that his understanding of these three qualities—like everything else in his philosophy—was based on direct knowing. In this sense, he denied that his metaphysical positions were speculative or indeterminate. Anyone who made the effort to see with complete attentiveness could confirm the truth of these qualities. But even the unenlightened person could grasp these ideas conceptually and see how they were supported by empirical evidence. Awakening added the depth, clarity, and certitude that could not be had by conceptual understanding alone.

The three marks of existence were impermanence, insubstantiality, and insatiability. In the Buddha's understanding, these three qualities were interrelated. Each implied the other two. We will take up each characteristic in turn and discuss its meaning and function in the Buddha's worldview. We will begin with impermanence.

Impermanence

To say things change is such a truism that for the Buddha even to point it out seems almost trite. Everyone knows that the world and the things in it are constantly changing. The Buddha's understanding of impermanence, or *anicca* to use the Pali term, was, however, significantly different from the run-of-the-mill idea that things undergo change. What distinguished the

Buddha's vision of impermanence was its completely thoroughgoing nature. He applied the idea of impermanence to absolutely everything in existence and insisted that happiness depended on the direct apprehension and un- qualified acceptance of that fact.

For the Buddha, change was not merely what happens to an entity over the course of time. Change was not simply the birth, growth, decay, and death of an organism, the kinds of changes that are ordinarily perceptible. The Buddha saw that birth, growth, decay, and death also occurred at ev- ery instant in a manner difficult to discern without the skills of meditation. Meditative practice made it possible to sharpen perceptive attention to such a degree that one could have a direct knowledge of the momentary aris- ing and passing away of all reality. When viewed this way, as the constant coming and going of transitory events, any perception of stability or per- manence was only apparent. A deep, penetrating awareness of the world revealed that all things were concatenations of events happening so rapidly that they seem to be stable or changing only very slowly.

Although a tree appears to be a more-or-less stable thing in the world, in fact it is a grand parade of processes happening in swift succession at every level of the tree's existence. At any moment, leaves may be engaged in the process of photosynthesis as chlorophyll interacts with the light of the sun; sap may be flowing through its xylem and phloem carrying nutrients from the soil throughout the tree's body; minute cells composing its bark are dying and sloughing off as new cells are born to replace the old. And of course, the atoms and their subatomic components that compose these cells and systems are themselves in a wild, mind-boggling state of transforma- tion. From this perspective, a tree is not—and cannot be—the same from moment to moment.

But neither is it completely different. The tree that appears at one moment in time bears a close resemblance to the tree at the moment just preceding it and to the tree at the moment just succeeding it. The resem- blance between the successive moments of the tree's life is the result of what the Buddha called "conditioning." The tree at moment 1 conditions the tree at moment 2, which conditions the tree at moment 3, and so on. In this context, conditioning means that one event (or collection of events) greatly influences, but does not completely determine, the next. Moment 3 is what it is because of the character of moment 2, which is what it is because of the character of moment 1. Because of conditioning, there is *continuity* between the tree's successive moments in time, but there is not identity, constancy, or sameness.

Now, let us push this view even further. The Buddha's understanding of change was so far-reaching, so thoroughgoing, that ultimately it meant there were no "things" in the world at all. This is not to say he thought that the universe was a complete illusion, a mere creation of some mind without objective reality; no, for the Buddha, the world was real enough. But he thought that no item in our experience—no thought, feeling, or physical object—endured long enough from one moment to the next for us to say it was a "thing." By "thing," I simply mean an entity that has its own existence in space and time. Because change occurs so rapidly and so thoroughly, and because all items of experience are dependent on other items, just as photosynthesis depends on the sun, it is misleading and technically wrong to call a tree a thing. There is nothing about a tree that warrants saying it has its *own* existence, since it depends on so much that is not-tree, like air, light, soil, and water, and since no particular form of it endures over time—not even a moment, however that would be defined. Imputing thinghood to these, these (one wants to say "things"!—and that proves the point) these "aspects" of experience is a function of our language and thinking processes. That is what the Buddha wants us to see by means of this doctrine of impermanence. Our minds, conditioned as they are by our language, tend to reify, or regard as concrete things, matters that are better understood as events or occurrences. Most of the time, it is perfectly okay that our minds do this. It is certainly more convenient to say, "Look at that tree over there" than to say "Look at that complex concatenation of successive events engaged in the processes of photosynthesis, the transport of nutrients, the death and birth of new cells, and the swirl of electrons. Isn't it beautiful?" The danger arises only when we *forget* that talking and thinking about "things" is a mere convenient contrivance. The true reality of the world of existence is something that cannot easily be captured by our thought and language.

To summarize his understanding of impermanence, let us say the Buddha did not think that things changed; he thought that change was the only thing there was. The attribution of "thinghood" to any aspect of our experience is merely a habit of thought and a function of language, based on our need for convenience in negotiating this complex existence.

Insubstantiality

By observing the radical depth of the Buddha's vision of impermanence, we have already begun to make our acquaintance with the mark of insubstantiality. As we have seen, the transitory nature of existence led the Buddha to deny the existence of things, in the ordinary sense that we think of thingness. Because nothing maintained sameness or identity over successive moments or existed independently of other realities, the idea of a thing, an entity enduring through time and having its own existence, was just a misleading habit of the mind. This denial of thinghood, or what medieval philosophers called "quiddity," is the basic meaning of the quality of insubstantiality. When the Buddha said that insubstantiality is a mark of existence, he was simply saying there is no such thing as a thing.

"Insubstantiality" is the way I am interpreting the Pali term *anatta*, a word that literally translates as "no-self" or "no-soul," a point seen more clearly in the Sanskrit word, *anatman—no atman*. No-self is the denial of thinghood, or permanent substance or essence, to what is ordinarily called the "self" or "soul." Human beings, in other words, are not exempt from impermanence; insubstantiality characterizes the *whole* of existence, including persons.

Suggesting that persons are no exception to the rule of change may sound unremarkable or hackneyed, but consider how often exceptions are actually made. Virtually all religions acknowledge the fact of change, but despite that recognition, almost every religious worldview posits an immortal soul or some version of a substantial self in which the personality has a core identity. No-self was directed specifically at the Hindu conception of the atman, the immortal self that the *Upanishads* claimed to be identical with the ultimate reality called *brahman*. All things pass away, report the *Upanishads, except* this singular reality. But other worldviews also hypothesize the existence of an essential or permanent self and are therefore vulnerable to the Buddha's critique. Certainly, the ancient Greeks believed in it, as did traditional Zoroastrianism, Christianity, Islam, and other religions that suggest that an enduring soul faces eternal paradise or perdition after death or at the end of days. Even some modern views in psychology maintain the existence of a "true self" that underlies so many false selves or masks of our personality. Each of these worldviews holds a perspective on the self that the Buddha found untenable. He could find no reason to excuse *any* aspect of personhood from the principle of impermanence. Even more, he thought the chief cause of human misery was the tendency to deny the pervasiveness of change by sneaking permanence in through the backdoor with the idea of selfhood.

Of all the aspects of the Buddha's teaching, no-self has been the feature most prone to misunderstanding. It was a stumbling block to the first Western interpreters of Buddhism, who saw it as a token of nihilism. On the face of it, the Buddha seemed to be saying that the human person did not exist or was unreal. Yet, if *anything* seems real to us in this world, surely it is our own selves. The French philosopher René Descartes even said that everything in existence could be doubted except the doubting subject itself, which gave him the necessary leverage to make his famous claim, "I think,

therefore I am." There seems to be something counterintuitive about denying the existence of the self. The Buddha, however, was not trying to suggest
that human beings do not exist, or that our souls are somehow annihilated
when one dies or attains nibbana, the goal of the Buddha's practice.

Rather, he merely refused to affirm the belief in an enduring, essential
self or soul. He was not proposing another concept in its place. No-self is a
not concept; it has no content. Therefore, it would be incorrect to say that
the Buddha "believed in no-self," as is sometimes said. No-self means he
declined to believe in the soul. After years of practice, culminating in his
awakening, the Buddha was convinced that the soul was an irredeemably
flawed concept. This idea, he insisted, was an unwholesome and problematic way of thinking.

Like the rest of existence, what we conventionally call "self," "I," or
"me" clearly has reality, but our language and ordinary ways of thinking are
incapable of adequately expressing that reality. We exist, the world exists, to
be sure, but not the way we *think* they do. This failure of thought is in part a
consequence of our native ignorance of the world and in part a consequence
of the nature of language, which necessarily reifies, separates, and imputes
substance to the flow of experience.

On one occasion, the Buddha explained why describing human personality was so difficult. He said:

> This world for the most part depends upon a duality—upon the
> notion of existence and the notion of nonexistence. But for one
> who sees the origin of the world as it really is with correct wis-
> dom, there is no notion of nonexistence in regard to the world.
> And for one who sees the cessation of the world as it really is
> with correct wisdom, there is no notion of existence in regard
> to the world.[25]

Although he intended it in a different context, President Bill Clinton was actually quite correct when he famously said, "It depends on what the meaning of the word 'is' is."[26] The Buddha's vision of "is" was simply inexpressible
in the conventional duality supported by conventional language; his vision
of reality was beyond the alternatives of being and not being. He would

25. "*Nidanavagga: The Book of Causation*" in Bodhi, trans., *Connected Discourses
of the Buddha*, 544.

26. Clinton's actual quotation: "It depends on what the meaning of the word 'is' is. If
the—if he—if 'is' means is and never has been, that is not—that is one thing. If it means
there is none, that was a completely true statement . . . Now, if someone had asked me
on that day, are you having any kind of sexual relations with Ms. Lewinsky, that is,
asked me a question in the present tense, I would have said no. And it would have been
completely true." *Communication from Kenneth W. Starr*, 125n1091.

have regarded Hamlet's famous question, "To be or not to be," as a false dilemma. The Buddha did not want to say the self "is." That would suggest that it is a thing, something fixed, unchanging, and separate from the rest of reality. At the same time, he was reluctant to say the self is *not*, which seems untrue to our experience, and which can be interpreted as a kind of nihilism. His strategy was to be silent if he thought his words might be misunderstood, or to use language very carefully if the listener was prepared to comprehend what he had to say. If he thought his listener could correctly grasp it, he might deny the existence of the self, if it were clear that the self he denied was understood to be a mere fabrication, an illusion. Part of the problem was that people so completely identified with this fabrication that they thought a denial of selfhood was a denial of personhood, which is not at all what the Buddha intended. The great Buddhist philosopher Nagarjuna (ca.150-250 CE) compared the concept of no-self and insubstantiality to a poisonous snake. You must know how to handle it, or you might be bitten and killed.

For the Buddha, the person is real but, like all conditioned realities, is a concatenation of successive events, different from one moment to the next. We can examine this assertion more clearly by considering what the Buddha regarded as the component dimensions of the person. To the Buddha, the human being was a compound of five processes that he called the aggregates of being.

These aggregates were materiality, sensation, perception and apperception, conceptual constructs, and consciousness. Materiality simply refers to our bodily natures, the fact that we inhabit the world in a physical form. Sensation means the feeling tone of our experience of the world. We are constantly judging our experiences as pleasant or unpleasant or occasionally as neither pleasant nor unpleasant. Perception and apperception refer to the process of perceiving the items of our experience in a certain way. I perceive this hard, smooth, brown object at which I sit as being a desk. Conceptual constructs are mental and volitional formations, the domain of intentions and desires. Finally, there is consciousness, the faculty and process of awareness.

The Buddhist tradition has a massive array of literature covering each of these aggregates in exhaustive detail, but for our purposes, we need only note several important features about this compendium of human components. First, they are all rapidly changing processes. Like everything else in existence, the body, sensation, apperception, mental fabrications and intentions, and awareness are never the same from moment to moment. As with the rest of his teaching, the Buddha invited his listeners to examine their own experience and confirm this fact for themselves. Second, the Buddha maintained that these five processes were the complete constituents of the human being. There are no other aspects of personhood than those denoted by these aggregates. Finally, none of these five processes or any combination of them contains a shred of substance or anything that could be identified as "self" or "soul."

The Buddha challenged his audiences to corroborate the absence of selfhood by introspection. He asked his listeners to consider systematically each of the five aggregates to determine whether or not it contained a self, soul, or directing agent. One by one, the Buddha asked if each component was under the control of the person, to which the answer was always no. Then he drew the inevitable implications:

> If the body constituted a self, then it would not give us any trouble, and it would be possible to manipulate the body by making determinations such as *Let my body be this way, let my body not be that way*. So, because the body does not constitute a self, it *does* give us trouble, and it is *not* possible to manipulate the body by making determinations such as *Let my body be this way, let my body not be that way*.[27]

If my body were my "self," I could will it not to be sick or to appear a certain way. As it is, I have extremely limited control over my body, and I have absolutely no control over its ultimate demise. The Buddha proceeded to make the same point about each of the other aggregates. Because we are not in complete control of any of the components of our being, he simply could not imagine a "self," in any meaningful sense, as being part of human personhood. He advised, therefore, that every aspect of what we are "should be seen with thorough understanding of what it is: *This is not mine, I am not this, this is not my self*."[28] There was simply nothing about what we conventionally call ourselves that corresponds to what is ordinarily meant by the self.

Insatiability

For the Buddha, the problem with the concept of the self was not just that it was empirically unverifiable or unavailable to our experience, but that it gave rise to the third characteristic of existence—insatiability. Insatiability is my translation of the Pali term *dukkha*.

---

27. Wallis, trans., *Basic Teachings of the Buddha*, 31.
28. Ibid., 32.

Dukkha is one of those notorious words whose meaning, as they say, gets lost in translation. Usually translated into English as "suffering" or "unsatisfactoriness," the meaning of *dukkha* is actually far richer than a single English word, or even a cluster of English words, can express. It is often rendered as "illness," "anguish," "sorrow," "unease," "distress," "unsettledness," "lamentation," "pain," "grief," "despair," and "disappointment." Certainly all of these terms can be associated with dukkha. The term "insatiability" is not a replacement for these other words but an effort to augment and represent them. I selected "insatiability" not only because it nicely fits my alliterative scheme that includes impermanence and insubstantiality; but also because it nicely captures what is at the root of the experience of dukkha: that *you can never get enough of what you don't really need.*

In the Pali, *dukkha* is the opposite of *sukha*, a word that means "happiness" or "contentment." Now, happiness and contentment are not to be confused with pleasure, which in the Buddha's view was a fleeting sensation or feeling. Happiness for the Buddha meant essentially "the supreme state of sublime peace," the deep, abiding contentment that was not dependent on circumstances. Happiness, he thought, was possible whether one's sensations were pleasant or unpleasant. This kind of contentment, this happiness, was what all beings really, truly wanted. All beings, in their many and various ways, seek it. Perhaps everything we do can be traced back to this fundamental aspiration. The Buddha was not alone in this view. A great number of philosophers and spiritual teachers, including Aristotle and Thomas Aquinas in the West, have regarded the quest for happiness as the primal impulse of human activity. Aristotle said happiness was the one thing we seek for itself and not as a means to something else.[29]

The Buddha certainly saw nothing problematic with the will to happiness per se, but he did see grave problems with how we go about trying to satisfy it. Because of our mistaken beliefs about the nature of the world and the human person, particularly our failures to understand impermanence and insubstantiality, we inevitably go about the pursuit of happiness in the very ways that thwart its fulfillment. Without awakening to the true nature of reality, we look for contentment in the wrong places, and because we can never find it, our thirst for satisfaction intensifies and worsens. It is like trying to put out a fire with gasoline.[30]

29. Bartlett and Collins, trans., *Nichomachean Ethics*, by Aristotle.

30. Mark Epstein relates the tale of a man who sits in a marketplace crying his eyes out with a plate of peppers on the ground before him: "Steadily and methodically, he reaches for pepper after pepper, popping them into his mouth and chewing deliberately, at the same time wailing uncontrollably. 'What's wrong, Nasruddin?' his friends wonder, gathering around the extraordinary sight. 'What's the matter with you?' Tears

Most people seek their happiness in two basic ways: through acquisition, which is the preferred method in the modern world, and through aversion, trying to avoid life's unpleasant situations. The quest for contentment through acquisition leads one to try to enhance the self by surrounding it with fine material possessions, fancy diplomas and trophies, and other markers of well-being and achievement. If you have ever gone shopping to cheer yourself up, then you know what I mean. But acquisitiveness need not focus only on material things. One can seek happiness by having unique and interesting experiences—including spiritual experiences—or by holding the right religious or political beliefs or by identifying with an organization or a country or cause. One can seek happiness through the love of other beings, both human and divine. There is no end to the ways we pursue contentment by means of getting and having. So what is the problem with trying to make ourselves happy in this way? Lots of things, really, but much of it has to do with the ephemeral nature of reality. Deep, abiding contentment cannot be gained by clinging to transient things. Possessions break or decay, interesting experiences become mere memories, the persons we love leave or die or stop loving us. Even if acquiring something we really want satisfies us for a while, it does not last. Soon, we start wanting something else.

Sometimes, we seek satisfaction by avoiding unpleasant situations or things or people. But a life principally motivated by fear is not a happy one. The problem with trying to find your happiness through avoidance, just like the problem of trying to find happiness through acquisition, is the nature of reality. Reality simply does not allow us to evade unwanted experiences. We might escape a few, but we cannot avert them all, including the great facts of life that impelled the Buddha on his journey to enlightenment—sickness, old age, and death. If our strategy has been to flee from unpleasant circumstances, when they come to meet us, as they surely will, our suffering will be great indeed.

The whole approach to contentment through acquisition or aversion is fundamentally misguided, the Buddha would say. Clearly, the Buddha's own biography informed his analysis. He was the man who had everything and the man who gave up everything. Both circumstances were unable to afford him any peace. Rather than bringing the satisfaction we so deeply want, acquisition and aversion only serve to frustrate us and increase our anguish and disappointment. Instead of questioning these methods themselves, we foolishly think, in our unawakened state, that we simply have not acquired

---

stream down Nasruddin's face as he sputters an answer. 'I'm looking for a sweet one,' he gasps." Epstein, *Open to Desire*, 1.

or averted the right thing. When one thing does not bring us happiness, we simply look for another. In other words, we are insatiable.

These situations are encompassed by this rich Pali word, *dukkha*. That single term denotes this fundamental, frustrating, and voracious quality to our unawakened existence. The Buddha thought that *dukkha* did not characterize merely episodes or aspects of existence; rather, it was pervasive and insidious. Like impermanence and insubstantiality, there are no exceptions to *dukkha* in the world of life as we ordinarily know it.

In its most obvious forms, *dukkha* manifests as simple forms of suffering such as anguish, fear, and grief. But clearly, all of life is not anguish, fear, and grief. It is important, therefore, to recognize the less apparent aspects of *dukkha* in order to grasp the Buddha's point fully. In its less obvious forms, it appears as frustration, annoyance, and irritation. Now the breadth of the concept becomes clearer. *Dukkha* names every aspect of experience in which there is the slightest twinge of anxiety, fear, or disappointment. With eyes wide open, the Buddha thought that anyone could see that all existence bore those qualities, even if it was nothing more than the awareness that the pleasantness one is now experiencing must eventually subside.

Dukkha is intrinsically related to the two other marks of existence. The failure to apprehend that the world and human persons are completely subject to impermanence and insubstantiality gives rise to *dukkha*, and the experience of *dukkha* in turn reinforces our misapprehensions. By attributing selfhood where there is none, we effectively believe ourselves to be separate, individual entities whose fragile existences must be propped up by possessions, achievements, beliefs, and relationships to convince ourselves that we are safe and protected from the vicissitudes of life. But this is an illusion. None of these things can give the security, the sense of well-being, the contentment that we really desire, and neither can our trying to avoid unpleasant and unwanted things and situations. Conditioned existence simply will not satisfy our deepest longings for happiness. When we awaken to the world "as it is," we discover, paradoxically, that the only way to find happiness is to relinquish these feverish efforts to protect and empower this mistaken belief we call the self.

Getting to the Farther Shore

The Buddha likened the difference between samsara, the conditioned realm of existence, and nibbana, the unconditioned absolute, to the two banks of a river. Getting from this samsaric side to the farther shore of nibbana was a mighty task that required personal effort and discipline. He regarded his dhamma, his teachings, as a seaworthy craft for making the journey. But his vessel was more like a raft than a motorboat. It required the energy and careful attention of the voyager to make it to the other side. In no uncertain terms, he told his students, "The Buddha only shows the way. You must make the effort yourselves." Even more, when one has reached the farther shore, the Buddha said the raft should be abandoned. Once it has served its purpose, it is no longer necessary. Like everything else, the Buddha's teachings should eventually be relinquished.

Spiritual Disciplines

Up to now, we have focused our studies on the near shore. We have explored the Buddha's fundamental understanding of this world through its three key characteristics: impermanence, insubstantiality, and insatiability. We now set our sights on the farther shore and the means the Buddha offered for navigating the waterway between samsara and nibbana. Our conversation will take us into the Buddha's ethical and spiritual practices, for these observances constitute the way across to the other side. But we will begin our exploration not with the means to the end, but with the end itself. Starting with the destination might seem a bit unusual, but understanding the objective will greatly assist us in appreciating how the Buddha proposed we get there.

Nibbana

Although nibbana was the ultimate goal of his entire dhamma, the Buddha said very little about it, just as Confucius was reticent about his ultimate reality, heaven. When he did speak, the Buddha described nibbana in mostly negative terms, which of course contributed to the West's early impression that Buddhism was a dour worldview. Yet there were very good reasons why the Buddha took a negative approach in his account of the ultimate reality. Once again, the matter concerned the nature of language. If the Buddha found the dualistic character of language insufficient for describing the conditioned reality of life as we know it, that inadequacy was even more evident when it came to discussing the unconditioned absolute. Language is grounded in human experience in the samsaric realm. Its vocabularies, metaphors, and grammars all refer to and derive from unenlightened experience in conditioned existence. How could it possibly suffice to explain that which is beyond this realm? Yet without language, how could the Buddha even indicate that there was a reality beyond samsara?

To resolve the tension created by this dilemma, he resorted to a rhetorical technique known in the Western intellectual traditions as *apophasis*, or saying by way of negation. Accordingly, the Buddha's preferred way to speak of nibbana was to say what it was not, and this is what accounts for the negative tone of his description. He called nibbana the cessation of *dukkha*, the eradication of ignorance, the termination of the illusion of selfhood, the cooling of selfish desires, the end of attachments, and the conclusion of rebirth. Nibbana was not a negative reality; the Buddha merely thought that positive descriptions of it could be misleading. On those relatively few occasions when he spoke of nibbana in more affirmative language, the Buddha called it "the supreme state of sublime peace," perfect clarity of mind, and unexcelled freedom and happiness. The Buddha said enough about nibbana to make it clear that it was not a place, although some of the metaphors he used might suggest that. The image of the "farther shore" was not an actual location, of course, but a concession to the limits of unenlightened mind.

Nor was nibbana understood to be a reality attained only at death in the way some religious traditions suggest: that human fulfillment comes only in a postmortem existence like heaven or paradise. In fact, one "sees" nibbana, to use a traditional phrase, while yet alive. The Buddha himself saw nibbana on the night of his final awakening, and everyone who awoke in this way was thought to have attained the end of suffering in their lifetimes. A person who had thus awakened was known as an "arahant," one who has "laid the burden down." Upon death, the arahant entered parinibbana, the final nibbana. The distinction between nibbana and parinibbana was a significant one, and it turned on the matter of karma. When one fully awakened to the world as it is, *dukkha* ceased, but the karmas that have driven existence to that point had not yet been spent. Nibbana entailed the cessation of new karma, since all self-centered desires, the source of karma according to the Buddha, had been eliminated. But the ripening of old karmas, the consequences of actions performed prior to awakening, had to take their due course. When all the karmic energies that had sustained conditioned existence had been completely exhausted, the arahant realized parinibbana.

Nibbana is thus the end of all the factors that condition insatiability. The illusion of a permanent, substantial, separate self is gone, and so is the craving and the attachments that arise to sustain and prop up this fantasy. When craving and attachments have been fully relinquished, one surrenders clinging to life or yearning for death. One is set free from the cycle of rebirth, never to be reborn again.

Wisdom and Compassion

It is difficult for those of us on the near shore to imagine what life is like for the arahant on the other side because it is ultimately unimaginable. Our best clues come from the specific ethical and spiritual practices prescribed by the Buddha for those who would find an end to *dukkha*. Nibbana is essentially the perfection of these practices. By examining these exercises and understanding them as countermeasures to *dukkha*, we can better glimpse the nibbanic life for those who have successfully reached the farther shore.

Throughout the Pali and other canons, one can find a wide array of specific techniques and observances taught by the Buddha that qualify as ethical precepts and spiritual exercises. We will only be able to sample some of the most important of these. But our coverage of these topics is made simpler by noting that the practices the Buddha encouraged were directed toward the cultivation of wisdom and compassion, the two primary virtues of the dhamma. Perfecting wisdom and compassion, to put it as concisely as possible, is the way to nibbana and the end of suffering.

For the Buddha, "wisdom" meant to know the world as it is, as constituted by the qualities of impermanence, insubstantiality, and insatiability. As we have mentioned on several occasions, knowing these characteristics meant more to the Buddha than just grasping these ideas conceptually. It also entailed directly comprehending their thoroughgoing, radical nature and living life in light of their truth. With wisdom, in this sense, we have become quite well acquainted.

Compassion, on the other hand, is a new term in our study of the Buddha's philosophy. Compassion, which translates the Pali word *karuna*, meant to empathize with a being's suffering and to be strongly moved to alleviate it. Living compassionately meant to think and act without putting ourselves at the center of the universe, without believing that "It's all about me."

In the Buddha's view, wisdom and compassion were dialectically related; each reinforced the other. When we see the world as it is, we cannot help but feel compassion for all beings. The more we recognize the depth and breadth of pain and anguish throughout the world, and the more we see beings struggling and failing to overcome dukkha, failing to be free, the more we respond with a heartfelt willingness to see all creatures become happy. The *Karaniya Metta Sutta* compares this response with the love a mother has for her only child. At the same time, as we become more compassionate, we grow in wisdom, in our capacity to see reality more clearly. For the Buddha, the illusion of the self keeps us in bondage. The way out of this prison is through the practice of compassion, through cultivating, in the words of the *Karaniya Metta Sutta,* "a limitless heart with regard to all beings" and "good will for the entire cosmos." This practice helps unfetter us from the delusion of selfhood, the principal source of *dukkha.* Compassion for others helps us to see the world more clearly.

Perfecting Wisdom and Compassion

By the time we can be held accountable for our actions, we have already endured years of conditioning. We have learned to act and think in self-centered ways for so long that selfishness seems natural. Because our habits of self-centeredness are so deep and ingrained, the Buddha thought that persons needed a gradual, gentle discipline to reverse the effects of years (or even lifetimes) of conditioning. We cannot expect radical transformation to happen overnight, nor can we expect to be the persons we wish to be simply by willing. Willing must be accompanied by deliberate action. By acting compassionately and wisely, it becomes easier to will to be compassionate and wise, and the stronger our determination to be wise and compassionate, the easier it is act wisely and compassionately. Buddhist spiritual practice, therefore, is a matter of training and reconditioning: learning and acting to be the wise and compassionate persons we truly are.

In many ways and in many places throughout the written record of his teaching, the Buddha offered precise techniques for realigning the heart and mind to liberation. The classic statement of this training is the Noble Path of Eight Parts. The Buddha's spiritual disciplines were not limited to the practices contained in this statement, but all of his exercises, including the Noble Path, can be related to the goal of perfecting wisdom and compassion. Rather than attempt a comprehensive analysis of all of these techniques, we will consider a select number of them to demonstrate how they serve to cultivate wisdom and compassion and how perfecting these virtues leads to the ultimate goal of nibbana. Our selection follows a traditional threefold typology of spiritual practices in Buddhism. The first is training in moral conduct, and under that category we discuss what is known as the Five Precepts and the practice of generosity. The second division is known as mental cultivation. As representative of these techniques, we examine loving-kindness meditation. Finally, there are exercises that cultivate wisdom, seeing the world as it is, and here we study sitting meditation. All three types of practices strengthen and mutually reinforce one another.

Moral Conduct

The Buddha taught that establishing sound moral conduct was foundational for spiritual advancement. One would be unable to develop the mind properly and gain insight into the true nature of reality without first mastering the rudiments of the ethical life. Advanced forms of spiritual practice required a basis of calmness and tranquility that cannot be experienced by anyone who routinely engages in immoral behavior.

Instilling moral behavior, of course, is a basic feature of most—perhaps all—spiritualities developed during and after the Axial Age. But unlike many other religions, morality in the Buddha's worldview was not grounded in the commands of a god who issues specific rules for human behavior, since there is no such god in Buddhism. Rather, the Buddha related moral behavior to the quest to end suffering, that is, to all beings' desire for happiness. Like Confucius, the Buddha thought that ethical conduct ought to be founded on the human desire to realize the good rather than on the fear of retribution. In this sense, moral behavior is also a spiritual practice in Buddhism because it is vitally connected to the ultimate objective of seeing nibbana.

Five Precepts

Cultivating moral virtue takes the form of aspiring to noble conduct. At its most basic, aspiration to noble behavior for the Buddha meant vowing to follow the Five Precepts of wholesome action. In the beginning, one follows the precepts rather imperfectly. When one fails to live up to the ideal, he or she simply acknowledges the failure and endeavors to do better next time. Moral failure is not considered a sin. Gradually, by resolving to start afresh each time one falls short, the skill to adhere to the precepts becomes increasingly stronger, to the point where acting otherwise becomes unthinkable.

These foundational precepts follow the principle of nonharming, an idea that resounds throughout the world's philosophical and ethical traditions. These traditions recognize that at its most fundamental level, moral behavior is not a matter of what one *does* but of what one *refrains* from doing. Confucius's formulation of the Golden Rule was expressed in this fashion: "What you do not want done to yourself do not do to others." Imagine the kind of world we would have if everyone followed the simple principle to do no harm. The first precept of the Buddha's ethics states this principle in its basic form: "I promise to refrain from harming sentient beings." Sentient beings are creatures with the capacity to feel pain and pleasure. In short, the first step toward ending suffering is by refusing to inflict suffering on others, as well as on oneself. According to the law of karma, violence begets violence. Historically, some Buddhists interpreted this precept strictly and practiced vegetarianism, but not all did. The Buddha permitted his monks and nuns to eat meat or fish if it were offered as a gift and if the animal was not killed specifically for the monastics' benefit. It is not easy to live in the world without harming or killing some sentient life; when one finds it necessary to compromise this ideal, at least the individual can strive to minimize the amount of harm she or he does. Following this precept not only avoids the negative karmic effects of violence but also sharpens one's awareness of the magnitude of the world's suffering, a consciousness that arouses the deeper sense of compassion.

The other foundational precepts work in a similar fashion and take a similar form: "I will refrain from stealing and coveting"; "I will refrain from sexual misconduct"; "I will not lie or use false speech"; "I will not use substances that impair my mind or body." Obviously, each of these vows serves to curtail the distress of others and oneself simply by limiting the infliction of harm. But each also serves to deepen wisdom and compassion. By intentionally determining not to harm, one develops a greater awareness of the vulnerabilities of all beings and of their desire to be happy. The precepts also help to dispel the illusion of the self by refusing to perform activities that perpetuate and reinforce it. We might call these kinds of activities "selfing" in order to indicate that certain behaviors help to convince us that the "self" is a reality rather than an illusion. Any behavior that serves this purpose—such as stealing, lying, or lust—is a form of selfing. The Buddha intended his ethical precepts to weaken the selfing function and to bring the aspirant's life into greater alignment with reality.

Dana

As the practice of the precepts demonstrates, much is accomplished merely by doing nothing. But doing nothing is not so easy, since our lives have been so deeply conditioned into self-absorbed behavior. To help retrain the mind towards a wiser and more compassionate disposition, the Buddha suggested many other practices. One of these was *dana*, or generosity.

The virtue of *dana* is not difficult to understand. It essentially means to give to others without expectation of return, to give freely and liberally with no strings attached. Ordinarily, the observance of *dana* involves giving material goods, and it probably originated with the practice of the householders of the Buddha's day providing the basic necessities of life for the men and women who had gone forth into homelessness, seeking the way to liberation. The samanas, of course, had no possessions or means of support other than what the ordinary folk provided them. The Buddha recognized this virtuous activity and encouraged it. Still today, one of the primary meanings of *dana* among Buddhist practitioners is to give food, clothing, and other essentials to the monastics. But *dana* has a wider meaning than this. It pertains to any act of generosity performed in a compassionate spirit to benefit other beings. The Buddha said that an act as humble as throwing "the rinsings from a pot or cup into a village pool or pond, wishing that the living beings there may feed on them,"[31] would qualify as an act of *dana*. The value of such practices in the Buddhist framework is readily apparent. The act of giving without expectation loosens the attachments we may have to our money and possessions, which relaxes the sense of self that money and possessions shore up. For the Buddha, the great benefit of acts of generosity is not principally in the material transfer of goods to a needy person, as beneficial as that may be, but in the spiritual transformation of the mind. It *is* better to give than receive.

The Buddha considered these ethical practices powerful enough to ensure a positive rebirth, whether or not the practitioner followed the other aspects of the dhamma or was even a follower of the Buddha's dhamma at all. Anyone—Buddhist, Hindu, agnostic, atheist—benefits by living the moral life. The Buddha claimed:

> Another person has practiced the making of merit by giving as well as by moral discipline to a high degree; but he has not undertaken the making of merit by meditation. With the breakup of the body, after death, he will be reborn among humans in a favorable condition. Or he will be reborn in the company of the devas of the Four Great Kings.[32]

Mental Cultivation

Transformation of thought is also the purpose of *metta*, or lovingkindness, meditation, one of the practices of concentration. The lovingkindness contemplation involves conjuring mental images of various persons in one's life and wishing for each of them freedom from illness, suffering, and fear and a sense of ease, contentment, and well-being. The practitioner usually

31. *Anguttara Nikaya* 3.57, from Nyanaponika and Bodhi, *Numerical Discourses of the Buddha*, 58.

32. "The Way to a Fortunate Rebirth," in Bodhi, trans., *In the Buddha's Words*, 167.

begins this contemplation by wishing for his or her own happiness, with phrases such as: "May I be healthy"; "May I be safe"; "May I experience no fear"; "May I live with ease." Then the exercise moves to thoughts about someone for whom the practitioner deeply cares. With an image in mind, the practitioner offers the same wishes for that person's happiness. Next, the meditator imagines another individual about whom he or she has no strong feelings, positive or negative—perhaps the clerk at the grocery store—and pronounces the list of wishes with as much sincerity as can be summoned. Then, the exercise focuses on a person for whom the practitioner has strong negative feelings, perhaps someone whose image evokes anger or hatred. And again, with as much earnestness as possible, the meditator wishes them great happiness. Finally, the practice concludes by evoking this same wish for all beings, with none excluded. The intent of this exercise in compassionate contemplation is obviously to work with the mind to help channel its patterns of thought into more wholesome and kindhearted ways. Over time, according to the Buddha, this practice helps the mind to see the suffering of all beings with greater sensitivity and to develop a kinder disposition toward them all.

Developing Wisdom

The Buddha encouraged meditative practice in a variety of forms toward different specific ends. Just as *metta* meditation was a means to shape a more compassionate mind, sitting meditation was intended to sharpen the mind and increase awareness. Sitting meditation is probably the spiritual exercise most often associated with Buddhism, since the Buddha is most frequently depicted in this posture in Buddhist iconography.

The basic sitting practice taught by the Buddha was established on the technique he remembered using as a boy sitting under the rose-apple tree. That practice involved finding a quiet place, stilling the body with crossed legs and an upright spine, and bringing concentrated awareness to the breath as an anchor for one's attention. Inevitably, as one begins this practice, the mind begins to stray, or the body and its feelings and perceptions demand attention. Almost reflexively and without awareness, the mind loses its concentration on breathing and begins to entertain a thought or to focus on an emotion or sensation. Soon, the mind has completely forgotten about the breath and is instead thinking about lunch or contemplating a vacation in Florida. That's the way the undisciplined mind works. It is an immensely powerful organ, but it is terribly unruly. The meditation practice begins when one becomes aware of the mind's waywardness and gently redirects it back to attending to the breath. The goal of this exercise is not to *prevent* thoughts or sensations from arising but to become aware of the moment they do arise and to learn to let them go. The continual observance of this technique gradually disciplines the mind and the body, helps sharpen the consciousness, and trains the practitioner in the art of relinquishing thoughts, the vast majority of which are not even worth the mental energy it requires to think.

The Five Precepts, *dana, metta* meditation, and sitting practice are four of the dozens of techniques taught by the Buddha for the development of wisdom and compassion, the two virtues that best represent the nibbanic life. Although oriented toward different factors that contribute to *dukkha*, the practices all work together to loosen the bonds that inhibit ultimate freedom and clarity of mind. The Buddha's approach to spirituality was to enlist an arsenal of practices to remove incrementally the impediments that hinder us from being wise and compassionate—ignorance, cravings and aversions, attachments, and most especially the delusion of the self. Because each person's conditioning is different, the Buddha prescribed different techniques to assist each practitioner along the path to nibbana. The Buddha's skill in offering specific exercises suited to the needs of individuals was one of the traits that made him such an effective teacher.

How the Buddha Taught

"What had to be done has been done," thought the Buddha when he saw nibbana. The quest was over; all self-interested desires had been exhausted; perfect bliss had been achieved. What does one do when all that had to be done has been done? That's not a question that I expect to be pondering—at least not in this lifetime. But it is one that a Buddha must consider. One option is to do nothing but enjoy the fruits of one's labors. For several weeks after his awakening, this was exactly what the Buddha did. But as he contemplated his next step, he considered another alternative—sharing the fruits of his labors with others. The Buddha gave the matter a great deal of thought. Initially, he concluded that trying to teach his dhamma—his vision of reality and liberation—would be futile. He said to himself: "This Dhamma that I have attained to is profound and hard to see, hard to discover . . . [If] I taught the Dhamma, others would not understand me, and that would be wearying and troublesome for me."[33] But he had a change of heart when one of the great gods suggested that some beings in the world have "only a little dust on their eyes" and are languishing because they do not know the

33. Ñāṇamoli, *Life of the Buddha*, 37.

way to freedom. The Buddha thought of his former teachers, Alara Kalama and Uddaka Ramaputta, and agreed that perhaps they and others might be prepared to receive the instruction he could offer. So, out of compassion for those still suffering in samsara, he decided to teach his Noble Path to those who might be ready to benefit from it.

Shortly after resolving to teach others out of compassion for their well-being, the Buddha determined to seek out his past teachers and share his dhamma with them. He soon learned, however, that both had recently died. Then he thought about the students who left him when it appeared he had forsaken the ascetic way. Having learned that the five were residing in a Deer Park near the holy city of Benares, the Buddha set out on foot to find them. Still upset by what they regarded as his betrayal, the five samanas decided not to show him any of the usual courtesies when they saw him approaching. Yet as he got nearer, they could perceive a visible difference in his countenance and bearing. When at last he reached them, they were unable to abide by their agreement and practically stumbled over themselves to welcome him and make him comfortable. He told them that he had discovered the way to the farther shore and had come to share his findings. Judging by his serene appearance, they recognized that their former mentor had indeed undergone a profound transformation, and they invited him to speak. And so the Buddha began his first lesson as a fully awakened being.

Setting the Wheel of Dhamma in Motion

His talk was brief and to the point. Its form was philosophical and particularly suited for longtime seekers of truth, like the five samanas. It was not a discourse for beginners. Yet it had been so carefully crafted that it became the touchstone of the Buddha's whole dhamma. The tradition called this inaugural address "Setting the Wheel of Dhamma in Motion." The image of the wheel, which is the oldest icon in Buddhist art, would have called to mind the chariot wheel, long associated with the power of royalty. Just as a king set chariots in motion by declaring a war of conquest, so too did the Buddha commence the conquest of samsara by the force of his dhamma.

The Buddha explained to the samanas that he had ascertained four essential facts about life. He presented these facts, not as propositions that could be debated or as faith statements that should be accepted as true, but as the discovery of incontrovertible realities, just as a physicist might discuss the four fundamental forces of nature.[34] In other words, the Buddha

---

34. The four forces are the strong nuclear force, the weak nuclear force, the electromagnetic force, and gravity.

regarded his "Four Noble Truths," as they are usually known, as having the same reality as we today attribute to gravity. Just as gravity is a universal governing force in nature that operates irrespective of our opinion about it, so too the Noble Truths were considered universal principles governing reality whether we recognize them or not. As with everything he taught, the Buddha expected his audiences to verify his claims for themselves by means of their own experience.

The basic form of the Four Noble Truths followed the medical model of diagnosing and treating a disease. The Buddha began with an objective description of the symptoms afflicting human beings and proceeded to explain their root cause. Then he offered a prognosis and continued by prescribing a treatment. Earlier in our study, we became acquainted with the gist of the Noble Truths but in a different format, so much of the following exposition should seem familiar.

The first point of the Buddha's initial discourse was that *dukkha* is a fact of unenlightened existence. To put the Buddha's assertion as succinctly as possible, we might state it this way: Disappointment and dissatisfaction pervade life as we know it. We all want happiness, but we cannot seem to find it. Dissatisfaction, disappointment, discontent—these are the manifest symptoms of what ails us.

The Buddha's second point identifies the source of our misery. Essentially, we suffer disappointment and dissatisfaction because we fail to apprehend the impermanent and insubstantial nature of all reality, especially what we call our "selves." Consequently, we act in self-centered ways and develop unhealthy attachments to persons, ideas, and all manner of things. When change occurs—as it always does—our attachments cause us to suffer. To be concise, our belief in self leads us to expect too much from the world, and that expectation leads to dukkha.

The third point is the good news that the prospects for our cure look bright. Although *dukkha* appears to be inherent in the way things are, it is not. There is an escape from *dukkha*, and it lies on the farther shore. Dissatisfaction, disappointment, and discontent are not necessary. Samsara can be overcome.

Finally, the Buddha offered a treatment for curing our distress. His prescription covered a variety of mutually supporting disciplines designed to diminish the harm we cause, cultivate moral conduct, sharpen awareness, weaken craving, and relax our white-knuckled grip on the many things that support our illusions about what we really are. Practicing these exercises brings wisdom and compassion and leads to ultimate freedom.

The Sangha

According to the Pali Canon, at the very moment he completed his discourse, the news of the dhamma reached the realm of the highest gods. The universe "shook and quaked and trembled while a great measureless light surpassing the splendour of the gods appeared in the world."[35] The entire cosmos recognized the significance of this event. The wheel of dhamma had begun to turn. At the same moment, one of the five samanas was immediately enlightened, simply by hearing the dhamma "well-proclaimed." Shortly afterwards, the other four became arahants, bringing the number of Awakened Ones in the world to six. These first five recipients of the Buddha's dhamma formed the core of the sangha, the monastic community that developed during the remainder of the Buddha's life and continued beyond it, to the present day.

After his Deer Park teaching, the Buddha began to teach others. His teachings were offered to samanas and householders, men and women, and persons of all castes. The dhamma was especially attractive to members of the lower castes and to women, in part because the Buddha believed that nibbanic life was available to anyone. In the Buddha's world, the usual marks of status—gender, class, wealth, ethnicity—meant nothing.

Growth of the Sangha

One poignant story illustrating this egalitarian spirit involved a poor untouchable known as Sunita, who was a road sweeper, or scavenger, as such persons are often called. Like many untouchables, Sunita was required to hide in the presence of persons of high caste lest his shadow fall upon them and make them unclean. Failure to so do might result in a beating. One day, as Sunita was sweeping a dirty road, the Buddha approached with a large retinue of monks and nuns. Finding no place to hide, the untouchable could only stand with his palms together in the traditional gesture of reverence as the Buddha walked toward him.

The Buddha stopped and said, "Friend, would you like to leave this work and follow me?"

Sunita was deeply moved and replied, "Sir, I have always received orders but never a kind word. If you will accept a dirty scavenger like me, then I will come."

The Buddha ordained Sunita and accepted him as a full member of the sangha.

35. Ñāṇamoli, *Life of the Buddha*, 45.

The first female to join the order was the Buddha's own aunt, Queen Mahapajapati, the woman who had raised him when Queen Mahamaya died seven days after giving birth. Queen Mahapajapati was later joined by Yasodhara, the wife of his youth, and many other women. His son Rahula, born shortly before Siddhattha's departure from his own father's house, had preceded his mother and grandmother as an ordained member of the sangha.

Of course, the monastic life was not for everyone. Many who heard and accepted the Buddha's dhamma continued to live as laypersons, or house-holders as they were called, and helped support the monks and nuns with their gifts of *dana*. And not all who heard the teachings accepted them. As in the case of Confucius, Jesus, and Muhammad, many walked away from the Buddha's teaching unwilling to support his movement or his message in any way. The Buddha felt no urge to compel anyone to accept his teaching. If anyone criticized his dhamma, he responded calmly and politely and tried to explain why he did what he did and thought what he thought. He told his students, "If anyone should criticize me, the dhamma, or the sangha, do not be angry, resentful, or upset. For if you were, that would darken your judgment, and you would be unable to know whether what they said was right or wrong."[36]

The Personal Qualities of the Buddha

To those who were ready to receive his teaching, a personal encounter with the Buddha was transformative. Once, one of his senior students met a man on the road whose face exuded serenity.

The student said, "Householder, your senses are calmed, your complexion is clear and radiant. Have you talked today face-to-face with the Blessed One?"

"How could it be otherwise, sir?" the man replied, "I have just now been sprinkled with nectar."[37] Such was the charisma of the Buddha that simply to be in his presence and hear him speak was often sufficient to enable some listeners to see nibbana. A student described being in the Buddha's presence like this:

> When he is teaching the Dhamma to an assembly, he does not flatter them or berate them; rather he instructs, uplifts, inspires, and encourages them. The sound that comes from his mouth

36. *Digha Nikaya*, 1.3, my rendering.
37. *Samyutta Nikaya*, 3.2, my rendering.

has eight qualities: It is distinct and intelligible, sweet and au-
dible, fluent and clear, deep and resonant. His voice does not
extend beyond the assembly. After being instructed, uplifted,
inspired, and encouraged, the assembly rises from their seats
and departs reluctantly, keeping their eyes upon him, concerned
with nothing else.[38]

The Buddha's physical appearance was certainly no liability in keeping his
audiences' attention. The Suttas indicate that he was about six feet tall with
coal black hair and a golden complexion. He was described by one Brahmin
as "handsome, good-looking, and pleasing to the eye . . . He has a Godlike
form and countenance."[39]

But like everything else, the charisma that could help midwife liberation could also become an obstruction to spiritual progress. Once, a
Brahmin by the name of Vakkali became totally captivated by the Buddha's
beauty. The Brahmin followed him everywhere, just to gaze at him; today
we might call it a "man-crush." Finally, the Buddha had to confront Vakkali
and command him to leave. The forced departure initially took the Brahmin
to the brink of suicide, but fortunately he came to his senses and, having
broken his attachment to the Buddha's good looks, became an arahant.

A Day in the Life of the Awakened One

Apart from his charismatic appeal, the Buddha's daily life seemed much like
that of any of the monks in the sangha. Like other monks, he wandered
about northeastern India for nine months of the year, and settled down only
during the rainy season. When possible, he preferred to sleep in the open,
often at the root of a tree. Occasionally he might take shelter in a potter's
shed. During the rainy season, he took residence in one of the small huts
that had been constructed for his use in various parks that had been do-
nated to the sangha by generous patrons.

The Buddha arose in the early morning after a very brief sleep—perhaps only an hour—and practiced meditation. At daybreak, he strolled
through his surroundings and often spoke with visitors or members of the
order. Later in the morning, he took his begging bowl—one of the few things
that he or any other monk owned—and walked to the nearest town or village to receive food for the one meal he ate each day. With his bowl held
with both hands, he would stand silently at the door of a home to receive
whatever the residents might offer. If he received nothing, he silently moved

38. *Majjhima Nikaya*, 2.140, my rendering.
39. *Digha Nikaya*, 1.115, my rendering.

on to another place. Frequently, he was invited to a home for the daily meal, where the hosts would often serve elegant foods. But even during these occasions, he maintained his simple way of living: he ate moderately and afterwards washed his own hands and bowl. As is still customary in much of South Asia, he would take a brief nap after the midday meal.[40] Later in the day, the Buddha received visitors and gave instruction to monks. At night when everyone else was asleep, the Buddha sat in meditative silence and sometimes, the legends say, the gods would appear and ask him questions about the dhamma. When at last he slept, he assumed what was the called the lion posture, reclining on his right side, with one hand under his head and his feet placed on each other.

The Buddha loved solitude. But his position in the sangha and the demands made upon him as a teacher rarely afforded him time alone, except in the early hours of the day. When he was able, he slipped into seclusion for an extended period and encountered only those who brought him food and drink. In this respect, he was much like Jesus and Muhammad, both of whom sought long periods of solitude.

Such was the general pattern of the Buddha's life in the years after his awakening. This quiet existence was of course punctuated by many noteworthy events. It is not possible to discuss them all, naturally, but let us mention a few remarkable occasions to help complete our portrait of the Buddha as a person and as a teacher.

Angulimala

One of the more unusual episodes in the Buddha's life involved a mass murderer by the name of Angulimala. As the story goes, Angulimala was a high-minded youth who excelled at his studies. His fellow students, however, were extremely envious of his skills and their teacher's fondness for him. They concocted a story about how Angulimala had attempted to seduce the teacher's wife. In anger, the teacher dismissed him as a student and demanded that he pay the tuition fee, which the teacher set as one thousand human fingers. Angulimala began to fulfill his teacher's request by murdering innocent victims and severing one of their fingers. He took the fingers and strung them to make a garland, which he wore around his neck. The name Angulimala literally means "finger-necklace." It is not completely clear why

---

40. I fondly remember my own experience teaching in India when the faculty and students would all return to their rooms to have a short rest after lunch before proceeding with classes. The world might be a nicer place, I came to believe, if we would all observe the spiritual discipline of the afternoon nap.

the young man actually followed through on the teacher's outrageous request. Some texts suggest he was predisposed to violence as result of karma from a previous birth; others suggest he was simply honoring the vow to be unquestioningly obedient to his teacher. In either case, the mild-mannered youth was turned into a raging, bloodthirsty killer. As he was looking for his one-thousandth victim, Angulimala saw the Buddha and ran toward him wielding a sword. The Buddha simply walked away in slow, measured steps. But Angulimala, running as fast as he was able, could not catch the Buddha. Astounded, the murderer demanded the Buddha to stop, at which point the Buddha turned and said that he *had* stopped and that Angulimala should also stop. When Angulimala asked for clarification, the Buddha explained that had stopped harming other beings and that Angulimala was still harming them. After hearing this, Angulimala changed his ways, joined the sangha, and soon attained arahantship. This story is another illustration of the Buddha's capacity to utter a timely and compassionate word in such a way that its transformative effects were immediate. But even more, the story emphasizes the power of the dhamma to liberate even the most hardened hearts. A person who has killed a thousand human beings can still be freed from samsara.

Ubbiri and Kisagotami

Earlier we observed in passing that throughout world religious history, the spiritual quest is usually prompted by an experience of tragedy, loss, or disillusionment. Such was the case for Ubbiri, the wife of a ruler in the state of Kosala. Not long after giving birth to a beautiful daughter, whom Ubbiri named Jiva, the child died and Ubbiri plunged into inconsolable grief. Each day she visited the river bank where Jiva's corpse had been cremated and grieved her lost daughter. One day, after these visitations had gone on for some time, the Buddha met her as she wept. Through her tears, she told him her story. After listening, the Buddha responded: You cry "Jiva, my daughter" in the forest. Come to your senses, Ubbiri. Eighty-four thousand daughters all named "Jiva" have been burned in that cremation ground. For which of them do you grieve? The response of the Buddha was exactly what Ubbiri needed to hear. With just a few well-chosen words, he was able to open her eyes to the ubiquity of grief and the reality of impermanence. Awakened to these facts, Ubbiri was suddenly relieved of her sorrow. Later, she wrote these words, preserved in the *Therigatha*, a collection of poems from the earliest Buddhist nuns:

> Pulling out

—completely out—
the arrow so hard to see,
embedded in my heart,
he expelled from me
    —overcome with grief—
the grief
over my daughter.

Today—with arrow removed,
    without hunger, entirely
    Unbound—
to the Buddha, Dhamma, & Sangha I go,
    for refuge to
the Sage[41]

Ubbiri's story is not unique in the Pali Canon. There were many such accounts in which a woman was devastated by the death of a child. This was a time, of course, when the infant mortality rate was very high, and grieving mothers were not uncommon. In another instance, the Buddha met Kisagotami, a mother who carried around the corpse of her child, pleading for someone to bring him back to life. The Buddha offered to do so if Kisagotami could bring him a mustard seed from a household that never knew grief. Kisagotami began her quest but eventually realized that there was no such home. She returned to the Buddha without the mustard seed but with the understanding that sorrow and death are universal and inevitable in conditioned existence. The knowledge was sufficient to soothe her sadness, and at last she allowed her child to be buried. She joined the Buddha's sangha and became an awakened one.

The Buddha's Pedagogy

In this all too brief overview of the Buddha's very long teaching career, we have sampled a variety of the ways the Buddha taught. In each instance, his lesson was tailored to the particular needs of his auditors and delivered at a timely moment. The Buddha claimed that he only taught about suffering and the end of suffering; but in many respects, he also taught much about how to teach.

41. "III.5—Ubbiri," http://uwf.edu/wmikulas/webpage/leaves/website/canon/khud-daka/therigatha/thig3.html/.

For the samanas who heard the discourse that set in motion the wheel of dhamma, the Buddha spoke in systematic philosophical terms. His concise outline of the way to attain the supreme state of sublime peace was imparted to them with the authority and clarity of someone having direct knowledge of the subject. Perhaps such direct knowledge is not important in teaching some things, but for the sage who teaches wisdom and compassion, it is essential. As the Indian poet Kabir said, "I speak only the words of experience; anything else is untrue."[42] The depth of the Buddha's knowledge is evidenced in the simplicity of the Four Noble Truths. The ability to make the complex simple—but not simplistic—is surely a mark of a great mind and, in this instance, a great teacher.

But not everyone learns by listening to philosophical discourses. Other temperaments require other approaches. Some respond to the simple display of compassion, as in the case of Sunita the road sweeper, whose entire life was transformed by the Buddha's human touch and an invitation to envision a life of freedom beyond the restrictions imposed by society. Some whom the Buddha taught were so filled with fear and terror that neither philosophy nor kind invitations would have had any effect. For Angulimala, the depth of rage and torment was so great that only a display of an equal measure of fearlessness and calm could have disarmed him. And on occasion, the best lesson may be the one that seems the harshest and the least compassionate. Vakkali, the Brahmin with the man-crush, could only make spiritual progress when he was commanded by the Buddha to leave the community. Sometimes it takes a sledgehammer to get through, but the lessons of the sledgehammer can be long enduring. Sometimes it only takes a gentle reminder of the facts of life to bring the lesson home. The grieving mothers Ubbiri and Kisagotami needed only someone to redirect their attention to the way things really were for them to see the truth. A gesture toward the charnel ground and an errand to fetch a mustard seed were sufficient. In each of these teaching moments, the Buddha revealed himself to be an astute observer of the human condition and a skillful communicator of wisdom.

Devadatta

We have already examined many of the noteworthy events of the Buddha's postawakening life, including his personal qualities and skills as a teacher. Before we move on to discuss his final nibbana, let us consider one more episode from this portion of his life—his relationship with his cousin

42. Bly, trans., *Kabir Book*, 37. I have edited Bly's version slightly.

Devadatta. We are not exactly certain when these events occurred, but the texts intimate that they happened late in the Buddha's life.

Devadatta had grown up with young Siddhattha Gotama and from an early age tried to compete with him. The legends tell several stories of Devadatta's efforts to embarrass or defeat Siddhattha. But despite—or perhaps *because* of—Devadatta's competitive spirit, he became a monk in the sangha shortly after the Buddha's awakening. In his early days, Devadatta was a good monk known for his abilities to use the extraordinary psychic powers that can be developed through meditation. But in spite of his meditative skills, he was unable to attain the ultimate goal of arahantship. Perhaps out of frustration, he became self-absorbed and sought worldly power and renown. Increasingly, he became envious of the respect and fame the Buddha received.

When he asked to be named the leader of the sangha, the Buddha flatly denied his request, and Devadatta vowed to destroy his cousin. Devadatta's first effort was to hire someone to kill the Buddha. But when the hired murderer approached the Awakened One, he lost the nerve, abandoned his weapons, and took refuge in the Buddha. Then Devadatta himself tried to kill the Buddha by pushing a huge boulder off a peak as the Buddha was walking below. As it careened downward, the rock struck another rock, causing it to veer off course and miss the Buddha. Devadatta's third attempt involved feeding liquor to a fierce killer elephant until it was drunk. When the elephant saw the Buddha coming in the distance, it charged. The Buddha remained calm and generated feelings of compassion for the raging beast. Suddenly, the elephant halted in its tracks and became quiet and serene. The Buddha stroked its trunk and spoke softly. In a gesture of respect, the elephant removed the dust on the Buddha's feet with its trunk and scattered it over its own head. Once again, murderous rage proved no match for the Buddha's serenity and compassion.

The point of these stories is not really that the Buddha's self-composure saved his own neck, but how his peaceful radiance brought tranquility to others. According to the traditions, a Buddha acts solely out of compassion for others. Even Devadatta was saved by the Buddha's compassion. Shortly before he died, the would-be assassin repented of his misdeeds. The ripening of his evil karma, however, prevented him from seeing the Buddha to make amends. But before he died, he professed a commitment to the Buddha's teaching. That act, coupled with the merits he acquired as a young monk, ensured that Devadatta would eventually become an arahant in a future birth.

The Death of the Buddha
and the Development of Buddhism

The Buddha's Parinibbana

Throughout his teaching career, the Buddha told his listeners: "All things in existence are subject to decay; everything that is born necessarily dies." This was a preeminent and ineluctable truth about the nature of reality. Although he had attained the highest level of fulfillment of which any being was capable, the Buddha, too, was subject to this truth. Having been born into existence, it was certain that he would decline and die. Death came to the Buddha sometime around 410 BCE, forty-five years after his awakening.

The last days of the Buddha's life are described in one of the great texts of the Buddhist tradition, the *Mahaparinibbanasutta*. According to this sutta, in his eightieth year the Buddha increasingly felt the effects of aging and was afflicted by serious illnesses. He knew his life was near the end. His foster mother, Mahapajapati, Yasodhara, the wife of his youth, and his son, Rahula, had all predeceased him. He told his personal assistant, Ananda:

> I am now old, worn out, . . . one who has traversed life's path,
> I have reached the term of life, which is eighty. Just as an old
> cart is made to go by being held together with straps, so the
> Tathagatha's [another title for the Buddha] body is kept going
> by being strapped up. It is only when the Tathagatha withdraws
> his attention from outward signs, and by the cessation of certain
> feelings, enters into the signless concentration of mind, that his
> body knows comfort.[43]

Existence had become painful and tiresome for the Buddha. When the writer Stewart Alsop was contemplating his own death from leukemia, he wrote, "A dying man needs to die, as a sleepy man needs to sleep, and there comes a time when it is wrong, as well as useless, to resist."[44] This was the Buddha's recognition. When he had come to this awareness, the sutta tells us, he "renounced the life principle,"[45] that is, he chose to allow the natural processes of decline to take their course. He predicted he would take final nibbana within three months' time.

---

43. "*Mahaparinibbana Sutta: The Great Passing*," in Walshe, trans., *Long Discourses of the Buddha*, 245.

44. Alsop, *Stay of Execution*, 299.

45. "*Mahaparinibbana Sutta: The Great Passing*," in Walshe, trans., *Long Discourses of the Buddha*, 247.

He continued to maintain his accustomed pattern of life until his shortly before his death. At that time, he accepted a meal from a blacksmith near the village of Kushinagara and soon became violently ill. It is not clear of what the meal consisted; the ancient texts call it "hog's mincemeat," which obviously suggests pork, but could also suggest the "food of pigs" or "pig's delight," which many scholars have interpreted as some kind of mushroom. The symptoms of his disease suggest that he may have contracted dysentery or food poisoning. In any case, it was clear that the meal was not intended to cause the Buddha harm. Indeed, as he approached the end of life, the Buddha made a special effort to assure the blacksmith that he was in no way responsible for the Awakened One's death.

Despite his intense pain, the Buddha did not complain but faced his illness in full awareness and complete equanimity. As his death approached, he asked Ananda to prepare a bed for him out in the open between two sala trees. You will recall that the Buddha was born as his mother reached for the branch of one of these flowering trees in a grove near Lumbini. He positioned himself in the lion's posture, in which he customarily slept, and his monks and nuns gathered around him. He asked the members of the sangha if they had any lingering questions about the dhamma. Three times he asked, and three times there was silence. Satisfied that his followers had understood his teachings, the Buddha uttered his final words: "All conditioned things are impermanent. Strive for liberation with diligence."[46] Then, he peacefully passed through the four states of deep meditation known as the *jhanas* and from there entered parinibbana, or the great final liberation. At once the earth began to tremble, and thunder clapped, in recognition of the great being's passing. It was during the night of the full moon of the month of Vesakha when this occurred, the same time of the year when he was born and when he was enlightened.

The Final Nibbana

The final nibbana is presented as a great, triumphant event. It was the Buddha's ultimate conquest of samsara. The legends indicate that gods from throughout the universe made their way to Kushinagara to witness this event. Like the crucifixion of Jesus, the Buddha's death was a lesson for his followers. This is why the *Mahaparinibbanasutta* describes the end of his life in such great detail; the text is one of the longest in the Pali Canon. The Buddha's dying lesson was that for those who have awakened to the reality as it is, death is nothing to fear. And if there is nothing to fear in death, then

46. *Digha Nikaya*, 6.7, my rendering.

there is nothing to fear in life. The Buddha's death was as placid a departure as one could hope for.

But where did he go? Even some of the Buddha's own students wanted to know what would occur to a fully awakened being at the time of death. In the *Majjhima Nikaya*, the monk Malunkyaputta confronts the Buddha, complaining that the Awakened One never explained this matter in any of his discourses. Malunkyaputta threatened to leave the community unless the Buddha stated his position unequivocally. The monk gave the Buddha four choices and demanded that he explicitly indicate which was the case. First, was it the case that the Tathagatha—that is, a perfectly enlightened being—exists after death? Or was it the case that the Tathagatha does not exist after death? Or, does the Tathagatha *both* exist *and* not exist after death? Or does the Tathagatha *neither* exist *nor* not exist after death?[47] Those options would seem to cover all the possibilities, but apparently they did not. The Buddha simply refused to answer Malunkyaputta's point-blank questions. The monk's questions were premised on the same dualistic way of thinking that the Buddha dismissed: the concept that something either exists or does not exist. Malunkyaputta's mind was still caught up in that web of thought, and he could not see beyond it. The Buddha knew that any answer he might give would serve to reinforce this flawed pattern of thinking.

As with seeing nibbana, the realization of parinibbana can only be described apophatically, with language that indicates what it is not. The parinibbana is the final depletion of all energies that have sustained existence. The five components of human life—physical matter, sensations, perceptions, mental fabrications, and consciousness—have been spent. Because the processes making up samsaric existence are no more, rebirth no longer occurs. Samsara is over.

The image often associated with parinibbana is the extinguishing of a candle flame. The flame is a consequence of various elements coming together: the wick, oxygen, and heat. When these constituents are exhausted—when the supply of oxygen is cut off, when the wick is burned out, when the heat has been cooled—the flame is gone. It makes as much sense to ask, "Where does the Buddha go after death?" as it does to ask, "Where does the flame go?" The flame is not an entity that can "go" anywhere. The Buddha is simply not here.

---

47. Sutta 63, *Majjhima Nikaya*.

The Cremation and Distribution of Relics

Just before he died, the Buddha directed his followers to treat his remains in the same manner as a "Great Wheel Turner,"[48] or universal emperor. Accordingly, the body of the Great Master lay in state for six days after his death. On the seventh day, after the body had been honored with perfumes and garlands, the Buddha's remains were wrapped in oil-soaked cloth and burned on a pyre of aromatic wood at a sacred shrine near the site of his parinibbana. Following the cremation, the ashes and other irreducible parts of the body, including a skull bone and some teeth, were collected and distributed to representatives from significant places in his life, including his birthplace; the site of his enlightenment, the location of his first teaching after enlightenment, and the site of his parinibbana. These artifacts were then taken back to these locations and buried in massive earthen mounds known as stupas, pre-Buddhist structures in which royalty were entombed.[49]

The earliest stupas were probably very simple constructions, but the structures became more ornate as the significance of these reliquaries increased in Buddhist life. Stupas soon became pilgrimage sites for those following the Buddha's Middle Way. Monks, nuns, and ordinary householders began to travel great distances just to be able to glimpse these reliquaries and to come into physical proximity to them. The stupa was a physical representation of the dhamma, functioning something like the way the crucifix or cross represents the gospel for Christians. As a central part of their pilgrimage, Buddhists circumambulated the stupa—in the same manner that Muslims walk around the Kaaba in Makkah as part of the Hajj. Coming to the stupa and circling it came to be considered a meritorious action that could improve the circumstances of one's next birth. Some Buddhists even believed the bodily relics could confer release from suffering or actual healing.

The Role of Relics

To one born into a religious tradition that venerates relics—such as Catholicism or Eastern Orthodoxy—their allure is probably quite familiar. Yet for one who was not brought up in such a tradition, the significance of relics and reliquaries may not be immediately apparent, and such things may be viewed with great suspicion. Let us, therefore, try to demystify them a bit.

---

48. The Pali term is *chakravartin*.
49. The oldest known prototypes date to ca. 700 BCE.

Matters of the spirit are by definition intangible, immaterial, and hence very difficult to conceive. The human mind, therefore, craves something tangible, something physical that it can use as an aid to understanding, even if that thing must ultimately be given up. Images, icons, religious architecture, scriptures, and the bread and wine of the Christian Eucharist all serve this function. Of course, there is no better mode of sacred tangibility than something closely associated with a great person who embodied the ideals of one's aspirations. And what can be more closely associated with such a person than fragments of his or her very body?

Consider for a moment the vast cults of celebrity throughout the world. Unfortunately, most societies today do not revere sages and noble persons as much as we worship television and movie actors and professional athletes. Think about the way one might prize an autograph or a piece of clothing from one of these celebrities—or even just a store-bought jersey with the name of a professional athlete embroidered on it. In my home city, Memphis, Tennessee, one can visit Graceland, the home of Elvis Presley, and view acres of memorabilia associated with him, including his cars and the jumpsuits he wore in his later years. Elvis's mansion is a magnet for people from all around the world who make the pilgrimage to get close to the relics of the King that lie interred on the Graceland grounds in a location aptly named the Meditation Garden. Perhaps these analogies will help illuminate the role of relics in a more sacred context. Something of the charisma of the individual with which they are connected is believed to be mediated through such objects.

Institutionalization and Dissemination

Within several months of the Buddha's parinibbana, five hundred fully awakened monks met in the north Indian town of Rajagaha to confer about the future of the dhamma and the sangha. The Buddha did not appoint a successor to lead the sangha but directed his followers to allow the dhamma itself to guide the community. Thus, it was essential for the sangha to agree upon the content of the Buddha's teaching. It was here that his assistant Ananda stood before the assembly and recited the Buddha's discourses, establishing the oral tradition that later became the Pali Canon. A few other councils were held later to resolve a number of doctrinal and practical issues. Since the Buddha left governance and interpretation of the dhamma in the hands of the sangha as a whole, disputes of this nature were almost inevitable.

Buddhism was not especially popular in the immediate centuries following the life of the Buddha. For many years, it was merely one of many
sects in ancient India. It was a demanding way of life and lacked many of
the elements that would make it a more attractive religion for ordinary folk,
such as belief in gods and community rituals. The cessation of suffering simply did not involve worship of the divine realm. The Buddha certainly never
suggested that *he* should be the object of prayers or rituals.

It was not until the reign of Emperor Ashoka the Great (304–232 BCE)
that Buddhism spread throughout the Indian subcontinent and attained the
status of an international religion. Ashoka's role in the history of Buddhism
should not be underestimated. Initially a ruthless conqueror, Ashoka converted to the Buddha's way after witnessing firsthand the massive atrocities
caused by his own insatiable quest for power and lands. In the aftermath of
the Battle of Kalinga, the horrifying spectacle of over one hundred thousand
human bodies prompted him to renounce war and embrace the dhamma.
Ashoka became as zealous a supporter of the Buddha's teaching as he had
been a conqueror. Legend says he had the original stupas opened to recover
the relics and divided them to create eighty-four thousand new reliquaries.
Most significantly, he sent missionaries throughout India, Sri Lanka, the
area now known as Afghanistan, and other parts of Central Asia. Under his
patronage, Buddhism became a dominant cultural and religious force in
India until the twelfth through the fourteenth centuries CE, when it became
all but extinct in the country of its birth.

The Forms of Buddhism

Like the development of any religious institution or school of philosophy,
Buddhism experienced a number of disputes concerning spiritual practice
and the finer points of doctrine. At one time in the early history of Buddhism there were at least eighteen different schools that looked to the Pali
Canon as their definitive source. Today, of these eighteen, only the Theravada school remains, making it the oldest extant Buddhist tradition and
probably the closest to the way Buddhism was practiced around the time of
the Buddha. Theravada, which means the way of the elders, is found mainly
in Sri Lanka, Burma, Cambodia, Laos, and Thailand.

Somewhere around the time of Jesus, another Buddhist movement
began to coalesce in the monasteries of North India. This development represented a much more significant division of thought than Buddhism had
experienced in its first five hundred years. The Mahayana, or the Great Vehicle as it came to be called, was based on a collection of texts purported to

contain teachings of the Buddha that had only been revealed to a select few of his students. These Mahayana sutras, their advocates claimed, had been kept concealed until the time was appropriate for them for them to come to light, and they provided a superior understanding of the Buddha's teaching. From one point of view, the Mahayana texts furnished a considerably different understanding of the Buddha and his role in bringing liberation to the world; from another perspective, this understanding can be seen as the further development of ideas inherent in the earliest Buddhist schools.

Two developments in particular helped distinguish the Mahayana from the Theravada school. The first was its view of the Buddha. Theravada had always maintained that Gotama Buddha was a human being, who had by his own efforts attained the status of Buddhahood. According to the Mahayana, Gotama Buddha was the manifestation of a transcendent reality known as the *dharma-kaya*, or the body of truth. As the Buddha of this era, Gotama was a *nirmana-kaya*, an appearance body of this cosmic principle. All Buddhas, in fact, were manifestations of the *dharma-kaya*. This conceptual development gave the Buddha a more divine, god-like status.

The second distinguishing mark of the Mahayana was its interpretation of the Bodhisatta. In Theravada, the Bodhisatta was simply the title given to the Buddha prior to his awakening. It was an epithet reserved only for Gotama and the other rare individuals destined for Buddhahood. In the Mahayana, the Bodhisatta—or Bodhisattva, to use the Sanskrit preferred by the Mahayana school—was an enlightened being who choose to forgo entry into final nibbana in order to stay within the world of samsara to enable others to achieve awakening. With this interpretation of the Buddha and the Bodhisattva, the Mahayana began to take on the qualities of a savior-religion. Interestingly, these developments took place at the same time another great savior-religion was taking shape in West Asia—Christianity.

The Mahayana was the form of Buddhism that was exported to China during the Han Dynasty, in the early centuries of the current era. From there, Buddhism later spread to Korea, Japan, and Vietnam. Over time, the Mahayana became the most popular variety of Buddhism and has so remained. Of course, it too has fragmented as new schools emerged from within it. One well known Mahayana sect was Ch'an, better known by its Japanese name, Zen.

A third form of Buddhism, the Vajrayana, developed from the Mahayana around the fifth century CE in North India. This particular version of the Buddhist tradition contains elements of the Indian yogic practice known as Tantra, an esoteric practice of harnessing the body's energies to promote enlightenment. Vajrayana, or the Diamond or Thunderbolt Vehicle, was first taken to Tibet in the seventh century CE, where it was influenced by

Bön, the indigenous Tibetan religion characterized by its interest in magic. Today, Vajrayana is still practiced in Tibet and Mongolia but also in Nepal, Bhutan, and India, the home of many Tibetan refugees, including Tenzin Gyatso, the fourteenth Dalai Lama.

Through these three traditional forms, Buddhism has traversed virtually the entire continent of Asia. Even when the inhabitants of these regions did not identify themselves as Buddhists, they were influenced by the perspectives of the Buddha and his interpreters, in much the same way that Westerners have been influenced by Christianity whether or not they consider themselves Christians. At present, Buddhism ranks as the world's fourth largest religion, and over one-half of the world's population lives in an area where Buddhism was or is a principal cultural force.

Today, a new form of the Buddhism appears to be arising in the Western world. This evolving variety of the tradition has no specific name beyond perhaps "Western Buddhism," but it seems to be taking a distinctive shape. This emerging Buddhism is the result of several older varieties of the tradition taking root in a new and very different culture, in the way Buddhism has done ever since Ashoka first sent missionaries beyond the borders of India. Western Buddhism's growth derives from an influx of Asian practitioners who have come to the West in the past few centuries and from an increasing number of Westerners who have adopted Buddhism as their own.

With this brief overview of the development of the Buddhist traditions, we bring to a close our study of the Buddha. We shall return to his life and teachings when we commence our comparative investigations of the four sages. In the next chapter, we will take up the sage with whom the Buddha is most often compared: Jesus of Nazareth.

3

JESUS

The Jewish and Roman Worlds of Jesus

Jesus of Nazareth lived at the intersection of two very different cultures: ancient Judaism and the Roman Empire. Each of these contexts in different ways decisively shaped his life and teachings. Yet he became convinced later in life that these two worlds were about to be replaced by an altogether new reality, the kingdom of heaven.

Ancient Judaism

Ancient Judaism was a great deal more than what most people today mean by the word "religion." It not only determined what one believed about the divine and what rituals one performed on holy days; it thoroughly inundated every aspect of life. It structured the daily routine, regulated one's diet, determined how people interacted with others, governed business transactions, defined criminality, shaped family relationships, and provided the fundamental concepts that formed the common worldview. So closely intertwined were what the modern world calls "religion" and everything else that the ancient Jews had no special word to designate the "religious" dimension of life. Religion and culture were identical.

What is today known as Judaism traces its roots to the persons and traditions described in the Torah, the first five books of the Tanakh, the most sacred collection of Jewish writings. According to these legendary accounts, the Jewish faith began when a nomad named Abram responded to the call of the god Yahweh (often rendered into English as "the LORD") to leave his home in Mesopotamia, in what is now present-day Iraq, and journey to a new land called Canaan and later known as Palestine. The LORD promised to give this land to Abram and his descendants in exchange for allegiance to Yahweh as their god. Abram accepted the invitation, thus beginning the long and complex narrative of the Jewish people's relationship with this god.

The ensuing saga includes many of the individuals and events that are well known in Western culture; they have become part of the common stock of our cultural literacy. Included in that story are the names of the great patriarchs and matriarchs who were the immediate descendants of Abram, or Abraham, as he was later called. Among them were Ishmael and Isaac; Jacob, who was given the name Israel, and his brother Esau; Joseph, the son of Jacob, who was sold into slavery by his envious brothers and later reconciled with them in the land of Egypt. Generations later, there was Moses who, under the guidance of the LORD, led the descendants of Joseph and his brothers out of Egypt and back to the land promised to Abraham. The story continues with the Israelites' struggles to establish a community in Canaan and to remain faithful to their god. They contended with the other peoples living in the promised land and with the temptations posed by the other gods of the land, who frequently seemed more accessible than the elusive Yahweh. Over time, what was initially a confederacy of small tribes living in Canaan was forged into the kingdom of Israel, united under the rule of Saul, David, and Solomon. But the cultural and political tensions between the groups became too great, and the kingdom was eventually split in two at the death of Solomon. The northern kingdom continued to be known as Israel, and the southern kingdom took the name Judah, after the dominant tribe of the realm. It was from the name Judah, which was later known as Judea, that the terms "Jew" and "Judaism" were derived. But the citizens of both kingdoms regarded themselves as the children of Abraham and as the chosen people of the god Yahweh.

Almost from the beginning, the relationship between this god and his chosen people was tempestuous, to say the least. Poets and prophets likened it to a marriage—a marriage that was sometimes tender and loving, and sometimes on the verge of divorce. The people found it hard at times to remain faithful to their commitment to the LORD as their sole god, and they frequently went "whoring after other gods," to use the biblical language. Yahweh himself was often frustrated with his people, allowing them to suffer the consequences of their infidelity to him and threatening them with harsh punishments.

When the kingdom split into the northern and southern realms, it began to appear increasingly likely that Yahweh was about to make good on his threats. Both kingdoms were tiny and highly vulnerable to the massive empires surrounding them. Prophets arose to warn the people of both territories to get right with their god or face the unpleasant consequences. In the eighth century BCE, Israel, the northern kingdom, fell victim to the armies of Assyria and was destroyed. There would no longer be a political entity known as Israel until 1948. The southern kingdom, Judah, survived longer than Israel, but it too suffered a major blow at the hands of the Babylonians in the sixth century BCE. In both instances, the devastation wrought by these great empires was widely construed as the work of Yahweh exacting punishment on a people who neglected to live up to their side of the ancient agreement negotiated with Abraham.

In 587 BCE, the Babylonian army marched into Judah, took tens of thousands of Jews captive, and carried them back to Babylon, in Mesopotamia. Many died on the nearly one-thousand mile trek. This event, referred to as the exile or the Babylonian captivity, was a turning point in Jewish history, marking the start of the diaspora, the dispersion of the Jews outside of Canaan.

It was during the exile and afterwards that Judaism acquired many of the features that characterize it today. Prior to the deportation to Babylon, religious life centered on the temple in Jerusalem, which had been built by Solomon, King David's son. At the temple, members of the priestly caste offered animal sacrifices to Yahweh on behalf of the nation, and performed various rituals for individuals. But the exile temporarily brought that practice to an end. Solomon's temple had been destroyed by the Babylonians, and the Jews living in the diaspora would have been unable to worship there anyway. In response to their displacement, certain key features of Jewish practice were newly created and others altered. During this time, the institution of the synagogue was formed, which allowed Jews to worship their god while physically removed from the temple in Jerusalem. The synagogue was an assembly of at least ten Jewish males over the age of thirteen, who constituted a *minyan*, or quorum. The development of the synagogue increased the importance of the rabbi, or teacher. Worship of god in the synagogue centered on reading and interpreting the Torah rather than on the system of sacrifice that had characterized worship in Judaism's early history. It was during the exile that the sacred writings began to be compiled and edited. By the time of Jesus, rabbinic Judaism that centered on the synagogue was well established in the Jewish homeland and was the form of Judaism that most profoundly shaped Jesus's own life.

These developments did not mean, however, that sacrifice and worship at the temple in Jerusalem were made obsolete. The Persians conquered the Babylonians in 539 BCE and permitted the Jews to return to their homeland in 538 BCE. Most Jews stayed in Babylon, but some returned to Canaan. When the small contingent of former exiles arrived in the promised land, they rebuilt the temple, now referred to as the Second Temple, and tried to establish strict devotion to Yahweh and his Torah. Since they interpreted the exile as the LORD's punishment for their failure to obey his commandments, they were zealously determined to maintain the traditions of the past, including animal sacrifice, and to remain faithful to Yahweh to avoid a future catastrophe of this magnitude. Many of the individuals associated with the rebirth of the temple insisted that it was *only* at the Jerusalem temple that Yahweh could be properly worshiped. Since the Persians who liberated the Jews from Babylon did not allow them to reestablish an independent monarchy, the priests, by default, emerged as the dominant authority. Consequently, the importance of the temple and the priesthood was amplified, generating tensions between the temple supporters and those living in the areas at a distance from Jerusalem, such as Galilee and Samaria, the region located where the old kingdom of Israel had once been.

In 333 BCE, two centuries after the return of the exiles from Babylon, the Jewish homeland was subjugated again, this time by the armies of Alexander the Great. Alexander's campaign of conquest, which extended as far as northern India, brought Greek culture and language throughout his empire. This expansion of Greek political and cultural influence is known as Hellenization. Many of the Jews welcomed Greek culture and adopted Greek philosophy, Greek dress, and the Greek language. A gymnasium was even built in Jerusalem, and some Jewish men tried to remove the marks of circumcision. But many others resisted Hellenism and tried to remain loyal to the traditional customs and practices of the descendants of Abraham.

On the whole, Greek rule was initially benign. Alexander was a relatively tolerant ruler who allowed conquered peoples a large measure of political and cultural autonomy. But after his death, his successors did not always adhere to that policy. One Greek king, Antiochus IV "Epiphanes" (reigned 175–164 BCE) was particularly cruel to the inhabitants of Palestine and was determined to force the Jews to give up their distinctive customs and traditions. Antiochus desecrated the temple in Jerusalem and stole its sacred ritual implements;[1] he forbade sacrifices to Yahweh;[2] and according to some stories, he compelled some Jews to eat pork, which they regarded as unclean. Antiochus's actions prompted a military response from a Jewish militia led by Judas Maccabeus. Under his leadership, the Jews overthrew Greek rule and established an independent nation governed by his family,

---

1. 1 Macc 1:21–28.
2. 1 Macc 1:45–50; 1:56–61.

the Hasmoneans. The Hasmoneans ruled an independent Jewish kingdom from the mid-second century until the mid-first century BCE. Judas Maccabeus reclaimed the temple for the Jews and restored its sacred status. This triumph is still celebrated by Jews today during the festival of Hanukkah.

Although dedicated to a single god, religion in the Jewish homeland during Hasmonean rule and through the time of Jesus was not at all uniform or homogenous. In fact, the religion of the Israelites and Jews was probably *never* homogenous, despite the efforts of some to make it so. There were several major groups with differing opinions about what constituted correct practice of the faith. The most prominent of these sects were the Pharisees, the Sadducees, and the Essenes. When Christianity emerged in the middle part of the first century CE, it was simply regarded as another one of these Jewish sects.

To the readers of the New Testament the group known as the Pharisees will surely be familiar. They were often portrayed in the Christian scripture as the sanctimonious rivals to Jesus. But the Pharisees probably had more in common with Jesus than is ordinarily thought. Some scholars, in fact, have argued that Jesus himself was a Pharisee or had been a part of the sect at one time. Pharisaism arose in the second century BCE, near the rise of the Hasmonean monarchy, as a movement among lay Jews—that is to say, Jews who were not part of the priesthood. The Pharisees believed in the authority of what was called the Oral Torah, a collection of traditions and commentaries that helped interpret the Written Torah. This oral tradition was eventually written down by rabbis in the second century CE and preserved as the body of writing called the *Mishnah*. The Pharisees were also resistant to the idea of the priesthood. They believed that all Jews were to be priests and that the nation was to be a "kingdom of priests," to quote the Tanakh. Laws that were originally intended for the priests, such as the regulations governing ritual purity, the Pharisees believed, should be observed by *all* Jews. The Pharisees also maintained a belief in the resurrection of the dead, an idea that developed rather late in ancient Judaism; it is not mentioned in the earliest Jewish scripture. Rabbinic Judaism of today—Orthodox, Conservative, and Reform—is directly descended from Pharisaism.

The Pharisees were opposed to the group called the Sadducees. Like the Pharisees, the Sadducees came into existence in the second century BCE, but they were primarily associated with the ruling class and the temple priesthood rather than the laity. They rejected the authority of the oral tradition and insisted on a strict interpretation of Torah, whereas the Pharisees preferred a loose construction of the scripture. Because they viewed the Torah as the sole authority for faith, the Sadducees also denied any belief in the resurrection of the dead, which is not found in that text. Because of its close connection with the priesthood, the Sadducee sect disappeared after the Romans destroyed the Second Temple in 70 CE.

Less popular than the Pharisees and Sadducees was a diverse group collectively known as the Essenes, who also arose in the second century BCE. The Essenes were not mentioned in New Testament, but they have received a fair amount of scholarly attention since the twentieth century because of the Dead Sea Scrolls, which some have argued were part of the Essene library of texts. There is no consensus among scholars today as to whether or not that claim is true. But it is likely that some Essenes lived at Qumran, the location near the Dead Sea where the scrolls were discovered. The Essenes were not unlike later Christian monastics who also lived in small communities and practiced celibacy. They were decidedly apolitical, and they were deeply concerned with maintaining ritual purity. They also objected to animal sacrifice, which put them at odds with the temple priesthood. Some historians have speculated that Jesus or John the Baptizer may have been associated with the Essenes for a time, but there has been no convincing evidence to support that notion.

Each of these sects existed into the first century CE and was a part of the world of Jesus. Yet most Jews of his day were probably not aligned with any of these groups. Nonetheless, these sects are important to understand Jesus's life and teaching and to appreciate the divided context in which he lived.

The Roman Empire

The rule of the Hasmonean Dynasty was brought to an end in 63 BCE, when the Roman general Pompey captured Jerusalem, and the Jewish homeland became a client state of Rome. By the time Jesus was born, around 4 BCE, Palestine, as the Romans called this region, had been under their domination for over half a century.

Roman control of and presence in Palestine had profound ramifications for the daily life of its inhabitants. For one thing, the Roman Empire was the latest in a centuries-long series of foreign conquerors of this tiny region. The Jews had become weary of being pushed around by alien behemoths. Frustration was on the rise. Roman domination exacerbated the existing class divisions and tensions within Jewish society. A small fraction of the Jewish populace—no more than 1 to 2 percent—were charged by Rome with the responsibility for governing the region, which meant maintaining order and exacting heavy taxes to be paid to the Empire. The members of this small ruling class were beholden to Rome, which allowed them to live extravagantly at public expense, as long as they efficiently discharged their duties. The ruling elite were supported by another small class comprising about another five percent of the population. This group was composed of various government officials and bureaucrats, the religious hierarchy, the military leadership, and the businesspeople who furnished them goods and services.

By far the largest class, however, was the peasantry, who made up at least 90 percent of society in Roman-occupied Palestine. Most of the peasants were farmers. A few owned the land they worked, but most were tenant farmers and day laborers. Also included in the peasant class were fishermen, craftsmen, and servants. Jesus of Nazareth was born into this class. Just below it was the very bottom rung of society: the destitute; the lepers, the blind, and the lame; those possessed by demons; prostitutes; and the ritually unclean. To borrow a word from the world of the Buddha's time, these were the untouchables.

This social structure effectively constituted a caste system. At the top were the wealthy and powerful, who lived comfortably and often lavishly in the larger cities and towns, and down below were common folk, largely uneducated, who worked hard in the country and on the waters to eke out a livelihood that barely sustained them. As usually happens in such systems, the small top tier took a large portion of what the peasantry produced to fund their privileged lives and to pay the fees required by the Roman Empire. Some estimates suggest that the commoners had to forfeit one-half to two-thirds of their annual productivity to Rome and its Jewish collaborators. Peasant life was obviously precarious; a drought could easily thrust a peasant family into the lowest stratum of society, reducing them to begging for alms. The life expectancy for a peasant was a mere thirty years.

This tenuous existence became even more precarious under the reign of King Herod the Great, one of the client rulers appointed by Rome to govern Palestine. He ruled this region in the three decades before the birth of Jesus. Herod, who was half Jewish, sought out and was given the title the "King of the Judeans" by the Roman senate. Despite his honorific title and Jewish heritage, he was not particularly sensitive to the plight of other Jews. Although he rebuilt the temple in Jerusalem to ingratiate himself with his subjects, he also sponsored campaigns to exterminate Jewish rivals and movements that resisted Roman rule. He even executed one of his own wives, who was a Hasmonean princess, and three of his own sons. During his regime, Herod confiscated peasant lands by means of foreclosure on debt and permitted other wealthy Jews to do so as well. Farmers were now required to work for large estates and grow crops determined by the landowners. No longer could the peasants raise their own food and barter their surplus with others; hence, they were no longer self-sustaining. As many of the peasant class lost their lands, they were forced into debt, which often resulted in imprisonment or indentured servitude. What was a hardscrabble life under the best of circumstances was made even worse by Herod.

When Herod died in 4 BCE, many of the Judeans who suffered during his tenure used the occasion to lodge protests against Roman rule. Widespread revolts erupted throughout the kingdom, and legions of imperial soldiers were dispatched to silence the rebels. By now, the political resistance movement directly opposing Roman rule had become more organized and prevalent. Among the political insurrectionists were the Zealots and an even more extreme faction called the *Sicarii*, probably a Zealot splintergroup. This latter sect is particularly interesting for our study. The *Sicarii* were so-called because each carried a dagger, or *sicarius*, with which they stabbed their enemies: the Roman occupiers and their Jewish collaborators. Some scholars have suggested that Judas Iscariot, the follower who betrayed Jesus, may have been a member of this group. They contend that the name "Iscariot" is a Greek transformation of the *sicari-ote*, that is, a member of the *Sicarii*.[3]

The uprisings that broke out after Herod's death were quickly snuffed. Two thousand insurgents were crucified in Jerusalem to express Rome's opinion of the insurrection. Because of its gruesome and public nature, crucifixion was almost always reserved for those convicted of sedition against the empire. But despite the effort to provide a graphic deterrent to future rebellions, the resistance movement continued to grow and to prove itself a thorn in flesh of the Romans.

After his death, Herod's kingdom was divided by Rome into three smaller regions, each governed by one of his sons. Galilee, in the northern part of Palestine, was given to Herod Antipas; and Judea, the Roman name for Judah, plus the area called Samaria, between Galilee and Judea, was given to Archelaus. The third son, Philip, was given a province northeast of Galilee. Archelaus's reign lasted only ten years. He was replaced by a number of Roman prefects, including the most famous, Pontius Pilate. During the rule of these Roman governors, the chief priest of Jerusalem and his associates, known as the elders, were appointed by Rome and given the responsibility of managing internal Jewish affairs and of maintaining peace in the province. This arrangement meant that the chief priest and his colleagues both managed the temple, which was so important to Jewish life, and reported to the Roman prefect. Their position brought them great power and wealth, yet their status was extremely precarious. One misstep

3. Eisenman, *James, the Brother of Jesus*, 179.

and they could incur the ire of the Roman overlords or incite the masses to rebellion. They had ample reason to try to pacify both groups.

The World of Jesus

Thus, Jesus was born into a world full of tension, a world on edge. The strain existed on a variety of levels. On the political level, ordinary Jews living in Palestine resented the Roman occupation. They despised their fellow Jews who collaborated with the empire. The Roman occupiers had virtually no interest in internal Jewish affairs but were centrally concerned with maintaining the *Pax Romana*—the Roman peace—and ensuring the abundant flow of tributes to Rome. On the economic level, the tension between rich and poor was greater than it had ever been as the rich kept getting richer at expense of the poor. On the cultural level, another conflict existed between those loyal to the ancient traditions of Abraham's descendants and those attracted by ways of the Greeks and the Romans. At the religious level, there were quarrels between those who championed the centrality of the temple in Jerusalem, its priesthood, and its system of sacrifice and those who did not regard the temple as essential and who were resistant to the authority of the priests. There were also debates about the ways to interpret the sacred texts and apply them to daily life and differing beliefs about life after death.

Politically, economically, culturally, and religiously, ancient Palestine was stretched to the breaking point. Something had to give.

The Historical Jesus

Few persons in history have been subject to such a wide range of interpretations as Jesus. The array is so diverse that it almost seems as if everyone has their own "personal Jesus," to quote the title of a song by Depeche Mode.

There are clear reasons for this broad spectrum of views. One concerns the nature of the sources we have for understanding Jesus. The only texts that relate historically relevant material about his life are the four gospels in the Christian New Testament and the noncanonical Gospel of Thomas, yet each of these accounts presents different viewpoints on who he was and what he taught. Sometimes the dissimilarities are minor, and sometimes they are substantial. But the careful reader of these writings cannot mistake the variations in perspective, style, and occasionally the presentation of facts. From the very beginning of his public activity, Jesus was seen and understood in disparate ways by those who knew him, and he was aware of this difference of opinion.[4]

But another—and perhaps more important—reason for these countless interpretations is the role that Jesus has played in human history and Western culture in particular. Almost from the start of what can be called Christianity, many followers of Jesus not only regarded him as a savior or as the incarnation of the god of the Jews, but also understood him to be the very personification of ideal humanity. Jesus was—and is—considered by those in the Christian traditions as manifesting the supreme qualities of what a human being should be. He was "perfect in manhood," to cite a phrase from the Chalcedonian Creed. When Christians looked at Jesus, they saw the image of what *their* lives should be. This dynamic had a profound bearing on the way Jesus has been interpreted throughout the years, especially in recent centuries in which scholars have attempted to gain access to the historical Jesus: the individual who lived in first-century Palestine apart from the many layers of tradition that accrued after his death. Because Jesus functioned as the representation of ideal humanity for many, those who interpreted his life were apt to impute their own values and beliefs to the man. In every era for the last two thousand years, and in every culture that finds him meaningful, Jesus has been envisioned in ways that fit that society's or that individual's understanding of what is ideal. There is little wonder the life and teachings of Jesus have been so diversely understood.

Just as we are challenged to re-create the historical Confucius and the historical Buddha, so we face difficulties in getting to the historical Jesus, the real individual who lived and died in human history. The primary sources offer various portraits of the man. Furthermore, the ways that we and others since his time construe those literary portrayals is profoundly shaped by both acknowledged and unacknowledged preconceptions. Even the most optimistic academic Jesus scholar today is cautious about drawing sharp and firm conclusions about the life of this teacher. There is much about the historical Jesus we just do not know, and much that we simply cannot know with the resources we have available currently.

The Bare Details

So what *can* we say with reasonable certainty? First, virtually all credible scholars believe there actually was a person living in ancient Palestine whom modern people now know as Jesus. Few historians doubt that he existed.

---

4. Matt 16:13–20; Mark 8:27; Luke 9:18–21.

But this individual was not known to his contemporaries by the name Jesus. "Jesus" is a relatively recent rendering of a number of other names by which he has been known. In 1629, the King James Version of the Bible began to spell his name as J-E-S-U-S, and the corresponding pronunciation "Jesus" soon followed and remained the standard in the English-speaking world. But the original version of the King James Bible, first published in 1611, followed the Latin tradition of spelling his name I-E-S-U-S, which would have been pronounced "ye-soos." "Iesus" was actually a bit closer to the way his name was probably pronounced in the first century, but not quite. The Latin spelling relied on the Greek, which added an *s* to the end of his name because all masculine names in Greek ended in *s*. In Greek, his name was pronounced "ee-ay-soos." But this was still not the pronunciation of his name in Aramaic, the language Jesus and his contemporaries spoke. In Aramaic, the name would lack the "s" on the end, and so could be pronounced as Yeshu, Eesho, or Eshoo. There were many dialects of Aramaic, so it is difficult to know which pronunciation is exact. "Eshoo" was the Aramaic version of the Hebrew name, Yeshua, a shortened form of Yehoshua, or Joshua as English has it today. Yehoshua is a venerable Hebrew name meaning "god is salvation" or "god saves." But by whatever name history has known him, there was a real person behind it.

There are just a few other things we can say with some confidence. Jesus was born into the peasant class and may have worked as a *tekton*, a common laborer who made things like doors and window frames. Based on archaeological discoveries about first century peasant life in Palestine, we can say that he was probably about five feet tall and weighed about 110 pounds. But beyond this, we have no idea what he looked like. The gospels do not consider it important to describe his appearance. He would have been considered an adult around the ages of thirteen to fifteen and lived to be around thirty-three. We are uncertain whether he was literate or had any formal education.

He grew up in the village of Nazareth in Galilee, a province ruled by Herod the Great's son, Herod Antipas. Nazareth was only about four miles from the largest and most important city of Galilee, Sepphoris. An ancient Christian tradition maintains that this city was the hometown of the Virgin Mary and her parents, Anna and Joachim. Surprisingly, Sepphoris is not mentioned in the Bible at all, yet it was within an hour's walk of Jesus's hometown. What makes this omission so curious is the fact that Sepphoris was a wealthy, thriving city with such amenities as a four-thousand-seat amphitheater probably built at the time of Jesus's youth. The proximity to Nazareth suggests that Jesus almost certainly visited the city. In Sepphoris he would have been exposed to the forms of Greek and Roman culture and to a cosmopolitan life that would have been unavailable in Nazareth. But how growing up so close to this important cultural center affected Jesus is not clear.

Sometime within the last three years of his life, he began to work publicly as an itinerant teacher, preacher, and healer. His public career garnered him a modest following and eventually led to his execution as an insurrectionist against the Roman Empire.

Beyond these bare biographical details, the story of Jesus's life and teachings rests on a less certain historical basis. Critical academic scholars debate which words reported in the gospels can be taken as authentic, and there is no absolute consensus about these. There are also debates about which events reported in the New Testament actually occurred and which have been embellished or invented to make particular theological points.

The Sources

When it comes to deciding what is and is not historical about Jesus's life, one of the first distinctions we need to make concerns the gospels themselves. Most historians believe that the so-called synoptic gospels—Mark, Matthew, and Luke—contain more historically reliable material than the gospel of John. Most scholars view John's account of Jesus's life primarily as theology told as biography. In other words, the significance of John is its theological message, not its historical accuracy, which most historians think is slight. The synoptic gospels, on the other hand, appear to be rooted in traditions that contain some authentic memory of Jesus's life and teachings. Based on philological analysis, most biblical scholars think the gospel of Mark was the first gospel and was written down around 70 CE, near the time of the Roman destruction of Jerusalem. Matthew and Luke were written a decade or two later and clearly use Mark's narrative as a source. Both Matthew and Luke quote whole sections of Mark verbatim or with slight changes. Matthew and Luke also appear to have used another common source that no longer exists. Scholars call this theoretical text Q, short for *Quelle*, the German word for "source." A fifth gospel, that of Thomas, was not included in the Christian canon of scriptures, yet about 75 percent of Thomas is also found in the synoptics.

Thus, Mark, Matthew, Luke, and Thomas relate similar aspects of the life of Jesus. But these gospels are by no means identical, nor does their similarity mean that they always relate historically precise material about the actual life of Jesus. Much in these texts is almost certainly based on the historical Jesus, but much is also fabricated by the authors or the oral traditions on which they relied. Invented sayings attributed to Jesus or his-torically doubtful events in these gospels are intended not to deceive but to make important theological statements.

The Birth Narratives

To illustrate this point, let us examine the stories of Jesus's birth. This study will serve two purposes. First, it will allow us to appreciate the differences between the various sources we have for constructing our portrait of Jesus and thereby help us understand a part of the reason that he has been subject to such wide-ranging interpretations throughout history. Second, it will provide us with material about Jesus's heritage and birth, which we will later consider in comparison with our other sages.

Every year children in North America and other parts of the world perform adorable Christmas pageants at their churches, retelling the story Christians know so well. That story describes how Mary is visited by an angel who tells her she will give birth to a son; sometime later, she and her husband, Joseph, travel to Bethlehem and, unable to find a room for the night, take lodging in a stable. That night, Jesus is born, placed in a manger, and visited by shepherds and three wise men from the East bearing gold, frankincense, and myrrh. Then a heavenly host descends and fills the world with angelic singing. This is the cherished and venerable Christmas story; it is not quite, however, the biblical story. The Christmas pageant retelling is actually a blending of elements from two very different stories in Matthew and Luke, the only two gospels in the New Testament that tell about Jesus's lineage, conception, and birth.

Matthew's Story

Matthew's account of Jesus's nativity begins with a genealogy that traces Jesus's ancestry from Abraham through King David to his earthly father Joseph.[5] Then the narrative turns to describe how Mary, a young virgin en-gaged to marry Joseph, came to be pregnant by the LORD's holy spirit. When he discovers his fiancée is expecting a child that he knew was not his, Joseph decides to break off the engagement quietly. But before he can, he is visited by an angel who counsels him against the plan, and Joseph reconsiders his decision.[6] The author of Matthew then concludes: "All of this has happened

5. Matt 1:2–17.
6. Matt 1:18, 21.

so the prediction of the Lord given by the prophet would come true."[7] Then he quotes a passage from the prophet Isaiah, words familiar to all Christians:

> Behold, a virgin will conceive a child
>
> And she will give birth to a son
>
> And they will name him Emmanuel (which means "God with us").[8]

This quotation is the first of many passages from the Tanakh that Matthew cites as ancient predictions of the messiah, the anointed one sent by Yahweh to restore his people. Matthew's intention is evident. He is attempting to show that Jesus fulfills Jewish expectations of this anointed one, the *christos,* as he was called in the Greek translation of the Tanakh.

On the angel's instruction, Joseph marries Mary, believing that her child was of divine origin. In due time, Mary's son was born in the town of Bethlehem in the province of Judea, and Joseph named him Eshoo, or Jesus. What is missing in Matthew's account is the story of Mary and Joseph's trip to Bethlehem from their hometown of Nazareth, in the northern province of Galilee. The gospel lacks this journey episode because it assumes that Mary and Joseph were *from* Bethlehem. We learn just a few verses after the announcement of Jesus's birth that Mary and Joseph are living in a house.[9] This is where Jesus was born, according to Matthew. There is no mention of a stable, as there is in Luke, or a cave, as later tradition believed.

The next scene in the narrative involves the *magi,* the famed wise men from the East who show up in Jerusalem inquiring about the new "King of the Judeans." These wise men are astrologers who had discerned from the stars that a child of great significance had been born, and they want to honor him. The text does not indicate that there were *three* wise men, as popularly believed; it gives no number at all. When King Herod the Great heard about the astrologers, he summoned them and carefully interrogated them. He found out the exact time the special star associated with the new king appeared in the sky. Then Herod consulted with his advisors, who informed him that the prophets predicted the *christos* would be born in Bethlehem, a short distance from Jerusalem.[10] So Herod sent the astrologers to the village and there they discovered Jesus, living with his parents in a house. They present him with their gifts, pay their respects, and return home without reporting back to Herod as he had asked.

---

7. Matt 1:22 in Miller, ed., *Complete Gospels,* 60.

8. Matt 1:23 in ibid.

9. Matt 2:11.

10. Matt 2:1–6.

When Herod realizes that the *magi* had deceived him, he is enraged and issues a command that all boys under the age of two in Bethlehem and vicinity should be put to death.[11] Herod's monstrous response obviously indicates that he is gravely threatened by the birth of the new "King of the Judeans." After all, the Roman senate had named *him* "King of the Judeans." The age of Herod's intended victims is worthy of note. Since he ordered the killing of children two years of age and younger, and since he knew the precise moment the new king was born according to the astrologers' calculations, we can infer that the visitation of the *magi* took place about two years after Jesus was born, not on the night of his birth, as the Christmas pageants tell us.[12]

Fortunately, it is highly unlikely that this horrifying slaughter of the innocents that Matthew describes actually occurred. There is no mention of such an event elsewhere; even Luke's birth narrative fails to mention it. More probably, the tale serves as a literary contrivance. It certainly reveals something of the character of Herod. Although this particular episode probably did not happen, it is consistent with what we know of him. He had his *own* sons executed for treason, after all! But the story is intended to suggest more than just Herod's paranoia; it also recalls a similar episode from the Tanakh: the time when Pharaoh in Egypt ordered the murder of the baby boys of the Israelites to keep the slaves from becoming too powerful. Moses, readers of the Bible will remember, survived the massacre because of his mother's resourcefulness and the compassion of the Pharaoh's daughter, and went on to become Israel's deliverer.

Matthew's comparison of Jesus and Moses is deliberate. This intent is confirmed in the next episode of the story, in which the angel appeared again to Joseph and told him to flee with his family to Egypt to evade Herod's persecution. Joseph did as he was told—again, as Matthew says—to fulfill a prophecy.[13] The story concludes with Mary, Joseph, and Jesus returning from Egypt to the promised land after Herod's death and settling in Nazareth in Galilee, rather than their original home in Bethlehem.[14] Again, the parallels with Moses and the exodus are purposeful. Throughout Matthew's gospel, Jesus is portrayed as the new Moses. He is even depicted as delivering a new law to the Jews—the Sermon on the Mount—just as Moses delivered the old law from Mount Sinai.

11. Matt 2:16–18.

12. It was a great relief for me to figure this out. Growing up, I could never understand how these wise men could get to Bethlehem from "the East"—wherever that was—in a single night. I could only imagine they had some superfast camels.

13. Matt 2:13–15.

14. Matt 2:19–23.

Luke's Account

Luke, however, has another story to tell. In Luke's gospel, the angel announces the pregnancy to Mary, not Joseph. In fact, in Luke, Mary's role is central and Joseph's is peripheral—just the opposite of Matthew's perspective. Luke's genealogy of Jesus is also quite different from Matthew's, and the line is traced back past Abraham, all the way to Adam.[15] In distinction to Matthew's emphasis on Jesus's Jewishness, as suggested by a pedigree that includes ancient Israel's most illustrious figures, Luke highlights Jesus's universal significance by invoking the name of humanity's first father.

Even the political background of Luke is different from Matthew's. Rather than setting the story of Jesus's birth in the context of Judea and the reign of Herod, Luke places the story against the backdrop of the Roman Empire and reign of Emperor Augustus. Luke's setting serves to underscore the universal importance of Jesus and to provide a striking contrast to the humbleness of Jesus's origins. Caesar Augustus was not just the ruler of the known world; he was also a son of god, an incarnation of the divine. His many titles included "the One who Brought Peace to the World," the lord, and the savior—some of the very titles Luke reserves for Jesus. But in the eyes of Luke, the baby born to peasant parents in an animal shelter in a cultural backwater—not the imposing emperor in Rome—is the world's true ruler and benefactor. That contrast foreshadows an important theme throughout Luke: Jesus's coming means the overturning of conventional values.

Caesar's call for a census was the occasion for Mary and Joseph to leave their hometown—which Luke thinks is Nazareth—to travel to Bethlehem. Importantly, both Matthew and Luke agree that Jesus was born in Bethlehem, the city of David. But in point of fact, many scholars think Jesus was probably born in Nazareth, his boyhood home, and that the story of a birth in Bethlehem is an addition to support the claim that he was the messiah. In any event, it was there in Bethlehem, amid animals and fodder, that Luke says Jesus was born and laid in a feeding trough,[16] quite a different setting from the home-birth of Matthew.

The visitors that night were not the wise men but common shepherds, who had been visited by an angel and informed of the savior's birth. The presence of the shepherds in the Luke's account accents the theme of humility and lowliness. Shepherds were regarded as among some of the lowest members of Judean society. From the very beginning, Luke associates Jesus

15. Luke 3:23–38.
16. Luke 2:2–7.

with the commoners and the disenfranchised. In view of the role of women in this patriarchal society, the prominence of Mary and her cousin Elizabeth, the mother of John the Baptizer, also reinforces this Lucan theme.

After Jesus's birth, Luke mentions his ritual circumcision and an incident at age twelve when he was discovered conversing with teachers and scholars in the temple at Jerusalem. This is all the New Testament has to say about his early life. The next we hear of Jesus in the Bible is at the time he begins his public activity of healing and proclamation, around the age of thirty. The relative lack of information about the first thirty years of his life obviously indicates that the first Christians thought his greatest significance was in his teaching and, most especially, his death and resurrection, two events that all four biblical gospels report.

What This Difference Means

Our comparison of Matthew and Luke's birth narratives should suffice to make it clear that there are, at the least, substantial differences of emphasis in the two accounts. The only common elements in both stories are the idea of a divine conception, the names of Jesus's parents, a birth in Bethlehem, and Nazareth as Jesus's boyhood home. Beyond these details, the stories are quite dissimilar.

Do those differences really matter? One might argue that the differences are inconsequential because the accounts are reconcilable. Just because Luke does not mention the *magi*, or Matthew does not mention the shepherds, does not mean the authors are telling different stories. The authors just report what they think is essential about one single story. If this is true, then we should at least acknowledge that what they think is vital is shaped by their theological presuppositions and intentions. In other words, they are not simply relating an objective description of what happened. The gospels are selective in what they report; else Matthew and Luke's account would be much closer in detail.

Yet, there are still problems with arguing that the stories are reconcilable. Matthew regards Mary and Joseph as residents of Bethlehem, and Luke sees them as visitors. They cannot both be right. And how could one author omit a matter that the other considered crucial? How could Luke fail to mention something as momentous as Herod's massacre of the children or the family's flight to Egypt? How could Matthew neglect Jesus's birth in a stable?

It is more plausible to say that these are different stories, addressed to different audiences, and intended to convey different ideas about who

Jesus was. They may have been based on the same oral traditions about the early life of Jesus, such as his birth in Bethlehem and his childhood home in Nazareth, but the authors cannot really be saying the same things. Neither account is interested in objectively reporting events as they actually occurred; each is a mixture of historical fact as recounted by oral tradition and imaginative embellishment. Matthew's account focuses on Jesus's Jewishness: the gospel sees him as fitting ancient predictions about an anointed one and suggests ways he parallels another Jewish deliverer and law-giver, Moses. It would be logical to infer that Matthew intended his story for a Jewish audience. Luke, on the other hand, stresses Jesus's universal significance and aims to undermine the political theology of the Roman Empire. It would make sense to suggest that his story was written primarily for a non-Jewish audience. Matthew plays up Jesus's kingship; Luke highlights his humbleness.

In Jesus's own lifetime, those who knew him had a great many ideas about who he was and what he meant when he taught and performed mighty deeds. A half century later, when the gospels of the New Testament were being written down, the diversity of viewpoints about his life and teachings remained unchecked. Since that time, the interpretations have only continued to amass.

Our analysis of these birth stories brings to the foreground several important points about the study of Jesus. First, the resources we have available for understanding his life and teachings can present very different portraits of the man. Matthew and Luke, who in many respects offer very similar narratives about Jesus, nonetheless have different purposes and perspectives in mind when they relate his story. Second, the historical accuracy of these the biblical texts about Jesus is questionable. There is a bare-bones plot to Jesus's life that seems indisputable, but on other matters, including the content of his teaching or the facticity of actions attributed to him, there are doubts about the gospels' reports. Third, contemporary interpretations of Jesus's life are clearly colored by often unconscious beliefs that interpreters have about ideal human character. Thus, descriptions of who Jesus was are commonly shaped by the interpreters' own beliefs and values.

The First Thirty Years

There is very little that we can say about Jesus's first thirty years. The Gospel of Mark tells us nothing at all about his first three decades, and most of what Matthew and Luke relate about this period is quite slim and not wholly reliable. Beyond the stories of Jesus's birth, we have only the mention of his circumcision and an incident at the temple in Jerusalem when he was found astounding the scholars with his wisdom.

The Gaps in Jesus's Life

Our curiosity naturally urges us to wonder about many things. What did Jesus look like? What was he like as a child? How did he treat his parents and other family members? Was he educated? Could he read and write? Did he live in Nazareth up until he began his public work? Was he married and, if so, why do the gospels fail to mention his wife? These were questions that concerned some of the earliest Christians as well. Ultimately, these questions must remain unanswered. We simply do not know enough based on the evidence we now have available. It is possible that some new archaeological find might unearth a cache of texts that would answer these questions to our satisfaction; but that find has not yet been made.

So in the absence of information, the human imagination, of course, steps in. Tradition has been very happy to try to satisfy our curiosity. A number of captivating stories endeavor to fill in the gaps about Jesus's early life. In each instance, these tales are mainly conjecture, usually told to advance a particular point of view. No serious Jesus scholar takes these speculative stories as being historically factual, but they are interesting to convey the variety of early viewpoints on Jesus' life.

The Infancy Gospel of Thomas

Let us begin with a fascinating set of stories about Jesus as a young boy growing up in Nazareth. The Infancy Gospel of Thomas is one of about twenty gospels we know of that were not included in the New Testament canon. This gospel is different from the Gospel of Thomas mentioned earlier as containing some historical material about Jesus. The Infancy Gospel briefly describes Jesus during his first twelve years, the time about which the Bible is completely silent. This short collection of tales was probably written in the latter half of the second century CE, well over one hundred years after the death of Jesus. Apparently, they were written to satisfy a curiosity among Christians about Jesus's early life. What makes the stories so interesting is that they take seriously both the divinity *and* humanity of Jesus, as affirmed in the Christian creeds, by imagining what divine nature would look like in a preteenager. In other words, think about what your typical boy would be like if he had god-like powers.

In one story, Jesus is helping his father Joseph build a bed for a rich patron. After cutting two pieces of lumber that were supposed to be of a particular length, Joseph realized one piece was shorter than necessary, and he was perplexed as to what to do. Jesus told Joseph to hold one end of the shorter board while he held the other end. Then Jesus pulled on the board and stretched it until it was the exact length as the other. Joseph, of course, was astounded at the miraculous feat.[17]

According to another story, when Jesus was five, he and some other boys were playing in a stream on the weekly holy day. Jesus took some mud and molded it into twelve sparrows. When a villager saw what Jesus had done, he went and told Joseph: "See here, your boy is at the ford and has taken mud and fashioned twelve birds with it, and so has violated the sabbath."[18] Joseph immediately went to Jesus and asked him "Why are you doing what's not permitted on the sabbath?"[19] Jesus didn't answer but simply clapped his hands and shouted: "Be off, fly away, and remember me!"[20] And the sparrows took off and flew away.

Later, a boy running through the village accidentally bumped Jesus on the shoulder. The jostling angered Jesus, and he cursed the other boy, who instantly fell down and died. The villagers who saw the incident were shocked, and wondered "Where did this boy come from?" When the parents of the dead boy learned what Jesus had done, they came to Joseph and blamed him and begged him to teach Jesus how to bless rather than curse. So Joseph confronted Jesus and scolded him, but Jesus was obstinate and said "those people must take their punishment,"[21] at which point the parents of the dead boy became blind. Then everyone in Nazareth became fearful of Jesus's powers. Joseph got angry and pulled Jesus's ear very hard; Jesus became enraged and said to Joseph, "Don't you know that I don't really belong to you? Don't make me upset."[22]

There are over a dozen such stories in the Infancy Gospel. A final tale involves Jesus and a friend playing on the roof of a house, when the other boy accidentally fell off and died. Given his reputation in the village, the parents of the dead boy arrived and accused Jesus of killing him. Jesus, rightly, insisted on his innocence. He suddenly jumped down from the roof and shouted at the dead boy: "Zeno! . . .Get up and tell me: Did I push

17. Infancy Gospel of Thomas 13:1–4.
18. Infancy Gospel of Thomas 2:4, in Miller, ed., *Complete Gospels*, 371.
19. Infancy Gospel of Thomas 2:5 in ibid.
20. Infancy Gospel of Thomas 2:6 in ibid.
21. Infancy Gospel of Thomas 5:2 in ibid., 372.
22. Infancy Gospel of Thomas 5:6 in ibid.

you?"[23] Suddenly Zeno returns to life and says, "No, Lord, you didn't push me, you raised me up."[24]

Obviously, stories like these attribute to the boy Jesus the powers he was believed to have as an adult, and they show how others were awed by his deeds. The stories draw upon some features we read about in the New Testament gospels but then add to that the element of immaturity. This is how the stories take Jesus's humanity seriously. They describe him as a real five- or six-year-old boy who at times can be sweet and helpful and at times an absolute menace who cannot control his temper.

As we said, scholars think these stories contain little historical fact—except the setting of Nazareth and naming Joseph as Jesus's father. What is important to note here is the apparent process by which the Infancy Gospel was written. It is evidently an imaginative tale based on a few historical details and then elaborated in a way consistent with the author's understanding of who Jesus was. The author made almost no effort to be historically accurate; the important feature of the text was its theological affirmation of Jesus's divinity and humanity. The gospel subordinates history to theology. Yet, the image of the boy Jesus may have been just a little too human to be included in the New Testament.

Jesus in India

Throughout the last two thousand years, many have speculated about Jesus's life during the thirty-year span between his birth and the beginning of his public proclamations. One persistent idea has been that as a young man, Jesus traveled to India, where he studied under Hindu and Buddhist gurus, and then returned to Palestine to preach a Judaized version of these religions. Advocates of this view point to the remarkable parallels between Christianity and the form of Buddhism that was beginning to develop in the first centuries CE, the Mahayana. Recall in our discussion of the Buddha that in the development of the Mahayana, the Buddha began to be viewed as having more divine qualities and functioning more as a savior to assist others in reaching the end of suffering. A different version of this story suggests that Jesus escaped death on the cross and made his way to Kashmir in northern India. There, *he* taught the Buddhist and Hindu scholars, who Indianized *his* theology. Still today, one can visit the reputed tomb of Jesus in the city of Srinagar in Kashmir. Modern critical scholars of Jesus think both versions of the Jesus–India connection are highly unlikely.

23. Infancy Gospel of Thomas 9:4, ibid., 375.
24. Infancy Gospel of Thomas 9:5, ibid.

Was Jesus Married?

One final area of speculation that is worth mentioning has received a good deal of renewed attention in the last half century: whether or not Jesus was married. In recent years, this question became a matter of public controversy as the result of Martin Scorsese's film *The Last Temptation of Christ* and the popular novel and later movie *The Da Vinci Code*. These releases indicate that Jesus was in fact married to Miriam of Magdala, or Mary Magdalene. But these recent works were not the first to suggest a married Jesus. In 1970, a Bible scholar named William E. Phipps published *Was Jesus Married?*, in which he argued that it was highly probable that Jesus was married since the Bible mentions nothing to the contrary. Phipps proposed that marriage was taken as such a matter of normal behavior in ancient Judaism that had Jesus *not* been married, the New Testament would surely have to explain it. If he were married, on the other hand, there would have been no reason to make mention of it. Phipps's contention was an argument from silence. The New Testament has absolute nothing to say about Jesus's marital status. It neither affirms nor denies that Jesus was married. Phipps had a point; it would have been highly unusual for Jesus to have been a bachelor all his life. It is possible that he was widower by the time he began his public work. But the argument from silence is a weak one and has not convinced most scholars. Bachelorhood may have been rare, but it was not impossible. The idea of a marriage between Jesus and Mary Magdalene is even less convincing. But what is interesting about the whole idea of a married Jesus is the way the suggestion meets with such resistance from many. They find the notion that Jesus may have had a wife to be repugnant, as evidenced by the debates generated by *The Last Temptation of Christ* and *The Da Vinci Code*. Why? I think these controversies have less to do with the issue of marriage and more to do with sexuality. There is nothing particularly problematic with the idea that Jesus may have participated in an ancient and honorable human institution. But the hint that he may have had sex upsets a good many people because it clashes with their idea of divinity, and perhaps of ideal humanity. In other words, many people find something so troubling about the whole sexual dimension of human experience that they regard it unworthy of the one they consider truly god and truly human. Once again, we see how preconceptions about divinity and humanity can inform and perhaps even skew an interpretation of Jesus.

Jesus and John

Any real knowledge we have about the historical Jesus does not start until the debut of his public activity near the age of thirty. This in fact is near the point at which Mark, the oldest gospel, begins. Mark disregards any mention of Jesus's life prior to the start of his ministry. The inauguration of his work as a teacher, preacher, and healer is closely connected with John the Baptizer. The New Testament gospels all report that Jesus and John had a special relationship, but the four accounts discuss that association in slightly different ways from one another.

The New Testament gospels all regard John the Baptizer as Jesus's forerunner. They all identify John with a figure from the book of Isaiah, who shouts in the wilderness: "Prepare the way of the Lord."[25] On the basis of this identification, they describe John as someone whose role is to ready people for the coming of Jesus. In this role, John called the people of Palestine to repent of their ways and submit to baptism, a ritual symbolizing the washing away of sins. John performed his baptisms in the Jordan River, in the wilderness of Judea, where he lived an ascetic life, wearing a camelhair shirt and eating raw honey and locusts. The Baptizer's unconventional lifestyle has led some to speculate that he may have been one of the Essenes, who observed similar practices. But it also placed him in line with some of ancient Judaism's greatest prophets, who preached fiery messages of repentance.

There are hints, however, that John's relationship to Jesus was more than simply that of a herald or harbinger. According to Luke, Jesus told his followers, "among those born of women, none is greater than John."[26] Luke also suggests they were second cousins, but that claim is doubtful. No one else indicates they had a familial relationship. Each of the four gospels says that John began his public activity before Jesus began his. John had a message to proclaim. According to Matthew, John's proclamation was concise: "Repent, for the kingdom of heaven is at hand."[27] That message brought Judeans out of the city and the countryside to hear John and to accept his baptism. Mark and Matthew indicate that Jesus himself went to John and was baptized by him. Sometime after Jesus's baptism, John was arrested by King Herod Antipas because John was critical of Herod's marriage to his brother's ex-wife, a violation of Jewish marital laws. It was at the moment of John's arrest and imprisonment that Jesus began his own work as a preacher and healer. Matthew writes "Now when Jesus heard that John had been

25. Isa 40:3, NRSV.

26. Luke 7:28, in Miller, ed., *Complete Gospels* (p. 134).

27. Matt 3:2, NRSV.

arrested, he withdrew to Galilee. He left Nazareth and made his home in Capernaum by the sea."[28] "From that time Jesus began to proclaim, 'Repent, for the kingdom of heaven is at hand.'"[29]

It is important to observe that Jesus does not begin his public work until John is unable to continue his. Furthermore, when Jesus *does* begin to preach, his message, according to the earliest gospels, is precisely the same as the Baptizer's: the kingdom of heaven is near, and everyone needs to live in accord with this fact. These observations suggest that John was not just Jesus's precursor but was also his mentor and teacher. On this view, Jesus was first a disciple of John's and then took up where John left off when the latter was arrested.

This interpretation of Jesus's relationship to John helps to clear up a baffling event in Jesus's life: his baptism. John called the Judeans to submit to baptism as a sign of their repentance to receive forgiveness for their sins. But why did Jesus go to John to be baptized if he were, as the later Christian tradition asserts, the sinless son of the LORD? Mark's gospel does not try to answer the question at all, but Matthew indicates that Jesus's acceptance of the ritual was to do "what is fitting and right,"[30] a rather vague and not very satisfying answer. Luke suggests that Jesus was baptized, but perhaps by someone other than John; the identity of Jesus's baptizer in Luke is unclear. Like Mark, Luke does not try to explain the baptism. The Gospel of John does not mention Jesus's baptism at all. What is going here?

It is likely that Jesus was one of many in Palestine who were attracted to John's message about the coming of the kingdom of heaven. He was baptized by John and became one of the Baptizer's disciples. When John was imprisoned by Herod, Jesus took over his work and began to proclaim the message about the kingdom. Jesus's own disciples, some of whom may have originally been with John, continued the custom of baptizing, as indicated by the New Testament. Later, particularly after his death and resurrection, when Jesus's significance was greatly magnified in the eyes of his followers, his earlier relationship with John became a bit of a problem. If Jesus were the messiah or the sinless son of god or god incarnate, to cite a few Christian claims about him, his baptism and his discipleship with John might seem an embarrassment. So, the later traditions, including the four New Testament gospels, cast John as a forerunner, a precursor, a herald of Jesus—but not his mentor—in order to keep John's role subordinate to that of Jesus. Thus the baptism is simply neglected in the Gospel of John, perhaps performed

28. Matt 4:12–13, NRSV.

29. Matt 4:17, NRSV.

30. Matt 3:15, Miller, ed., *Complete Gospels*, 63.

by someone else in Luke, or done because Jesus declares it is "appropriate" in Matthew. These treatments are ways of mitigating the potential claim that John's baptism implied his superiority over Jesus.

To be clear, this interpretation is not a historically verifiably fact but a theory, a way to try to make sense of the various reports about Jesus and John's relationship. We are obviously not reading the gospels at face value; the tensions among the gospel texts invite us to look for a deeper reading. This theory tries to provide a plausible explanation for why Jesus submitted to baptism, why he waited until John's arrest to begin his public activity, and why their messages were the same. Viewing John as Jesus's mentor clarifies each of these questions.

The Divine Kingdom

But however we understand the nature of their relationship, the synoptic gospels—Mark, Matthew, and Luke—report that Jesus and John both proclaimed the coming of god's kingdom. Despite how simple it is to say that, the meaning of that declaration is anything but simple. Scholars of Jesus agree that the coming of this kingdom was the substance of Jesus message, but there has been much debate about the details of that message.[31] Among the issues that have been discussed are these: what exactly did Jesus mean by the kingdom of god? Was this kingdom an earthly or a heavenly reality? What did Jesus mean when he said the kingdom is "at hand"? Did he think it had arrived or was coming shortly? What changes would the kingdom entail? How did he understand his own role in the coming of this new reality? Was he simply warning people about its inevitable arrival, or did he think that he himself was doing something to bring it about? These are far from easy questions to answer because Jesus never addressed them directly. Rather than providing straightforward explanations, Jesus tried to illustrate the meaning of the kingdom by means of parable and paradox and to demonstrate it by acts of healing, exorcism, and flouting the religious customs of his culture, such as ignoring its purity laws. Even his closest associates did not always grasp what he was trying to communicate when he offered a parable to help them understand the kingdom to come. Frequently, the gospels depict his followers coming to him in private asking for a clearer interpretation of one of his stories. Sometimes he would try to spell it out for them; sometimes he just would lament how dense they were.

---

31. "I must proclaim the good news of the kingdom of God," Jesus told a crowd, "for I was sent for this purpose" (Luke 4:43, NRSV).

In the gospels of Mark and Luke, the expression "kingdom of god" translates the Greek phrase *basileia tou theou*. Matthew, however, uses slightly different words, *basileia ton ouranon*, which is usually rendered as the "kingdom of heaven." Both expressions mean the same thing. Matthew probably used the word "heaven" as a euphemism for "god" or "the LORD" since this gospel was addressed primarily to a Jewish audience, and Jews customarily avoided using their god's name. In ancient China, we recall, "heaven" and "god" were sometimes used interchangeably. In any event, neither "kingdom of heaven" nor "kingdom of god" should be understood as "heaven," if by heaven one means the abode of the divine being and his angels. For Jesus, the kingdom of heaven was not a place where the streets were paved with gold and Saint Peter guarded the pearly gates. In fact, this kingdom was not a place at all. In the Greek, *basileia* is defined by rule or power, not territory. In this sense, "kingdom" is a misleading translation. Biblical specialists have been aware of this problem for quite some time and have tried to come up with more suitable expressions. Some of these include "the reign of god," "the dominion of god," and "the LORD's imperial rule." These phrases have the benefit of removing the territorial connotations of "kingdom," but they still carry the disadvantage of referring to a form of governance that most of us no longer experience. Hence, the metaphor lacks the evocative power that the word "kingdom" had for Jesus's listeners. But not having a completely satisfactory alternative, we will continue to use the word "kingdom," with "reign" or "dominion" thrown in occasionally for variety.[32]

The important thing to bear in mind is that for Jesus, the kingdom of heaven was not a location. When members of the Pharisee sect asked him when the kingdom would come, Jesus told them:

> You won't be able to observe the coming of God's imperial rule. People are not going to be able to say, "Look, here it is!" or "Over there!" On the contrary, God's imperial rule is right there in your presence.[33]

The kingdom, for Jesus, was an invisible or intangible reality. In the Gospel of Thomas, Jesus told his followers:

> If your leaders say to you, "Look, the [Father's] kingdom is in the sky," then the birds of the sky will precede you. If they say to

---

32. I do that as much for sentimental reasons as anything. My grandmother used the expression all the time. She used to say things like "I don't care if you cry till kingdom come; it won't do you any good."

33. Luke 17:20–21, in Miller, ed., *Complete Gospels*, 157.

you, "It is in the sea," then the fish will precede you. Rather, the [Father's] kingdom is inside you and outside you.[34]

Jesus's statement in Thomas intimates another characteristic of the kingdom. Even though god's reign is not localized to a *particular* place, it is understood to be an *earthly* reality. It is not territorial, but it is terrestrial. Contrary to the popular mythology of later Christianity, Jesus never spoke of human beings going to heaven. He said nothing about souls being transported to the celestial regions after death. He did, however, indicate that the kingdom of heaven would come to earth. It was here that the divine reign would be realized, not somewhere beyond the skies. The point is evident in the well-known words of the Lord's Prayer: "Thy kingdom come; thy will be done in earth as it is in heaven."[35] The kingdom comes to people; people do not go to the kingdom.

Everything Jesus said about it suggested that the divine kingdom was a utopia, a blessed state of affairs free of suffering and poverty, in which justice and harmony flourished. To put it in the language of Jesus, the kingdom was the state in which the LORD's will for the world prevails. It was *shalom*, the condition of peace, plenty, and well-being. It is hard *not* to think of Jesus's use of the phrase "kingdom of god" as a deliberate affront to the kingdom of Rome, or what we might call for the sake of parallelism, the "kingdom of man." As we noted in our discussion of the birth narratives, the Roman Empire, as manifested in the reign of King Herod and Augustus Caesar, was the imposing backdrop against which the life of Jesus began and the power by which it ultimately ended. Rome's occupation of Palestine was a ubiquitous reality that caused deep and extensive suffering for the vast majority of Judeans and Galileans. Jesus's descriptions of and analogies for the reign of the LORD seemed to suggest that it was the exact opposite of the reign of Caesar.

The Blessings and Curses

One of the best-known descriptions of the kingdom is the passage known as the Beatitudes, which appears in different forms in Luke and Matthew. In this classic piece of world literature, Jesus tells his listeners what the kingdom will be like. Try to hear these words with the ears of those whose lives had been brought low by the imperial power and its local collaborators. In Luke, Jesus declares:

34. Gospel of Thomas 3:1–3, in ibid., 305.
35. Matt 6:10, KJV.

Congratulations, you poor!

God's domain belongs to you.

Congratulations, you hungry!

You will have a feast.

Congratulations, you who weep now!

You will laugh.[36]

To those being crushed by Roman power Jesus's proclamation would have indeed been received as gospel, that is, as good news. Luke adds a complementary pronouncement of curses just after this series of blessings:

Damn you rich!

You already have your consolation.

Damn you who are well-fed now!

You will know hunger.

Damn you who laugh now!

You will learn to weep and grieve.[37]

Again, it is hard to neglect the political overtones of Jesus's message; certainly they were not lost on his listeners.

The juxtaposition of these blessings and curses in Luke intimates the paradoxical character of god's dominion as Jesus understood it. I am using the word "paradox" in its original sense as something contrary to expectation or received belief. The kingdom of heaven contravenes the common values of the world. In the eyes of the world you may be poor and wretched, but when the kingdom comes, it will belong to you, *not* to those the world considers rich. You may be grieving now, but when divine dominion arrives, you'll be laughing. On the other hand, those who are complacent and well-fed, who don't give a second thought to anyone but themselves, those who are rich and powerful: they will get their comeuppance. From the perspective of the LORD's kingdom, what the world calls wealth, prestige, fame, success, and power is nothing.

The Parable of the Good Samaritan

Paradox abounds throughout the teachings of Jesus, particularly in his parables, the brief engaging stories he told to communicate the meaning of the kingdom. Take, for instance, one of the best known parables: the story

36. Luke 6:20–21, in Miller, ed., *Complete Gospels*, 130; cf. Matt 5:3–10.

37. Luke 6:24–25, in ibid., 131.

of the Good Samaritan. On the road to Jericho, a Judean was accosted by robbers who beat him, stripped him, and left him for dead. A priest and later a Levite traveling the same way saw the beaten man and each crossed to the other side of the road to avoid him. But at last a Samaritan saw the man and had compassion for him. The Samaritan administered first-aid, put the victim on his own donkey, and took him to an inn and nursed him. The next day, the Samaritan gave the innkeeper some money and asked him continue to care for the beaten man in his absence. The Samaritan promised to reimburse the innkeeper for any extra expense he might incur.

For such a concise narrative, this parable is rich in significance, as almost all of Jesus's parables were. And hence it has been subject to myriad interpretations. We will not even begin to try to do it justice with a comprehensive reading. Let us only observe what makes this a characteristic parable and an effective teaching device. The real point of this story is not that people should *be* compassionate to one another, although that of course is implied. Simply to derive a "moral" from the tale as if it were a fable of Aesop flattens a parable and reduces its impact. The deeper significance of a parable lies in the response it provokes in the listener, the sense of surprise—and even shock—that it induces, and it is that *response* that likens the story to the kingdom of heaven. To the first-century listener, the surprises of the Good Samaritan story would come in several ways. The first is the way the priest and Levite completely ignore the robbers' victim. Not only were these two Judeans—that is, fellow countrymen of the fallen man—they were also specialists in the Judean religion. How could they possibly ignore him? Most likely, the priest and Levite shunned the wounded man to preserve their ritual purity. To touch a dead body or blood was to become polluted and would require a ritual restoration of cleanliness. Better to turn a blind eye. These are men who have allowed their devotion to institutions and religious beliefs to get the better of their compassion. The second surprise comes when the beaten man's true benefactor arrives: a Samaritan, a citizen of the region between Galilee and Judea, and a descendant of the inhabitants of the ancient kingdom of Israel that was destroyed by Assyria seven hundred years earlier. Although the Samaritans professed to worship the god of Abraham, Isaac, and Jacob, they believed that Yahweh chose Mount Gerizim in their country, rather than the temple at Jerusalem, as the center of worship and sacrifice. In the time of Jesus, the Samaritans were regarded as impure and were despised by the Judeans. Jesus's listeners would have been astounded—and perhaps incensed—that Jesus told a story in which the hero turned out to be a Samaritan. This reaction would have contributed to the story's effectiveness. It is hard to forget such a story.

Imagine a story about an American soldier wounded in World War II who was ignored by fellow Americans who feared risking their lives to save him. Instead, a member of the Gestapo put *his* life on the line to save the fallen soldier and nursed him back to health. The Good Samaritan is that kind of story. The parable disrupts conventional beliefs and expectations. Those who would have been assumed to assist the beaten man walk right on by, but the detested Samaritan stops to render aid. This is how it will be in the coming kingdom: things as they are will be upended; what the world calls power will be revealed as weakness; the losers will be declared winners; customary hierarchies will be shaken up; the first shall be last. The kingdom of heaven will not be what you expect.

The Parable of the Mustard Seed

Let's consider another of Jesus's stories, the parable of the mustard seed. We discussed another mustard seed story in our study of the Buddha. Jesus's tale is much different. In fact, it is not much of a story at all; it is more of an expanded simile. Jesus said:

> What is God's imperial rule like? What does it remind me of? It is like a mustard seed that a man took and tossed into his garden. It grew and became a tree, and the birds of the sky roosted in its branches.[38]

This is a baffling statement. Perhaps the most obvious meaning is that the heavenly kingdom starts out as something small, even insignificant, like a mustard seed, one of the smallest of seeds, and develops into something great. On that level, it is an acceptable story. Insignificant beginnings yield immense results. Some interpreters have taken this anecdote as a metaphor for the growth of the Christian church throughout history, but I doubt that is what Jesus had in mind. Here is what complicates this story. Jewish law recorded in the *Mishnah* actually forbade growing mustard seeds in a garden.[39] Mustard was a highly invasive weed; it did not actually grow into a tree but a shrub, and was extremely difficult to eradicate, like bamboo. Planting it in a garden would be foolish, as well as illegal. It would soon take over the garden and overpower the vegetables. Then it would provide shelter for the birds of the sky. Nice image, but who wants *birds* in their garden? Isn't that why they invented scarecrows? Finally, mustard was wild and grew everywhere. Why would *anyone* actually cultivate it? These points would

38. Luke 13:18–19, in ibid., 150.
39. *Mishnah*, Kilaim 3:2; *Tosephta*, Kilaim 2:8.

not be lost on the peasants who listened to Jesus. Imagine *their* responses to the story. First, think of their surprise at comparing the reign of the King of the Universe to a common weed. "Hey Jesus, we were expecting something a little more like the Garden of Eden, not a garden that needs weeding!" Then imagine how they might ponder the violation of the law. Does he mean the kingdom comes in defiance of our regulations and the authority of our teachers? But even if there were no laws against it, what person in his or her right mind would actually *introduce* weeds and birds into a garden? Does this mean the kingdom comes in foolishness?

This is the way Jesus's parables worked. They implicitly invited those who heard them to contemplate their significance. Rarely did a parable have a single, straightforward meaning. Their intention seems to be deliberately to provoke unconventional, unaccustomed thinking, to stimulate the imagination, to envision new possibilities, and to disrupt habit. Certainly some of Jesus's listeners must have just walked away from one of his sermons shaking their heads, thinking the man must be crazy. Others may have sat there with their mouths agape, trying to figure out these bewildering sayings. Even some of his closest associates would approach him later and ask Jesus to explain the meaning of his parables. Sometimes the gospels report that he would accede and provide his disciples with some allegory, but I suspect these allegories were added by the gospel writers to help dispel the parables' mysteriousness. When the writers try to explain the story, it becomes flat and loses its evocative and imaginative power. It is like telling a joke and then having to explain what it means when someone doesn't get it. The explanation is never as effective as the joke itself.

The "Powerful Acts"

Jesus's message of the LORD's kingdom was conveyed not only in parables and anecdotes but also in his actions. His deeds were a way of expressing his understanding of what the divine reign would be. Healings and exorcisms were all ways of dramatizing the message of the kingdom, as were what are sometimes called his "miracles," but what the gospels call "signs" and "powerful acts." Let's examine one of these powerful acts, the well-known story of turning water into wine at a wedding celebration at Cana.[40] According to John's account, shortly after Jesus began his public activity, he and his students attended a marriage feast in the village of Cana. This was not simply the ritual in which the marital vows were solemnized, but was the party that took place after the ceremony. Sometimes these celebrations would last for

40. John 2:1–11.

a week. Such feasts were very important occasions in the lives of the peasants of Palestine. Weddings provided welcome relief from their hard lives, a holiday in which the food and wine were plentiful, work was temporarily forgotten, and music and dance abounded. At some point during the festival, the wine ran out and Jesus's mother, who was also attending, asked Jesus to do something about it. For some reason, Jesus responded to her rather brusquely, "Woman, what is it with you and me? It's not my time yet."[41] But she let his rather disrespectful comment pass and directed the servants to do whatever he said. Jesus told them to take the huge stone jars that were used for ritual purification and fill them with water. After the servants had done so, Jesus instructed them to give some of the water, now become wine, to the caterer, who tasted it and was astonished at how good it was. Then the caterer called the groom aside and asked why the best wine had been served last, contrary to usual practice.

Like one of Jesus's parables, this story has many levels of meaning and admits of divergent interpretations. In recent years the story has sometimes been cited to show that Jesus endorsed marriage as the union of one man and one woman in order to challenge the idea of gay marriages. In the past, particularly during prohibition, it was used to argue that Jesus approved of drinking alcohol. But to focus on these ancillary aspects of the story tends to detract from the way it illustrates the coming of the kingdom. God's reign will be like a feast, a holiday, with music and dance and plenty to eat and drink. In fact, Jesus keeps the party going: his powerful act ensures that festivities will not be halted because provisions run out. Jesus's idea of the kingdom was earthy; there were no angels floating around, strumming harps of gold. And it all happens contrary to expectation: the best wine comes at the end; Jesus is abrasive with his mother but does what she asks; and he performs his mighty deed using, of all things, the jars that contained the foot-washing water. This is a plot with several twists and a happy ending.

The Healings

Like the parables and his powerful signs, Jesus's healings and exorcisms served to reveal the character of the kingdom of the LORD. The New Testament gospels relate the stories of dozens of such cures. Jesus's fame in Palestine, in fact, depended mainly on his reputation as a healer and exorcist. The masses seemed to flock to him to experience his healing power. Jesus even referred to himself as a physician, yet he occasionally seemed to get annoyed by all the requests for cures. The texts report that in addition to casting out

41. John 2:4, in Miller, ed., *Complete Gospels*, 203.

demons, he cured a wide variety of ailments, including blindness, deafness, fever, leprosy, paralysis, seizures, and chronic hemorrhaging. The New Testament also mentions three occasions when Jesus brought individuals back to life after they had died.[42]

The healing stories have been variously interpreted throughout Christian history. Ordinarily, they were taken as indicative of Jesus's divine power. The seventeenth-century English philosopher John Locke argued that Jesus's healings and miracles constituted empirical proof of Jesus's divinity.[43] Many today would argue the same point, just as others would dismiss such an argument on the assumption that spontaneous healings and acts like transforming water into wine simply cannot occur because they violate our scientific understanding of the world. Interestingly, Locke made his argument *because* he believed these miracles were scientific evidence for Jesus's supernatural origins and thus verified Christianity.

Whatever one may conclude about the historical facticity of the accounts of these events, it is hard to dispute that many persons experienced a healing power in Jesus's presence. The real issue is what *significance* we attribute to Jesus's remarkable powers. Did they mean that Jesus was divine—that he was a god incarnate, as the later Christian tradition asserted? It is difficult to draw such conclusions for one simple reason: stories of healings, exorcisms, powerful acts, and miracles are not unique to Jesus. Even the stories of resurrections were not unusual. There are such accounts throughout the Bible and in literature from across the centuries and cultures. There were even miracle workers in Galilee at the same time as Jesus, such as Rabbi Chanina ben Dosa, who was credited with numerous healings and nature miracles. I can think of no principle by which to dismiss other reports of powerful deeds as false while accepting those about Jesus as true. In other words, it is hard to think that the stories of Jesus's extraordinary powers confirm claims about his unique oneness with the Jewish god. That does not mean I deny the claim, only that miracles do not suffice to prove it.

What the miracles *do* suggest is how Jesus understood the divine dominion. When the kingdom comes, the world will be a very different place. The demons and illnesses that afflict us will be banished. Pain and suffering will be no more. The end of suffering does not just imply the well-being of individuals; it portends a new kind of relationship among people. In Jesus's day, illnesses and demon possessions were not merely unfortunate events that happened to individuals. They often implied impurity and untouchability. Compounding the pain of leprosy or hemorrhaging was ostracism from

---

42. Matt 9:25; Luke 7:13–15; John 11:43–44.

43. Locke, *Reasonableness of Christianity, and A Discourse on Miracles.*

society. The sick and demon-possessed had to endure the sense of shame that came with being a social outcast. In the new age that Jesus proclaimed, the division of pure and impure would be obliterated, along with the categories of rich and poor, powerful and weak, sick and healthy. Jesus acted as if he were abolishing these distinctions by his very words and deeds. He ignored the purity practices by touching the untouchables, he promised that the hungry would be fed and the poor would be vindicated, he cast out demons and cured the afflicted, and he kept a party going by making sure there was plenty of wine to drink.

Back to the Future

The first part of Jesus's message was an announcement: the reign of god is near. The second part of his message was an admonition: begin to live your lives accordingly. As Matthew's gospel reports, Jesus urged his listeners, "Change your ways because Heaven's imperial rule is closing in!"[44] The coming of the new world demanded a response. But exactly what kind of response did Jesus expect? In what ways did Jesus want his listeners to change? The answer was simple enough: think and act as if the kingdom were *already* here. Jesus wanted his followers to live as subjects of the divine rule even before it arrived in its full manifestation.

But what did living in the kingdom really mean? To explore this question requires that we move deeper into our understanding of Jesus's teachings and practices. For this discussion, we will return to the fundamental categories that guided our study of Confucius and the Buddha and that will inform our consideration of Muhammad: the ideas of ultimate reality, anthropology, spirituality, and ethics. These topics will help shape our image of Jesus's vision of life in the approaching new age.

The God of Jesus

The ultimate reality for Jesus was of course the god of ancient Judaism, the deity worshiped by Abraham, Isaac, and Jacob. There is little, if anything, in Jesus's teachings to suggest that he departed in any way from the Jewish traditions in his thinking about the LORD. We can find parallels to everything Jesus taught in the teachings of other Jewish sages. Jesus certainly believed that the god of the Jews was the world's creator and king, that he was profoundly moral and interested in the welfare of his people, and that he often

---

44. Matt 4:17, in Miller, ed., *Complete Gospels*, 64.

intervened in the affairs of human beings, directing the course of history in ways that suited his purposes. All of this is implied in Jesus's proclamation of the kingdom.

Like other Jews, Jesus also believed that god formed relationships with persons. Earlier we mentioned how ancient Israel conceived of its relationship with its god as a marriage: the Israelites thought of themselves as Yahweh's bride. In the Tanakh, the Israelite god usually dealt with his people collectively rather than as individuals, but occasionally he established close relationships with exceptional persons such Abraham, Jacob, Elijah, and Moses. The book of Exodus declares that "the LORD used to speak to Moses face to face, as one speaks to a friend."[45] Both the corporate and individual forms of divine relationships contrast with the formal and distant way the Chinese approached their gods, as we saw in our study of Confucius.

It is evident that Jesus understood his relationship with his god as an intimate one, of the sort attributed to Moses. But Jesus thought of god not as a friend but as a father. Calling the LORD father is one thing that critical scholars are virtually certain was an authentic practice of the historical Jesus. *Abba*, one of the terms translated as "father," is one of the few Aramaic words that the Greek New Testament preserves in its original form. That is one clue that the word goes back to Jesus himself. In the synoptic gospels Jesus addresses or refers to his god as the Father over forty times. Using the metaphor of father for god, however, is hardly unique in the history of the world's religions. But it was used relatively infrequently in ancient Judaism, which preferred images such as creator, king, and judge for the divine reality. The synoptic gospels alone have twice as many references to god as father than does the entire Tanakh.

Jesus's usage of the paternal trope emphasizes his sense of radical dependence on god as well as the close nature of their relationship. The use of the English word *father*, in fact, may not fully convey their intimacy as Jesus understood it. Today, *father* often carries a more formal tone than the word Jesus used. Some of the other words we use to address our fathers may actually be closer to Jesus's sense of his relationship to his god. "Daddy" or "papa," words that are structurally similar to *abba*, would probably be closer to Jesus's meaning than "father." *Abba* is almost baby talk.

Such language suggests that Jesus thought of the divine as very close, almost palpable. For Jesus, god was not remote or disinterested. Such a sense of his god's nearness, it seems, could only be based on profound experiences that Jesus identified as holy. The Tanakh, as well as the history of human religiousness, relates many such personal experiences of the divine.

45. Exod 33:11, NRSV.

Whatever one may think about such experiences—whether they are purely psychogenetic or actual encounters with some transcendent dimension of reality or something else entirely—they are quite vivid and convincing to those who have them. They are also quite transformative. Such religious experiences often yield momentous changes, not unlike the way the Buddha's awakening to the realities of existence prompted him to walk away from his comfortable life to seek an end to suffering.

The New Testament gives us few clues as to when Jesus's religious experiences led him to conceive of the divine in such intimate terms. Some might argue that Jesus came into the world with a vivid god-consciousness. As "the Word made flesh," they might say, Jesus was born with full awareness of the LORD and of his own divine mission. Not only do the synoptic gospels *not* say this, but they suggest quite the opposite: that Jesus's spiritual and intellectual development, like his physical growth, was a gradual process. Luke writes: "And Jesus *increased* in wisdom and stature, and in favor with God and others."[46]

It is quite possible that Jesus's sense of intimacy with the divine was connected to his discipleship with John the Baptizer. Perhaps Jesus left home sometime in his twenties to join John in the Judean desert to fulfill a yearning for deeper spirituality. The ancient Jews often encountered their god in the wilderness, whether they were seeking him or not. We cannot be certain about what influence, if any, John's mentorship had on Jesus's religious experiences, but it is interesting to observe that Mark and Matthew report one of these experiences just after Jesus's baptism. The heavens opened, the divine spirit descended like a dove, and he heard the voice of his heavenly Father announcing his approval.[47]

What is clear from the New Testament accounts of Jesus's religious experiences is that he understood god as present reality. Jesus believed he shared an intimate connection with his god, and he invited his followers to regard the divine in the same way. Because Jesus's theology was informed by these profound experiences, his followers sensed in him the sacred presence of which he spoke. As many remarked on numerous occasions, they were astounded at his teaching because he taught as one having authority, not as one of their religious scholars.[48] Such authority is grounded in existential experience, not mere belief or hearsay.

46. Luke 2:52, my rendering, my italics.

47. Matt 3:16, 17; Mark 1:10.

48. Mark 1:22.

Anthropology

Like Jesus's understanding of god, his convictions about human nature and the problems besetting humanity were not out of the ordinary for someone shaped by ancient Judaism, particularly by its prophetic tradition. Jesus did not spend much time articulating his beliefs about human existence in the abstract. But from his words and actions, it is clear that he thought something was terribly askew in the human situation of his day. To put it simply, he believed people no longer cared about what the LORD cared about. Jesus seemed to think that people had gotten absorbed by trivialities and an inordinate concern for themselves. This disordering of values was manifested in the tremendous suffering he saw all around, from the Jewish purity system that graded people like cuts of meat, to the Roman occupation that stole food from people's mouths to satisfy the palates of the well-to-do. The world's anguish was self-inflicted because human beings had departed from the way of their god.

Ethics and Spirituality

If the basic problem with human beings was their failure to care about the things god cared about, then the obvious solution was for them to reorient their lives to the divine. This seems to be the whole point of Jesus's endorsement of the summary of the Torah: "You shall love the Lord your God with all your heart, and with all your soul, and with all your strength, and with all your mind; and your neighbor as yourself."[49] If anything qualifies as a synopsis of how Jesus thought one should prepare for the kingdom, this statement would be it. For Jesus, the holy life, life in the kingdom, was more important than anything. If it meant giving up everything else—including one's life—to participate in that reality, it would be worth it. He said, "the kingdom of heaven is like a merchant in search of fine pearls; on finding one pearl of great value, he went and sold all that he had and bought it."[50] The first step toward the life in the divine domain was a radical commitment to the values of the Father.

But as the Buddha and Confucius also knew, making promises was of little worth unless those pledges were enacted and reaffirmed continually. Reorienting one's life in the divine was not a one-time event. Jesus himself regularly practiced disciplines of spirituality to maintain and foster his sense of intimacy with the Father and to focus on life's most important matters.

49. Luke 10:27, NRSV.
50. Matt 13:45–46, NRSV.

Prayer

Foremost among these spiritual exercises was prayer. As a Jew, Jesus's fundamental approach to prayer would have been shaped by the traditions of ancient Judaism. In his day, it was customary to pray at dawn, in the evening, before meals, and at synagogue on the Sabbath. But Jesus's prayers were not limited to these times. The gospels indicate that he prayed frequently, at various times, according to diverse needs and circumstances. Jesus seemed to view prayer principally as a discipline for subordinating his desires to divine wisdom rather than as an opportunity to enlist the divine Father's assistance in fulfilling a personal wish-list. As he anticipated his impending death, Jesus prayed, "*Abba* . . . all things are possible for you! Take this cup away from me! But it's not what I want (that matters), but what you want."[51] Even the Lord's Prayer, the model prayer Jesus provided for his disciples, petitions the Father for the basic requisites to align one's desires and deeds to those of god. Daily bread, forgiveness, and deliverance from evil—these were no more than the necessary things for living in the kingdom.

Although Jesus prayed publicly, his clear preference was to do so in solitude, with an economy of words, and perhaps even silence. He advised his listeners:

> But whenever you pray, go into your room and shut the door and pray to your Father who is in secret; and your Father who sees in secret will reward you. When you are praying, do not heap up empty phrases as the Gentiles [the non-Jews] do; for they think that they will be heard because of their many words.[52]

The New Testament relates that Jesus, like the Buddha and Muhammad, craved solitude and used every opportunity to steal away from the crowds to be alone.[53] We know nothing, of course, of the content of his prayers during these periods of isolation, but we can imagine that much of his time was spent in complete silence, in what some Christians today call contemplative prayer. Contemplative prayer is the practice of simply allowing the mind to settle and become quiet and receptive by focusing on a phrase or the breath. It is not unlike the form of sitting meditation taught by the Buddha.

On at least one occasion, and perhaps on others not recorded, Jesus retreated into solitude deep into the wilderness and fasted for an extended period. The gospels state that one such instance occurred just after his baptism. After Jesus had experienced forty days of prayer and fasting, Satan

51. Mark 14:36, in Miller, ed., *Complete Gospels*, 48.

52. Matt 6:5–7, NRSV.

53. E.g., Luke 5:16.

appeared to Jesus for the first time and attempted to disrupt his spiritual quest. Just as Mara, the Buddhist tempter figure, tried to lure Siddhattha Gotama into forsaking his goal of complete awakening, so too did Satan aim to upset Jesus's aspiration to live the holy life. First, Satan suggested that Jesus try to satisfy his hunger by turning stones into bread. When Jesus refused, Satan whisked him away to the highest point of the temple and dared him to jump to see whether the Father would protect him. Again Jesus declined. Finally, Satan produced a vision of all the kingdoms of the world in their glory and offered them all to Jesus in exchange for worshiping the prince of darkness. For the third time, Jesus rejected the offer, and Satan accepted defeat for the moment.[54] In each instance, Satan's temptation was an invitation for Jesus to indulge his own desires: to give in to his wish for food, to assuage the doubts he may have had about god's endorsement of his mission, and to accept the easy glory of the kingdom of man rather than the arduous path to the kingdom of god. This retreat, and perhaps others like it, served the purpose of heightening Jesus's awareness of the divine and fortifying his spirit against the onslaughts of selfish desire, represented by the figure of Satan.[55]

Communal Meals

Jesus observed the disciplines of prayer, fasting, and retreat as an individual, but another practice was decidedly communal: taking meals. Like Confucius and the Buddha, Jesus regarded eating as an activity with profound spiritual significance. For Confucius, eating in certain ways expressed one's respect for self and others and the rules of decorum. For the Buddha, taking

---

54. Matt 4:1–11.

55. I once visited the place where tradition claims that Jesus spent his forty-day retreat after his baptism. Today Christians call it Mount Temptation, just west of the ancient city of Jericho. There was something so intriguing and compelling about the sight of that desolate and barren place that I decided to have a taste of that experience of solitude and hunger for myself. Some years later, I spent three days and nights alone in a desert canyon in the panhandle of Texas, without food or companion. There are many things about that time that I could comment upon, but the observation that impressed me most was that stripping away all the familiar markers of my life heightened my awareness of space, time, and self. With no one talk to, no meals to look forward to, and no newspapers, Internet, or other distractions to occupy my attention, my sensation of the external world was sharper than it had ever been. My sense of time slowed to a snail's pace. And my mind penetrated deep into forgotten nooks and crannies. I became conscious of how much my daily routine had insulated me from a deeper awareness of my own life and the world surrounding it. I can easily understand why the sages loved the solitude of nature to intensify their experience of living.

only one meal a day and consuming it in quiet mindfulness was essential to maintaining the Middle Way. For Jesus, meals represented something quite different. A meal was an enactment of the kingdom to come.

Jesus apparently loved feasts. We have already mentioned his pivotal role at the wedding celebration in Cana. Many of Jesus's powerful deeds involved food, such as the occasion in which he fed over five thousand listeners with five loaves of barley bread and two fishes.[56] Many of his parables and aphorisms were drawn from the experiences of growing, preparing, and eating food. Jesus's fondness for feasting also became a bone of contention for those who sought to criticize him. They referred to him disparagingly as "a glutton and a drunkard."[57] But Jesus was unmoved by their complaints; the banquet was the symbol par excellence of the divine reign. The Christian church still remembers that with its sacrament of the Eucharist.

The practice of the taking of meals was important to Jesus's vision of the kingdom for many reasons. Foremost was the inclusive nature of his eating customs. Jesus adamantly refused to discriminate among his mealtime companions. Anyone—from the wealthy elites to the "sinners and tax collectors"—was welcome. This practice scandalized those in his culture who were strict about maintaining the rules of ritual purity. They could not grasp how someone who professed to be on such close terms with the LORD would allow himself to be contaminated by eating with the unclean. From Jesus's perspective, the distinction between pure and impure was a humanly contrived system. Not only did the LORD not recognize it, but he positively opposed it, and Jesus made this point by deliberately flouting purity laws.

Meals also symbolized and fostered the sense of community that was a hallmark of the kingdom. By sharing common food that will be incorporated into their individual bodies, the meal represents a bond among people and their common dependence on the same earthly elements for sustenance. We all must eat to live. Eating together has a way of breaking down many of the barriers we impose among ourselves. The fine Danish film *Babette's Feast*, based on a story by Isak Dinesen, conveys some sense of this point. Babette is a French housekeeper working for two elderly sisters who belong to a strait-laced Christian sect on Jutland. After many years in their employ, Babette suddenly comes into a tidy sum of money, and she decides to splurge the whole of her small fortune on preparing and serving a single exquisite banquet, the likes of which the Danish sisters could not even imagine. They and their guests, mostly members of the same puritanical religion, agree to participate in the meal but determine to resist enjoying its

56. John 6:1–14.
57. Matt 11:19.

sensual pleasures. Babette's extraordinary gifts as a chef, however, dissolve their distrust and apprehensions. Soon the diners begin to enjoy the exceptionally fine food and wine, and a new spirit of life settles over the table. Old grudges are forgotten and old loves are rekindled. The dreaded supper becomes a banquet of joy. That's the way Jesus imagined the new age.

The Ethics of the Kingdom

Jesus's teachings and spiritual disciplines were oriented to sharpening an awareness of the divine reality and galvanizing the will to care about the things the LORD cared about. And what he cared about, Jesus thought, was human fulfillment and happiness, abundant life for every human being, the prevailing of justice. Life in the kingdom therefore meant acting in some extraordinary ways, ways that were unconventional and dangerous. This is part of the reason Jesus's teachings were oriented toward surprising and shocking listeners, and why his spiritual disciplines functioned to take practitioners out of the routine and the familiar. As we have said before, the kingdom is not what you expect.

Of the many remarkable features of Jesus's ethics for the new dominion, three principles stand out as especially important. Each of them is striking in the way it contrasts with our ordinary proclivities. They are nonretaliation, generosity and nonpossessiveness, and forgiveness.

I do not know if I was born with it or conditioned into it, but for as long as I can remember I have had a reflexive impulse to punch the lights out of anyone who insulted me, hurt someone I cared about, or tried to steal something that was mine. Jesus thought I should not do that. He said, "We were once told, 'An eye for an eye' and 'A tooth for a tooth.' But I tell you, Don't react violently against the one who is evil."[58] Jesus was right. He says, do not react *violently* to evil, but he does *not* say do not act. Nothing in Jesus's teachings suggests that humans ought in any way to cooperate with evil or allow it to flourish. He did not, however, think it was necessary to answer evil with evil or violence with violence. The surprising nature of coming kingdom meant that new possibilities were available and that persons attuned to creative thinking were bound to discover them.

Jesus also had a lot to say about wealth and possessions—a lot! And what he taught was not the gospel of prosperity that many television preachers attribute to him today. Jesus was quite clear that wealth was a serious impediment to participation in the LORD's kingdom. On numerous occasions, he urged those with wealth to give it all away and those without it

---

58. Matt 5:38–39, in Miller, ed., *Complete Gospels*, 67.

to be happy with what they had. Contemporary interpreters in the affluent West seemed to have a dozen ingenious ways to mitigate the severity of Jesus's denunciation of wealth. The gospels are clear that Jesus preached non-possessiveness and generosity. He taught others to not acquire possessions[59] and to give away lavishly and extravagantly: "if anyone wants to sue you and take your coat, give your cloak as well; and if anyone forces you to go one mile, go also the second mile. Give to everyone who begs from you, and do not refuse anyone who wants to borrow from you."[60]

Finally, there is forgiveness. Forgiveness means relinquishment. To relinquish something is to release whatever power it holds over us. If I forgive someone for a wrong done to me, I no longer allow that event to determine how I treat the other person. I may remember the wrong or I may forget it, but either way I have disarmed it. It no longer determines my actions, thoughts, or words. Forgiveness in this sense is rarely easy or quick. Because of its difficulty, forgiveness has to be practiced. It is less an act than a way of living, a discipline, a cultivated skill. I think this is why Jesus told his students to forgive "seventy times seven."[61] True forgiveness often comes only at the end of an inner struggle. We forgive to be free, to be liberated from the destructive power of anger and hatred. Of course, it is much easier to nourish the thoughts of indignation. It is hard to surrender the delicious feeling that we have suffered unfairly. But ultimately that sense does us no good.

All my life I have heard people talk about how Jesus helped them get their lives in order, which generally meant they gained social respectability. But I often wonder if taking Jesus seriously would not more likely turn somebody's life upside down, since so many of his teachings and practices seem to go against the grain of social and religious convention.

Jesus's Christology

Christology is the branch of Christian thought that seeks to understand the nature and deeds of Jesus. The systematic study of the person of Jesus did not actually begin until after his death and resurrection, although his first disciples were certainly trying to comprehend who he was from the very beginning of their relationships with him. After he was gone, the efforts to understand his significance intensified and became more sophisticated. Ultimately, these christological endeavors culminated in the great creeds of the church that pronounced Jesus as fully god and fully human, the second

59. Matt 6:19.
60. Matt 5:40–42, NRSV.
61. Matt 18:21.

person of the Trinity. Yet, christology did not end with these statements of faith. The work of understanding who Jesus was and what his significance is continues to be a vital part of Christian theology today as Christians still seek to know Jesus.

As a theological enterprise, christology has always been the work of Jesus's followers. But now we will pose, and attempt to answer, what might seem to be an odd and certainly anachronistic question: What was *Jesus's* christology? In other words, what did Jesus think about himself? Did *he* regard himself as the messiah, or the *christos*, to use the Greek term? Did he think he was a divine incarnation or the son of god? Why did he refer to himself as the son of man? What, if anything, did he think his death on the cross would accomplish?

When and How the Kingdom Will Arrive

We have observed that Jesus's teaching and actions centered on the coming of the reign of the LORD. Our first approach to Jesus's christology, then, is to consider how he understood his role in this new order. Did he think of himself as simply a messenger warning others of the approaching new age, or did he believe he was playing—or would play—a role in making it an actuality? To answer this question requires that we delve into one of the most hotly debated areas of modern Jesus scholarship: when and how did Jesus think the kingdom would come?

The Impending Perspective

Since the last century most critical scholars have thought that Jesus believed the new age would be established within a few years of his lifetime by a spectacular event initiated and directed by the LORD himself. These theologians took seriously Jesus's proclamation that the kingdom was "near" or "at hand."[62] In the Gospel of Mark, for example, Jesus declared, "Truly I tell you, there are some standing here who will not taste death until they see that the kingdom of God has come with power."[63] Later in the same gospel, Jesus predicted:

> . . . in those days . . . the sun will be darkened, and the moon
> will not give its light, and the stars will be falling from heaven,
> and the powers in the heavens will be shaken. Then they will see

62. Mark 1:15.
63. Mark 9:1, NRSV.

"the Son of Man coming in clouds" with great power and glory. Then he will send out the angels, and gather his elect from the four winds, from the ends of the earth to the ends of heaven. . . . Truly I tell you, this generation will not pass away until all these things have taken place.[64]

Matthew and Luke record similar statements. Even the apostle Paul, writing to the Thessalonians in the mid-first century, believed the kingdom would arrive before some of his fellow Christians had died.[65]

The belief that Jesus taught that the rule of the Father would soon appear helps explain certain beliefs and practices of the earliest Christians. For instance, it would account for the great sense of urgency that inspired Jesus's followers to spread his gospel throughout the empire, and for the fact that it was almost a half century before Jesus's story was committed to the written word. It would help clarify Paul's exhortation for Christians not to marry and to practice celibacy. If the new world were truly near to hand, what need would there be to change one's marital status or risk being consumed with lust? Why record Jesus's story if the heavenly dominion were about to dawn? It would be far better to focus all efforts on preparing for the kingdom. Theologians called this outlook an "interim ethic," a way of life appropriate for persons expecting the complete transformation of the earth at any moment. Jesus's expectation of the imminent arrival of the kingdom also accounts for the significant differences between Jesus's teachings and later developments in Christian theology and practice. When the spectacular coming of the kingdom did not occur as Jesus anticipated, the church had to revise its understanding of Jesus and his teachings.

The Involvement Perspective

This interpretation has been the dominant view among most liberal biblical scholars for at least a hundred years. But of course, there have been other interpretations. One such reading suggests that Jesus believed the kingdom was a *present* reality, already available to anyone willing to be a part of it. In other words, the kingdom would not arrive in a dramatic display of the LORD's cosmic powers but would rather quietly and almost imperceptibly appear as more persons committed themselves to living as subjects of heaven's rule. Advocates of this perspective cite such passages as the one in

---

64. Mark 13:24–30, NRSV.

65. 1 Thess 4:15.

which Jesus declares, "the kingdom of God is among [or within] you."[66] Here it seems that Jesus is suggesting that the kingdom is here; one only needs to change one's way of perceiving in order to see it. From this standpoint, Jesus's mission was to teach others how to see and live in the kingdom because the full manifestation of the divine rule on earth depends on the human willingness to accept it. Jesus's healings, exorcisms, and powerful acts were all ways to demonstrate participation in this new reality. Not only did Jesus perform these acts, but he also commissioned some of his disciples to go out and do the very same things he did: healing, casting out demons, and proclaiming the new dominion. When Jesus urged his listeners to follow him, he intended for them to respond by helping him to make the kingdom a reality. Without human cooperation, the rule of the LORD could not be established. But by collaboration, human beings could bring the kingdom into being at this very moment.

Which Is It?

It is difficult to adjudicate between these interpretations of Jesus's view of the kingdom. At first glance, they seem at odds with one another. In the first view, which we might call the *impending* perspective, Jesus would have believed that his principal calling was as a prophet or messenger to urge his contemporaries to prepare for the glorious transformation of the world to be produced by the Father at any moment. Those who failed to change their ways and get right with their god were liable to find themselves excluded from the new world. The second view, which we can call the *involvement* perspective, suggests that Jesus's primary role was to inspire and enable others to see the possibilities of a new way of living, free from the sufferings and disappointments of life as we now know it. As more people shared this vision and participated in it, the more the reign of heaven would become an actuality.

As frameworks for interpreting Jesus, both the impending and involvement perspectives have their merits and drawbacks. Both have support from the earliest texts we have about the historical Jesus. Advocates of either view can bring forth passages from the gospels to support their argument. The impending view seems to fit well with apocalyptic expectations of the time and is consistent with the preaching of John the Baptizer. The involvement view may seem more appealing from a Christian theological perspective. It avoids having to say that Jesus was mistaken about the kingdom's

66. Luke 17:20.

timing and gives modern Christians a focus for their faith by encouraging the continuation of Jesus's advocacy of justice.

Is it possible that *both* viewpoints are true, that Jesus preached a kingdom that was both coming and yet in some sense already here? This was the thesis of several prominent New Testament scholars of the last century, who argued that as a result of Jesus's life, death, and resurrection, divine reign on earth had been initiated but still awaited its final consummation at some point in the future.[67] Today, most evangelical scholars support this point of view. This outlook is attractive because it obviates the need to emphasize some of Jesus's sayings over others. Yet, it is not clear how it resolves Jesus's and the early Christians' belief that the kingdom would be fully manifested within their generation.

The Titles of Jesus

What one decides about Jesus's understanding of the coming of the kingdom will in large measure determine what one believes about his christology. The impending viewpoint suggests that Jesus regarded himself mainly as a prophet of the end-times. The involvement model implies that Jesus saw himself more as a teacher whose role was to educate others about a new way of life. Throughout the New Testament, he is referred to in both ways. While certainly these titles were appropriate, the gospels are also quite clear that these were not the *only* ways that Jesus was thought of—or that he thought of himself. Examining these other designations might shed light on Jesus's understanding of his role in the new age and illuminate his own christology. We will consider the most of prominent of these titles: messiah, son of god, and son of man.

Messiah

The title by which Jesus has been most commonly known throughout history is the Christ, or the messiah. So closely associated have been the words "Jesus" and "Christ" that the terms are often used interchangeably. Many people today are even unaware that "the Christ" is a title applied to Jesus just as "the Buddha" was given to Gotama. The fundamental Christian affirmation is that Jesus of Nazareth was the Christ. But what is the Christ, and did Jesus understand *himself* that way, as his followers obviously did?

67. In particular, Hans Conzelman and Joachim Jeremias. Oscar Cullman used the analogy of the difference between D-Day, when the decisive phase of World War II began, and V-E Day, when the victory was finally achieved and seen to be achieved.

The word *messiah* derives from Hebrew and Aramaic terms that mean "anointed one," and an anointed one was literally someone on whom holy oil had been ritually applied. This ritual of anointment symbolized divine appointment to a sacred task. Throughout the Tanakh, the Jewish scripture, numerous individuals are called messiahs, including King David and King Cyrus of Persia, the emperor who liberated the Jews from their Babylonian captivity.

But by the time of Jesus, the term *messiah* had acquired a more specific meaning. Under the domination of Greek and then Roman rule, many Jews in Palestine began to expect or yearn for a new messiah who, like King David and King Cyrus, would be an exceptional military hero and who would restore the kingdom of Israel to its former greatness. This hope was partly based on passages from the apocalyptic book of Daniel that refer to an approaching anointed prince, a descendant of King David, who would lead his troops "to restore and rebuild Jerusalem."[68] The expectation did not necessarily involve the idea that the messiah was god incarnate or divine, only that he was designated by the LORD for a special purpose. This may not have been the only way the new messiah was envisioned, but it was the dominant view. There seems to have been an extensive belief in Jesus's time that matters had gotten so dire that this messiah would appear very shortly. Perhaps in response to the common hope, a whole series of persons appeared in the first century claiming to be the Christ. Was Jesus of Nazareth one of them?

Let us be clear: We are not asking, *was* Jesus the messiah? We are merely asking, did the historical Jesus *claim* to be the messiah? Others will disagree, I am sure, but I do not believe that how we answer the second question necessarily determines how we answer the first.

For some readers of the New Testament, perhaps even most, the answer is as plain as day. Of course Jesus declared himself to be the Christ. The Gospel of John reports a well-known story about Jesus's encounter with a Samaritan woman at a public well. After a conversation, the woman challenges Jesus about one of the issues separating the Judeans and Samaritans—the appropriate place to worship the LORD. Jesus responds by telling her, "the time is coming—in fact, it's already here—for true worshipers to worship the Father as he truly is, without regard to place."[69] "The woman continues, 'All I know is that the Messiah, the one called Anointed, is going to come; when he does, he'll tell us everything.' Jesus says to her, 'You've been talking to [the Anointed] all along; I am he.'"[70] Several other passages

68. Dan 9:25, NRSV.

69. John 4:23, in Miller, ed., *Complete Gospels*, 207.

70. John 4:25–26, in ibid., 207.

from John make the same point. Indeed, John's gospel goes even further, to suggest that Jesus was more than just the Father's anointed. He was the Lord's "Word made flesh."

Critical biblical scholars, as we have noted, have grave doubts about the historicity of most of John's gospel. Very few aspects of John can be certified as historically probable according to the standards of modern historiography. This is not the place to discuss those issues in detail, but let me mention a few factors that contribute to this judgment. First, John's gospel was written later than the synoptics, at the end of the first or beginning of the second century; by that time, christological developments had been in process for sixty or seventy years. As we have seen in the cases of the Buddha and Confucius, as time proceeds, the biographies of charismatic individuals tend to acquire greater legendary and even mythic qualities. Second, John neglects to mention most of the events and teachings contained in Mark, Matthew, and Luke. John contains no parables, no reports of exorcisms, and no discussions of the end-time. John mentions the heavenly kingdom only twice. It is hard to account for these omissions if John had access to the same historical material that the synoptics used. There are other factors involved, of course, but the consensus among academic biblical specialists who apply the methods of modern historical study is that John contains little historical fact and few, if any, authentic sayings of Jesus. Accordingly, most critical scholars doubt that the historical Jesus actually identified himself as the Christ, as the Gospel of John describes.

But what of the synoptics? Mark, Matthew, and Luke are generally believed to contain material that came from Jesus himself. Is there evidence in these texts that Jesus laid claim to the title *messiah*? In these earliest gospels, Jesus refrains from declaring outright that he was the Christ. On a few occasions, however, *others* make that assertion. But he himself appears hesitant to accept the title. This motif is referred to by scholars as the "messianic secret."[71] The most noteworthy expression of this theme occurs in Mark:

> Jesus went on with his disciples to the villages of Caesarea Philippi; and on the way he asked his disciples, "Who do people say that I am?" And they answered him, "John the Baptist; and others, Elijah; and still others, one of the prophets." He asked them, "But who do you say that I am?" Peter answered him, "You are the Messiah." And he sternly ordered them not to tell anyone about him.[72]

71. Wrede, *Messianic Secret.*
72. Mark 8:27–30, NRSV.

The other gospels report similar events or other occasions during which Jesus gives ambiguous answers to questions about his identity. If indeed the messianic secret is historically accurate, that is, factually goes back to Jesus's life, what could possibly explain it? One plausible answer is that Jesus was concerned that his followers might misunderstand what messiahship truly meant. If the common hope was for a political hero along the lines of King David, then Jesus did not want the masses attempting to coerce him into that role. As we noted, there were other messianic claimants at the time, many of them associated with violent revolutions. Perhaps Jesus wanted to avoid these connotations to forestall distractions to his genuine mission. Another possibility is that what Jesus considered true messiahship could not be revealed until his death and resurrection. In short, he urged his followers not to speak of him—and perhaps even to *think* of him—as the messiah until his crucifixion and resurrection disclosed the true nature of messiahship. A third possibility has to be that Jesus never actually claimed to be the messiah. The messianic secret was a literary device used by the synoptic gospels to explain why Jesus never made messianic claims even though Christians were claiming he *was* the Christ.

In the final analysis, it is hard to state with confidence that Jesus unequivocally accepted the title the Christ. Even if it were clear that Jesus had embraced that designation, it is not altogether evident what he would have meant by it.

Son of God

Let us consider another title often attributed to Jesus: the son of god. With respect to this appellation, the attestations in the synoptic gospels seem clearer, and it seems likely that Jesus *did* think of himself as god's son. One fairly obviously example is the way Jesus constantly referred to god as "the Father," particularly in prayer.[73] In Mark's gospel, whenever Jesus performs an exorcism, the demons typically call him son of god. But despite these attestations, discerning Jesus's understanding of this title is not easy. Throughout the biblical literature and the Mediterranean area, various permutations of the expression "son of god" conveyed many different meanings. In the Tanakh, "son of god" or "sons of god" could refer to angels, to humanity as a whole, or to particularly noble individuals. But there are suggestions, espe-

---

73. "I praise you Father, Lord of heaven and earth . . . My Father has turned everything over to me. No one knows the son except the Father, nor does anyone know the Father except the son—and anyone to whom the son wishes to reveal him." Matt 11:25–27 in Miller, ed., *Complete Gospels*, 77-78.

cially in noncanonical Jewish texts, that the anticipated messiah would also be called the son of god. Furthermore, as we observed in our discussion of the stories of Jesus's birth, Augustus Caesar was called "son of god," as well as "god," "god from god," "redeemer," "liberator," and "savior of the world." Unfortunately, the lack of primary sources in Aramaic about the life of Jesus makes it impossible to determine whether he himself or others referred to him in that language as "*a* son of god" or as "*the* son of god." Almost certainly, Jesus thought of himself as a son of god, but there is little definitive evidence to compel us to say that he thought of sonship as a unique relationship that only he had with the Father.

Son of Man

One of the most frequently used expressions for Jesus in the synoptic gospels was the "son of man." It may also be one of the most obscure. There is little doubt that Jesus actually used this term to refer to himself; there is none of the ambiguity that we find with messiah or son of god. In Mark, for instance, Jesus called himself the son of man when he referred to his own fate: "The Son of Man is to be betrayed into human hands, and they will kill him, and three days after being killed, he will rise again."[74]

Many Christians today believe "son of man" indicates Jesus's humanity, as compared with his divinity. Historian Geza Vermes believes that "son of man" was not really a title but just a polite way in which people referred to themselves.[75] These interpretations may both be correct, but it is also true that in the Tanakh and the New Testament, the expression could have a more technical meaning.

According to the book of Daniel, at the end of the world, a figure known as the son of man would descend from heaven to play a decisive role in the annihilation of evil and to return the world to the path of righteousness. Daniel writes of his vision:

> I saw one like a human being [or son of man] coming with the clouds
>   of heaven.
> And he came to the Ancient One and was presented before him.
> To him was given dominion and glory and kingship,
>   that all the peoples, nations, and languages should serve him.
> His dominion is an everlasting dominion that shall not pass away,

74. Mark 9:31, NRSV; cf. Matt 20:18–19.
75. Vermes, *Jesus the Jew.*

and his kingship is one that shall never be destroyed.[76]

Was this what Jesus had in mind when he called himself the son of man? It is quite possible he did. Shortly after he told his followers that he would die and rise again, Jesus said to them: "Then they will see 'the Son of Man coming in clouds' with great power and glory."[77] Or as Matthew tells it, Jesus said, "the Son of Man is to come with his angels in the glory of his Father, and then he will repay everyone for what has been done. Truly I tell you, there are some standing here who will not taste death before they see the Son of Man coming in his kingdom."[78]

As we near the end of this discussion, let me observe that we have hardly reached any conclusions. Indeed, we have more raised questions than provided answers. Our purpose has been to provide a glimpse into the diversity of perspectives that characterizes current scholarship on Jesus and the complexity of the issues involved. Soon, we will try to put these puzzle pieces back together again. But before we do, we need to consider one final aspect of Jesus's life: his death and resurrection.

The Last Days in Jerusalem

Jesus's death and resurrection were without doubt the most important events of his life, according to the New Testament. All four gospels relate detailed stories of these occurrences. The apostle Paul, whom I consider the chief founder of Christianity, based his entire theology on Jesus's crucifixion and resurrection without ever mentioning his teachings. For two millennia, many Christians have followed Paul's example. Although other Christians have certainly given far more attention to Jesus's life and teachings than did Paul, on the whole they have still concurred with Paul's belief in the centrality of the death and resurrection.

The emphasis on this aspect of Jesus's life is directly related to his function in Christianity. Jesus is considered by Christians to be the atonement for human sinfulness and the means by which salvation is made possible. As Paul wrote, Jesus "was handed over to death for our trespasses and was raised for our justification."[79] That has been the dominant view of the meaning of Jesus's crucifixion and resurrection among Christians for centuries.

---

76. Dan 7:13–14, NRSV.

77. Mark 13:26, NRSV.

78. Matt 16:27–28, NRSV; cf. Luke 21:28.

79. Rom 4:25, NRSV.

But in this discussion, we shall develop another understanding of these events, one focusing on what we know of their historicity and their significance for the message that Jesus proclaimed: the coming of the LORD's kingdom. I will not suggest that my interpretation and the dominant interpretation of Christians are necessarily incompatible. I simply intend to demonstrate the continuity of the crucifixion and resurrection with the rest of Jesus's life and teaching as we have studied it thus far. From that vantage point, we will discuss these events in the same manner as we have considered the parables, the healings and exorcisms, the miracles, and his prayers and feasts—as enactments of life in the kingdom. Rather than view Jesus's death and resurrection as a divinely planned transaction conferring the forgiveness of humanity's sin, let us think about them in relation to the central message of Jesus's life.

Jesus urged his contemporaries to prepare for the new age and to begin living as if it were a present reality. He believed god's reign would disrupt the values and priorities of the current state of affairs and bring a qualitatively new reality to the world characterized by a radical commitment to the things the LORD cared about. In this new way of life, there would be plenty of resources for everyone and freedom from every kind of bondage. The world would be at peace and the qualities of fairness, compassion, and imagination would prevail. When Jesus decided to leave the relative safety of Galilee, where his public activity had centered, and journey to Jerusalem during the Passover festival, it was with the intent both to dramatize this message of the kingdom and to set in motion the events that would signal its coming in final fullness.

Holy Week

The choice of both place and time were deliberate. Jerusalem was, of course, the symbolic center of ancient Judaism, the location of its temple and its traditions. It was also the home of the high priests and the council of elders and the heart of Judean collaboration with the Roman Empire. The Passover was one of major celebrations of the Jewish people, one of three festivals in which Jews from all over Palestine made pilgrimage to Jerusalem. Passover, of course, commemorated the Israelites' exodus from Egypt, specifically the night Yahweh spared the children of Israel from the tenth and final plague, the killing of the firstborn. Jesus chose to go to Jerusalem at the time the Jews were celebrating their freedom from Egyptian domination, surely an occasion in which they were particularly cognizant of the contrast between liberation from Egypt and their virtual enslavement to Rome. Jesus would also have known that Jerusalem would have been especially crowded. Perhaps he saw that as an opportunity to reach a greater audience with his message. But he could not have been unaware that the city would also be packed with Roman soldiers, who would have been dispatched for crowd control. Passover would have been a prime opportunity for a rebellion to erupt, the last thing the Romans wanted; they would take extra precautions to ensure that order was maintained. In fact, Jesus was surely aware that the Roman prefect, Pontius Pilate, and the Roman reinforcements would parade into the city at the start of holiday from his headquarters on the Mediterranean coast to pointedly remind the Jews of Roman presence and power.

We can be confident that Jesus was aware of the Roman procession because he staged another, very different parade at about the same time. From the opposite end of the city, Jesus entered Jerusalem riding on a donkey, symbolizing another power and another kingdom. Jesus's entry, celebrated by the churches each year as Palm Sunday, was a dramatic allusion to the words of the prophet Zechariah:

> Rejoice greatly, O daughter Zion!
>   Shout aloud, O daughter Jerusalem!
> Lo, your king comes to you;
>   triumphant and victorious is he,
> humble and riding on a donkey,
>   on a colt, the foal of a donkey.
> He will cut off the chariot from Ephraim
>   and the warhorse from Jerusalem;
> and the battle-bow shall be cut off,
>   and he shall command peace to the nations;
> his dominion shall be from sea to sea,
>   and from the River to the ends of the earth.[80]

Jesus's procession into Jerusalem enacts the entrance of a humble king to mark the start of his peaceable kingdom, in glaring contrast to the ostentatious march of the Roman military in all its glory.

During the days following his entry into the city, Jesus continued to speak of the kingdom of heaven and to perform acts to symbolize it. One of the memorable incidents occurred within the temple precincts when Jesus drove out the sellers and buyers and overturned the tables of the moneychangers and dove sellers so that no one could carry anything through the temple. Then he began to teach to those present. He declared, "Is it not written, 'My house shall be called a house of prayer for all the nations'?

---

80. Zech 9:9–10, NRSV.

But you have made it a den of robbers."[81] It would be a mistake to read this story as an indictment of mixing commerce and religion, as it is usually interpreted. When Jesus declares that the temple has become a "den of robbers," he is not directing his condemnation to the moneychangers and dove sellers, who, after all, were providing an essential service for pilgrims to the temple and may not have been making all that much money. Briefly bringing temple business to a halt by overturning the tables was simply a way for Jesus to stop the commotion and get attention to state his message, which was intended for the priests, those who were in charge of the temple and who were the chief collaborators with the Romans. The phrase "den of robbers" is taken from the prophet Jeremiah, who was deeply critical of the ancient Jews for failing to live up to their god's standard of social justice by oppressing foreigners in their midst, allowing the orphans and widows to go uncared for, and for shedding innocent blood.[82] For Jesus, the real robbers were the priests and temple authorities, who benefited by the Roman occupation and refused to resist the imperial exploitation of the poor and destitute. Mark says that just after this incident, the chief priests and scribes—*not* the moneychangers and dove sellers—began to look for a way to kill him.

The Last Supper

On Thursday evening of Passion or Holy Week, as the church now calls it, Jesus celebrated his last meal with his disciples. The New Testament reports that two important events occurred at this last supper. First, Jesus instituted the ritual of the Eucharist, or the Lord's Supper, by offering bread and wine to his companions. The meaning of that ritual, of course, would become the subject of fierce debate among Christians for centuries to come. The second event was Judas Iscariot's departure during the meal to inform the temple authorities of Jesus's whereabouts. Judas's role in Jesus's death is an enigma, and the gospels struggle to explain his motivations. Luke can think of nothing better than to say the devil made him do it. John suggests he was motivated by money—thirty pieces of silver. Neither is a satisfying answer. More recent interpretations suggest that Judas became disappointed when he discovered that the kingdom Jesus had in mind was not the one that Judas wanted. Others have thought he was cowardly and sought to avoid the consequences that Jesus appeared headed for. The recently released translations of the noncanonical Gospel of Judas suggest that Judas and

81. Mark 11:17, NRSV.
82. Jer 7:5–7.

Jesus conspired to arrange Jesus's arrest so he might complete his mission on earth. In this interpretation, Judas was Jesus's closest and most important disciple. Whatever was historically the case with Judas, it is clear that early Christians could not decide how best to explain him. The books of New Testament do not even agree on how he died. Matthew says he hung himself, and the book of Acts says he fell in a field and spilled his guts. Regardless of his motives and demise, the gospels do agree that he played a central role in Jesus's arrest. But he was hardly the cause of Jesus's death. The stories suggest that Jesus was fully aware of what might happen to him by taking his message to Jerusalem during the Passover.

It was late in the night when the temple police arrived at the Garden of Gethsemane at the foot of the Mount of Olives to arrest Jesus. He had been praying there with some of his followers since supper. The New Testament relates a heart-wrenching scene in which Jesus struggles to accept what he believes is the Father's will. Luke says "his sweat became like great drops of blood falling down on the ground."[83] When the temple guards arrived, Jesus offered no resistance and allowed himself to be taken into custody. His followers, however, abandoned him.

Trial and Condemnation

What happened after his arrest is unclear. The gospels report that Jesus was taken to Caiaphas, the high priest, and a hearing was conducted before the temple authorities. Several witnesses were brought forth, but they were unable to present consistent testimony against Jesus. Finally, the high priest simply asked point-blank: "Are you the messiah, the son of the blessed one?"[84] Jesus's answer was far from lucid. Most English translations of Jesus's response in Mark's gospel report his answer as "I am." But that phrase in Greek could just as correctly be rendered as "Am I?" Matthew and Luke preserve the ambiguity with "You have said so"[85] and "You say that I am."[86] Then Jesus said a curious thing. Mark expresses it this way: "you will see the Son of Man seated at the right hand of the Power, and 'coming with the clouds of heaven.'"[87] Jesus gives an ambiguous answer to the question about his messiahship, but seems to accept for himself the title Son of Man. As we noted in our discussion of Jesus's christology, these appellations were

83. Luke 22:44, NRSV.
84. Mark 14:53–61, NRSV.
85. Matt 26:64, NRSV.
86. Luke 22:70, NRSV.
87. Mark 14:62, NRSV.

ordinarily understood to mean two very different figures: one, a military hero; the other, a figure appearing from the heavens at the end-time. In any event, it was enough for the high priest to declare Jesus a blasphemer and ask the council for a recommendation. They judged him deserving of death.

At dawn on Friday, Jesus was taken to Pilate, who was staying at Herod the Great's former palace. It is likely that the temple authorities were not allowed to condemn a criminal to death. That would have been the sole prerogative of Rome. Hence, it was necessary to get the prefect's approval to put an end to Jesus's life. Pilate asked Jesus if he were the king of Judeans. Pilate's question was probably full of sarcasm as he looked upon the bound and beaten Galilean: "*You* are 'the King of the Judeans?'" Jesus gave a curt, evasive answer: "If you so say,"[88]—again, not exactly a resounding affirmation. In Mark, the chief priests make other accusations, but Jesus remains completely silent until he is crucified; Jesus's silence at this time seems to be a gesture of contempt for Roman authority. The New Testament suggests that Pilate did not want to execute Jesus and tried to get out of the situation gracefully without stirring up a riot. Mark tells how Pilate tried to escape his predicament by offering to release Jesus in accord with a Roman custom of freeing one prisoner at Passover. But the crowd chose Barabbas, a convicted insurgent, over Jesus. The whole Barabbas episode is highly unlikely. It is hard to believe that the Romans would really release a man convicted of insurrection at a time when rebellion could erupt in a flash. The story is more likely a literary device to show how the Judeans preferred the path of violent insurrection to the nonviolent resistance represented by Jesus. Whether the Barabbas story is a fiction or not, it is true that Pilate ordered Jesus's crucifixion as an insurrectionist against the empire, probably as a matter of expediency. Better to kill one man than risk an uprising.

Crucifixion

Jesus was turned over to the Roman soldiers, who began to treat him without mercy. They picked up on the charge that Jesus claimed to be the king of the Judeans, and they mocked him accordingly, giving him a purple robe and a crown of thorns, and prostrating themselves before him. After they had their amusement, they forced him to march up to Calvary, a very public location just outside the city wall, carrying a wooden crossbeam. There, he was stripped naked, nailed to the crossbeam, and hoisted up to the vertical post on which the horizontal beam rested.

88. Mark 15:2, in Miller, ed., *Complete Gospels*, 49–50.

Crucifixion was meant to be both painful and humiliating. Those who were crucified ordinarily died a slow, agonizing death; it often took days for the victim to succumb. Death could have been caused by blood loss, exposure, dehydration, asphyxiation, infection, or a combination of these. Because it was excruciating and public, crucifixion was reserved for those convicted of sedition against the state and for chronically disobedient slaves. Obviously, it was intended as a deterrent to future acts of defying authority.

According to Mark, Jesus was crucified around nine o'clock in the morning, between two Judean insurgents.[89] At noon, a great darkness began to cover the earth. This literary symbol should be interpreted in the same way as the great lights and earthquakes that accompanied significant moments of the Buddha's life, namely, as the cosmic recognition of the significance of these events. By midafternoon, Jesus was approaching his death. At the moment of his death, around three o'clock in the afternoon, a Roman centurion who watched him die said, as Mark tells it, "Truly this man was God's Son!"[90] It is doubtful that the centurion's announcement was a historical event, but there is tremendous theological significance here. First, there is the immense irony. The symbol of Roman might and oppressiveness is the mouthpiece by which Jesus's identity is revealed to the world. But equally important is the *moment* at which the announcement is made. It was only when the soldier "saw that in this way he breathed his last,"[91] that he was moved to declare Jesus's relationship with the Father. We are led to conclude that there was something in the way Jesus died that prompted the pronouncement, but Mark isn't clear about what it was. Perhaps it was the courage and nobility revealed in the way he faced death that touched the centurion. Perhaps it was Jesus's willingness to proclaim a message of justice in the face of the Roman and Judean authorities—even though it meant his death—that impressed the soldier. But whatever the reason, the declaration serves to reinforce the idea we mentioned earlier—that Jesus's death was one of the two most important aspects of his life, according to the later Christian tradition.

Jesus's body was removed from the cross and placed in a tomb shortly before sunset on Friday, which would have been the start of Shabbat. Once the sun had set, the corpse would have had to remain on the cross until the end of the sabbath. The arrival of Shabbat meant that the usual preparations for burial could not be undertaken before the body was entombed. That is why the women who followed Jesus to Jerusalem and had cared for him in

89. Mark 15:25.

90. Mark 15:39, NRSV.

91. Ibid.

Galilee had gone to his tomb early in the morning on Sunday. Their plan was to anoint his body for burial, which they had been unable to do on the day of his death.

Resurrection

The four gospels all offer different accounts of what happened on that Sunday morning. The earliest gospel, Mark, presents a terse description with an abrupt ending.

> When the sabbath was over, Mary Magdalene, and Mary the mother of James, and Salome bought spices, so that they might go and anoint him. And very early on the first day of the week, when the sun had risen, they went to the tomb. They had been saying to one another, 'Who will roll away the stone for us from the entrance to the tomb?' When they looked up, they saw that the stone, which was very large, had already been rolled back. As they entered the tomb, they saw a young man, dressed in a white robe, sitting on the right side; and they were alarmed. But he said to them, 'Do not be alarmed; you are looking for Jesus of Nazareth, who was crucified. He has been raised; he is not here. Look, there is the place they laid him. But go, tell his disciples and Peter that he is going ahead of you to Galilee; there you will see him, just as he told you.' So they went out and fled from the tomb, for terror and amazement had seized them; and they said nothing to anyone, for they were afraid.[92]

There are several puzzling aspects of this account. To begin, it is rather curious that the women consider the obstacle of the stone only *after* they were on their way to the tomb. When they arrive, they only encounter a young man who tells them that Jesus is not there but instructs them to tell the other followers that Jesus will meet them in Galilee. But the whole event scares them, and they flee and do not tell anyone. This is the point at which the original gospel of Mark ends. Apparently, later Christians found this conclusion unsatisfying, because they added an alternative ending, with stories of Jesus's appearances. But critical scholars are fairly certain that the original text ends with the women fleeing the empty tomb, determined not to tell anyone.

The stories of Matthew and Luke differ significantly from Mark in several details. The most important difference is the account of Jesus's appearances. In both Matthew and Luke, some of his disciples see Jesus after his

92. Mark 16:1–8, NRSV.

resurrection. In Matthew, the women who had gone to the tomb encounter Jesus en route to tell the other disciples of the empty grave. Immediately, they fell at his feet and worshiped him. Later, the remaining eleven apostles visit a mountain back in Galilee, and they too see Jesus. Matthew concludes his story with these parting words from Jesus:

> Go therefore and make disciples of all nations, baptizing them in the name of the Father and of the Son and of the Holy Spirit, and teaching them to obey everything that I have commanded you. And remember, I am with you always, to the end of the age.[93]

Matthew's account of Jesus's appearance adds one very interesting detail: "When they saw him," Matthew writes, "they worshiped him; but some doubted."[94] In other words, even seeing Jesus after his death was not sufficient to convince some apostles that he had indeed been raised by the Father.

Luke tells of other stories in which Jesus's followers see him. Interestingly, Luke does not mention the women seeing him, as Matthew does. When the women returned to the apostles with the news, the men refused to believe them. Then Peter ran to the tomb and discovered that it was indeed empty. Later, Luke reports what I think is the most fascinating of the appearance stories. On Resurrection Sunday, two followers of Jesus were walking away from Jerusalem to a village called Emmaus, and Jesus suddenly began to walk alongside them. They were discussing Jesus's death and the story of the empty tomb. Jesus conversed with them for quite some time, and yet they did not recognize him. As they approached the village, they invited Jesus to share a meal with them, an invitation he accepted. Then, as Luke tells the story:

> When he was at the table with them, he took bread, blessed and broke it, and gave it to them. Then their eyes were opened, and they recognized him; and he vanished from their sight.[95]

There are two important features of this story. First is the fact that Jesus was not immediately recognized by these disciples, even though he had walked with them and spoken with them at length. Second is the setting during which they finally *do* identify Jesus: at a meal, one the great symbols of the kingdom. But just as soon they recognize him, he vanishes from their midst.

---

93. Matt 28:19–20, NRSV.
94. Matt 28:17, NRSV.
95. Luke 24:30–31, NRSV.

Luke also says that shortly afterwards, Jesus appeared to the eleven while they were gathered in Jerusalem, not in Galilee as Matthew tells it. At first, they "thought they were seeing a ghost,"[96] until Jesus invited them to touch him and feel his flesh and bones. During the entire experience, the apostles felt terror, joy, disbelief, and wonder. Luke ends the story by describing how Jesus was carried up to heaven in an event known in the Christian tradition as the ascension.

In John's gospel, Jesus first appears to Mary Magdalene, who mistakes him for the caretaker of the garden where the tomb is located. Later in the day, Jesus appears to the apostles, except for Thomas, who is not among them. When they tell him that they have seen the Lord, Thomas retorts that he will not believe their story until he himself is able to touch Jesus. A week later, Thomas sees Jesus and loses the skepticism that had earned him the title Doubting Thomas. John continues to describe several other occasions on which Jesus's followers saw and interacted with him.

How Jesus Became Christ

What are we to make of the stories? Did Jesus *really* appear to his followers or did the gospel writers make that up? What do these resurrection stories really mean? Can we take them as evidence of Jesus's divinity, or do they perhaps indicate something else?

What Really Happened?

These extraordinary stories of Jesus's empty tomb and appearances to his disciples invite us to inquire into their historical basis and their significance for those who accepted them as true. Let us begin with the question of history. What really happened in the days after Jesus's death?

As our overview of the gospels' accounts suggests, there is little agreement among the sources as to what occurred and to whom. But that *something* happened seems hard to deny. It is difficult to account for the fervent movement that began to coalesce among Jesus's followers without positing some powerful experience that convinced them that their teacher had been vindicated by his god and lived on, in some fashion, despite his death. In my view, the simplest and most plausible explanation of this experience is that some of the disciples—perhaps individually, perhaps collectively—saw Jesus or perceived his presence after his death. The exact nature of these

96. Luke 24:37, NRSV.

perceptions—whether dreams, visions, auditory hallucinations, or some other phenomenon—cannot be determined. But I see no reason to deny that the crucified Jesus was seen, heard, and even felt by several of his closest companions after his entombment. Experiences of this sort, while not completely understood scientifically, are widely attested both in history and in our own era. In Hinduism, for instance, sightings of the god Krishna are relatively commonplace, as are visions of the Virgin Mary in Roman Catholicism. There is no good reason to dismiss such reports as merely pathological or pure fabrications. Such experiences are often had by individuals who are no more neurotic than the average person. Therefore, I am quite comfortable affirming that the stories of Jesus's resurrection appearances are rooted in actual historical events—namely, the disciples' experiences of him following his crucifixion.

That does not mean, however, that we should affirm that the selfsame individual who died on Good Friday was brought back to life the following Sunday morning and then visited with his disciples until he was taken up into heaven. The gospels themselves indicate that the post-Easter Jesus was different from the Jesus they had known as their teacher and mentor. In several accounts of his appearances, Jesus was not immediately recognized, indicating that the experience was not a simple resuscitation of a dead individual. Jesus was perceived as somehow transformed in a profound way. Yet at the same time, what they saw and heard was sufficiently familiar for the disciples to identify him as Jesus and not as an angel or someone else. The apostle Paul, writing before the gospels were written, called the resurrected form a "spiritual body" and distinguished it from a "flesh-and-blood" body.[97] The idea of a spiritual body is almost oxymoronic, and it is not immediately evident what Paul intended by it. But it is clear that this concept was distinct from the traditional Greek view of the immortality of the soul. The early Christians believed that resurrection entailed a raised body, but a body that had been transformed in some substantial manner. It was no longer the identical body that belonged to the individual prior to death.

However we might understand what "really" happened on Easter Sunday, it is significant that Jesus's followers referred to the event as a "resurrection." Whether or not there was such a reality as resurrection was a matter of considerable debate during Jesus's time. The Pharisees and Sadducees argued about it. The issue at stake was whether human beings collectively would be raised from the dead *at the end of time*. Neither the Pharisees nor the Sadducees seemed to think that "resurrection" indicated an *individual* person brought back to life during the normal routine of history. The

97. 1 Cor 15:44, 50.

general resurrection of humanity at the day of judgment would have been the predominant understanding of the concept in Jesus's time. The fact that the early Christians used the term "resurrection" suggests that they considered what happened to Jesus to be an eschatological event, that is to say, as an occurrence associated with the end of days. The apostle Paul seems to have construed Jesus's post-Easter appearances in just this manner. He called the resurrection of Jesus the "firstfruits of those who have died," indicating that God's raising of Jesus was the inauguration of events that would culminate in the resurrection of all the dead and the final establishment of the kingdom of the Father.[98] Paul's view was consistent with the early Christian belief that Jesus would return from heaven shortly and that the new reign would bring an end to all suffering and want and would destroy humanity's ultimate enemy, death itself. As Paul wrote in his first letter to the Corinthians:

> What I am saying, brothers and sisters, is this: flesh and blood cannot inherit the kingdom of God, nor does the perishable inherit the imperishable. Listen, I will tell you a mystery! We will not all die [before the kingdom comes], but we will all be changed, in a moment, in the twinkling of an eye, at the last trumpet. For the trumpet will sound, and the dead will be raised imperishable, and we will be changed. For this perishable body must put on imperishability and this mortal body must put on immortality. When this perishable body puts on imperishability, and this mortal body puts on immortality, then the saying that is written will be fulfilled:
> "Death has been swallowed up in victory."
> "Where, O death, is your victory? Where, O death, is your sting?"
> The sting of death is sin, and the power of sin is the law. But thanks be to God, who gives us the victory through our Lord Jesus Christ.[99]

The Interpretation of Paul

The name of Paul signals a new stage in the development of christology. In Paul, we have a person who seems to have regarded Jesus in a way significantly different from the way Jesus thought of himself. Because of the substantial christological shift represented by Paul, and because of his decisive

98. 1 Cor 15:20–28.
99. 1 Cor 15:50–57, NRSV.

influence on the evolution of thinking about Jesus, I have suggested that he is rightly considered as the chief founder of Christianity. Paul's own experience of the post-Easter Jesus appears greatly to have shaped his theology. At first a persecutor of the nascent Jesus movement, according to the book of Acts, Paul is suddenly blinded by a bright light while traveling on the road to Damascus and hears the voice of Jesus saying,

> I have appeared to you . . . to appoint you to serve and testify to
> the things in which you have seen me and to those in which I
> will appear to you. I will rescue you from your people and from
> the Gentiles—to whom I am sending you to open their eyes so
> that they may turn from darkness to light and from the power of
> Satan to God, so that they may receive forgiveness of sins and a
> place among those who are sanctified by faith in me.[100]

Although he had never met the pre-Easter Jesus, Paul now believed that he too, like some of Jesus's original followers, had a personal encounter with the resurrected Jesus, probably several years after Easter Sunday. From that moment onward, Paul took as his appointed mission to deliver the gospel to the Gentiles, the non-Jews. It is largely through Paul's efforts that the Christian movement eventually became overwhelmingly Gentile.

The gospel that Paul took to the Gentiles was, however, significantly different from the gospel proclaimed by Jesus. Examining the nature of these differences will help us appreciate the developments that transformed Jesus of Nazareth into Jesus Christ, the only son of god, and eventually god incarnate.

The divergence between Jesus and Paul can best seen in their respective proclamations. As we have observed, the substance of the message of the historical Jesus was the coming of the heavenly kingdom and the necessity to live life in light of this new reality. Paul's gospel was expressed differently. A passage from Paul's Letter to the Romans is often taken as a concise summary of his teaching:

> For I handed on to you as of first importance what I in turn
> had received: that Christ died for our sins in accordance with
> the scriptures, and that he was buried, and that he was raised
> on the third day in accordance with the scriptures, and that he
> appeared to Cephas [i.e., the apostle Peter], then to the twelve.
> Then he appeared to more than five hundred brothers and sis-
> ters at one time, most of whom are still alive, though some have

---

100. Acts 26:16–18, NRSV.

died. Then he appeared to James, then to all the apostles. Last
of all, as to someone untimely born, he appeared also to me.[101]

Many scholars regard the core of this statement as the oldest part of the New
Testament, reflecting perhaps the earliest creedal formulation of Jesus's followers. The key elements of this proclamation were incorporated into later
Christian creeds: that Christ died for human sins, was buried, was raised
from the dead, and appeared to his followers.

The message has clearly shifted. Whereas the historical Jesus promised a new state of affairs centered in the Father's reign, Paul declared that
the forgiveness of sin centered in Jesus, who is now called the Christ, the
messiah. Jesus urged his listeners to amend their ways and live in accord
with the new reality being enacted in his words and deeds and coming im-
minently in its fullness. Paul told his listeners to believe in Christ Jesus to
be saved from the wrath of the LORD that would be directed against the
ungodly when Jesus returned to earth to establish the kingdom. Paul writes:
"if you confess with your lips that Jesus is Lord and believe in your heart that
God raised him from the dead, you will be saved."[102] The messages of Jesus
and Paul are not necessarily incompatible with one another, but they are not
the same message.

A Theory of Jesus

As we move toward concluding our discussion of Jesus, it is time now to try
to provide a concise summing up of his life and teachings and their influence on his immediate followers. In so doing, I want to offer a "theory" of
Jesus. By "theory" I mean exactly the same thing meant by that term in the
natural sciences: a coherent explanation to account for a set of phenomena.
In this instance, the set of phenomena comprises what we have learned in
our analysis of the life of the historical Jesus and the development of interpretations of that life by his earlier followers. The term theory is appropriate,
I believe, because the final answers to the questions of Jesus's identity and
self-understanding are not currently—and may never be—available to us.

Many of the elements of this theoretical sketch have been presented
previously, but other aspects have yet to be provided. Thus far, we have seen
that Jesus was a Galilean Jew born of peasant parents in Roman-occupied
Palestine near the beginning of the first century CE. Of the first thirty
years of his life we know virtually nothing, except what can be reasonably

101. 1 Cor 15:3–8, NRSV.
102. Rom 10:9, NRSV.

conjectured based on what we know of others in his social, economic, and cultural situation two thousand years ago, and on the way his life eventually unfolded. Jesus grew into adulthood with a keen sensitivity to the presence of the god of the Jews as well as to matters of social justice and human suffering, an abiding concern of the Jewish god, according to many interpreters. Both traits put Jesus within the Jewish prophetic tradition that includes such figures as Jeremiah, Isaiah, and Amos. Both characteristics were probably decisive in leading Jesus to John the Baptizer. In John, Jesus found a teacher who shared his passion for the sacred and the possibilities of creating a righteous and wholesome society. John also became a paragon of a meaningful life for Jesus. John demonstrated great courage in criticizing the immoral behavior of King Herod Antipas, a virtue that led to his imprisonment and eventual execution. It is very likely that John helped shape Jesus's theology and spirituality and inspired his bravery in confronting the political powers of his day.

But it is also quite probable that Jesus's skills and spiritual acumen transcended those of John. Jesus was more than just John's lieutenant who took over when the Baptizer was beheaded. Jesus was apparently an individual of marvelous intellect and imagination whose creativity and wit made him a charismatic teacher. In his parables and aphorisms, we see clear evidence of these traits. Jesus used his creative abilities to craft intriguing stories and sayings designed to stimulate the hearer's own imaginative capacity to envision a better life beyond the present one. In ways like the Buddha, Jesus tried to enable others to see the truth for themselves and break out of habitual patterns of thought. His imaginative and often paradoxical messages are part of what has made Jesus subject to such a wide range of interpretations and why he remains so elusive.

Jesus was also more than just a prophetic figure. Unlike John, he was a healer, exorcist, and wonder worker. In his presence, people sensed a sacred, restorative power. It is difficult to accept many of the stories of Jesus's "mighty deeds" at face value, such as his raising Lazarus from the dead or his calming a raging storm on the Sea of Galilee. I can only read such accounts as fictions intended to express the extraordinary qualities that Jesus possessed. It is not difficult to believe that Jesus *was* an individual with extraordinary qualities, including a deeply compassionate nature that provided many with a sense of wholeness and acceptance.

But what did Jesus think of himself? Earlier, we examined some of the titles by which he has been known, particularly messiah, son of god, and son of man. We noted that in the most historically reliable accounts Jesus tended to resist the title Christ, or messiah, and we offered some possible reasons for that reluctance. We also noted that Jesus almost certainly thought of himself as a son of god, but whether or not he considered himself *the* son of god was an open question.

My own opinion is that during the course of his public activity, Jesus came to regard himself as the son of man who would play a key role in the final act of the inauguration of the kingdom of heaven. This is the title he used most frequently to refer to himself in the earliest gospel, and it is almost assuredly authentic to the historical Jesus. The hypothesis that Jesus thought of himself as, or as becoming, the son of man, provides a compelling explanation for his decision to leave Galilee to teach his subversive message in Jerusalem at a highly volatile moment. Jesus probably knew full well that his presence in Jerusalem during Passover would result in his execution, but also I think he believed that his death would be necessary to initiate the complete manifestation of the kingdom. It is quite possible that Jesus viewed his impending death not as a human sacrifice to effect the forgiveness of sins, as Paul and other Christians would later regard it, but as a vital part of his task as the son of man. According to the prophecies, the son of man would descend from heaven on clouds to establish the divine reign and to eliminate evil for good. Jesus's death and ascension into heaven, he may have thought, would prepare him to return to earth at the end of time. This belief may have contributed to the disciples' widely held expectation that his return was imminent. There is also an important sense in which Jesus's execution in Jerusalem made a bold statement about the nature of the LORD's kingdom. Like other nonviolent resisters, Jesus willingly allowed himself to suffer humiliation and death at the hands of Rome and its collaborators in order to dramatize graphically the oppressive nature of their rule. Throughout his teaching career, Jesus made a point of illustrating, by his deeds, the destruction created by the human neglect of justice and mercy, as well as the possibilities of life when one lived in accordance with the will of the Father. Jesus died a martyr's death, bearing witness to the failings of the kingdom of man. I think Jesus considered his crucifixion to be his final statement to the world before what he thought would be his glorious return as the son of man.

Did Jesus *think* of himself as the Christ? Probably not. The concept of the messiah was simply too laden with militaristic and violent overtones for the historical Jesus to embrace that idea as referring to himself. The idea of the messiah, as generally understood at the time, was not consistent with Jesus's ideals and comportment. If he did think of himself as the Christ, it was in very different terms than what other Jews were expecting. Yet regardless of whether Jesus considered himself the Christ, it is quite clear that his followers *did* and that they chose this title as their principal way to refer to him. It is equally clear that the disciples understood this title to mean something other than the standard interpretation. Exactly what they intended when they called Jesus the Christ, however, is not completely evident. Perhaps they were suggesting that the true path to Israel's restoration lay in the way of the cross, the willingness to resist evil in a nonviolent manner. But it is not altogether obvious why the followers would use a title that Jesus did not seem to accept outright and that was commonly understood as symbolizing a way to freedom that Jesus forthrightly rejected.

Did Jesus think he was god? I think the answer to that question is almost certainly no. Even if he had considered himself to be the *son* of the Father or the messiah, those titles would not necessarily have amounted to a claim of a divine incarnation. The Romans were comfortable with the idea that a god could assume human form, but that notion is essentially alien to Judaism. The historically reliable gospels never portray Jesus claiming to be god, and it is hard to imagine that Jesus, as a devout Jew, ever thought of himself that way. The idea that Jesus was a divine incarnation is a christological development that appears many decades after Jesus's death, long after the Christian movement had gained a foothold in other parts of the Roman world. It is probable that his followers began to think of Jesus as a divine incarnation only under the influence of Greek and Roman religious beliefs.

It might appear that if Jesus never thought of himself as the messiah nor as god, then the central claims of the Christian tradition would be undermined. But as I indicated earlier, it is not necessary that such must be the case. The messiah was a concept generated within ancient Judaism. Although there was a predominant expectation among Jews as to what this messiah would be, there was no official definition or job description. The Jews who followed Jesus had as much right to reinterpret the concept and declare Jesus the *christos* as others had to declare their favorites the messiah or to deny Jesus's Christhood because he did not fulfill the common hope for what the messiah would do. By posthumously naming Jesus as the Christ, his disciples were acting in the same manner as when the church declares an individual a saint. Such a person might not think of himself or herself as a saint while he or she is living; he or she might deny such a label altogether. Yet, in the judgment of others, the title "saint" is appropriate, perhaps even necessary. Confucius, you will recall, did not consider himself a sage, but "sage" is precisely the title most frequently given him. In the same manner, Jesus may not have regarded himself as the messiah, yet in the way his followers came to judge his significance, the title was warranted.

A similar consideration obtains when we evaluate the Christian assertion of Jesus's divinity. Jesus may not have thought of himself as god, but his followers may have discovered the divine through him to such a degree that it seemed fitting to them to call him "the incarnation of god." But that claim of divinity need not imply that Jesus was omniscient or omnipotent. It need not imply that Jesus was incapable of making mistakes, such as miscalculating the timing of god's kingdom. He was, after all, a human being, and Christianity expressly affirms that, although it has sometimes had a hard time taking its own affirmation seriously. In such instances, Christianity has allowed preconceptions of what god is determine how it understood who Jesus was, when in fact the tradition indicates that the process ought to move in the opposite manner: It is *Jesus* who reveals the true nature of god.

In making these statements, I am neither affirming nor denying the traditional Christian assertions about Jesus. I am only suggesting that what we know about the historical Jesus need not threaten those claims outright. History can neither prove nor disprove those claims. Affirming or denying Christianity's declarations about Jesus must be done on other grounds.

The stories of Jesus leave us in this rich, ambiguous territory. Like one of his parables, the meaning of the life of Jesus is hard to pin down. The significance of Jesus is elusive and subject to multiple interpretations. Perhaps Jesus's life is itself a parable, a story told to stimulate our imaginations, to envision new possibilities, to break our patterned ways of thinking of our existence and of the ultimate reality.

4

MUHAMMAD

Arabia in the Days of Ignorance

Like Jews and Christians, Muslims trace their spiritual lineage to the great patriarch Abraham. According to traditional Islamic belief, Abraham, who is known by Muslims as Ibrahim, was neither a Jew nor a Christian but simply a devoted worshiper of the one true god, known in the Arabic language as Allah.[1] The Qur'an relates that Abraham and his son Ishmael (or Isma'il) established the Kaaba—the house of god—in the city of Bacca and brought to Arabia the pure monotheistic faith. As the centuries passed, Bacca, which was later called Makkah, became a center of pilgrimage for the many Arabs who embraced the religion of Abraham. But gradually, Arabia lapsed into a dark age of religious bewilderment and moral confusion. Enchanted by allure of tribal gods and goddesses, all but a few Arabs abandoned the ancient monotheism of Abraham and Ishmael. Eventually, the Kaaba became the home of the Arabian pantheon, housing the physical representations of over three hundred local deities. Although Allah was still recognized as the god supreme, he had now become one of many. Only a small remnant of monotheists, called the *hanifs* (or *hunafa*), remained faithful to Abraham's religion and worshiped Allah alone.

Muslims refer to this age of polytheism and religious iconography as *al-Jahiliyyah*, the days of ignorance. It was during this era that the Prophet Muhammad was born. But by the time of his death in 632 CE, the age of

1. Allah is a simplification of *al-Lah*, a transliteration of the Arabic that means "the deity."

religious bewilderment had drawn to a close, and the faith of Abraham had been restored to the Arabian Peninsula. Our study of Muhammad thus begins with an examination of the *Jahiliyyah*, his immediate cultural context and the world in which Islam was first proclaimed.

Historical Sources

Apart from Muslim sources, not a great deal is known about Arabia prior to the seventh century CE when Islam was established, or reestablished, as the tradition would have it. The sources available to the historian for understanding this period are restricted to artifacts gathered in a few modern archaeological excavations and to written material from Egypt, Persia, Greece, and the Roman Empire. Arabic literature written before the Islamic era is quite meager, limited to a small number of inscriptions from the area of Yemen and a handful of poems found inside the Kaaba. Pre-Islamic Arabia was a decidedly oral culture. The Qur'an was essentially the first work of any significance written in Arabic. Recollections of the pre-Islamic period were put in writing after Islam's ascendancy and thus reflect Muslim perspectives on the state of affairs in Arabia prior to Muhammad.

Geography

Although the Arabian Peninsula is considered a rich land today due to its vast oil and gas reserves, sources from the ancient world tell us that it was regarded by residents of other territories as a desolate wasteland—and for good reason. The land was mostly desert and very difficult to cultivate for food. Starvation and malnutrition were constant threats to the well-being of its inhabitants, particularly for the nomads who lived in the peninsula's interior, caring for their livestock. The sedentary agriculturalists who lived near springs and oases fared only somewhat better than their nomadic cousins. Lacking adequate resources, the Arabs depended heavily on trade, bartering what few items the region was able to produce—dates, wheat, and resins for incense and perfume—in exchange for other necessities of living. Life in ancient Arabia was so hard that the great empires of the region, Persia and Byzantium, had no ambition to conquer it. The land was considered inhospitable and its occupants wild barbarians. For the most part, the world simply ignored Arabia.

Social Structure

Its reputation as an uncivilized territory was shaped by its social structure and the culture it produced. Arab society comprised large, autonomous tribes and smaller subgroups of clans based on kinship. These collectives were extremely close-knit, and loyalty to one's kinship group was essential to an individual's well-being. In the harsh environment of Arabia, the individual would easily perish without the protection of the larger group. There was no central authority or government enforcing a common law to regulate tribal or intertribal affairs. Each group was responsible for caring for its own and promoting its own welfare. The tribal chief ensured the equitable distribution of the sparse resources to care for the weaker members.

The scarcity of goods for life fostered sharp competition and outright hostilities among the tribal groups. The tribes, in fact, were at constant war with one another. Raiding caravans or the settlements of other tribes was a common practice and, in the words of one scholar, a "national sport."[2] Stealing from social groups other than one's own was not regarded as immoral or wrong; theft was only unethical when it was committed against a member of one's own group. Because of the intense rivalries, tribes would often create alliances with other tribes for mutual protection. Such covenants were frequently secured by marriages between members of the allied groups. Nonetheless, social associations were in constant flux; alliances between clans and tribes were like the shifting sands of the Arabian Desert.

The Tribal Ethic

The structure of Arabian society and the absence of a central governing authority stimulated the development of a unique ethical and religious culture based on the supreme importance of the tribe. Without pan-Arabian kings or councils, each tribe was left to enforce its sense of justice. Crimes committed against the tribe were requited by the tribe, a practice known as blood vengeance. If a tribe were to suffer the slaying of one of its members, for example, it would in turn kill a member of the killer's tribe. It was not necessary to exact justice on the actual killer. To satisfy the demands of blood vengeance, a tribe need only kill a member of the killer's tribe. Failure to avenge an injury would weaken the image of a tribe and render it vulnerable to future attacks by other tribes. This deeply engrained custom of tribal vendetta made the cycle of violence vicious and prevented the social groups from uniting and working together to solve their common problems.

2. Armstrong, *Muhammad*, 60.

The tribal ethic also included a number of important virtues that individuals were expected to uphold. Among the most important of these were hospitality and generosity. The poems of this era frequently extolled the merits of taking care of one's guests. Some stories tell of magnanimous hosts who sacrificed their own well-being to provide for a guest, even a stranger. The best hosts always ensured that their visitors were given plenty of food and beverage, especially wine. In Arabic, one of the words for "vineyard" and one for "generosity" are derived from the same root and pronounced and spelled almost identically. Although Islam did not continue the ancient custom of lavish drinking, it did retain the great virtues of generosity and hospitality. Promise-keeping was another. Abiding by one's promises and covenants was closely associated with one's sense of self-worth and integrity. Failure to keep one's promises resulted in a deep sense of shame and dishonor. Legends relate how certain individuals would sooner accept the death of their children or the destruction of their households than break a covenant. Finally, tribal survival depended deeply on the virtue of *muruwah*, which is commonly translated as "manliness."[3] In pre-Islamic Arabia, *muruwah* specifically meant courage in fighting adversaries, endurance in bearing adversity, a willingness to avenge a wrong committed against the social group, and the readiness to defend the weak and oppose the powerful. These ethical ideals seem to have significantly informed the development of Islamic morality. Some Muslim commentators have even suggested that the prevalence of these virtues was a chief factor in Allah's selection of the Arabs as the people to whom he entrusted his final revelation.

Be that as it may, Muslims also remember the days of ignorance as an age of depravity, a time in which Arabs lacked the moral compass of the one true god. During this period, say the Muslim interpreters, the worship of numerous local gods and goddesses led the Arabs into an ethical morass that Islam was later compelled to repudiate. Among the prevailing sins of *al-Jahiliyyah* Muslims include racism and ethnic bigotry, as reflected in the tribal structure of society; the practice of usury, or charging exorbitant interest rates on loans; female infanticide; and sexual licentiousness. Concerning the charge of sexual immorality, we know very little about practices of the pre-Islamic culture that Muslims later found objectionable. In the Qur'an, Allah commands the wives of the Prophet: "And make not a wanton display like the lewd displays of the times of ignorance."[4] In this instance, Muhammad's wives were counseled to dress modestly, which suggests that

3. Izutsu, *Ethico-religious Concepts in the Qur'ān*, 27.

4. Sura 33:33, quoted in al-Oadah, *Islam and Secularism*, 3. http://www.ummah.com/forum/showthread.php?231797-Islam-amp-Secularism/.

part of what was judged as sexual immorality was provocative clothing. It is instructive to observe that some Muslims in the modern age have begun to refer to the lifestyles of the Western world as *Jahiliyyah*.[5] This new usage of the concept illustrates that the days of ignorance represent more than just a bygone era for Islam; it can also be regarded as a psychological or cultural state of godlessness and decadence. This understanding yields insight into the disposition of many Muslims towards the West, which some regard as racially and ethnically biased, obsessed with money and the material world, and sexually permissive—precisely the grievances against the Arabs in the original time of ignorance.

The Spirit World

According to traditional Islamic interpretation, these moral shortcomings were merely symptomatic of a deeper problem inherent in the *Jahiliyyah*— the worship of false gods. According to tradition, as we noted earlier, the days of ignorance commenced when the Arabs began to forsake the exclusive worship of Allah and started to devote themselves to local, tribal deities. Although these Arab "pagans," as they are usually called, never denied the existence of Allah, they apparently found him increasingly remote and ultimately irrelevant to their daily concerns, so they turned to the gods they found more accessible. In the days of ignorance, Allah was understood to be the creator and supreme deity. He was a powerful god to invoke when swearing an oath, but never a god to trouble for ordinary matters. Only in times of great peril would he be called upon for help. On most other occasions, it was more expedient to turn to his underlings, the lesser gods and goddesses of the pantheon. Perhaps the most important of these subordinate divinities were the three goddesses known as the "daughters of Allah." They were al-Lat, or simply "the goddess"; al-Uzza, whose name means "the mighty" and who was probably a manifestation of the Egyptian goddess Isis; and Manat, the goddess of fate. These goddesses had no mythologies, so it is unclear why they came to be regarded as Allah's daughters. Each of these deities had her image inside the Kaaba as well as her own shrine in the vicinity of Makkah. They functioned as mediators with Allah and were very powerful in their own right. It was to these goddesses that most Arabs prayed when they needed rain, when they were sick, and when they were about to engage in battle or embark on a dangerous journey.

In addition to the daughters of Allah, the interior of the Kaaba bore witness to a host of other pre-Islamic deities, many of them adopted from

5. E.g., Seyyid Qutub and Mawlana Mawdudi.

cultures surrounding Arabia. Among them were Hubal, the god of the moon, who was probably introduced to Arabia from Mesopotamia. Hubal was a favorite of the Quraysh, the custodians of the Kaaba and the tribe into which Muhammad was born. Even images of Jesus and his mother Mary were enshrined there. Tradition suggests that there were 360 divine images housed in the Kaaba, representing all of the gods of the peninsula. Because of its correspondence to the days of the year according to some reckoning systems then in use, that number almost certainly had astrological significance for the ancient Arabs. Many of the gods kept there were in fact associated with various planets and astral bodies. Although Allah was widely regarded as the creator and highest god, he was not represented by a physical image in the Kaaba, and Islam fervently maintains this iconoclastic stance.

Besides the various gods and goddesses, the spirit world comprised innumerable demons, angels, nature spirits, ancestors, and a class of beings called the jinn. The jinn, or "genies" as they are better known in the West, were spiritual creatures made of smokeless fire who were believed to possess free will and thus were able to perform good or evil deeds. They were also intelligent creatures, although less intelligent than humans, and very powerful. Because of their capacity to do evil and lead humans astray, the jinn were often feared by the Arabs, who made a point of avoiding their desert haunts.

The Kaaba

In the sixth century CE, during which the Prophet Muhammad was born, the focal point of Arabian religion was the Kaaba. In those days, the Kaaba was a simple cubic structure made of granite stones and mud and sunk into the sand. Its four walls were probably much lower than they are now. At its base, there were two small doors, allowing entry into the inner sanctum where the images were kept. Some sources indicate that the exterior of the Kaaba was covered in symbols representing the myriad demons, angels, and jinn that were prominent inhabitants of the spirit world.

Long before the time of Muhammad, the Kaaba had been a center for pilgrimage. Each year during the Arabian holy months, all tribal warfare was temporarily halted and pilgrims from all over the peninsula came to Makkah to worship their deities and pray for health and prosperity. During these holidays, Makkah swelled with visitors, and great bazaars and fairs sprang up in the area surrounding the sacred precincts. Makkah was not only the religious center of Arabia but the commercial center as well.

At the Kaaba, the Arabs conducted their sacred rituals, which included the recitation of poetry, dancing, offerings, and circumambulating the Kaaba seven times, a practice whose origins are obscure. Some scholars have suggested the original intent of this observance may have been to imitate the motion of the heavenly bodies, symbolizing the belief that the Kaaba was the center point of creation, just as the earth was at the center of the universe. This pre-Islamic custom of pilgrimage, known as the *Hajj*, was retained after the Kaaba was restored to what Islam considered its pristine function, the worship of Allah as the only god. The seven circumambulations (*tawaf*) of the Kaaba are still the primary ritual of the annual *Hajj*.

The precise history of the Kaaba prior to the advent of Islam is not known. Some ancient legends say the shrine was constructed by Adam, the first man, and then destroyed by the Great Flood described in both the Bible and the Qur'an. Afterwards, it was rebuilt by Noah and his sons and then forgotten for centuries. The patriarch Abraham discovered its foundations while visiting his son Ishmael and Ishmael's mother Hagar (Hajar), whom Abraham had banished at the behest of his chief wife, Sarah. The book of Genesis describes their expulsion from Canaan as the result of Sarah's envy of Ishmael's firstborn status when her own son, Isaac, was born. Ishmael and Hagar wandered in the wilderness until they came to the region that was later called Makkah. When he visited with them in the Arabian wilderness, Abraham discovered the ancient sanctuary and restored it according to Allah's instructions. The Qur'an says:

> As Abraham and Ishmael built up the foundations of the House [they prayed], "Our Lord, accept [this] from us. You are the All Hearing, the All Knowing. Our Lord, make us devoted to You; make our descendants into a community devoted to You. Show us how to worship and accept our repentance, for You are the Ever Relenting, the Most Merciful. Our Lord, make a messenger of their own rise up from among them, to recite Your revelations to them, teach them the Scripture and wisdom, and purify them."[6]

Muslims believe that in the life of the Prophet Muhammad Abraham and Ishmael's prayer for a messenger to the Arabs has been answered.

Modern history is unable to verify these stories about the origins of the Kaaba. Because of the lack of literary records from the pre-Islamic period, critical historians cannot state with any certainty who initially built the Kaaba or even determine how long it has been in existence. There is no

---

6. Sura 2.127-129, in Haleem, trans., *Qur'an*, 15.

doubt, however, that the shrine long antedates Islam and that it has been repaired and rebuilt many times both before and after Muhammad.

Religious Practices

Like the religious culture of Confucius's China, pre-Islamic Arabian religion was decidedly this-worldly. The Arabs had little concept of an afterlife or a sense of individual destiny beyond this existence. The tribe, not the individual, was the highest value; immortality meant the endurance of the tribe. Religious concerns of the day were much more immediate: Which god will make it rain or bring us to water? Who can be relied upon to protect us from our enemies among the other tribes? What deity can cure our afflictions?

Ancient Arabian religion hardly constituted an orderly system of beliefs and practices. Like other ancient religions that are loosely described as "pagan," it had no creed or scripture or uniformly defined approaches to practice. It also had no developed priesthood or hierarchy. There were, however, individuals known as *kahanah*, who functioned as priests at local shrines. The *kahanah* performed sacrifices and offered prayers, as priests do, but they also functioned as soothsayers and oracles. They were able to fall into ecstatic trances and reveal divine communications through poems of rhyming couplets. The *kahanah* did not communicate directly with the gods but gained accessed to them through the jinn and other spirits. These poet-priests came from every social and economic stratum in Arabia, and included women as well as men. Through their ecstatic trances, the *kahanah* interpreted dreams, found lost animals, foretold the future, and settled arguments. Many Arabs believed that the clothing, hair, and saliva of the *kahanah* contained a potent curative power, and hence they were sought out for their healing skills. The *kahanah* also provided protection against the dreaded evil eye. The concept of the evil eye was—and still is—a widespread belief throughout the Middle East, the Mediterranean region, Africa, and South Asia. Those who fear the evil eye believe that envious looks from certain persons can have detrimental consequences for the person who is being envied. The Qur'an tells its listeners to "take refuge" from "the ill of the envious when he envies."[7] Various cultures have devised assorted ways of warding off the evil eye. The *kahanah* probably used amulets and spells to neutralize the effects of the evil eye. Although the Qur'an recognizes the phenomenon, Muslims are forbidden to use such charms and are advised to call upon Allah to avert the effects of the evil eye.

7. Sura 113.5, in Cleary, trans., *Qur'an*, 301.

Jews and Christians

Any description of the religious landscape of ancient Arabia would be incomplete without mention of Judaism and Christianity, both of which played important roles in the early history of Islam. Some scholars trace the Jewish presence in the peninsula to the Babylonian exile in the sixth century BCE, the beginning of the Jewish diaspora. It is likely that there were also other, and probably more significant, migrations after the Roman destruction of Jerusalem in 70 CE and the Bar Kokhba rebellion in the second century CE. By the time of Muhammad, the Jews had been almost completely assimilated into the culture of pre-Islamic Arabia. Throughout the peninsula, there were Jewish traders and nomads, Jewish agriculturalists and warriors. They adopted Arab names and Arab dress and spoke Arabic as their primary language. The religion they practiced was loosely based on traditional Jewish beliefs and customs, but they also participated in aspects of the popular religion of the Arab pagans, such as the use of magic, charms, and divination. There was even a Jewish counterpart to the Arabian *kahin* (the singular form of *kahanah*) known as the *kohen*, who also functioned as a priest and soothsayer. The words *kohen* and *kahin* are etymologically related.[8]

There were also some Arab tribes that practiced Christianity. In the Hijaz, the coastal region bordering the Red Sea, the majority of Christians were of the Nestorian sect, now known as the Assyrian Church of the East. The Nestorians believed that Jesus Christ existed as two separate persons, the man Jesus and the divine son of god, rather than as divine and human natures in one person. That divergence may seem to be theological hairsplitting, but it was enough to get the Nestorians condemned as heretics by the Roman Catholic Church. In Yemen, on the southern side of the peninsula, the Christians were Syrian Orthodox. In the sixth century CE, Christianity in the region of Najran in southwestern Arabia was prominent enough to have a bishop, monks, nuns, and priests. Najran was also ruled by a Jewish king.

Muhammad felt a great affinity for the Jews and Christians of ancient Arabia because of their devotion to Allah, whom he thought of as the same god described in the Tanakh and the New Testament. Arab Jews and Arab Christians both referred to their god as "Allah," that is, "the god." According to Qur'anic tradition, Muhammad was a *hanif*, a member of the remnant still devoted to the faith in one god established by Abraham and Ishmael.[9]

8. Interestingly, *kohen*, the word for "priest," is the basis of the popular Jewish surname Cohen.

9. Sura 10.104.

Thus the tradition asserts that throughout his life, Muhammad never followed his contemporaries in their polytheistic practices and their infatuation with divine images. He preferred instead to retreat to the hills for periods of quiet contemplation and prayer, apart from the din and clamor of the world below. It was on one of these retreats that he received a message from Allah that would profoundly change his life and forever alter the course of human history.

The Trustworthy One

The stories of Muhammad's birth and early life, like those of Confucius, the Buddha, and Jesus, portend his future greatness. Many of these stories, of course, have a legendary quality, telling of events that cannot be confirmed by modern historiography. But their significance concerns beliefs about the Prophet and his role in Islam that transcend mere factual details. They are told not to set forth historical information but to create a portrait of the individual who most embodies the spirit of Islam and whose very life offers to Muslims an unparalleled example of faith.

The Sources

Although many stories of his life cannot be verified according to the standards of modern history, there is sufficient material for constructing a reasonably sure account of the historical Muhammad. The most reliable source is the Qur'an, the holy book revealed to Muhammad over a period of twenty-three years. Although he is mentioned by name only four times in this scripture, the Qur'an offers many insights into his life and the issues with which he struggled as the Islamic community, or *ummah*, evolved. Of immense importance to the faith, but of less value for historical purposes, are the *hadith*, the reports about his sayings and vignettes of his life that were kept in oral tradition by his followers and written down over a century after his death. The actual historical value of this source is the subject of considerable debate in the contemporary scholarship on Muhammad. Some researchers claim that the traditions contained within the collections of *hadith* are all inventions of later Muslim writers, in the way most of the *Analects* of Confucius is believed to be the work of later Confucians. Other scholars maintain that many of the *hadith* contain a core of historical material even if many of them are spurious. Within Islam itself, particular collections of *hadith* are asserted to be valid in their entirety and are used as important supplements for understanding the Qur'an. Nevertheless, Muslims have never accepted all putative *hadith* as historically authentic. Because of the importance of *hadith* in Islam, some less-than-scrupulous individuals have even been known to create their own "traditions of the Prophet," such as the self-serving onion seller who amazingly "discovered" a *hadith* that promoted the benefits of buying onions.[10] As a consequence of such abuses, the tradition has insisted that only *hadith* that can be traced back to Muhammad through a trustworthy chain of transmission (*isnad*) can be accepted as legitimate. This safeguard has not been foolproof, however, since even links to reliable authorities can be and have been counterfeited. There are several major collections of *hadith*, the most important of which, at least for most Muslims, is called *Sahih Bukhari*, which was compiled by Muhammad al-Bukhari in the ninth century. Al-Bukhari whittled down over three hundred thousand *hadith* to a set of just over 2,600 that he regarded as authentic. The Sunnis, members of the largest branch of Islam, consider the nine volumes of the *Sahih Bukhari* to be the most important book next to the Qur'an itself and a principal guide to the life of Muhammad and the practice of the faith.

Historians also depend on the early biographies of the Prophet. Such biographies began to be written relatively early in Islam. There were at least two dozen texts written within three centuries of the Prophet's death that narrate all or part of his life story. The earliest biography comes from Ibn Ishaq, who composed his *Life of God's Messenger* about a century and a half after Muhammad's death. Ibn Ishaq reputedly relied on oral traditions that went back to the Prophet and his acquaintances. Original copies of Ibn Ishaq's biography no longer exist, but the biography has been transmitted through history in a version edited by Ibn Hisham in the ninth century. We are unable to know, however, just how accurately Ibn Hisham transmitted the original. And since there are no non-Muslim sources from near the start of Islam that mention Muhammad, there is no external confirmation or disconfirmation of Islamic interpretations of the Prophet's life. As they are with the study of our other sages, scholars are cautious about what facts and interpretations about Muhammad can be authenticated.

Birth and Childhood

Ibn Hisham reports that Ibn Ishaq determined that Muhammad came into the world on a Monday evening on the 12th day of the third month of the "year of the elephant." Because the Islamic calendar is based on the rhythms of the moon rather than the sun, it is hard to pinpoint the day and month of his birth on the Western solar-based calendar. The "year of the elephant,"

10. I am indebted to my colleague John Kaltner for making me aware of this story.

refers to a time in Arabian history when a ruler from the southern part of the peninsula marched on Makkah with a massive army and a white elephant, intent on destroying the Kaaba. But the elephant refused to enter the sacred precincts and simply knelt down, as if worshiping at the shrine. Unable to make the elephant move forward, the army was forced to return home unsuccessful. The year of the elephant is traditionally reckoned to correspond to the year 570 CE. But today, historians generally believe it occurred nearer to 560 CE. It is probably true that Muhammad was born in or around 570, but in not in the year of the elephant, as Ibn Ishaq maintained.

Like the stories about Confucius, the Buddha, and Jesus, the biographies of Muhammad ascribe to him a noble lineage. He was born in Makkah into the Banu Hashim clan, which was part of Arabia's leading tribe, the Quraysh. The Banu Hashim had been a highly respected family, especially among the other Quraysh. Although once very powerful, by the time of Muhammad's birth the clan had fallen on hard times and had begun to lose some of its earlier prestige.

Like stories of Confucius, the Buddha, and Jesus, legends suggest unusual circumstances surrounding Muhammad's conception. There are slightly different versions of the narrative, but the basic story involves Muhammad's father, Abdallah, his mother, Aminah, and another woman. One telling of the story has Abdallah on his way to consummate his newly arranged marriage with Aminah. En route, he is accosted by the other woman who tries to detour him into her own bed. Since it was his wedding day, after all, Abdallah declined the invitation, but promised to return on his way home the next day. He proceeded to Aminah's house and stayed the night, during which Muhammad was conceived. On his way back to his own home the next morning, he stopped by the residence of the woman who had waylaid him the day before to see if the invitation was still in effect. This time, the woman refused him, saying that earlier there had been a bright light blazing between Abdallah's eyes, but now it was gone. In some versions, the woman goes on to interpret the light as a sign of the coming of the Last Prophet. When she notices the light has disappeared from Abdallah's face, she realizes that another woman has taken the honor of conceiving the new messenger. The major difference among the variant narratives is the other woman's identity. In one, she is unnamed; in another, she is Abdallah's chief wife; in a third, she is the sister of Waraqa ibn Nawfal, a monotheistic *hanif* who later figures prominently in Muhammad's story. Regardless of who she was, the narrative's purpose is clear: to suggest divine intention in Muhammad's birth, an important theme in the accounts of Jesus's birth as well. But notice how strikingly these stories contrast in their views on sexuality!

Muhammad never knew his father and was technically considered an orphan at birth. Abdallah died while on a trip to Yathrib—later known as Madinah—when Muhammad's mother Aminah was two months pregnant. Her pregnancy, according to Ibn Ishaq, was accompanied by numerous "strange signs" and the birth was remarkably easy (as was the Buddha's, according to legend). After seeing a vision that announced the child would be the master of his people, Aminah gave her son the name Muhammad, which means "he who is worthy of praise." Ibn Ishaq claims Muhammad was a very unusual name at the time, although today it is one of the most popular names in the world.[11] In this same vision, Aminah was also instructed to place the infant under the protection of Allah to shield him from the evil eye. His paternal grandfather, Abd al-Muttalib, was overjoyed at the birth and recalled an oracle from a *kahin* who had told him that one his descendants would rule the world. Immediately, he took the baby to the Kaaba as an act of gratitude.

As was the custom in Makkah at the time, children were entrusted to Bedouin families, who would raise them in the nearby desert, acquainting them with nomadic life, before returning them at a later age to their parents in the city. Desert life, as we have noted, was difficult and precarious, and this practice was intended to accustom children to face the rigors of Arabian life. Muhammad stayed with his Bedouin family for four years before he was returned to Aminah. Halimah, his Bedouin foster mother, reported unusual occurrences that led her to believe that Muhammad was a special child. On one occasion, she related how her own son witnessed two men in white laying the four-year-old Muhammad on the ground, splitting open his chest, and removing something from inside it. Muhammad himself confirmed the story. Fearing for his life, Halimah returned the boy to his mother in Makkah. Interestingly, Aminah was not surprised by the story and in fact recounted similar events. Years later, Muhammad says that the men had removed a black clot from his heart in an act of spiritual cleansing.

Muhammad remained with his mother for only two years. When he was six, Aminah died, leaving the child bereft of both parents. His grandfather, Abd al-Muttalib, who was now eighty, immediately brought his grandson into his own household, but then two years later, Abd al-Muttalib himself died. But before he did, Muhammad's grandfather charged his son Abu Talib—Muhammad's uncle—to continue to raise and care for the boy. Apparently, Abu Talib admirably discharged his responsibilities as a foster

11. "List of Most Popular Given Names." *Wikipedia.* https://en.wikipedia.org/wiki/List_of_most_popular_given_names/.

father. Muhammad would later reflect fondly on the care he received from his uncle and the uncle's wife, Fatimah.

These early experiences seem to have decisively shaped Muhammad's outlook on life. His childhood acquaintance with poverty, vulnerability, and loss made him familiar with the tenuous nature of life and, in adulthood, would heighten his sensitivity to the weaker members of society, especially the parentless, the poor, and women. In one of the shortest chapters of the Qur'an, Allah pointedly reminds the Prophet of these childhood experiences and draws a moral that Muhammad took to heart:

> Did God not find you an orphan and give you shelter and care?
> And He found you wandering and gave you guidance. And He
> found you in need, and made you independent. Therefore, do
> not treat the orphan with harshness, Nor repulse the one in
> need; But the bounty of the Lord—rehearse and proclaim![12]

At a time when children most need to feel the secure presence of the adults in their lives, the young Muhammad had to negotiate a world in which his caretakers were frequently changing. This early experience may have kindled within him a deep longing for a source of constancy beyond his ever-shifting circumstances.

His time among nomads was also an important element in shaping Muhammad's character. Bedouin culture was steeped in a rich oral tradition, and the members of the nomadic tribes were renowned as poets and master storytellers. No doubt Muhammad's facility with language was refined by his exposure to this tradition and its bearers. In later life, his mastery of spoken Arabic would be put to use in his struggles to articulate in words the revelations he received, many of which came to him through intense experiences barely on the edge of language.

Desert life seems also to have influenced his relationship with the natural world. Like Jesus and the Buddha, Muhammad spent long periods alone in nature, and it was during these times that he often received the revelations that would comprise the Qur'an. For Muhammad, nature was also a revelation of another sort. He viewed nature as a cipher of the divine. The Qur'an speaks of the created order as rich with the marks of the creator for those perceptive enough to recognize them:

12. Sura 93:6-11, in Ali, trans., *Holy Qur'an*, http://wikilivres.ca/wiki/The_Holy_ Qur%27an/Ad-Dhuha. I have modernized the archaic language in the translation.

> He has made subject to you the Night and the Day; the sun and
> the moon; and the stars are in subjection by His Command:
> [truly] in this are Signs for [ones] who are wise.[13]

Nature appears to have taught Muhammad the value of silent contemplation and the observation of objects and events to understand their deeper
significance. Later in his young life, Muhammad became a shepherd tending flocks just outside Makkah, where his skills of mindfulness and discernment were further cultivated.

Beyond assumptions we might make about his experience with his
Bedouin foster family, we know virtually nothing about his formal education—or even if he received a formal education. Islamic tradition insists that
Muhammad was unable to read or write but possessed a fine memory and
excellent speaking skills. Some Western scholars, however, question this
tradition and assert that Muhammad probably had a basic literacy, since he
would need rudimentary skills in reading and writing in his adult work as
a trader.[14]

Adolescence

As an adolescent, Muhammad experienced two events that are often recounted to foreshadow his call to be the Last Prophet to humanity. At age
twelve, Muhammad accompanied his uncle Abu Talib on a caravan to Syria.
As it approached the ancient town of Busra, about a hundred miles south of
Damascus, the caravan was observed by a Christian hermit named Bahira,
who saw what appeared to be a cloud hovering over the procession and
protecting it from the sun. Intrigued, he invited the members of the caravan
to stop for a meal, and they accepted. Bahira was inexplicably drawn to the
boy Muhammad and took him aside to get to know him better. After asking about his family and his early experiences in life, Bahira asked to see
his back. Muhammad complied with the request. Bahira reported that he
saw a growth of skin between the boy's shoulder blades, which the monk
interpreted as "the seal of prophethood." Like the stories about the physical
marks discovered on Prince Siddhattha, this legend suggests that signs of
Muhammad's spiritual achievements were inscribed on his very body.

Another account from this stage in Muhammad's life concerns his at-
tendance at the negotiation of an important tribal alliance, around the year
590 CE. As we noted previously, the tribal arrangements characteristic of

---

13. Sura 16:12. Ali, http://wikilivres.ca/wiki/The_Holy_Qur%27an/An-Nahl.
14. E.g., Maxime Rodinson. See Rodinson, *Muhammad*.

pre-Islamic Arabia were taking their toll on the well-being of Arabian society. Groups appeared locked in a wearisome cycle of intertribal warfare and constantly reconfiguring social alliances. In an effort to curtail the violence and lack of order, the chief of one prominent tribe, the forward-thinking Abdallah ibn Ja'dan, summoned all interested parties to meet for the purpose of establishing a covenant of justice that would transcend tribal affiliations. The result of that meeting was an agreement known as the Alliance of the Virtuous. In it, the participating tribes committed themselves to respect universal principles of fairness and to intervene collectively to establish justice in intertribal disputes. The pact was written and placed inside the Kaaba to signify its sacred status and to put it under the protection of the gods. Today, the United Nations considers the Alliance of the Virtuous one of the first human rights statements and one of the antecedents for its own Universal Declaration of Human Rights.[15] The event made a lasting impression on the young Muhammad. In later life, he favorably recalled the agreement, not only because he valued its fundamental principles of fairness and equity, but also because it acknowledged the possibility of a system of ethics that all persons, regardless of ethnic or religious affiliations, could affirm.

Young Adulthood and Marriage

The virtues of fairness and honesty were to guide Muhammad throughout his life. As he entered young adulthood, he became widely known for these qualities. Those who knew him called him the "Trustworthy One." A well-known story about this time in his life is often told to illustrate how profoundly he embodied these traits. When he was a young man, the Quraysh tribe, the caretakers of the Kaaba, decided to refurbish the sacred shrine by razing it to its foundations and reconstructing its walls. As the construction was taking place, the time came to reset the holy Black Stone that had formed part of one of the exterior walls. The Black Stone had long been an important feature of the Kaaba and was believed by many to have fallen from heaven in the days of Adam and Eve. Indeed, many scholars today believe the stone is a meteorite. During their circumambulations, pilgrims would stop and kiss the stone, which was placed in the wall about five feet above ground. Legends say the stone was originally a brilliant white but over the years turned black because it absorbed the sins of humanity. When it was time to secure the Black Stone in the newly constructed wall, a dispute arose among the clans as to which would have the honor to put it back

15. United Nations Public Information Office, of Public Information, *Universal Declaration of Human Rights*, http://www.un.org/en/universal-declaration-human-rights/.

in place. The conflict was about to erupt into violence when Muhammad entered the precincts and was asked to settle the quarrel. After listening to the arguments of the clans, he asked for a cloth, put the stone upon it, and invited all the clan chiefs to carry the stone together and lift it in place by holding the edges of the fabric. In this way, the honor of each clan was upheld and all parties were satisfied.

As a young adult, Muhammad had left his job as a shepherd to work as a trader. His reputation for honesty had attracted the attention of one of the prominent caravan owners in Makkah, a wealthy widow named Khadija bint Khuwaylid, one of his distant relatives. According to tradition, Khadija was forty when, at the recommendation of Abu Talib and others, she hired the twenty-five-year-old Muhammad to lead her caravan to Syria. Although Muhammad had little business experience, his honesty and skill in fair dealing served him well, and he returned to Makkah with twice the profits Khadija had expected. Khadija was so pleased with Muhammad's accomplishment that she asked him to accompany a second caravan to Yemen the following winter.

Over time, Muhammad continued to impress her. Her interests in him became more than simply commercial in nature, and, eventually, she sought to marry him. Marriage was not an easy decision for her to make. Khadija had been married twice, and each time lost her husband during the intertribal wars. Until she met Muhammad, she had no intention of marrying a third time, although she had received proposals from many highly respected men throughout the peninsula. That she overcame this reluctance and set aside the offers of more prominent men attests to the great impression Muhammad made on her. She sent a friend as an emissary to Muhammad to see what he thought about marriage in general and Khadija in particular. Muhammad told the friend that he was too poor to contemplate marriage. When she mentioned Khadija's name, Muhammad indicated he was very interested, but again, he could not imagine how he could even consider such a relationship, given his lowly status. Without telling him that she had been sent by Khadija herself, the emissary assured Muhammad that she would discreetly act on his behalf. When Khadija was informed of Muhammad's openness to marriage, she invited him to her home and proposed. And Muhammad accepted. After consulting their uncles about the propriety of the arrangement, the two were married.

They lived together as husband and wife for approximately twenty-five years, until her death. Apparently, their marriage was one of great love and devotion. During his time with Khadija, Muhammad took no other wife. She became his confidante and was the first to embrace Islam when he began to receive revelations from Allah. After her death, he took many other wives, but he always remembered Khadija with great affection and wistfulness, which occasionally stirred up no small resentment among his newer wives.

According to the Sunni sources, Muhammad and Khadija had six children together, four daughters[16] and two sons.[17] Both sons, however, died early in their lives. Because of the number of children they had, some scholars have questioned whether Khadija was actually forty at the time of her marriage to Muhammad, as tradition maintains. Some have suggested that she may have been closer to thirty. Sources from the Shi'a branch contend that Khadija and Muhammad had only one daughter, Fatimah (named for Muhammad's aunt), and that the other three were nieces or orphans whom they adopted. If that were the case, then the age of forty seems less problematic. In any event, there is no doubt that Khadija was many years older than the Prophet.

The sources from all traditions indicate that Muhammad greatly enjoyed family life and found much fulfillment as a husband and a father. Not only did he father at least one child of his own, he also adopted several others, including his young cousin Ali, whose father—Muhammad's uncle, Abu Talib—was suffering financial difficulties. When he was only ten, according to some sources, Ali was the first male to embrace Islam. Later, Ali became Muhammad's son-in-law when he married Fatimah, Muhammad's daughter by Khadija.[18] Muhammad also adopted a young man named Zayd, whom Khadija had given to him as a slave. Muhammad gave Zayd his freedom and accepted him as a son.

As Muhammad neared middle age, his stature as a devoted family man, an honest merchant, and an individual with sound judgment increased. By the time he was thirty-five, many supposed that he would assume leadership of the Banu Hashim. But at the time, Muhammad had little interest in civic affairs. He preferred to spend his time with his family and in occasional retreats into the wilderness surrounding Makkah, where he could enjoy his solitude and pray. But during one of these desert excursions, Muhammad had an experience that would forcefully thrust his life in a new direction and ultimately lead him to the place where evading leadership was no longer an option.

16. Their names were Zaynab, Ruqayya, Fatima, and Umm Kulthum.

17. Their names were Qasim and Abdallah.

18. Sunni Muslims consider 'Ali as the fourth and final Rightly Guided Caliph, while Shī'a Muslims regard 'Ali as the first Imam and consider him and his descendants as the rightful successors to Muhammad. This dispute about Ali's status split the Muslim community into the Sunni and Shī'a branches.

"I am Only a Messenger"

Muhammad was not certain about what was happening to him when he began to receive the revelations that became the Qur'an. According to the traditional account, they started in the month of Ramadan in the year 610 CE, when Muhammad was forty, during one of his regular retreats to the wilderness for prayer and solitude. He was abruptly awakened from his sleep in a small cave on one of the mountains[19] surrounding Makkah by what seemed to be an overwhelming presence. Then he heard the command, "Read!" When he responded that he could not read, he felt as if he were being violently squeezed to the point that he could barely breathe. When the force bearing down on him subsided, the voice again commanded him to read; again he said he was unable; again, he felt himself being crushed. This exchange was repeated for a third time, after which Muhammad was told:

> Read, in the name of your Lord, who created, created the human from a clot of blood. Read, and your Lord is most generous, who taught the use of the pen. He teaches man what he never knew.[20]

Frightened for his life and not knowing what else to do, Muhammad began to repeat the words he heard. He later reported that he thought he was being possessed by a jinni and was becoming a *kahin*, one of the entranced pagan soothsayers. One biographer even suggests that the thought of becoming a *kahin* filled Muhammad with such despair that he attempted to throw himself from the mountaintop but was prevented from doing so by the sight of an angel standing on the horizon. Instinctively, he turned and rushed home to Khadija. Trembling, he begged her, "Cover me, cover me!" and she wrapped him with a cloak and held him until he regained his composure. After Muhammad told her of the experience, Khadija tried to assure him that he was not possessed. From the very moment she heard his story, Khadija was confident that the voice he heard spoke words from god.[21]

Shortly after Muhammad's return, Khadija went to see her cousin Waraqa bin Nawfal, an older and much revered *hanif*. Some accounts say she went alone; others say Muhammad accompanied her. In any event, when Waraqa was told of the experience, he replied: "This is 'Namus,' the angel entrusted with divine secrets whom Allah sent to Moses." Waraqa interpreted the incident as a sign that Muhammad was being called as a

---

19. *Jabal an-Nur*, Mountain of Light, also known as Mt. Hira.

20. Sura 96:1–5, my rendering.

21. *Sahih Bukhari*, Vol. 1, Book 1, Number 3. http://www.sahih-bukhari.com/Pages/Bukhari_1_01.php

prophet to the Arabs. At the Kaaba, Waraqa later told Muhammad that he would suffer great hostility from the Makkans, a prediction that in fact came to pass.[22] A prophet, as Jesus said, is never welcome in his own hometown.

Eventually, Muhammad would accept Waraqa's conviction that Allah had called him to be a prophet. But Muhammad struggled with the idea for a long time before he was able to accept it. Meanwhile, he told no one else about the occurrence on the mountain. He received a few other revelations shortly afterward, but no one knows precisely how many. Then, suddenly, they stopped. It would be about two years before Muhammad heard the voice of the angel again. This was a period of grave self-doubt and even suicidal despair. He interpreted the abrupt absence of revelations as an indication that Allah had decided he was unworthy to receive the divine message. At last, he heard the voice speak words of reassurance that dispelled his uncertainty:

> By the glorious morning light,
> And by the night when it is calm,
> Your guardian Lord has not forsaken you, nor is he displeased:
> hereafter will be better for you than what has been before.
> Soon your guardian Lord will give you what shall make you
>   content.[23]

Thenceforth, Muhammad had no uncertainties about the source of his revelations or his mission. The revelations continued sporadically over the next two decades and were usually occasioned by specific situations in his life that required divine insight.

Muhammad had well over one hundred such experiences, although we are unsure of the exact number. The voice did not always speak with the clarity and distinctness of the first revelation in the cave. In one of the *hadith*, Muhammad describes the nature of the revelations: "Sometimes," he said, "it comes to me like the reverberations of a bell, and those are the hardest on me; the reverberations stop when I am aware of their message. And sometimes the Angel takes the form of a man and speaks to me, and I am aware of what he says."[24] The Qur'an identifies this angel as Gabriel (Jibril). As Muhammad's description indicates, sometimes the aural experiences were accompanied by a visual perception of Gabriel, but very often the revelations came as indistinct and overpowering sensations that required

22. Ibid.

23. Sura 93:1-5 in Cleary, trans., *Qur'an*, 298. I have edited the translation slightly.

24. *Sahih Bukhari*, Vol. 1, Book 3, in Lings, *Muhammad*, 2nd ed. I have modernized the archaic language.

great effort to render into language. In these cases, the process of articulating the revelation was not unlike the way a poet might struggle to find just the right words to give expression to deep feelings that lie below the surface of consciousness. One of the Qur'anic passages reporting an early revelation admonishes Muhammad to attend carefully to the complete depth of the experience and allow the words to come to expression in their own good time.[25] He was once quoted as saying, "Never once did I receive a revelation without thinking that my soul had been torn away from me."[26] Even today, some Muslims think there is a bit of Muhammad's soul in the Qur'an. Thus, Muhammad occasionally experienced the divine voice as coming from without and occasionally as coming from within. But either way, Muhammad always identified the source of the revelation as a reality beyond his individual self.

In the past, many scholars from outside Islam have felt compelled to provide a naturalistic explanation of Muhammad's revelations. One such theory suggests that Muhammad suffered from epilepsy,[27] which would account for the trancelike states and occasional loss of consciousness he underwent during these moments of inspiration. Other analysts contend that he lapsed into states of greater sensitivity to the contents of his unconscious mind such as occurs during dreaming.[28] Both hypotheses imply that the source of the revelations was none other than his own mind, but neither necessarily means that Muhammad was disingenuous in claiming that the revelations came from outside him. In other words, as the argument goes, Muhammad may have genuinely believed the words of revelation were from Gabriel even if they originated by means of his own mental processes. Considering the intense opposition he later faced, it is difficult to believe that Muhammad would have been willing to risk his life—and the lives of others close to him—for the sake of something he knew to be a sham.

A naturalistic explanation for Muhammad's experiences, however, need not be incompatible with the traditional Muslim conviction that Allah is the ultimate author of the revelations. There is no reason why Allah could not work by means of epileptic seizures or the unconscious mind as media through which to communicate. In *Saint Joan*, George Bernard Shaw's play about the life of Joan of Arc, the heroine tries to persuade Robert de Baudricourt to lend her his men so she might raise a siege against Orléans. When

25. Sura 75:16-18.

26. Quoted in Rodinson, *Muhammad*, 74.

27. Taxil, *Traicte de l'Epilepsie*, Livre I, Chapitre 15. http://asklepios.chez.com/taxil/Livre1_Chap15.htm

28. Watt, *Muhammad*, 238.

Robert asks her about the source of this plan, she tells him: "I hear voices telling me what to do. They come from God." Robert replies: "They come from your imagination." "Of course," responds Joan. "That is how the messages of God come to us."[29] It is a mistake to assume that tracing the source of an idea to the human mind rules out the possibility of divine inspiration.

Just as some have tried to discount the authenticity of Muhammad's revelations by offering a purely naturalistic explanation, others have sought to discredit them by noting their similarity to the principles and precepts of other religions. There is no doubt that many of the revelations Muhammad articulated bear strong resemblances to stories and images in the Bible. As one scholar puts it, there was "nothing new" about the revelations.[30] And, indeed, Muhammad never claimed novelty for his message. To the contrary, he insisted the message was ancient, as old as Adam, humanity's first prophet. The novelty was the messenger. God had at last sent a prophet to the Arabs. In the Islamic view, the sanctity of Muhammad's revelations had less to do with the manner in which he received them and more with the fact that millions found—and continue to find—a living truth in them. Regardless of the mode of reception or the originality of its ideas and values, the Qur'an appeared to provide a framework for resolving many of the deep social tensions of Arabian society in Muhammad's day. In so doing, the revelations enabled the Arabs to break through to a new level of consciousness and establish a more just and equitable society.

Whenever Muhammad received a revelation, he committed the words to memory and recited them to his companions later. Several of these companions would also memorize them. Each year, during the month of Ramadan, he would repeat each of the revelations that he had received to that point and, in that way, fixed them in an oral tradition. Muslims believe that Muhammad did not alter the revelations by a single word. Islamic tradition maintains that some of the revelations were preserved in writing during the Prophet's lifetime, but it was only after his death that they were completely transcribed and put together as a physical book. The full text in the form it now exists may have been completed as early as twenty years after Muhammad's death, although some scholars argue for a later date, sometimes as late as the tenth century. The book comprises 114 chapters, or suras, of over six thousand verses. The suras are not placed in the order in which they were received by the Prophet but generally by length, from the longest to the shortest, a manner specified by Gabriel to reflect the order of the Qur'an as

29. Shaw, *Saint Joan*, Scene 1, http://faculty.smu.edu/bwheeler/joan_of_arc/olr/07_saintjoan_gbshaw.pdf, 35-36.

30. Armstrong, *Muhammad*, 86.

it exists in heaven. The length of the complete Qur'an is comparable to that of the New Testament.

Although the Qur'an is similar to the New Testament in size, the texts do not compare in terms of their function as scripture. In Christianity, the Bible is generally regarded as the written *witness* to god's revelation, which for Christians is Jesus himself. Traditionally, Christianity has asserted that Jesus is the divine Word made manifest; the Bible serves as a testament to that revelation. In Islam, the Qur'an serves the role that Jesus does in Christianity. The Qur'an is the divine Word made manifest, not as a human being but as a book. Yet, the Qur'an is not just a book in the sense of a written text; more precisely, it is an oral and aural book. The words of the Qur'an are most meaningful in spoken form. Some Muslims use a separate term— *Mushaf*—to designate the Qur'an in its textual form. "Al-Qur'an" literally means the recitation, and it is in spoken Arabic, Muslims believe, that the rich significance and beauty of the Qur'an is most fully conveyed. Indeed, a translation of the Qur'an into any language other than Arabic is not truly the Qur'an. Much of the transformative power of the book is surely attributable to the evocative quality of the words as they are chanted in a way that borders on music. The traditions tell of many individuals who converted to Muhammad's faith upon merely hearing the Qur'an recited. Umar ibn al-Khattab, whom some biographers say planned to kill the Prophet, embraced Islam when he heard a recitation of the revelations. "When I heard the Qur'an," he said, "my heart was softened and I wept, and Islam entered into me."[31] Even for those who are not proficient in Arabic, the verses of the Qur'an seem to touch a resonant chord within their hearts and lift them to a transcendent world. Anyone who appreciates the beauty of Gregorian chant may understand how the ethereal recitation of words—even in a foreign tongue—can move the spirit.[32]

After coming to terms with the trauma of the first revelations, and as the revelations began again following the period of silence, Muhammad became more willing to share the substance of the message with his family and friends. Khadija, as we have noted earlier, readily accepted his experiences as genuine communications from Allah. Now others began to embrace Islam as the Prophet quietly taught his message to those closest to him. His cousin and foster son, Ali, was among the first new converts,

31. Guillaume, trans., *Life of Muhammad*, 158.

32. In our time, the popularity of Henryk Górecki's Third Symphony may provide an analogue to this response to the recited Qur'an. Górecki speculated that "perhaps people find something they need in this piece of music . . . Somehow I hit the right note, something they were missing. Something, somewhere had been lost to them. I feel that I instinctively knew what they needed" (Steinberg, *Symphony*, 171).

as was Abu Bakr, one of Muhammad's longtime friends. But to his great disappointment, Muhammad's beloved uncle, Abu Talib, and other senior members of his clan were not willing to relinquish the old traditions to subscribe to Muhammad's monotheism. Nevertheless, Abu Talib remained Muhammad's protector, affording him much-needed security as the disenchantment with the Prophet's message grew, just as Waraqa predicted. Initially, the movement remained small. Over the next three years, the young Muslim community added only thirty to forty new members. Those who professed Islam were men and women from all clans and all social ranks. Not surprisingly, the message Muhammad spoke had a special appeal to the poor and the young, a fact that provoked more than a little derision from the more powerful members of the tribe.

As the hostility toward Muhammad increased, he received word from Gabriel that he should make the message of Islam more public.[33] Accordingly, he gathered together the heads of the clans and spoke to them from the top of a hill. He began with a rhetorical question: "If I were to tell you that down in this valley armed horsemen are advancing to attack us, would you believe me?" "Certainly," they answered. "You are the Trustworthy One, and you do not tell lies." Having established his credibility, Muhammad then proceeded to speak: "Then believe me when I tell you that I have come to warn you of violent torments. God has called me to admonish you to believe in the oneness of god. I am like the one who sees the enemy approaching and runs to tell his people, Beware! Beware!" The clan leaders were not impressed by Muhammad's lesson. His own uncle, Abu Lahab, was the first to ridicule Muhammad: "This is why you have gathered us together?" He immediately turned his back and walked away along with the rest of the assembly. The chiefs instantly grasped the significance of Muhammad's message and foresaw how it threatened tribal traditions as well as their own power and livelihood. From that moment, Muhammad began to speak more openly and forcefully.

Initially, it seems, Muhammad understood his mission in very modest terms. He was not being called to create a new religion, to be a new savior, or even to preach a universal message to the world. Rather, he regarded himself as one who has simply come to warn the inhabitants of Makkah of the dangers of deviating from the ideals of a just society. In this respect, he considered himself as just another of the 124,000 prophets that Allah had sent to the various peoples of humanity, all of whom had preached the oneness of god and his demands for justice and compassion. Eventually, Muhammad came to understand that he had been called to be not simply a

33. Sura 26:214.

nabi—an ordinary prophet—but a *rasul*—a messenger, the bearer of a major revelation, the revelation that would be humanity's last. Acknowledging his status as Allah's messenger would also become part of the *shahadah*, the Muslim profession of faith: "I bear witness that there is no god but Allah and that Muhammad is His Messenger."

The early revelations stressed the importance taking care of the poor and the orphaned and praised the virtues of simple living and almsgiving. By all accounts, Muhammad himself carefully abided by these values. Even after he became a man of great power, he continued to live frugally. His companions urged him to wear fine ceremonial robes befitting the messenger of Allah, but Muhammad continued to wear the plain, coarsely woven cloth of the common folk. Likewise, his home was spartan and often lacking in food because he gave away much of it to those who were hungry. Any gifts he received were promptly given to someone else. Even as his understanding of his calling evolved, Muhammad never departed from the basic message of the earliest revelations: a theology grounded in the oneness of the divine and an ethical vision of a just society based on the principle of human equality.

As the Prophet received new communications from Gabriel, the revelations began to speak increasingly of a Last Day, at which time the dead would be resurrected and all souls would be judged according to their deeds during life. This new eschatological dimension of Muhammad's message further alienated the Makkans. Resurrection was a novel idea to the Arabs. Traditional Arabian paganism made little allowance for an afterlife. The proposition that decomposed corpses would somehow arise from their graves struck the Makkans as absurd. The concept of a final judgment, furthermore, meant that *individuals* would be called to account before god; one's communal associations would mean nothing on that day. At the resurrection, the clan or the tribe could provide no protection; the person alone would be held responsible for his or her behavior. Thus, Muhammad's belief in the end time seemed merely an attempt to disrupt old traditions and replace them with an idea that made little sense to his contemporaries. It was to answer this skepticism that one of the early revelations seemed to be intended:

> Can man not see that We created him from a drop of fluid?
> Yet—lo and behold!—he disputes openly, producing arguments
> against Us, forgetting his own creation. He says, "Who can give
> life back to bones after they have decayed?" Say, "He who cre-
> ated them in the first place will give them life again: He has full
> knowledge of every act of creation. It is He who produces fire

for you out of the green tree—lo and behold!—and from this
you kindle fire. Is He who created the heavens and earth not
able to create the likes of these people? Of course He is! He is the
All Knowing Creator: when He wills something to be, His way
is to say, 'Be'—and it is! So glory be to Him in whose Hand lies
control over all things. It is to Him that you will all be brought
back."[34]

The deity who creates life from a drop of liquid can surely re-create it from
the dust it becomes after death.

Despite the rejection and ridicule the Prophet endured from the older
and more powerful Makkans, his movement eventually began to enjoy great
success. Within five or six years after the first revelation on the Mountain of
Light, it almost appeared as if Muhammad would succeed at bringing the
Quraysh to adopt his religious point of view. But apparently, some of the
Makkans who had become attracted to the message of Islam misunderstood
the stringency of Muhammad's monotheism. They had assumed that they
could continue to worship at the shrines of al-Lat, al-Uzza, and Manat—
the "Three Daughters of Allah"—while recognizing the supremacy of Allah and obeying his demands for social justice. When Muhammad made
it clear that Islam precluded the worship of these goddesses (and all other
gods), many of his recent converts renounced the faith and reverted to their
former paganism, which, in fact, they never actually left. It was one thing
merely to include Allah in everyday religious practice; but it was quite another thing to *reject* the other gods who had been revered by the community
for so long. Muhammad's denunciation of the goddesses exacerbated the
Makkans' disenchantment with the Prophet and his radical theology, which
they considered tantamount to atheism.

At last, the most powerful members of the Quraysh sent representatives to Muhammad's uncle Abu Talib, asking him to relinquish his protection of the Prophet, which would have left Muhammad easy prey for anyone
who wished to kill him. Abu Talib was caught in a dilemma. He certainly
did not want to invite the wrath of the other clans, but neither did he want
to expose his nephew to such peril. When Abu Talib asked Muhammad
to desist for both their sakes, Muhammad tearfully replied that he could
not do that and would sooner die. Abu Talib then had a change of heart
and told Muhammad to speak as his conscience demanded, for the uncle
would never abandon his nephew. When Abu Talib refused to withdraw
his protection, the clan chiefs tried another tack. They sent another delegation to Muhammad himself and offered him money, political status, and

34. Sura 36:77-83 in Haleem, trans., *Qur'an*, 284.

material goods in exchange for his silence. The Prophet, of course, refused the offer and announced his willingness to accept the consequences of his refusal. This episode in Muhammad's life recalls similar events in the lives of the Buddha and Jesus, each of whom also withstood attempts to be lured away from his spiritual purposes with the enticements of worldly wealth and power.

When Muhammad proved impervious to bribery, the leaders of the clans resorted to insult and ridicule. They said he was possessed by a jinni and called him a homewrecker because he set children against parents, husbands against wives. His fellow Makkans began to ask him to perform miracles and provide them with proof of his claims. Some did this to mock him, others because they were half serious. Muhammad's response was simple: "I am only a messenger." Threats, bribes, and humiliation all proved ineffective.

While Muhammad enjoyed his uncle's protection, not all members of the Muslim community had the luxury of such security from a powerful clan leader. A great number of Muhammad's followers were down-and-outers, including many slaves. When those opposing the Prophet were unable to deter *him*, they began to persecute his followers. The slaves and the poor were most vulnerable, and they began to suffer greatly. Finally, a husband and wife were tortured and killed for refusing to renounce their faith. Islam had its first martyrs, and Muhammad began to seek a way to protect those who regarded him as Allah's messenger. The situation was becoming dire.

The Road to Madinah

The tribe and clan chiefs of Makkah had many reasons to want Muhammad silenced. As custodians of the Kaaba, the Quraysh had a vested interest in the yearly pilgrimage that brought thousands of Arabs from throughout the peninsula to worship their gods at the sacred shrine. If Muhammad were to persuade the Makkans to worship Allah alone and reject the other gods, then surely the profit and prestige gained from the pilgrimage would suffer immensely. Yet, commerce was not the only thing at risk. Muhammad's success could quite possibly bring down the wrath of the other deities. To be sure, Muhammad might be correct in proclaiming that Allah was the one and only god, but what if he was wrong? Dare the Makkans take that chance? When Rome was sacked in 410 CE by the Visigoths, many argued that the city's defeat was a punishment from the Roman gods who had been officially abandoned in favor of the god of Christianity. The Makkan leaders were probably unaware of this bit of Roman history, but they were certainly acquainted with the principle involved. Worship of the gods was not merely an individual's affair; the welfare of the entire community depended on the propitiation of the patron deities. Finally, the ethical demands of Muhammad's message were deeply unsettling and threatening to the ancient Arabian way of life. The revelations Muhammad received disrupted the traditional ways of viewing slaves, women, and other marginalized persons, ultimately challenging the whole tribal system. Any one of these reasons might have been sufficient for the Makkans to seek to put an end to the Prophet's proclamations or even his life. But since he was convinced of the authenticity of his message and was under the protection of his powerful uncle, neither prospect seemed likely. The Makkan leadership therefore turned to harassing, torturing, and even killing the members of Muhammad's new community of Muslims, the *ummah*. Muhammad needed to find a way to provide some security for his fledgling community.

His first effort to protect the Muslims was to send about a hundred of them to Abyssinia—present-day Ethiopia—to seek refuge with the Christian king who reigned there. Muhammad had hoped that the Abyssinian monarch, the negus, would be receptive to the Muslim exiles since they professed faith in the same god that the Christians worshiped and held the Christian messiah in high regard, considering him the greatest messenger next to Muhammad himself. Indeed, the negus welcomed the Muslims, and even refused to extradite them when the Makkan leaders sent a delegation to bring them back to Arabia. The king had been deeply moved by the beauty of the chanted Qur'an and the Muslims' affirmation of the virginal conception of Jesus. Later, it was said, the negus himself converted to Islam and maintained close ties with the Prophet. The Muslim exiles remained in Abyssinia for fifteen years until they rejoined Muhammad in Arabia under more favorable conditions.

But Muhammad remained in Makkah, and his teachings continued to frustrate the civic leaders, so they resorted to new measures. For three years, they imposed a boycott on the Banu Hashim, the Prophet's clan. During this time, other members of the Quraysh tribe were prohibited from having contact with the clan, engaging in trade relations with it, or negotiating marriages for their sons and daughters with the children of the Hashemites. The ban caused great suffering for the clan, but it was finally lifted in 619 CE when it became apparent that the sanctions were not having their intended effect. The end of the boycott meant a slight improvement in conditions for the Muslim community generally, but it also marked the start of what Muhammad called his Year of Sorrow. During that year, both Khadija and Abu Talib died. His wife had been the first to believe in him when he began to receive his revelations, and his uncle had been his steadfast guardian, even though Abu Talib never embraced Islam. Both had furnished Muhammad with immense encouragement during times of self-doubt and danger. He grieved their deaths profoundly.

The Night Journey

About this time in his life, Muhammad had an unusual experience, later known as the Night Journey. The Qur'an refers to this event only obliquely: "Glory to Him who made His servant travel by night from the sacred place of worship to the furthest place of worship [the Furthest Mosque], whose surroundings We have blessed, to show him some of Our signs."[35] The details are provided by the *hadith* and the Prophet's early biographers. According to these extra-Qur'anic traditions, late one night, while asleep near the Kaaba after a vigil of prayer, Muhammad was awakened by Gabriel and taken to a creature called the Buraq, a milk-white horse with wings, similar to Pegasus in Greek mythology, but smaller. Muhammad mounted the Buraq and flew, alongside Gabriel, to Jerusalem, the "Furthest Mosque." There he met with Abraham, Moses, Jesus, and other great prophets and prayed with them at the site where the Second Temple had stood. Afterwards, Gabriel escorted him to the heavens where he was given a vision of paradise and hell and received instructions to enjoin the Muslims to pray five times a day rather than three times a day, as had been their custom to that point. At that time, it was also customary for the Muslims to face Jerusalem when they prayed. A few years later, Muhammad received instructions to face the Kaaba in Makkah, to distinguish Islam from Judaism.

Nevertheless, Jerusalem remained a sacred place for the Muslims. In 691, the Umayyad Caliphate completed construction of a shrine on the site where Muhammad was believed to have met his predecessors. This shrine, which is now known as the Dome of the Rock, still stands in Jerusalem, just above the Western Wall, the most sacred site in Judaism. Within the dome is a massive boulder from which, many believed, Muhammad was taken into heaven. Muslims believe an imprint of the Prophet's heel is embedded in the stone. In 705 CE, a mosque was built near the site. It was called al-Aqsa, the "furthest mosque." Jerusalem is regarded as the third holiest city in Islam, next to Makkah and Madinah.

The real significance of the story, however, has less to do with Jerusalem and more with the centrality of prayer. This episode in the Prophet's life, which some Muslims regard as a physical occurrence and others as a vision or a dream, symbolizes the importance of prayer as a spiritual practice for

35. Sura 17:1 in Haleem, trans., *Qur'an*, 175.

Muslims. So essential was the five-times-daily prayer to Islam that Muhammad was given an exceptional experience to receive the revelation.

Following his journey into the heavens, Muhammad returned with Gabriel to the Temple Mount in Jerusalem and from there back to Makkah. Against the advice of one of his close companions, the Prophet reported his experience to fellow Makkans at the Kaaba. It is not clear how Muhammad expected them to respond, but the reaction of the vast majority was to conclude that Muhammad had lost his mind and was demonstrably insane. The story even alienated some Muslims, who subsequently left Islam.

The Quest for Sanctuary

Muhammad was now more vulnerable than ever and began to look beyond Makkah for a source of security for himself and the other Muslims. He sought help from the leaders of the nearby town of Taif, the home of the shrine to one of the daughters of Allah. But the chiefs scoffed at his claim to be a messenger of the divine and chased him out of town, hurling both insults and stones. But sometime later, during the annual pilgrimage, Muhammad met with a group of citizens from Yathrib, an oasis city just over two hundred miles north of Makkah, and succeeded in converting them to Islam. They returned home and began to preach the faith to others. A year later, probably 621 CE, they came back to Makkah and reported to the Prophet that the two main tribes of Yathrib had both embraced the faith and ended their ancient hostilities with one another. Furthermore, they offered to provide necessary protection for the Prophet and the women and children among the Makkan Muslims. This new association with the citizens of this city set the groundwork for one of the most important events in Muhammad's life: his migration from Makkah to Yathrib, which later became Madinah, the city of the Prophet. Although it would be a year or two before he himself arrived in Madinah, he immediately began to encourage other Muslims to leave Makkah quietly and to take up residence in this more hospitable environment.

In the meantime, Muhammad remarried. He first married Sawdah bint Zam'ah, a widow who had been part of the Muslim community in Abyssinia. About a year later, he became engaged to Aishah, the six-year-old daughter of his close friend Abu Bakr. According to the early sources, the wedding ceremony took place when Aishah was nine and Muhammad was around fifty.[36] After the wedding, according to tradition, Aishah continued

36. *Sahih Bukhari*, Vol. 7, Book 62, Number 64; http://www.sahih-bukhari.com/Pages/Bukhari_7_62.php.

to live with her parents and did not consummate the marriage until she had reached puberty. Some *hadith* relate that the marriage was a very happy one for both parties, and, with the possible exception of Khadija, Aishah was Muhammad's favorite wife. They remained married until the Prophet's death in 632. Throughout his lifetime, Muhammad had eleven or thirteen wives—the number varies according to the source. As was the practice in Arabia and other ancient cultures, most of these marriages were arranged to create or solidify political or kinship ties. Occasionally, the Prophet married to assist a woman in need. Many of his wives were older widows or women who had been abandoned by their husbands.

Marriage may have helped Muhammad cope with his grief during this period of his life, but it did little to ameliorate his situation with the Makkan leadership. As they became aware that Muslims had been secretly migrating to Madinah, the clan leaders decided it was time to put Muhammad to death. To avoid a vendetta or having to pay blood money to the Banu Hashim, the chiefs decided to organize an assassination squad composed of members from each of the clans. Before they could carry out the plot, however, Gabriel told Muhammad that he should prepare to leave for Madinah. Having also learned of the conspiracy against his life, Muhammad asked his foster son Ali to sleep in his bed while he and Abu Bakr made plans for the exodus from Makkah. At daybreak the next day, the would-be assassins were about to attack the Prophet, only to discover the ruse at the last minute. Muhammad and Abu Bakr had left Makkah in the middle of the night and begun their journey to Madinah, following an unconventional and dangerous route to confuse their pursuers.

The Hijrah

They arrived in the city of Madinah several weeks later amid the cheers and well-wishes of its inhabitants. The first order of business was to find a residence and begin construction on a mosque. Despite invitations from some of the Madinans to dwell with them, Muhammad declined their offers and allowed his camel Qaswa to determine the site of his home and the future mosque. The camel roamed freely for a while and finally came to rest on some property owned by two orphans. Muhammad paid them a good price and construction began immediately.

The migration to Madinah—or the *hijrah* as it is known in Islam—was a vitally important strategic and symbolic event in the life of the Prophet and the growing Muslim community. Its significance is reflected in the fact that Muslims now date the start of their calendar to the year of Muhammad's resettlement, which occurred in 1 AH, *anno hijrah*, or 622 CE. The *hijrah* represented a great act of faith. Like Abraham responding to the call of Yahweh to leave his home in Mesopotamia to strike out for the Promised Land, Muhammad's departure from Makkah required a deep sense of trust in Allah to venture forth into uncharted territory. On another level, the *hijrah* also connects Muhammad with Confucius, the Buddha, and Jesus, each of whom left his home as part of his own spiritual development. All four sages found it essential to their life's purpose to leave the familiar and open themselves up to the unknown. In Muhammad's case, the departure was both an exodus and an exile, to use as metaphors the two central events of the Hebrew Bible. As an exodus, he and his community were cutting themselves off from the painful circumstances of life in Makkah, just as crossing the Red Sea severed the ancient Israelites' ties to their hardships in Egypt. The *hijrah* was a community taking charge of its own liberation; it was a refusal to comply with an intolerable situation. But as an exile, the *hijrah* was a community forcibly alienated from its home. The Qur'an describes the Muslims being "driven out" of Makkah, as if obliged to leave against their will. That Makkah remained in the hearts of the Muslims was demonstrated in the revelation that Muhammad received in 624 CE, instructing the community to face the Kaaba whenever they prayed. Muhammad would eventually return to Makkah for the pilgrimage, but he lived out his days in Madinah, his adopted hometown.

Muhammad as Military Leader

After his arrival, Muhammad set about securing his new city as a safe haven for the *ummah*. He negotiated alliances with the neighboring tribes, including several Jewish tribes who were the descendants of the original settlers of Madinah. Muhammad's vision was to create a new community based on religious and ethical values rather than kinship. This was a largely unprecedented idea in ancient Arabia. Many of the Arabian pagans found Muhammad's dream appealing, in part because they were so weary of the old tribal hostilities, and so they converted to his monotheism. Initially, the Jewish tribes were also willing to participate in this novel arrangement, and a few even embraced Muhammad's faith. Yet, the Prophet never expected the Jews to change their religion. In his view, they had already received a genuine revelation from Moses and the other prophets, and he considered the Qur'an to be part of the same fabric. In the Qur'an, Muhammad received these instructions regarding the Jews and Christians:

> Say: "We believe in God, and in what has been revealed to us,
> and what was revealed to Abraham, Ishmael, Isaac, Jacob, and
> the Tribes; and in [the Books] given to Moses, Jesus, and the
> prophets, from their Lord. We make no discrimination between
> individuals among them; for we submit to God."[37]

In short, Muhammad regarded the Jews and Christians as "muslims" (with a small *m*), those who submit to the will of the one god. Evidently, Muhammad did not distinguish the Jews and Christians at first, considering them members of the same religion. As he came to understand both groups, he began to recognize the differences between them.

Despite the initial enthusiasm that greeted Muhammad's arrival in Madinah, not everyone remained happy about the presence of the Prophet. Apparently, many Madinans who had converted to Islam were less than sincere about the faith. Over time, their discontent with Muhammad and the migrant Muslims become increasingly evident. Abdallah ibn Ubbay, who was of one of the new converts, had been preparing to become the king of Madinah when Muhammad entered the scene. Now, he was beginning to feel he had been robbed of his crown. Although he remained a nominal Muslim, ibn Ubbay began to foment resistance to the Prophet. The subversive actions of ibn Ubbay and his associates earned them the name the Hypocrites. Many of the members of the Jewish tribes also joined the growing resistance. Upon reflection, they started to have grave misgivings about Muhammad. They came to believe that his revelations distorted the stories of their Torah, and they came to doubt his claim to be a prophet. In their mind, the age of prophecy had ended long ago. Muhammad was bitterly disappointed when the Jews failed to accept him as a messenger of the LORD in the tradition of Abraham and Moses. Not long afterwards, Muhammad received the revelation to face Makkah, rather than Jerusalem, during prayer.

Based on the earliest revelations in the Qur'an, it is clear that Muhammad had little interest in social and political leadership. He understood himself as a prophet in the biblical vein, calling his contemporaries back to the one god and to a just society. But after the *hijrah*, Muhammad became more overtly concerned with civic leadership. Even the quality of the revelations changed. The earlier revelations in Makkah were relatively brief, focusing on the majesty and mystery of Allah and his ethical demands. The later Madinan revelations were much longer, addressing practical, social, and political matters. This distinction, however, is not an absolute one; it simply reflects a shift in emphasis. But it does signal the way that Muhammad's attention was turning (or being turned) toward consolidating the

---

37. Sura 3:84 in Cleary, trans., *Qur'an*, 29; cf. Sura 29:46.

Muslim community and ensuring its survival. In Madinah, for the first time, the Qur'an began to speak of the legitimacy of battle:

> Those who have been attacked are permitted to take up arms because they have been wronged—God has the power to help them—those who have been driven unjustly from their homes only for saying, "Our Lord is God." If God did not repel some people by means of others, many monasteries, churches, synagogues, and mosques, where God's name is much invoked, would have been destroyed. God is sure to help those who help His cause—God is strong and mighty.[38]

In Makkah, Islam was essentially pacifistic. Now, as this passage indicates, Allah granted permission for the Muslims to engage in combat for a just cause. Specifically, this revelation allowed the Muslims who migrated to Madinah to seek compensation for the property they lost when they left Makkah and to take up arms, if necessary, to obtain it. This consent was based on the belief in the need for just persons to hold the wicked in check, lest chaos ensue and even religious institutions be destroyed. In short, the Muslim community had the right to defend itself against injustice.

In 623 CE, the Prophet sent two groups of emigrants to accost caravans en route to Makkah from Syria. The intent of the raids—which, as we noted earlier, were commonplace in ancient Arabia—was to recover for the Muslims some of the value of their homes that were confiscated when they left Makkah. These raids, like most, were not supposed to involve killing, since that would incur blood vengeance according to the old tribal codes. The first expeditions were not great successes. Later that year, Muhammad himself led two hundred Muslims in a raid on a huge caravan, but it also failed. Finally, the Muslims succeeded in ambushing a Makkan caravan during a month when fighting was strictly forbidden throughout the peninsula. The violation of the sacred truce repulsed many Madinans, and Muhammad later felt compelled to condemn the act, even though the raiders were acting on his orders. Although not especially successful, these caravan attacks put the Arabian tribes on notice that the Muslims were willing to put up a fight for their survival and to challenge what they considered an oppressive situation. Muhammad believed that it was important to demonstrate this attitude, lest the new community leave itself vulnerable to constant aggression. The *ummah* could not afford to appear weak. A confrontation with the Quraysh now seemed inevitable.

The first real battle between the Quraysh and the Muslims occurred in 624 CE. With an army of about three hundred, the Prophet planned to

---

38. Sura 22:39-40 in Haleem, trans., *Qur'an*, 212.

intercept a caravan at the Well of Badr, near the Red Sea. The caravan, however, was warned of the plan and sent word back to Makkah for help. More than a thousand Makkans responded to join the fight against the small Muslim army. After witnessing the arrival of reinforcements, Muhammad consulted his close companions and decided to press forward with the plan, despite being outnumbered more than three to one. Muhammad proved to be an impressive military leader, and the Muslims fought with such determination that the Quraysh were soon routed. When the battle was over, Muhammad spared the lives of all the prisoners but two who had been especially cruel in the conflict, and he equitably distributed the spoils of battle, both uncommon practices at the time. The win was a great moral victory for the Muslims, who viewed their success as a validation of their faith in Allah. Henceforth, the Muslim community was regarded throughout Arabia as a force to be reckoned with.

Shortly after the triumph at Badr, the Banu Qaynuqa, one of the Jewish tribes at Madinah, broke its covenant with the Muslims. Historians are not agreed about what precipitated the violation, but it was evidence of a growing disenchantment with Muhammad among the Madinan tribes. Around this time, Muhammad received another revelation that he interpreted as addressing this breach. He was told, "And if you learn of treachery on the part of any people, throw their treaty back at them, for God does not love the treacherous."[39] Muhammad quickly raised an army and defeated the Jews. But, as in the battle of Badr, Muhammad spared the prisoners of war and the other members of the tribe. He did, however, banish the entire tribe and kept their belongings, dividing them among the Muslims.

The Battle of Uhud, on the other hand, did not turn out so well for the Muslim community. In 625, a Quraysh army of three thousand men and three thousand camels began a march to Madinah to avenge their loss at Badr. Muhammad and his companions decided to meet them in Uhud, about five miles from Madinah, to prevent them from entering the city. Again, the Muslims were heavily outnumbered, but they seemed to be heady with the taste of their previous victories. Early on, it appeared as though the Muslims would win again, but the archers who had been posted in the hills above the battle began to observe that the foot soldiers on the front lines were prematurely collecting the spoils of war. Fearing they would not get a share of the plunder, the archers deserted their posts, and the entire battle fell into disarray. Muhammad was knocked off his horse and broke a tooth and sustained other injuries, prompting the rumor that he had been killed. Within a short while, the Muslims had lost the battle. In the face of

39. Sura 8:58 in ibid., 114.

defeat, Muhammad was able to retain composure and did not let his emotions control his actions. According to his biographers, he showed respect to his enemies and, despite his anger, was "neither brutal nor stern" with the archers who caused the loss.[40] A subsequent revelation, however, made it clear that the defeat was the result of the Muslims' greed and disobedience.

Muhammad's battle practices followed the guidelines of what ethicists call "just war theory." The principal objective in his military operations was to preserve and protect his community. Muhammad never fought out of pure aggression or anger. The Qur'an was clear about the limits of war:

> And fight for the sake of God those who fight you; but do not be brutal or commit aggression, for God does not love brutal aggressors ... [D]o not fight them in the precincts of the sacred mosque, unless they fight you there. If they fight you, then kill them; such is the reward of scoffers. But if they stop, God is most forgiving, most merciful. And fight them until there is no more strife and there is the religion of God. And if they stop, then let there be no hostility, except against wrongdoers.[41]

The just war was to be fought only for self-protection and to put an end to tyranny. A war motivated by greed could not be sanctioned by the Qur'an. Furthermore, the revelations enjoined the Muslims to spare the lives of women, children and noncombatants, and even crops and animals. Muhammad treated his prisoners humanely and prohibited the Muslims from mutilating or desecrating the corpses of the dead.

The migration to Madinah had prompted important changes in the character of Islam and the Prophet's understanding of his mission. Muhammad had become convinced that violence was necessary when the cause of justice demanded it. In the pursuit of justice, Allah aids the warrior, but even so, the use of force must always be contained by discipline. In this respect, the development of Islam remained consistent with the values espoused in the first revelations. Madinah and Makkah were not so far removed.

The Components of Muhammad's Metaphysics

Within a few years of Muhammad's resettlement in Madinah, the salient features of Islam had been defined by revelation and experience. The Prophet continued to receive messages from Gabriel until his death ten years after the *hijrah*, but most of the later Madinan suras addressed matters

---

40. Ramadan, *In the Footsteps of the Prophet*, 127.
41. Sura 2:190-93 in Cleary, trans., *Qur'an*, 14.

of communal polity as compared with the theological, ethical, and spiritual emphases of the revelations received in Makkah and the first years in Madinah. Since the Prophet's worldview had by now attained its essential character and form, this is an appropriate point in our study to discuss his teachings more systematically, using the same categories we have employed for each of the other three sages, namely, metaphysics, anthropology, ethics, and spiritual practices.

A passage from one of the suras revealed in Madinah provides a concise statement of the elements of Muhammad's metaphysical view:

> O you who believe! Believe in Allah and His Messenger, and the scripture [that] He [has] sent to His Messenger and the scripture [that] He sent to those before (him). Any who deny Allah, His Angels, His Books, His Messengers, and the Day of Judgment [has] gone far, far astray.[42]

Thus, the Qur'an makes clear that god, angels, prophets and messengers, revealed books, and a forthcoming day of judgment are vital beliefs in Muhammad's teaching about the nature of ultimate reality. These concepts will provide the essential points for our study.

God Is the Ultimate Reality

When he began to proclaim faith in Allah, Muhammad was not introducing a new deity to the Arabs. Rather, he was making a particular assertion about the nature of the ultimate reality. For his time and place, that claim was a radical statement, and it nearly got him killed.

Muhammad's provocative contention was that the fundamental character of ultimate reality is unity, oneness, or what is known in Islamic theology as *tawhid*. The very first words of the *shahadah*, the Muslim profession of faith, proclaim the doctrine of *tawhid*: "There is no god but Allah." The doctrine of *tawhid* is the bedrock of Islam. On the face of it, *tawhid* seems a rather simple and straightforward declaration of the principle of monotheism. But much more is involved in this conception than the simple denial of all gods but one. In one of the earliest revelations, Muhammad is told, "Say, 'It is God, unique, God, the eternal, not begetting or begotten, not having any equal.'"[43] This statement reveals that *tawhid* implies not just singleness but singularity, in the sense that Allah is incomparable, utterly unlike anything

---

42. Sura 4:136, in Ali, trans., *Qur'an*, http://wikilivres.ca/wiki/The_Holy_Qur%27an/An-Nisa. I have modernized the archaic language.

43. Sura 112, in Cleary, trans., *Qur'an*, 301.

else in human experience. "There is nothing like God," says Sura 42.[44] Other beings have limited life spans; Allah alone is eternal. Other beings are born and they reproduce; Allah alone has no progenitor and does not procreate; Allah relies on no one or nothing else. Other beings are members of species, of families of like beings; Allah is the only one of his kind. Other beings are composites, made up of parts; Allah alone is indivisible. *Tawhid* thus implies divine inscrutability. Because absolutely nothing compares to Allah, Allah infinitely exceeds human understanding. "No vision can grasp Him," says Sura 6, "but His grasp is over all vision: He is above all comprehension, yet is acquainted with all things."[45] These statements about the nature of Allah help clarify why Islam can tolerate no other gods and goddesses. To suggest that Allah is a deity like Hubal or al-Uzza would imply that god can be imagined, envisioned, or understood like these others, and that would diminish the majesty and mystery of the ultimate reality. Precisely to avoid this assumption, Allah was never represented with images and icons like the members of the Arabian pantheon.

To Muhammad, the doctrine of divine oneness was not only a revealed truth; it was readily apparent to anyone able to use their reasoning powers and read the signs of the sacred found through creation: "God has never had a child. Nor is there any god beside Him—if there were, each god would have taken his creation aside and tried to overcome the others."[46] In short, reason itself dictates that there can be only one supreme being; otherwise, the universe would be in complete chaos. As Sura 21 says, "If there were a deity besides God in the sky and earth, both would go awry."[47]

The singularity and inscrutability of Allah entails the claim that ultimate reality simply cannot be grasped or explained. Allah exists without place and bears no resemblance to his creations. He alone caused all things to exist and brought them into being out of nothing. The whole created order depends on god, but god needs the creation for nothing at all; he is "uniquely independent."[48] Everything that happens—good and evil—occurs because Allah wills it; yet, Allah is never unjust, not "in the least degree" says the Qur'an.[49] He never makes mistakes and is fully cognizant of the whole of reality:

44. Sura 42:11 in ibid., 238.

45. Sura 6:103 in Ali, trans., *Qur'an*, http://wikilivres.ca/wiki/The_Holy_Qur%27an/Al-Anaam

46. Sura 23:91 in Haleem, trans., *Qur'an*, 218.

47. Sura 21:22, Cleary, trans., *Qur'an*, 158.

48. Sura 6:133 in ibid., 69.

49. Sura 4:40 in Ali, trans., *Qur'an*, http://wikilivres.ca/wiki/The_Holy_Qur%27an/An-Nisa

> And whatever business you take part in, and whatever you read
> from the Qur'an, and whatever deed you do, We are witnessing
> you as you are immersed therein. And nothing on earth or in the
> sky is hidden from your Lord, even to the weight of an atom.[50]

While Muhammad's understanding of Allah explicitly affirmed the principle of mystery, it is also true that the Prophet spoke in terms that permitted a partial understanding of god, a concession to the limitations of the human mind. Islamic theology distinguishes between the divine essence, which is beyond comprehension, and the divine attributes, which name certain qualities that assist in appropriately orienting the mind toward god. Without such attributes, the divine reality cannot be spoken of at all. This distinction between god's essence and attributes is a common theological move in the history of world religions. It is a way of both affirming the final mystery of the ultimate reality of the universe and permitting the mind to have some ideas to work with as it attempts to draw closer to that reality.

The Qur'an and the *hadith* both attribute particular qualities to Allah but do so in ways that are intended to preclude compromising god's utter unknowability. A well-known list of Allah's qualities is the Ninety-Nine Most Beautiful Names. This inventory includes divine attributes that can only be ascribed to Allah and no other. Two of the most popularly invoked names are *Ar-Rahman*, the all-compassionate, and *Ar-Rahim*, the all-merciful. Every sura of the Qur'an (except Sura 9) begins with the recitation of these two attributes of Allah in a formula known as the *bismillah*: "In the name of God, the all-compassionate, the all-merciful." The *bismillah* is recited several times as part of Muslim daily prayers, and it is often spoken as one undertakes a new task. Some Muslims think the *bismillah* contains the very essence of the Qur'an. It certainly highlights what Muhammad took to be one of the defining qualities of Allah: complete compassion. The other beautiful names complement and supplement these attributes. Sura 59 offers a listing of about a dozen more of these superlative qualities:

> This is *the* God, other than which there is no deity: the Sovereign, the Holy, Peace, the Giver of Safety, the Protector, the Almighty, the Omnipotent, the Overwhelming; glory to God, beyond any association they attribute. This is God, the Originator, the Creator, the Shaper, to whom refer the most beautiful names, celebrated by everything in the heavens and on earth, being the Almighty, the Perfectly Wise.[51]

---

50. Sura 10:61 in Cleary, trans., *Qur'an*, 101.

51. Sura 59:23–24 in ibid., 273.

Scattered throughout the Qur'an, *hadith*, and other Islamic literature are many other such beautiful names. All of them, Muslims believe, have only one true referent: Allah.

Although these qualities can only be properly ascribed to Allah, human beings from the beginning of time have been inclined to misappropriate them, attributing them to realities other than the one to whom they rightly belong. Misappropriating the divine attributes is part of what Islam considers to be the most heinous of sins: *shirk*. The sin of *shirk* is at the root of all transgressions. Literally meaning "association," *shirk* is connecting with Allah something that is less than ultimate, or giving to that which is less than ultimate something that belongs to Allah alone. It is to draw comparisons between god and other realities. Concretely, *shirk* manifests in a variety of forms. To deny the doctrine of *tawhid* by believing in and worshiping deities other than Allah is committing *shirk*. To create a physical image or representation of Allah is *shirk*. To impute the attributes of Allah to anything other than Allah is *shirk*. The Qur'an calls *shirk* an "unpardonable sin," indeed, the *only* sin that Allah cannot forgive. Even so, *shirk* is unpardonable only if one dies in this state of unbelief. While yet alive, anyone can repent and be forgiven. Indeed, most of the first Muslims were considered idolaters until they embraced Islam.

Shirk is idolatry in its broadest sense. The Christian theologian Paul Tillich defined idolatry in very concise terms that seem to capture the spirit of the concept of *shirk*: "Idolatry is the elevation of a preliminary concern to ultimacy," Tillich wrote. "Something essentially conditional is taken as unconditional, something essentially partial is boosted to universality, and something essentially finite is given infinite significance."[52] The great danger of idolatry is not just that it denies the majesty of the divine by drawing it down to the level of the finite and conditional. Perhaps more important, it endangers the individual who places his or her faith in an object that is unable to sustain it. Idols will, by their very nature, disappoint us. By "idols" I do not necessary mean "images," although Islam would most certainly include physical representations of the divine under the category of idols. Rather, I simply mean whatever serves as our god, the locus of our highest values, that which we trust to provide our lives with meaning and worth. We can make anything our god—money, country, self, religion—whenever we invest it with ultimate significance in our lives. What Muhammad and Tillich would tell us is that the only reality worthy of such loyalty and faith is the inscrutable absolute, what Tillich called our "ground of being" and Muhammad called Allah.

52. Tillich, *Systematic Theology*, 1:13.

The Servants of Allah

Angels and prophets are the servants of Allah. They differ from one another by nature. The angels are beings created of light and can assume any form and travel great distances in an instant. Although they are sentient, angels lack the free will of human beings; they have no choice but to obey god. The Qur'an and *hadith* mention some of the angels by name and describe their responsibilities. Gabriel, of course, was the angel who revealed the Qur'an to Muhammad, but he was also the one who communicated divine messages to *all* of humanity's prophets. Michael is the angel who distributes rewards to those who live good lives. With a blast of his trumpet, Raphael will announce the coming of the last day. At the first sound of the trumpet, everything will be destroyed, and at the second, the dead will be resurrected. Islamic tradition also refers to an angel of death who is responsible for sundering the individual's body and soul at the end of life. It is said that the soul of a wicked person is ripped painfully from his or her body, while that of a good person is gently removed. Angels are also the custodians of paradise and hell and the recorders of a person's good and bad deeds.

Satan, or *Iblis*, is important figure in Islam, but he is not considered a fallen angel as suggested by Christian mythology.[53] *Iblis* is a jinni who was created from fire and was fervently devoted to worshiping Allah. His great misdeed, according to the Qur'an, was disobeying the divine command for all creatures to prostrate themselves before Adam, after Adam's creation from a lump of clay. Possessing free will, unlike the angels, *Iblis* refused to bow before Adam, and Allah cast him out of heaven.[54] At that point, *Iblis* assumed the title Shaitan, or Satan, and was promised punishment for his disobedience at the end of time, the day of requital. In response, he swore that he would spend the meantime roaming the world attempting to divert human beings from the straight path.

Angels and prophets both function as envoys of the divine, but prophets are human rather than celestial. Muhammad taught that Allah had sent prophets to every nation in the world at various points in history to preach the same basic message of Islam. There were slight variations in their proclamations because their words were directed to different audiences, but all the prophets taught the oneness of god and the necessity of submitting to the divine will. They were chosen by Allah and lived exemplary lives.

Only about two dozen prophets are named in the Qur'an. Many are figures also known from the Bible, although most are not regarded as

---

53. Certain passages (Sura 2:34 and Sura 15:31) suggest that Iblis was an angel, but his refusal to obey Allah gives him freedom of will, the quality of a jinni.

54. Sura 7:11-12.

prophets by Judaism and Christianity. They include Adam, Noah, Abraham, Ishmael, Isaac, Joseph, Job, Moses, David, Solomon, John the Baptizer, and Jesus. Although not named in the Qur'an, some modern Muslim communities regard Confucius and the Buddha as two of the prophets dispatched to humanity, although that is by no means a consensus opinion.[55] Muhammad was the "seal of the prophets," the final and most important emissary of Allah, sent not just to a nation but to all humankind. As we noted, some of the prophets are also known as messengers, if their revelations were especially significant. The Qur'an considers Abraham, Ishmael, Moses, Jesus, and Muhammad as messengers.

Prophet Jesus

Although not all Muslims would count Confucius and the Buddha among the prophets, there is no such dispute about Jesus, who is known in the Qur'an as 'Isa, the son of Maryam. The Qur'an leaves no doubt that Jesus was not only a messenger; he was among the greatest of all human beings. Like the New Testament, the Qur'an affirms he was born of a virgin and further declares that he was the *only* human ever born this way. It acknowledges that Jesus performed many miracles, including healing the blind, curing lepers, and raising the dead. It even attributes to Jesus certain miraculous phenomena that the New Testament does not mention, such as the ability to speak as an infant and bringing clay birds to life (compare to the noncanonical Infancy Gospel of Thomas). Yet—and the Qur'an is very emphatic about this—Jesus was not, and could not be, the son or incarnation of god. Sura 4 declares:

> People of the Book! Commit no excesses in your religion. Speak only the truth about God. Christ Jesus the son of Mary was no more than a messenger of God, and his Word, which he bestowed on Mary, and a spirit proceeding from him. So believe in God and his messengers. Do not say "Trinity"! Desist: it will be much better for you, for God is one God. Glory be to him: he is too exalted to have a son.[56]

The Qur'an's admonition rests on the doctrine of *tawhid*. Regarding Jesus as the son of god, as a person of the Trinity, or as a divine incarnation, in the view of Islam, violates the oneness of god and commits the sin of *shirk*.

---

55. E.g., the Ahmadiyya Community, according to Ahmad, *Revelation, Rationality, Knowledge, and Truth.*

56. Sura 4:171, my rendering.

Muhammad may have thought that identifying Jesus as divine was an error of only *some* Christians, that is, those who went to "excess in their religion." He may not have been aware that the divinity of Jesus is the sine qua non of Christianity. Muhammad also seems to have believed that the Christian Trinity comprised the Father, Jesus the son, and Mary the mother, rather than the father, son, and holy spirit, as the ecumenical Christian councils formulated it. In any event, the Trinity—however conceived—was a doctrine clearly at odds with Islam.

The Qur'an quotes Jesus as saying that he is only a human being devoted to the worship of Allah. His mission was not to die for the sin of humanity but to bear witness to the oneness of god and the necessity of submitting to the divine will. To be sure, Jesus was chosen and blessed by Allah and given a revelation to deliver to the Christians, the book known in Arabic as the *Injil,* or the Gospel. The *Injil,* however, is not identical to the New Testament or the four gospels. Most Muslims believe that the original book delivered to Jesus was lost or at least corrupted by his followers, which might explain why Christians, or at least some of them, went "to excess" and ascribed divinity to their messenger. The Qur'an also indicates that Jesus served as a forerunner to a future messenger named Ahmed, whom it identifies as the Prophet Muhammad.

The Ontology of the Qur'an

The Qur'an frequently uses the phrase "People of the Book" or the "People of Scripture."[57] The expression refers to those pre-Islamic nations who have received revelations from Allah in the form of a text. Generally, the People of Scripture are the Jews and Christians, but sometimes included are the Sabians, whose identity is unclear, and the Zoroastrians, members of the ancient religion established in Iran in the first or second millennium BCE. From among these groups, the Qur'an names four revealed books prior to the revelations to Muhammad: the Scrolls of Abraham,[58] the Torah,[59] the Psalms,[60] and the Gospel.

The Qur'an itself is the quintessential revealed book. We have discussed the Qur'an in some detail already, noting particularly its content and its transmission from Gabriel to Muhammad. But it is necessary to mention the Qur'an as an element in the Prophet's metaphysics. The Qur'an exists not

57. *Ahl al-Kitab.*
58. *Suhuf Ibrahim.*
59. *Tawrat.*
60. *Zabur.*

only as text and as oral scripture. For Islam, the Qur'an has an ontological status as the word of god, the very speech of Allah. There are even allusions in some revelations to a written Qur'an existing in the divine presence even before it was sent down to the Prophet.[61] One of the early controversies among Islamic theologians was whether the Qur'an was eternal or created, a debate that roughly paralleled a similar dispute about Jesus in ancient Christianity. The view that came to dominate theological opinion was that the Qur'an *is* eternal, having existed with Allah since before the beginning of time. The Qur'an delivered to the Prophet during the twenty-three years of revelation was identical to the eternal Qur'an. Muslims believe—and the Qur'an explicitly states—that it is not possible for a human being to produce a book like the Qur'an.

The Day of Requital

Like Jesus, Muhammad anticipated an end to the world as we know it. Some Qur'anic scholars regard the day of requital to be the "dominant message of the Qur'an."[62] On that day, the dead will rise and persons will be judged by their deeds and rewarded or punished accordingly. The time of this eschatological event is known only to Allah. Sura 7 says, "It will only come to you suddenly, as a surprise."[63] But, as Jesus also predicted, there will be certain signs preceding the final days. There will be a disruption of the created order manifesting as natural disasters and the rapid erosion of human morality, both harbingers of the end-time found in eschatological visions throughout the world.

When the last day finally comes, Raphael will give two blasts of his trumpet, the first to destroy all things and the second to signal the resurrection of the dead and the ultimate reckoning.[64] The Qur'an explains that each person, Muslim and non-Muslim, will receive a "book of deeds" that appraises his or her every action and word during life.[65] If the book is placed in the right hand, the individual will be permitted into eternal paradise.[66] If the book is placed in the left hand, he or she will be seized, bound, and destined for hell, where the person will be received by nineteen tormenting angels and exposed to burning fire. The sins that merit condemnation

61. Sura 43:3-4.
62. Smith, *Islamic Understanding of Death*, 63.
63. Sura 7:187 in Cleary, trans., *Qur'an*, 83.
64. Sura 69:13.
65. Sura 54:52-53.
66. The Arabic term is *Jannah*, which simply means "garden."

include lying and dishonesty, the denial of the *tawhid* and Allah's revelations, refusing to help the poor and hungry, usury, economic exploitation, and social oppression. Interestingly, extra-Qur'anic sources indicate that Jesus will play a judging role at the day of requital, similar to the function of the son of man in the Christian Bible.

After the final judgment, each individual must cross a bridge that leads over and across hell. The righteous will find the bridge a broad path over which they swiftly and freely move, led by Muhammad himself, into paradise. But for the wicked, the bridge becomes so sharp and narrow that they plummet into damnation. Yet the mercy of Allah is so great that he directs his angels and prophets to rescue those who have done some good, and those who have done just a little good,[67] and even those in whose hearts there is a single atom of goodness.[68]

Muhammad's metaphysical understanding is a comprehensive vision centered in a transcendent and ultimately mysterious reality that creates humanity and is intimately interested in its welfare. Although far beyond the capacity of the human mind to comprehend, this reality endeavors to make itself known by inspiring prophets to go to all the peoples of the earth with the message of god's oneness and compassion. While compassionate, Allah is also just and demands that human beings treat one another fairly and honestly. God's demand for justice is symbolized in the day of requital, the moment at which human beings will have to account for their lives and ultimately reap the consequences of what they have done. But even to the very end, Allah remains all-compassionate and all-merciful.

The Anthropology and Ethics of Islam

Muhammad's anticipation of the day of requital highlights the central importance of ethical behavior and the standards of justice in his teaching. But even from the start of the revelations, Gabriel made it clear that Allah had moral expectations of humanity. During the twenty-three years that Muhammad received them, the revelations continued to amplify and refine

---

67. Allah's Apostle said, "A prostitute was forgiven by Allah, because, passing by a panting dog near a well and seeing that the dog was about to die of thirst, she took off her shoe, and tying it with her head-cover she drew out some water for it. So, Allah forgave her because of that." (*Sahih Buhkari*, Volume 4, Book 54, Number 538, narrated by Abu Huraira, http://www.sahih-bukhari.com/Pages/Bukhari_4_54.php).

68. "(Each one) of you should save himself from the fire by giving even half of a date (in charity). And if you do not find a half date, then (by saying) a pleasant word (to your brethren)" (*Sahih Bukhari*, Volume 2, Book 24, Number 494, narrated by 'Adi bin Hatim, http://www.sahih-bukhari.com/Pages/Bukhari_2_24.php).

the ethics of Islam. We will examine the fundamental principles and ideals of human behavior as Muhammad understood them by means of the messages he received from Allah. We begin our study with the Qur'anic view of the human being, that aspect of theology called anthropology. As we shall see, the ethical precepts of Islam are intrinsically related to its fundamental understanding of the nature and purpose of humanity.

Adam, Eve, and the Problem with Humans

In Islam, as in Christianity, the world's first man and woman function as the archetypes for all human beings. An understanding of the Qur'an's perspective on humanity, therefore, begins with the story of Adam and Eve.[69] The Qur'anic narrative echoes many details and themes of the biblical account. Adam was created from clay and brought to life when Allah breathed his spirit into him. Although the Qur'an does not say so, some *hadith* indicate that Adam was made in the divine image. Adam possessed the knowledge of all things in creation and hence had the ability to name them. The first humans had no power to create like god, but they did have the ability to submit or refuse to submit to god's will. The capacity to know god's will and to decide whether or not to follow it distinguished humans from other animate creatures and made them responsible for their actions.

We all know how the story turned out, of course. Adam and Eve chose wrongly and had to bear the consequences of their choice. But the Qur'anic story offers some slightly different details from the Bible. Paradise, which derives from the ancient Iranian word meaning "garden," existed in heaven, not on earth, according to the Qur'an. When Adam and Eve partook of the forbidden fruit, they were exiled to the earth, where their descendants must now live until the last day. On that day, the good among the resurrected will return to the garden from whence Adam and Eve were banished. The nature of the first ancestors' sin is also interpreted differently in the Qur'an. The eating of the fruit is regarded as a mistake made in a state of forgetfulness brought about by the ploys of Iblis, the Satan. When Allah confronts the pair with their error, they confess, "Our Lord, we have wronged our own selves";[70] then immediately they beg for forgiveness. In Genesis, on the other hand, Adam instantly blames Eve, Eve points the finger at the serpent, and no one says they are sorry.

---

69. Eve is actually not mentioned by name in the Qur'an but she is referred to in other Muslim sources as Hawa. Mary, the mother of Jesus, interestingly, is the only woman the Qur'an calls by name.

70. Sura 7:23, Cleary, trans., *Qur'an*, 72.

The story of Adam and Eve defines what Muslims see as the fundamental human fault: forgetting Allah and his commands. Because of this tendency, Allah in his great compassion has provided countless signs in creation and has sent a vast succession of prophets to remind humanity of their fundamental purpose in life: to remember god[71] and submit to his will.[72] Allah intended human beings to give themselves wholeheartedly to their creator so they might flourish. This is the fundamental meaning of the word *Islam*: to relinquish one's own desires for the sake of the highest good. But human beings get distracted by the allurements of the world, particularly its material delights, and we ignore the true center and purpose of existence. It is the same tendency that leads human beings to create idols by putting the things of the world in the place that rightfully belongs to god.

Basic Morality

Near the end of his life, Muhammad gathered together members of the Muslim community and delivered his final public address, sometimes known as the Farewell Sermon. In that discourse, which is reported in several collections of *hadith*, Muhammad succinctly restated the understanding of humanity that underlies the entire Qur'an:

> You all descend from Adam and Adam was created from dirt. The most noble in the sight of God is the most pious. No Arab is superior to a non-Arab, except by their intimate consciousness of God [piety].[73]

For Muhammad, the descent of all humanity from the same ancestors entailed two important principles. First, all human beings are prone to the same heedlessness that led to the banishment from paradise; and second, all human beings are fundamentally equal before the supreme being. Tribal and clan affiliations are of no significance. Ethnicity and skin color mean nothing. The only distinguishing trait of any significance is whether or not one surrenders to Allah and acts with justice and humility. This is not, however, a distinction between those *called* Muslims and those who are non-Muslims. There were nominal Muslims, such as the Madinan group known as the Hypocrites, who embraced Islam in name but not in practice. By the same token, Jews, Christians, or the members of *any* religion who followed

---

71. *dhikr.*

72. Sura 51:56.

73. From Muhammad's Last Sermon, recorded in Ibn Hisham, *As-Sirah an-Nabawiyyah*, 6:9 and quoted in Ramadan, *Footsteps of the Prophet*, 196.

the will of Allah were accounted by Muhammad among the righteous and the heirs of paradise. To surrender to the will of Allah did not mean that one had to refer to the ultimate reality by that specific name. By revelation, Muhammad is told, "Invoke [Allah], or invoke the Benevolent: however you invoke the deity, the most beautiful names are appropriate."[74] This statement permits a certain latitude in the names by which the Absolute One is addressed, but it does not throw open the door to *any and all* names and attributes. The true god may not be called Allah in some languages, but the divine qualities of compassion, mercy, and justice must characterize the deity, by whatever name it is known.

And what did it mean to submit to the will of Allah? The specific elements of god's will as Muhammad knew them are scattered throughout the Qur'an and *hadith*, but one of the most comprehensive statements appears in Sura 17. Because this passage is fairly extensive, it is an excellent place to gain a good sense of the foundational ethical principles of Islam:

> Your Lord has decreed that you should worship only God, and be good to your parents. Whether one or both of them reaches old age with you, never speak to them harshly, and do not rebuff them, but speak to them in kindly terms . . . And give relatives their due, and the poor and the wayfarer, but do not squander wastefully. For squanderers are the brothers of the devils; . . . Do not kill your children out of fear of poverty; We will provide for them, and for you. Indeed, killing them is a great sin. And do not approach adultery, for it is an obscenity and an evil way. And do not take a life that God has made sacred, except for just cause . . . And do not approach the property of the orphan, except with what is better . . . and fulfill promises, for the promise will be questioned. And give full measure when you measure out, and weigh with an accurate balance. That is fair, and the best determination . . . listening, looking, and the impulse of the heart will all be questioned. And do not walk on earth insolently, for you cannot circle the earth and you cannot reach the mountains in height.[75]

Much in this passage compares with the moral statements of other traditions, especially the Bible. Injunctions to worship only one god, to be good to one's parents, and to refrain from murder and adultery are, of course, reminiscent of the Ten Commandments. Some admonitions recall other sages we have studied. Confucius urged his followers to speak gently and

---

74. Sura 17:110 in Cleary, trans., *Qur'an*, 141.
75. Sura 17:23-39 in ibid., 136-37.

humbly to their parents under all circumstances. Both the Buddha and Confucius emphasized the practice of humility, or not "walking on the earth insolently," as the Qur'an has it.

This adumbration also addresses ethical concerns more particular, but not exclusive, to the ancient Arabian context. Several statements concern the fair distribution of resources and issues regarding commerce and property rights. The passage makes special mention of the necessity of living frugally and of caring for the poor, the orphaned, and the sojourner. Indeed, the context of scarcity in which Muhammad lived necessarily made these matters the subject of explicit attention. The prohibition of killing children was also necessitated by Muhammad's historical context. During the days of ignorance, female infanticide was a common practice because the male was more highly valued than the female, and girls were considered an economic burden. The Qur'an specifically forbids the murder of infant girls,[76] and in a *hadith*, Muhammad declares the birth of daughters to be a blessing and not, as it was often taken to be, a source of grief. Here, the Qur'an prohibits the killing of any child for fear of impoverishment. The clear tenor of the stipulations in this entire passage is the obligation to care for society's weakest and most vulnerable members. The unnamed evils against which these regulations are directed are self-centeredness and materialism, two deeply disturbing trends that Muhammad had witnessed encroaching on Arab society in his day. Both materialism and self-centeredness, he believed, were rooted in the neglect of Allah. Rather than worship the true god, his contemporaries revered the idols of the self and the world.

This list of precepts, of course, does not exhaust the Qur'an's many statements about appropriate human behavior. Nor does the Qur'an address all possible situations demanding an ethical response. Rather, like the Bible and other scriptures, it provides both specific commands and general principles on the basis of which novel ethical situations can be evaluated and appropriate actions determined.

Women in Islam

One area of Islamic ethics that has received special attention in recent years is the role and status of women. The Qur'an has much to say about women and their relationships with men. In view of the importance of this issue for both Muhammad and modernity, and to illustrate the dynamics of the Prophet's ethical thought, we will consider some aspects of this vital matter.

---

76. Sura 16:58-59; Sura 81:8-14.

Let us begin by setting some parameters for this discussion. First, we will be concerned only with the Prophet's understanding of and relationship with women as revealed in the Qur'an and the *hadith*. We are not inquiring into the role and status of women throughout Islamic history, nor will we try to determine the extent to which Islam in the post-Prophet era converged with or departed from Muhammad's teachings. The position of women in Islamic cultures throughout history has varied greatly, and it would be a mistake to assume that all aspects of women's lives in these societies derive solely from Islam. That would be like saying the role of Christian women throughout history was determined exclusively by the teachings of Jesus. Second, we must note that the Qur'anic view of women and gender relations is the subject of divergent opinion among both Muslim and non-Muslim scholars. I will indicate where such differences exist to provide a sense of this range of views.

But let us start with a few fundamental issues about which almost all critical scholars are agreed. First, it seems undeniable that Muhammad regarded women and men as equal souls before Allah. Sura 4, titled "Women," in fact proclaims that men and women have been created from one soul.[77] At the day of requital, all persons will be judged according to the same standards of conduct and belief. This passage from Sura 33 summarizes the Qur'an's view of the spiritual equality of men and women:

> For the men who acquiesce to the will of God, and the women who acquiesce, the men who believe and the women who believe, the men who are devout and the women who are devout, the men who are truthful and the women who are truthful, the men who are constant and the women who are constant, the men who are humble and the women who are humble, the men who give charity and the women who give charity, the men who fast and the women who fast, the men who are chaste and the women who are chaste, and the men and women who remember God a lot, God has arranged forgiveness for them, and a magnificent reward.[78]

Second, many aspects of Muhammad's personal life indicate that his teaching was influenced but not determined by traditional thinking about gender.[79] Despite the highly patriarchal structure of pre-Islamic Arabia, for example, Muhammad accepted a proposal of marriage from a woman far wealthier and more powerful than he, and he treated her as a dear and in-

---

77. Sura 4:1.

78. Sura 33:35 in Cleary, trans., *Qur'an*, 107.

79. E.g., Armstrong, *Muhammad*; Ramadan, *In the Footsteps of the Prophet*, 24-25.

timate companion. While Khadija lived, he remained married to her alone at a time when polygyny was the norm. Even after he attained stature as Allah's messenger, he was not averse to performing domestic chores, the jobs culturally regarded as "women's work." Finally, virtually all historians of early Islam agree that the reforms Muhammad brought to ancient Arabia immensely improved the situation of women over their status in pre-Islamic society. Muhammad did believe, however, that men and women served different roles in society and, on account of this difference, men and women were given distinct rights and responsibilities. Whether these different social functions amount to social equality or inequality is a matter of debate. To examine the social changes Islam brought about during the life of the Prophet, we will consider three specific areas: marriage and divorce, inheritance rights, and dress.

Marriage and Divorce

Muhammad considered marriage a contract in which the woman's consent was essential. The contract was validated when the bride received her dowry,[80] which was often a set of expensive gifts given by the groom and his family. In pre-Islamic times, the dowry was regarded as the bride-price paid to her father, making marriage a virtual trade of property that was usually transacted without the woman's permission. The Qur'an, however, mandated that the bride herself was to receive and keep the dowry as her personal property, even in the event of divorce.[81] The possessions she owned before marriage, furthermore, did not transfer to her husband. According to the Qur'an, the husband's responsibility was to support his wife and family financially, but she was under no obligation to provide for the family out of her properties or from her income after marriage.

Muhammad envisioned marriage as a relationship of mutual rights and responsibilities. In his Farewell Sermon, Muhammad tells the men:

> O Believers, you have certain rights over your women, but remember, they also have certain rights over you. You have taken them as your wives only under Allah's trust and with his consent. If they respect your rights, then they have the right to be fed and clothed in kindness. Treat your women well and be kind to them for they are your partners and helpers.[82]

80. *mahr.*
81. Sura 4:20.
82. My rendering.

Since most of the Qur'an is directed to Muslim men, the ideals of marital relations focus on the rights and responsibilities of husbands rather than wives. Husbands are instructed to be kind even if they are averse to their wives. One sura says, "And associate with them considerately. And even if you dislike them, it may be that God has put much good in something you dislike."[83] In one *hadith*, the Prophet reportedly told his companions: "the best of you are those who are the best to their wives."[84] The Qur'an placed few restrictions on sexual expression within marriage, but it advises men to leave women alone during menstruation because "it hurts," says Sura 2.[85] Although the Qur'an permits a man to take up to four wives, it stipulates that he must be able to treat them all equally and fairly.[86] Although Islamic polygyny has been the subject of much criticism throughout Western history, the custom had a very practical and even humane purpose. Given the rampant intertribal warfare, women significantly outnumbered men, and without male protection and support, their lives could be miserable indeed. The Qur'an says: "Wed those among you who are unmarried, even the virtuous of your servants and maids. If they are poor, God will relieve them from the divine bounty."[87] In practice, Muhammad's teaching helped ameliorate the harsh conditions under which women lived by encouraging men to treat them with kindness and provide for those who especially needed it.

Muhammad recognized, however, that not all marriages were made in heaven, and so his teachings stipulated certain conditions under which divorce is possible. Divorce, however, is seen as an absolute last resort in the Qur'an and one that should not be pursued except for the most compelling reasons. In a *hadith*, the Prophet says: "among all the permitted acts, divorce is the most hateful to God."[88] Couples are instructed to pursue all possible remedies whenever their marriages are in danger. When husbands suspect their wives of disloyalty or lewd behavior, for example, the Qur'an advises first to "admonish them, then leave them alone in bed [in other words, deny them their conjugal rights], then [discipline] them. And if they obey you, then seek no means against them."[89] If these approaches fail, the couple should appoint two arbiters, one from his family and one from hers, to try to

83. Sura 4:19 in Cleary trans., *Qur'an*, 38.

84. Sultan, *Qur'an and Sayings of Prophet Muhammad*, 197.

85. Sura 2: 222, Cleary, trans., *Qur'an*, 17.

86. Sura 4:3.

87. Sura 24:32, Cleary, trans., *Qur'an*, 173.

88. *Hadith* from Abu Dawud, "Talaq," 3, cited in Buyukcelebi, *Living in the Shade of Islam*, 320.

89. Sura 4:34 in Cleary trans., *Qur'an*, 40.

bring about reconciliation.[90] When all else fails, both partners have the right to end the marriage. Unquestionably, though, it was far easier for the husband to do this than the wife. He simply had to tell her "I divorce you" on three occasions. The wife, on the other hand, must either ask her husband to grant a divorce, in which case the marriage is dissolved by mutual consent,[91] or she may seek a court to nullify the marriage on specific grounds, such as cruelty or neglect of his responsibilities to her. Divorces are undoubtedly unfortunate, but they are not, according to the Qur'an, sinful.

Inheritance Rights

Under Islam, females were given inheritance rights that had been restricted to males during the pre-Islamic period. The Qur'an requires that parents bequeath their property to their daughters as well as their sons. The basic standard for the division of assets, however, was not the same. A daughter was to receive only half as much as a son. Islam justified this difference by noting that the financial obligations of women were much less than those of men. Men were required to support their parents, wives, children, and sisters, and to pay dowries, while women had no comparable responsibility.

Clothing

For many in the contemporary Western world, the clothing of Muslim women, particularly the *hijab*, or veil, symbolizes their religiously sanctioned subjugation by men. But that interpretation of female dress is rather simplistic and, according to many Islamic scholars, misleading.

The Qur'an sets out no highly specific rules regarding how women should dress. In a revelation, Muhammad was told, "And tell the believing women to lower their eyes and guard their privates, and not to show their ornaments except the obvious ones, and to draw their coverings over their breasts and not to show their graces except to their husbands" and other members of their family.[92] At the same time, men are also enjoined to lower their eyes and dress modestly. In his teachings, Muhammad considered modesty in dress to reflect modesty of the heart, which he took to be an essential aspect of the faith.[93] Elsewhere, the Qur'an directs Muhammad to

90. Sura 4:35.
91. Sura 4:128.
92. Sura 24:31 in Cleary, trans., *Qur'an*, 172–73.
93. Sultan, 121.

"tell your wives, your daughters, and the believing women to put on their outer garments; that is most convenient so they will be recognized and not molested."[94] The intent of this command is to give Muslim women a distinctive appearance to protect themselves from harassment from nonbelievers.[95] Modest clothing, in other words, was intended to signal a woman's commitment to chastity and fidelity.

The tradition of veiling, according to many Islamic scholars, is not mandated in the Qur'an. Wearing the veil was a pre-Islamic custom and was practiced by some Jewish and Christian women.[96] When the custom first came to Islam, only the Prophet's wives veiled themselves,[97] perhaps to symbolize their special status. Veiling was most likely adopted because of its association with the Prophet's wives, who were regarded by the tradition as exemplars of the faith. Today, many Muslim women defend the veil because they find it a deterrent to unwanted sexual attention from men, and they have resisted efforts in some Western countries to force them to remove it in public.

It would be an anachronism to suggest that Muhammad was a seventh-century feminist. But it is not inaccurate to say that his teachings greatly improved the situation of women in his time. Prior to the advent of Islam, women had no property or inheritance rights but were considered the property of their fathers or husbands. By instituting rights of property ownership, inheritance, and divorce, Muhammad gave women basic safeguards that they did not have previously. Some historians have even maintained that Muslim women in Muhammad's day were able to enjoy certain rights that Western women did not receive until relatively recently.[98] This is not to say, however, that the situation of women throughout Islamic history and in the Islamic world today has always been a happy one. The development of every religion through time involves departures from the original inspiration out of which it began. Often, the departures are not only serious but even directly opposed to the initial impulse of the tradition. No matter how one might judge the subsequent history of the religion of Islam, it is hard to see how the spirit of Muhammad's own teachings, as reflected in the Qur'an and *hadith*, point to anything other than an ethical vision based on the fundamental spiritual equality and dignity of all human beings, without exception.

94. Sura 33:59 in Cleary, trans., Qur'an, 209.

95. Lawrence, Qur'an: A Biography, 54.

96. Ahmed, Women and Gender in Islam.

97. Ibid.

98. Lewis, What Went Wrong?, 82–83.

The Greater Jihad: Spiritual Disciplines of the Prophet

Upon returning to Madinah from the Battle of Badr, at which the Muslims soundly defeated a Makkan army over three times its size, Muhammad was reported to have said, "We have returned from the lesser *jihad* to the greater *jihad.*"[99] The Arabic term *jihad* needs no introduction, of course, but the distinction between the lesser and greater *jihad* probably requires some clarification. Muslims and non-Muslims alike ordinarily take the word *jihad* to refer to military action on behalf of Islam.[100] For this reason, the word is often translated as "holy war." In its basic sense, however, *jihad* simply means "struggle" and can refer to the struggle to bring oneself or one's society into greater alignment with the will of Allah. It was in this sense that the Prophet spoke of the "greater" *jihad*. Muhammad was commenting on the greater difficulty and significance of the internal struggle of the soul as compared to the external battle with the sword. "Though one may conquer thousands upon thousands in battle," said the Buddha, "the one who conquers self is the noblest victor."[101]

In the West, much more attention has been given to the lesser than to the greater *jihad*. In our analysis, we will try to redress that imbalance by examining the components of the spiritual disciplines of Islam, for those make up the arsenal of the greater *jihad*. To appreciate fully the purpose and design of spiritual exercises in Islam, it is essential to bear in mind its understanding of the fundamental flaw in human existence: our propensity to forget about the Absolute One and the obligations incumbent upon us as Allah's creatures. We will consider the four most prominent disciplines in the life of the Prophet: prayer, fasting, generosity, and pilgrimage. These practices, along with the Muslim profession of faith, were eventually incorporated into a cluster of the fundamental elements of the religion known in the Sunni tradition as the Five Pillars of Islam. Each of these practices serves as a vivid and constant reminder of the ideal of the life centered in the divine will.

Prayer

Long before the angel Gabriel appeared to him on the Mountain of Light, prayer and contemplative retreats were regular observances for the Prophet.

---

99. The provenance of this *hadith* is controversial; some have questioned the authenticity of the *isnad* by which it was transmitted.

100. Lewis, *Political Language of Islam*, 72; Cook, *Understanding Jihad*, 165–66.

101. *Dhammapada* 103, my rendering.

We know very little about the exact nature of Muhammad's prayer life prior to Gabriel's arrival. We do know that his retreats into the hills above Makkah were frequent, and tradition tells us that his prayers were exclusively addressed to Allah, although some non-Muslim scholars are not wholly convinced that Muhammad had been a *hanif*, or monotheist, his entire life.[102]

The *hadith* indicate that after Gabriel initially spoke to Muhammad, he met the Prophet at the Kaaba and taught the proper forms of ritual prayer. Perhaps the most impressive aspect of the prayer that Gabriel taught was its intricate physical movements and gestures. For Muhammad, and later for the entire Muslim community, prayer was not only vocal recitations but also carefully choreographed postures that carried deep significance. Today the specific forms and recitations of the prayers vary somewhat according to context and tradition, but all ritual prayers contain specific elements such as making ablutions (*wudu*), facing the Kaaba, standing with open arms, kneeling, prostrating, and reciting specific passages from the Qur'an and other words of praise and petition.

Prayer always begins with ablution, or the ritual cleansing of the face, mouth, hands, and feet with water. These gestures are intended to create a state of ritual purity[103] and to prepare the devotee's heart for sincere prayer. The postures of standing, kneeling, and prostrating with the forehead on the ground are intended to embody the act of submission to Allah, the very meaning of the word *islam*. Ritual prayers are thus not only spoken; they are physically enacted. Each *rak'ah*, or unit of prayer, begins with an Arabic recitation of the first sura of the Qur'an:

> In the name of God, the all-compassionate, the all-merciful. Praise is proper to God, Lord of the Universe, the all-compassionate, the all-merciful, Ruler of the Day of Requital. It is You we serve, to You we turn for help. Show us the straight path, the path of those You have favored, not of those who are objects of anger, nor of those who wander astray.[104]

Words and gestures, mind and body thus coordinate to create a state of spiritual surrender to god.

Initially, Muhammad taught that ritual prayer should be practiced twice a day, in the morning and in the evening, the same pattern that Jesus and other Jews observed.[105] Eventually, however, Gabriel revealed that twice a day was not sufficient. The Prophet was told: "Pray regularly at the borders

102. E.g., William Montgomery Watt.

103. *Tahara.*

104. Sura 1, in Cleary, trans., *Qur'an*, 1.

105. Ramadan, *In the Footsteps of the Prophet*, 42.

of the day and the approaches of the night."[106] But then later, as you recall, Muhammad learned on his Night Journey that Allah expected prayer five times a day. Actually, according to an interesting, although non-Qur'anic, tale, Muhammad was initially told by god to require the Muslims to pray *fifty* times a day. When Moses learned of this new command back at the Temple Mount in Jerusalem, he told Muhammad to return to heaven and get the number reduced. Fifty times a day was simply too many! Muhammad then got the number cut to ten times a day, but Moses thought that was still too much. Muhammad returned to heaven again, and the number was reduced to five. Moses thought five times was *still* too many, but Muhammad was too embarrassed to ask Allah to change it, and so he returned to Makkah.[107] Obviously, the frequency of prayer is an important feature in Islam and clearly serves the purpose of reminding the faithful to continually reorient their lives to Allah. The Qur'an states: "Recite what has been revealed to you from the Book, and pray regularly; for prayer restrains from that which is evil and repulsive. And remembrance of God is even greater."[108]

Ritual prayers may be made alone at specified times of the day, which vary from day to day because they depend on the position of the sun. But Muhammad made it clear that prayer with others was better than individual prayer. He claimed that communal prayer was twenty-five times superior to praying in private.[109]

In addition to the daily ritual prayers, Muhammad was known to pray in other ways and at other times. He found praying in the quiet of the night especially meaningful. A revelation while he was still in Makkah explained the content and purpose of nightly prayer:

> Stand [to pray] by night, but not all night—half of it, or a little less, or a little more; and recite the Qur'an in slow measured rhythmic tones. We shall soon send down to you a weighty Word. Truly the rising by night is a time when impression is more keen and speech more certain. True, there is for you by day prolonged occupation with ordinary duties. But keep in remembrance the name of your Educator and devote yourself to him wholeheartedly.[110]

---

106. Sura 11:114 in Cleary, trans., *Qur'an*, 111.

107. Al-Gailani and Smith, *Islamic Year*, 90-94.

108. Sura 29:45 in Cleary, trans., *Qur'an*, 197. I have slightly altered the translation.

109. Phipps, *Muhammad and Jesus*, 58.

110. Sura 73:1-8, translated and cited in Ramadan, *In the Footsteps of the Prophet*, 42.

Before the revelation to pray five times a day, all Muslims were required to pray during the night, sometime between the hours of 1:00 and 4:30. The sura suggests the mind is especially receptive to the divine during this period of the day. After the establishment of the five-times-daily prayer, Muslims were no longer expected to observe nightly prayer, but Muhammad continued the practice. At one point, his wife Aishah suggested he might be overdoing it: "'Don't you take on too much [worship] while God has already forgiven all your past and future sins?' [she asked.] The Prophet answered: 'How could I but be a thankful servant?'"[111] Muhammad held himself to higher standards of spiritual discipline than he expected of all others.

Fasting

Like daily ritual prayer, fasting during the month of Ramadan is compulsory[112] for all Muslims beyond the age of puberty.[113] During this month, Muslims refrain from eating, drinking, sexual activity, and smoking from dawn to sundown. But the discipline of the fast is not limited to the holy month; it can be practiced voluntarily at almost any time, except on a few days when it is specifically forbidden.

The Prophet Muhammad fasted, according to tradition, each Monday and Thursday.[114] It is worth noting that Confucius, the Buddha, and Jesus also observed the fast at particular times in their lives. For Confucius, fasting was important during rituals of grief and mourning. The Buddha fasted zealously during his period of extreme asceticism, after which he began to take food in moderation, one meal a day. Fasting was not a *major* part of Jesus's life, but the gospels report that he fasted for forty days during his vision quest in the wilderness after his baptism.

The practice of fasting takes many forms and serves many purposes. In Islam, as part of the Ramadan celebration, fasting technically means not allowing anything to pass through the lips as well as abstaining from sex. But fasting can mean, and often does mean, more than this. In a *hadith*, Muhammad said, "When any one of you is fasting on a day, he should neither indulge in obscene language nor should he raise his voice; and if anyone

111. *Hadith* reported by Bukari and quoted in Ramadan, *In the Footsteps of the Prophet*, 111.

112. *Fard.*

113. *Takleef,* the age of accountability.

114. Sultan, *Qur'an and Sayings of Prophet Muhammad*, 100.

insults him or tries to quarrel with him, he should say 'I am fasting.'"[115] Fasting can also mean refraining from lustful or angry thoughts.

The principal purpose of the spiritual fast, I believe, is sharpening awareness, and I think this is generally true regardless of tradition. To go a day without food alters one's awareness of the body, sense of time and habits, and even perceptions of the world. Refraining from certain items in our routine experience can make us more conscious of ourselves and our world. The Qur'an says: "fasting is prescribed to you as it was prescribed to those before you, so that you may be conscious of God."[116] Fasting also serves to arouse a sense of compassion by enabling the practitioner to feel, even if only for a short while, the pangs of those who hunger and thirst, thereby cultivating greater awareness of those in need.

While fasting is only required during Ramadan, Muhammad encouraged his community to practice it more frequently, a minimum of three times each month, but no more than every other day.[117] Like the Buddha, moderation was important to Muhammad. Although Muhammad often fasted, he did not expect other Muslims to do so to the extent that he did,[118] and he exempted those who were sick or enduring hardship from the Ramadan fast.[119] Muhammad often tempered the letter of the law with the compassionate spirit that he believed was characteristic of Allah.

Generosity

I use the word "generosity" to translate the Arabic term zakah, a word that ordinarily refers to the practice of giving a portion of one's wealth to those in need or to serve the cause of Islam. Although the zakah is ordinarily collected as a tax in Islamic countries today, the word generosity, I think, aptly characterizes the actual intent of the practice as it was instituted by the Qur'an. The word literally signifies purification and is derived from the word that means "to thrive" or "to be wholesome."[120] This derivation suggests that the payment of zakah serves as practical way to support not only Islam's concern for the poor and dispossessed but also the spiritual function of purifying the soul of materialism and greed. The Qur'an tells believers:

115. Quoted in Sultan, Qur'an and Sayings of Prophet Muhammad, 101.

116. Sura 2:183 in Cleary, trans, Qur'an, 13; I have slightly altered the translation.

117. Sultan, Qur'an and Sayings of Prophet Muhammad, 100.

118. Ramadan, In the Footsteps of the Prophet, 111.

119. Phipps, Muhammad and Jesus, 126.

120. Glassé, Concise Encyclopedia of Islam, 430.

"spend in charity for the benefit of your own souls, for those saved from the covetousness of their own souls are the ones who achieve success."[121]

Because the zakah is an obligation on every Muslim who is able to pay it, it is usually levied as a tax collected by the state. Determining the precise amount of the zakah is a bit complicated. The amount is a percentage of the wealth one has over and above what is necessary for sustenance. The figure of 2.5% is often cited, but that formula applies only to liquid assets and would be different for other kinds of possessions such as livestock or farm produce. But these percentages are only the minima; what is given beyond the minimum is regarded as a pious and meritorious act.

Hajj

As our final example of the Prophet's spiritual practices, we will consider the pilgrimage to Makkah. As we have learned earlier, the yearly pilgrimage, known as the Hajj, was an ancient practice even in the time of the Prophet. Initially intended as a shrine devoted to Allah alone, the Muslim traditions contend that the Kaaba, the centerpiece of the pilgrimage, had degenerated into a house of idols during the days of ignorance. Some sources suggest that the pilgrimage during the pre-Islamic era was little more than a pan-Arabian carnival in which the tribes gathered to drink and boast of their own courage, strength, and hospitality while ridiculing the qualities of other tribes. Circumambulating the Kaaba, these sources say, was a farce. Men and women performed the circuits in the nude while clapping their hands, blowing horns, and whistling. (Whistling is associated with sorcery and vulgarity and is forbidden in Islam.) Animals were sacrificed and their blood poured on the walls of the Kaaba.

Despite these practices, which were later abolished by the Prophet, the Kaaba and the pilgrimage were deeply sacred to Muhammad. Early in his life he was drawn to the Kaaba and went there often to pray. He frequently performed the 'umrah, or lesser pilgrimage, which can be made at any time of the year. Even after he left Makkah to take up residence in Madinah, he fondly remembered the Kaaba and sought to return to make the greater pilgrimage. Just before the end of his life, he was able to visit the Kaaba twice, once in the year 7 AH to perform the 'umrah, and once in year 10 to perform the Hajj. A few months later, he died, as if to suggest that in his completing the greater pilgrimage, his life's journey had reached its end. His

---

121. Sura 64:16 in Ali, trans, Qur'an, http://wikilivres.ca/wiki/The_Holy_Qur%27an/At-Taghabun.

final Hajj provided many elements of the ritual as it has been practiced by Muslims since that time.

Muhammad's final pilgrimage, like the Hajj today, took place over a period of many days and involved several different undertakings. As with ritual prayer, his pilgrimage involved first entering a state of purity[122] to prepare the mind, heart, and body for its encounter with the sacred. Today, before they enter Makkah, pilgrims purify themselves and dress in white, seamless garments, which for men are two simple towels and for women long robes. The uniformity and simplicity of the clothing signifies the equality of persons before god. Differences of race, age, nationality, class, and culture, as we have noted before, are spiritually irrelevant in Islam. These ritual preparations also symbolize entrance into sacred time and space, an extraordinary reality that requires severing ordinary routines and conventions.

As the Prophet proceeded to Makkah, he and his companions recited the phrase that all pilgrims say as they enter the sacred precincts: "At Your service, My God, At Your service." As soon as the Muslims entered Makkah, Muhammad went directly to the Kaaba and circumambulated it seven times. On each circuit, he stopped to kiss the Black Stone, which he had helped peacefully to put in place years earlier when the structure was being renovated. He also stopped to pray at the Station of Abraham, another stone near the Kaaba that is said to contain an imprint of Abraham's foot, placed there as he was building the shrine with Ishmael. Pilgrims today still attempt to kiss the Black Stone and pray at Abraham's Station, but it is far more difficult now than ever before, given the great numbers of Muslims who perform the Hajj each year—nearly two million annually.

Muhammad remained in Makkah for several days before leaving the city and traveling to the Plain of Arafat, just outside the city. It was here that the Prophet delivered his Farewell Sermon. Since that time, pilgrims go to this site and stand in the blazing sun for most of the day, engaged in prayer and self-examination. Standing at Arafat is understood to be a foretaste of the day of requital. As Muhammad himself was performing this portion of the Hajj, he received a revelation: "Today I have completed your religion for you, and have fulfilled My favor for you, and approved Islam as a religion for you."[123] By completing the greater pilgrimage and incorporating it as a fundamental element of the faith, Islam had been perfected. Ever since, all

---

122. *ihram.*

123. Sura 5:3 according to Sunni *tafsir*. According to Shi'a *tafsir*, it refers to the appointment of Ali ibn Abu Talib at the pond of Khumm as Muhammad's successor, a few days later when the Muslims were returning to Madinah.

Muslims have been required to perform the Hajj at least once, if they can afford it.

Later, Muhammad traveled to nearby Mina, where he threw seven pebbles at each of three stone pillars in an act symbolizing resistance to the temptations of Iblis. He enacted this ritual many times over the next several days. Then he addressed the Muslims again and urged them to practice the pilgrimage as he showed them and to not revert back to Arabian paganism. Shortly afterward, he sacrificed sixty-three camels, one for each year of his life, had his head shaved, and returned to Makkah for a final series of revolutions around the shrine. Before leaving Makkah, he partook of water from the well of Zamzam, located near the Kaaba. According to tradition, this well appeared when Hagar and Ishmael depleted the water supply given to them by Abraham. In desperation, Hagar ran to and fro as Ishmael prayed to god for water. Suddenly, in answer to his prayer, water gushed forth out of the desert, making the sound *zam zam*, and it has flowed ever since.

At last, Muhammad returned to Mina, a few miles from Makkah, and stayed there several days before departing for Madinah. He never saw Makkah again.

To grasp the significance of the Hajj and the Kaaba for Muhammad and to appreciate its importance in Islam, let us discuss what makes pilgrimage such a powerful and popular spiritual exercise not just in Islam but in virtually all religions.

To begin, we note that pilgrimage, like Muslim prayer, engages the body as well as the mind. It is an enactment, a performance, and not merely the intellectual assent to beliefs and doctrines. It fully involves the senses in ways that other dimensions of religion, such as theology, do not. The physical actions of the pilgrimage both reflect and shape the interior dynamics of the soul. Movements of the body coordinate with movements of the spirit. This engagement of one's whole being makes the often abstract and intangible aspects of faith more palpable.

The lesser and greater pilgrimages in Islam, like many pilgrimages in other religions, are ritual reenactments of its primordial history. To go to Makkah, circumambulate the Kaaba, and kiss the sacred stone is to relive events performed by Adam, Abraham, Hagar, Ishmael, and the Prophet himself. It is also to participate in the long history of Muslims who have been to this place. Symbolically, going to the Kaaba for Muslims is, as it was literally for Muhammad, a return to one's true home, the center of being, and the source of life. The Hajj is thus a way vividly and memorably to bind oneself to a history, a community, and set of shared values. The feast of Passover functions in a similar way for Jews. Celebrating the Passover reminds the Jews of the events that liberated them from Egypt and encourages remembrance of their dependence on Yahweh. The Hajj and the Passover remind their celebrants of who they are and what the purpose of their lives should be.

The pilgrimage to Makkah for Muhammad—and for Muslims still today—involved discrete stages that facilitated individual and communal transformation. There is a pattern common to many, but by no means all, pilgrimages. To simplify a more complicated scheme, I would identify five basic stages: intention, separation, struggle, transformation, and return. The Hajj and other pilgrimages usually begin with an intention, or a decision to travel for a spiritual purpose, such as renewal, healing, or penance. Once one determines to make the pilgrimage, it is necessary to intentionally leave the place where one is. This involves a literal and a symbolic separation. At the Hajj, the pilgrim purifies him- or herself and puts on new clothes to ritualize the separation from ordinary life. Pilgrimages are not easy. They often involve overcoming obstacles of some sort or engaging in a struggle or contest. Such struggles symbolize the internal, spiritual effort. During the Hajj, standing at the plain of Arafat is a *jihad* with one's soul as the pilgrim stands before Allah examining his or her conscience. Throwing pebbles at the stone pillars represents the individual's striving against the devil. And the dangers are not only symbolic. Today performing the Hajj is more arduous than ever, given the vast numbers of pilgrims who descend on Makkah each year. Overcoming obstacles often allows transformation to occur. In the Hajj, transformation can be both personal and communal. The Hajj helps bind the Muslim community together in shared activities and reinforces the Islamic belief in the fundamental equality of all human beings. The individual often experiences a personal transformation, a cleansing of the soul, a new understanding or insight.[124] Finally, the movement of the Hajj is, in a sense, circular. The pilgrim usually goes back to the place from which he or she began. Muhammad returns to Madinah. But now that place is different because the pilgrim is different. Transformed by the experience, the pilgrim is not the same person who left.

Let us draw to a close this discussion of the spiritual practices of the Prophet by reiterating the features most common to them all: repetition and remembrance. Human beings are forgetful creatures, Islam tells us. We are so easily distracted by the delights of the world and our daily cares that we often fail to remember who we really are and what things in life are of true and lasting value. Praying daily, fasting yearly, practicing generosity, and performing pilgrimage all serve to prod the memory about those things.

---

124. The "Letter from Makkah" in X, *The Autobiography of Malcolm X* provides an excellent account of the profound transformative effects of the Hajj.

The world is big and our minds are small; we never cease needing to be reminded of what is really important.

The Triumph of Islam

Muhammad's final pilgrimage a few months before his death in 632 CE culminated a series of significant episodes in his life that led to the eventual triumph of Islam in Arabia. We will now discuss these events, covering the last seven years of his life, from the Muslim defeat at Uhud to his death in Madinah. Then we will briefly outline the developments within Islam in the post-Prophet era.

The King of the Arabs

As you will recall, within two years of the migration to Madinah, Muhammad and the Muslims finally faced the Quraysh in a major conflict at the well of Badr. Against the odds, and with Allah's help they believed, the Muslims defeated a Makkan army of over one thousand. Given their humiliating loss, the Makkans felt as if they had no choice but to avenge their defeat. A year later they squared off against the Muslims at Uhud, just outside of Madinah. This time, due to greed and a lack of discipline, the Muslims were beaten, and Muhammad handled the lost with equanimity. But the thrashing at Uhud was not quite the success the Makkans had hoped it would be. The Muslims had not been utterly destroyed as the Quraysh intended. The Makkans returned home victorious but not champions.

Upon their arrival, the Makkans began to plot another attack on Madinah aimed at completely eradicating the Muslim community. The leaders of the Quraysh sought to enlist the aid of nomadic tribes surrounding Madinah. Back in Madinah, Muhammad's strategy was to forestall a major confrontation with the Makkans by breaking up the very alliances the Quraysh were trying to establish. He kept surveillance on the other tribes in the region and immediately dispatched armed squads to disrupt any coalitions that were forming against Madinah. Muhammad proved he was extremely serious about protecting the Muslims from hostile alliances. When he discovered that Ka'b ibn Ashraf, the chief of a Jewish tribe in Madinah, had conspired with Makkans against the Muslims, Muhammad ordered Ka'b's assassination and later expelled his tribe from Madinah. Ultimately, however, Muhammad was unable to avert a confederation of his enemies, but he *was* able to contain its size while increasing the strength of his own army.

With the assistance of the Banu Nadir, one of the Jewish tribes banished from Madinah, the Quraysh were able to raise a force of ten thousand men and felt confident about the army's ability to crush the Muslims. The year was 627 CE, the fifth year of the *hijrah*. By now, Muhammad's army numbered about three thousand men, much more than before, but far less than the Makkans. The Prophet had been warned that the Makkan confederates were about to lay siege to Madinah and had about a week to prepare for their arrival. Knowing they were vastly outnumbered, the Muslims began to think creatively. Something about the knowledge of ten thousand armed soldiers marching to annihilate you is wonderfully effective in stimulating novel ideas. Thanks to a Persian convert to Islam, Muhammad learned of a defensive maneuver never before tried in Arabia: to dig a massive trench to protect the most vulnerable part of the city. In six days, every able-bodied Muslim assisted in completing the huge ditch on the northern side of Madinah. The rest of the city was surrounded by mountains and trees, which prevented a cavalry attack. The confederates were completely unprepared for the surprise tactic. The inability to attack with force, the shortage of food, the cold nights, and dissension within the ranks of the coalition, eventually led them to abandon the siege. In twenty-five days, the confederates packed up and went home. Their failure to defeat the Muslims resulted in a great loss of prestige for the Quraysh, and their commerce suffered as a result.

During the conflict—which is variously known as the Battle of the Trench, the Siege of Madinah, and the Battle of the Confederates—the Jewish tribe of Qurayza, who lived south of Madinah, had entered talks with the Makkans to join the confederates in their war against Muhammad. The Qurayza had committed themselves earlier to an alliance with the Muslims, and reneging on that treaty would have left Madinah vulnerable and subject to certain extermination. After the confederates gave up the siege, the Muslims accused the Qurayza tribe of treachery and attacked them. After twenty-five days holed up in their fortresses, the Qurayza eventually surrendered. All seven hundred men, apart from a few who converted to Islam, were executed, while the women and children were taken as slaves. This action was contrary to the clemency Muhammad had shown to his enemies in previous battles. Muslim apologists explain that Muhammad had gained a reputation throughout the peninsula as one who spared his prisoners of war, against the common practice of the time, and this led to his being viewed as weak, making the Muslims even more vulnerable to future attacks. Furthermore, many of the prisoners he spared had returned to their homes to instigate new wars against the Muslims, and this led to his being viewed as incompetent. Finally, the breach of covenant had been a serious threat to the survival of the Muslim community. Taken together, suggests this argument in defense of his actions, these factors had persuaded Muhammad to agree to this harsh penalty. One of the female captives became a member of the Prophet's household, either as his servant or his wife; the sources are not clear on this point. The treatment of the Qurayza made it known to all tribes that any act of aggression or treachery against the Muslims would be handled in a similar fashion. The rulers of other nations were also beginning to take notice. The Persians and Byzantines began to call Muhammad the "King of the Arabs."

Negotiations with Makkah

For years while in Madinah, Muhammad had longed to return to Makkah to perform the Hajj. The conflicts with the Makkans had obviously precluded that. But by 628, year 6 of the hijrah, Muhammad felt confident enough to attempt the *'umrah*, the lesser pilgrimage. He had been emboldened by a vision in which he saw himself with a shaven head, indicating his completion of the pilgrimage. With 1,400 Muslims and herds of sacrificial animals, he set out for the holy city. Scholars debate whether Muhammad's journey was motivated purely by spiritual purposes. Some have suggested that Muhammad's real intention was to fight the Makkans, but that on the way he decided against it and hastily converted the expedition into a pilgrimage.[125] Others argue that the Muslims were never sufficiently armed and always intended the pilgrimage to be peaceful.[126] The *hadith* agree with the latter view and quote Muhammad as saying that he wanted to avoid the shedding of blood in the holy city and had come only to perform the pilgrimage. He offered the Makkans a truce but also indicated his preparedness to fight if they did not accept it.[127] The Quraysh were fully aware of the military prowess of the Muslims by now and agreed to the terms of the treaty. The treaty stipulated that the fighting between the Muslims and the Quraysh would cease for ten years. In addition, Muhammad promised to return to the Quraysh any young man who had joined the Muslims without his father's or protector's permission. Finally, the Quraysh agreed to allow the Muslims to come to Makkah in the *following* year, unarmed, to perform the pilgrimage while the Makkans retreated to the hills for three days.

Not all the Muslims were happy with this pact, which was called the Treaty of Hudaybiyyah, named for the area outside of Makkah where it was

125. E.g., Bernard Lewis.

126. Andrae, *Mohammed*, 156; Watt, *Muhammad*, 183.

127. *Sahih Bukhari*, Vol. 3, Book 50, Number 891. http://www.sahih-bukhari.com/ Pages/Bukhari_3_50.php

concluded. Some were upset that the document did not refer to Muhammad as the messenger of god; some simply wanted to fight the Quraysh; others resented the return of some Muslims to their Makkan protectors. But after the treaty was ratified, Muhammad received a revelation telling the Muslims that the agreement should be regarded as a victory for Islam and promising them great benefits from it.[128] Over time, those advantages became apparent. Effectively, the treaty meant that the Quraysh had regarded Muhammad as an equal, and they were impressed by the Muslims' desire to incorporate the ancient pilgrimage into Islam. The benefits would eventually pay off.

In the years following the conclusion of the truce, Muhammad continued with sporadic military expeditions against assorted tribes in the region, particularly those he believed were stirring up hostilities against the community of Muslims. During this time, according to tradition, he also sent letters to the leaders of the Byzantine and Persian empires and Yemen, inviting them to embrace Islam. They declined. Muhammad and his community were also able to perform the lesser pilgrimage one year after the accord with the Makkans, who honored their promise to allow Muhammad to visit the Kaaba.

Life in Madinah

During this relatively quiet period, Muhammad enjoyed domestic life in Madinah. By now, he had married many other women in addition to Sawdah and Aishah. The exact number of his wives is not known and may have been as many as thirteen. Although the Qur'an specifically limited the number of wives to four, Muhammad received a revelation that permitted an exception in his case because of his status as Allah's messenger. Some of his marriages were happy, like the one with Aishah; others were not. At one point, Muhammad wanted to divorce Sawdah, but she persuaded him to give up the idea. As I noted earlier, many of these marriages were social or political arrangements, as was the custom at the time, and some were to provide protection to widows of soldiers who had died in battle. One or two may have been motivated by love. Each of his wives had her own small apartment attached to the mosque that served as his residence. The *hadith* say that Muhammad frequently spoke with his wives and even debated with them and asked for their advice. He assisted with the domestic chores such as cooking and sewing and often played with his children.

---

128. Sura 48, "The Victory."

Conquest of Makkah

The Treaty of Hudaybiyyah did not last for ten years, as it had stipulated. In 630, two years after the truce had been signed, the agreement was broken when one of the allies of the Quraysh attacked one of the allies of the Muslims. In fact, the Quraysh had probably abetted their ally in the attack. Muhammad asked the Quraysh to pay blood money, to break their association with the ally, or to consider the treaty with the Muslims invalid. Unwisely, they sent word to Muhammad declaring the Treaty of Hudaybiyyah nullified. Almost immediately, the Makkans regretted their action. Fearing the superior strength of the Muslims, Abu Sufyan, the leader of the Quraysh, went to Madinah to try to restore the agreement. Muhammad refused.

Muhammad was now committed to the conquest of the Quraysh. He mustered an army of more than ten thousand and marched on Makkah. As the Muslims advanced, Abu Sufyan shuttled back and forth between Makkah and the approaching Muslims, trying to avert what seemed to be an inevitable slaughter of the Quraysh. Just before the Muslims were about to besiege the city, Abu Sufyan embraced Islam, acknowledging that the patron deities of Makkah had been powerless before Allah. In response, Muhammad promised the Makkans that Abu Sufyan's home would be a safe haven. Anyone taking refuge there would be spared. He extended that promise to anyone who would stay in their own homes and lay down their arms. The Muslims essentially walked into Makkah unopposed. With just a few skirmishes and minimal bloodshed, Muhammad had conquered the city.

Accompanied by his closest companions, Muhammad made his way to the Kaaba, opened its doors, removed the images of the gods (or had them removed according to some accounts), and destroyed them. One report says he even found pictures of Abraham and Ishmael and demolished them as well. Then he quoted the Qur'an: "The truth has come, and falsehood has passed away: falsehood is bound to pass away."[129] He addressed the Makkans who had assembled outside the shrine and declared the Kaaba cleansed and rededicated to Allah. According to a *hadith*, he issued a general amnesty to all, invoking the example of Joseph, who forgave his brothers who had sold him into slavery to the Egyptians. "Go your way," he told the Makkans, "for you are free." Muhammad did, however, order the execution of ten persons who played especially nefarious roles in the years of conflict. Not all of the executions were carried out, for various reasons, and at least one of the condemned adopted Islam, as did most of the Makkans. As a result of the conquest, Muhammad's stature throughout Arabia grew, and

---

129. Sura 17:81 in Haleem, trans., *Qur'an*, 180.

his military power was widely recognized. Many tribes sent their representatives to declare their submission to the Prophet.

But some of the Arabian tribes were unwilling to submit to Muhammad's authority. Soon after the conquest of Makkah, a new coalition was amassing, led by the Hawazin tribe, who were the ancient enemies of the Quraysh. The inhabitants of Taif, who had thrown Muhammad out of their town when he still lived in Makkah, joined forces with the Hawazin. Muhammad's army met the coalition and severely defeated it, accumulating many spoils of war. Later the same year, Muhammad led an immense expedition into northwestern Arabia with the intent of engaging the Byzantines, who had, according to Muslim sources, become increasingly concerned by the growth of Islam and its military might. Upon arriving at Tabuk, the Muslims found no Byzantine army as they had expected. Contemporary Muslim sources say the Byzantines had fled upon learning of the approach of Muhammad's army, rumored to number around thirty thousand. There were no casualties as a result of this venture, but it did garner the Muslims greater prestige and more alliances in this part of the peninsula and probably set the stage for a later Arab-Byzantine conflict. By now, virtually all of Arabia had been unified by Muhammad. Not all of the tribes were persuaded by the superiority of Islam. Many acquiesced to protect themselves from attack or to gain a share in the war spoils. Many of the Bedouin tribes were particularly recalcitrant. They agreed to acknowledge Madinah's rule but tried to maintain their own honor codes and traditions.

After the conquest of Makkah, the Prophet chose to maintain his residence in Madinah. His final year of life was 632 CE, or 10 AH. It was during this year that he was visited twice by Gabriel for the purpose of reciting the Qur'an. Since the revelations began, Gabriel appeared to Muhammad once a year to rehearse the messages that had been given to that point. In the year 10, Gabriel came twice. Muhammad interpreted this anomaly as a sign that his death was imminent. Accordingly, he made plans to lead the Muslims on the greater pilgrimage to Makkah, believing that it would be his last. It was also his first genuinely Islamic Hajj, because now the Kaaba had been dedicated solely to Allah. As we noted previously, it was during this farewell pilgrimage that Muhammad instructed the Muslims on the proper performance of the Hajj and delivered his final public discourse.

On the return trip to Madinah, a seemingly innocuous event occurred that would later have profound ramifications for Islamic history. The caravan stopped near a pond called Khumm, between the two cities. There Muhammad made a public statement about Ali, his cousin, foster son, and son-in-law. Sources report that Muhammad declared, "Whoever has me as his *mawla*, this Ali is also *his mawla*. O Allah, befriend whoever befriends him and be the enemy of whoever is his enemy." *Mawla* is a word that often appears in the Qur'an in reference to Allah, and it is often translated as "protector." Shortly after the Prophet's death, a dispute arose among some of the Muslims as to the meaning of Muhammad's statement. One faction took it to mean that Muhammad was appointing Ali to be his successor, taking the word *mawla* to mean "master" or "one with authority." The other faction contended that Muhammad was merely defending Ali against unfair criticism and interpreted *mawla* to mean "beloved friend." The dispute eventually entailed a major split within the ranks of the Muslims. Those who regarded the statement as Muhammad's endorsement of Ali to be his successor came to be called the Shi'a, or "the followers," meaning the followers of Ali. Those who did not accept that interpretation became known as the "Sunni," those who follow the *Sunnah*, the words and example of Muhammad.

"Muhammad Is Dead"

Just a few months after the farewell pilgrimage, Muhammad became ill and suffered severe head pain for several days. He died in Madinah in Aishah's apartment on or around June 8, 632 CE at the age of sixty-three. Many Muslims refused to believe that he had actually died. As soon as he received the news, Abu Bakr, one of Muhammad's oldest and closest companions went to the mosque and announced: "Oh believers, if you worship Muhammad, then know that Muhammad is dead. But if you worship Allah, know that Allah never dies." Abu Bakr then recited a passage from the Qur'an: "Muhammad is only a messenger before whom many messengers have been and gone. If he died or was killed, would you revert to your old ways?"[130]

The Prophet was buried the next day at the same place where he died. According to Abu Bakr, "Allah does not cause a prophet to die but in the place where he is to be buried." His tomb now serves as a mosque and a visitation site, especially for pilgrims making the Hajj. It is the second holiest place in Islam, next to the Kaaba.

As directed by revelation, his widows never remarried. After his death, their stature in the community increased, and they became known as the "mothers of the believers." Aishah survived him by several decades and helped to collect the scattered sayings of and about Muhammad that would compose the *hadith*. His wife Hafsah assisted in putting together the first manuscript of the Qur'an. Some of the widows even became involved in

---

130. Sura 3:144, in ibid., 44-45.

Arabian politics and took sides when the internal dissension among Muslims increased.

Abu Bakr's words announcing Muhammad's demise effectively eliminated any possibility that Muhammad himself might be deified, although in view of his ardent emphasis on the oneness of the divine, such a development would likely never have occurred or been tolerated for long. Yet, Muslims have traditionally regarded Muhammad with tremendous affection and admiration. When Muslims say or write the name of Muhammad, or any other prophet in Islam, they usually follow it with the words "Peace be upon him."[131] The Qur'an calls him "a mercy to all peoples"[132] and says, "The Messenger of God is an excellent model for those of you who put your hope in God and the Last Day and remember Him often."[133] Although he was not divine, Islam asserts that Muhammad was the most perfect of god's creatures. The Prophet thus embodies the highest human qualities and serves as the model of true and complete humanity for Muslims, much as Jesus serves this function for Christians. In particular, Muslims stress his humility and simple life, his equanimity and dignity, his honesty and promise keeping, his courage and commitment to justice.

For many non-Muslims, the militarism of Muhammad's last years will no doubt cast a dark shadow on some of what they might consider his finer qualities. Apologists have used different arguments to mitigate this concern. Some writers note that Muhammad's military actions—even those that appear to be offensive rather than defensive—were motivated purely by the desire to preserve his community and hence true monotheistic faith.[134] After all, in the ancient Arabian context, raids and the collecting of spoils were necessary to preempt attacks by other tribes and clans. Others observe that Muhammad instituted important rules of warfare where there were none before. Finally, some contend that Muhammad's use of the sword was in effect no different from the practices of the ancient Israelites and their prophets, by whom he was inspired.[135] Muhammad and the ancient Israelites believed that god had sanctioned battle with their enemies and even fought on their behalf. Each of these arguments makes valid points, but whether these observations amount to justification for bloodshed is yet another matter.

131. *sallAllahu 'alayhi wa sallam.*

132. Sura 21:107 in Cleary, trans., *Qur'an*, 161.

133. Sura 33:21, Haleem, trans., *Qur'an*, 268.

134. E.g., Tariq Ramadan.

135. Esposito, *Islam*, 15.

Muhammad's death sparked a crisis in Arabia. The first issue to confront the community was determining his successor. Unlike the Buddha and Jesus, who established *religious* communities, Muhammad governed a political state as well as a religious institution by the time he died. Having only recently unified the peninsula and established a new order of things, Muhammad left Arabia in a precarious position; therefore, agreeing upon a *khalif*, or successor to the Prophet, seemed paramount. Two different views emerged about how the process unfolded. According to the Sunni view, Muhammad expected the Muslim community to elect a *khalif*, and he clearly favored his close friend, Abu Bakr. Abu Bakr was nominated and chosen by the Prophet's closest companions. The Shi'a view, on the other hand, contends that Muhammad had in fact appointed Ali at the pond at Khumm, several months before his death. For the Shi'a, Ali was the first *khalif*; for the Sunni, Abu Bakr was the first and Ali was the fourth successor to Muhammad. The dispute was never resolved and remains a point of disagreement between two branches of the religion. Today, the Sunni constitute about 80–85 percent of the Muslim population, and the Shi'a make up between 15 and 20 percent.

After uniting the Arabian peninsula, Islam continued to spread throughout the world. Within a few centuries, the religion and culture of Islam had moved beyond Arabia westward through northern Africa and into Spain; it had traveled north through Palestine and into Asia Minor and the Balkans, and through Persia eastward into northern India. Eventually, it traveled to China, through Southeast Asia and into Indonesia, which is today the nation with the largest Muslim population. Islam is currently the second-largest religion next to Christianity and the world's fastest-growing faith.

CONCLUSION

Up to now, we have focused our studies on the lives and teachings of Confucius, the Buddha, Jesus, and Muhammad within their particular historical contexts. This approach has allowed us to appreciate these teachers as individuals influenced by and responding to specific moments and settings within the human experience. It is time now to begin a new stage in our inquiry by considering their lives and teachings from a comparative point of view. Without losing sight of their rootedness in particular times and places, we will now put those contextual matters in the background so we might give greater attention to the similarities and differences in the patterns of their lives and teachings. Our ultimate purpose in creating this comparative study is to bring us closer to determining what significance these four have for our lives today. We will begin by looking at their life stories and then consider the similarities and differences in their teachings.

Their Lives Compared

Early on, we noted that Confucius, the Buddha, Jesus, and Muhammad were all born into old, well-established civilizations in the midst of momentous changes. The natures of those changes, however, were not the same. China in Confucius's day was struggling with political turmoil as petty kingdoms governed by selfish rulers and self-serving aristocrats began to vie for control of the region. Warfare was rampant, and human life was cheap. These developments necessarily shaped the issues with which Confucius and other Chinese had to struggle: questions about human harmony and proper governance.

The political situation in the Buddha's India was more stable than China at the time of Confucius, but it was undergoing an *intellectual* revolution, a complete shift in worldview. In the centuries just before the Buddha, Indians had adopted the view that life was governed by the principle of karma and that individuals were subject to an invidious cycle of birth, death, and rebirth. The value of the entire phenomenal world had been called into question, and the Buddha responded by discovering and teaching a way to be happy by accepting the impermanence and pervasive suffering of existence.

Compared to the cultures of Confucius and Muhammad, the Palestine of Jesus's day seemed closer to the India of the Buddha. In the initial decades of the first century CE, Palestine was not subject to the incessant warfare of ancient China and Arabia. But the relative calm in Judea and Galilee of the *Pax Romana* could not mask the subterranean tensions stretching and ripping the fabric of Jewish society. The stresses on that culture constellated around a number of oppositions: Jew and Roman, rich and poor, collaborators and rebels, clean and unclean, temple and synagogue, Sadducee and Pharisee. These tensions decisively shaped Jesus's outlook on life and informed his vision of a world in which such oppositions no longer existed.

Prior to Muhammad's birth, many ancient Arabs sensed that the old tribal and clan system and its virtues and code of honor were no longer serving the best interests of the Arabian people. As warfare continued to plague the tribes and clans, there was a growing, but mostly unconscious, intuition that something needed to change, yet insight into the nature of that change had not yet broken to the surface. It took someone of Muhammad's perceptive nature to respond to that yearning and to listen to the words from deep within in order to articulate a way to transformation.

In view of the nature of their cultural settings, part of the greatness of each of these teachers must lie in his attunement to the profound issues driving the changes in his society and the clarity of his vision to imagine a way through them. Certainly, that keen awareness was rooted in a heightened sensitivity to the suffering of others. Perhaps some are born with a more compassionate nature than others; perhaps these four came into the world with a greater measure of empathy than most of us. But in any event, they all tell us that concern for others—call it humaneness (Confucius), call it compassion (the Buddha), call it love (Jesus), call it mercy (Muhammad)—is a quality that can be—and must be—developed and matured.

We also observed that each of the four sages could claim a noble heritage but was unable or unwilling to take advantage of his ancestry. Confucius was born into a family of nobility who had at one time served the ruling duke of the Kingdom of Song. But the family had fallen on hard times and become impoverished. The only benefit Confucius received from this heritage was his entitlement to an education, of which he took complete advantage. The Buddha was born into the caste of nobility and warriors, although he was probably not a prince, as legend describes. He had every advantage his station in life could afford him, yet in the end he found that having everything was not enough. That heritage and its many benefits were simply not sufficient for Siddhattha Gotama, and he felt compelled to re-linquish them. The gospel writers Matthew and Luke trace Jesus's lineage back to Israelite royalty and to some of the luminaries of the Jewish faith. Although those genealogies were most likely fabricated, they serve the very important theological purpose of stating what constitutes genuine power and authentic humanity. The life of Jesus—in its humility and simplicity— was closer to the way of god than was the life of Caesar in all its power and glory. Muhammad, like Confucius, was born into a family that once com-manded some aristocratic prestige but, by the time of his birth, had fallen on hard times and had tarnished its reputation. His ancestry, therefore, did little to advance his way in the world. But by the end of his life, he was being hailed by some as the king of the Arabs.

While we might say that each of the four was born with a *claim* to noble heritage, what is more important is that they each tried to *redefine* nobility. All four came into cultures that understood nobility to be a status conferred by birth. An individual was *born* an aristocrat or a noble. But Confucius, the Buddha, and Muhammad all said that true nobility was a matter of *character*—how one acted and treated other human beings—and that real nobility was a possibility for anyone, not merely those born into a certain class, caste, or clan. Jesus did not use the term "nobility," but he argued and demonstrated the point in other ways. For Jesus, participating in the kingdom of heaven had nothing to do with being born into the priestly or ruling class, or being born a "clean" person, or being born a Jew. He il-lustrated that point by his subversive parables and his association with the outcastes. Being a subject in the Father's kingdom depended on embracing the divine qualities of forgiveness and compassion, not on the status of one's birth.

The histories of the early lives of our sages are sketchy at best. In some cases we have detailed and fascinating reports, but in most instances those accounts border on or enter into the mythic realm. In each case, the stories describe unusual circumstances surrounding his conception, birth, and parentage.

Confucius was born to a very old father and a very young mother (like Jesus), who conceived him in the fields. It is not clear if their union was even legitimate. But just as in the stories of the other three, there is the hint of divine intention in Confucius's birth. His parents had prayed for a child at a mountain shrine and regarded Confucius as the answer to their prayers. Like Muhammad, Confucius probably never really knew his father. Shu-liang died when Confucius was three; his mother lived longer, but she too died when he was only twenty-three.

For the Buddha, the stories of his mother's dream on the night of his conception and his birth in the grove of Lumbini point to the extraordinary significance of his coming into the world. Whereas Confucius and Muhammad lost their fathers very early in life, the Buddha lost his mother, Queen Mahamaya, who died one week after giving birth. But he was lovingly raised by his mother's sister and his natural father, who were heartbroken when he decided to leave their home to live the life of a samana. Of the four sages, only the Buddha seems to have had a close relationship with his father.

The gospels intimate that Joseph was not Jesus's real father, and the New Testament has almost nothing to say about their relationship. They *may* have been close, or maybe not; the gospels do not say. We are not even told when Joseph died; it may have been early in Jesus's life. The New Testament does say a fair amount about his mother Mary—as does the Qur'an. Both the Christian and Muslim scriptures indicate that Jesus's birth was accomplished with divine intention and by means of a virginal conception. Yet, we know very little about the nature of Jesus's relationship with his mother. We assume it was close, and there are some stories to support that, but sometimes it is portrayed as strained. In the gospels, Jesus occasionally makes what seems to be a harsh or rude statement to her, such as his retort to her at the wedding in Cana.

Muhammad came into the world as an orphan, since his father died before he was even born. The element of divine intention in the story of Muhammad comes in the anecdote where the bright light between his father Abdallah's eyes disappears when the Prophet is conceived. Muhammad essentially had two mothers: his Bedouin foster mother, Halimah, and his natural mother, Aminah. But his relationships with both were short-lived. He stayed with Halimah until he was four, and Aminah died when he was six. For much of his young life, he resided with his uncle Abu Talib and aunt Fatimah, who cared for him like a son.

Each of the four sages is the subject of stories about his early life that foretell his future greatness or indicate something about his mature outlook on life. Confucius was fond of playing at rituals. Astrologers predicted that Siddhattha Gotama would become a great emperor or a great sage. At age twelve, Jesus astounded the temple authorities in Jerusalem with his wisdom and wit. When he was four, two men opened Muhammad's chest and cleansed his heart, just as he would later open the Kaaba and cleanse it of its idols.

What do the comparisons of these stories really tell us about these four individuals or about their paths to wisdom? Overall, we would have to say, not a great deal. It is likely that each of these stories was created and transmitted by pious followers who were using fictional devices to convey their beliefs in the ultimate significance of their sage or his teachings. The stories tell us more about the impressions that Confucius, the Buddha, Jesus, and Muhammad left on their followers than anything of great significance about their historical lives. We are not even able to draw firm conclusions about how their lives in their families of origins may have contributed to the persons they were to become. One might be tempted, for example, to say that the absence of their natural fathers had a profound effect on Confucius, Muhammad, and perhaps Jesus. It is tempting to suggest that Jesus's relationship with his father—if it *were* disrupted by Joseph's death or perhaps his aloofness—may have driven Jesus to seek the comfort in a "heavenly" father as a form of psychological compensation. But that is to speculate where the Bible is silent. Furthermore, Confucius and Muhammad, who certainly had absent fathers, did not incorporate a divine father into their views. Muhammad scrupulously avoided even the *hint* that Allah had children. Perhaps it is significant that Confucius, the Buddha, Muhammad, and maybe Jesus each lost a natural parent or parent figure in their early lives. If so, this similarity might suggest their childhood losses made them particularly empathetic to the suffering of others. Beyond that bit of speculation, I find little in the historical lives of our four teachers to indicate that their extraordinary qualities were somehow determined in their families of origin. But perhaps that fact is meaningful in itself. No matter where we come from or the circumstances of our early lives, genuine humanity always remains within our grasp.

Aside from the fabulous birth narratives and the occasional anecdotes about their early lives, we are able to say very little about these four individuals prior to adulthood. I wish we had more information about these formative years, particularly about their educational experiences. We are reasonably sure that both Confucius and the Buddha had formal schooling, but we are uncertain about Jesus and Muhammad. But whatever the nature of their prescribed education, it is clear that *each of them had a thirst for understanding.* Confucius loved to read books and clearly derived much of his wisdom from the ancients. In his early life, the Buddha was trained in the Veda and the skills of warfare, as would have been appropriate for a boy of his caste. Later, he applied the discipline he gained in these pursuits to study himself. The Buddha's quest of wisdom was whetted by the desire for self-understanding. Jesus was a keen observer of society and human relationships. He was deeply sensitive to the ways the prevailing social arrangements of his time disrupted the love and concern for others that the Father had intended for humanity. Muhammad loved to look at and listen to the world in search of "signs" about the purpose of living. Much like the Buddha and Jesus, he spent copious periods in solitude—waiting, watching, and listening. Each of these four sages had clearly developed a *fearless love for the truth* that inspired them to endure hardships, such as persecution, exile, harsh asceticism, and even death.

In terms of marital and family arrangements, Confucius, the Buddha, Jesus, and Muhammad seem to represent the gamut of human possibilities. Confucius was married and had two children. But the sources tell us virtually nothing about his wife or children, an odd thing in view of the tremendous importance he placed on family virtues. But if the *Analects* and early biographies are to be taken as a guide, we would have to conclude that his marriage and family played a very small, if any, role in his development as a sage. In fact, Confucius may have divorced his wife, although that is not certain.

The Buddha was married early in life and had a son, Rahula, at age twenty-nine. But shortly after his son's birth, the Buddha left his family to continue the quest for freedom. After his discovery of the dhamma, he returned to his parents, wife, and son and shared his teaching with them. His foster mother, Mahapajapati, became the first nun, and Yasodhara, his former wife, as well as their son, Rahula, joined the sangha. The Buddhist tradition has always regarded Siddhattha's departure from home as a necessary act of compassion so that he might bring back to his family—and to all beings—the path to nibbana.

In all likelihood, Jesus never married or, if he did, he became a widower early in life. The New Testament reports that Jesus had close friendships with women and men, but determining the precise nature of those relationships can only be speculative. It is sometimes hard to judge Jesus's attitudes to marriage and family life. The gospels report numerous instances in which he appears to advocate a disruption of the traditional family structure. Mark, for instance, reports a scene in which Jesus ignores his mother and brothers and tells his listeners, "Whoever does the will of God is my brother and sister and mother."[1] It is quite possible that Jesus envisioned the coming of the kingdom of heaven as supplanting conventional familial arrangements.

Muhammad's marital and family life was the most complicated among the four sages. Throughout his life, he had around a dozen wives and several children, although some of his children died young; all but one or two predeceased him. We have noted before that the motivations for his marriages were diverse: some were political, some humanitarian, some perhaps romantic. We have also observed that some of his marriages were happy and some were not, but that he tried, according to the *hadith*, to treat all of his

---

1. Mark 3:31–35, NRSV.

wives with kindness and told his followers to do the same. It is also clear that Muhammad often consulted his wives—at least some of them—and sought their advice on important matters. Of our four sages, Muhammad seems to be the one who would most deserve the title of "family man."

Just as it is difficult to know the influences of their families of origin on their lives and teachings, so it is difficult to draw compelling conclusions about the role that marriage and children may have played in their spiritual outlooks. It would be wrong, I think, to say the marital and familial context was *unimportant* to that outlook, but it does not seem true that a *particular kind* of context was more favorable than another. Developing spiritual maturity, in other words, is possible in different sorts of marriage and family situations, even unhappy ones.

One area at which the lives of our sages do converge is in their adoption of a simple manner of life. All four were eventually committed to a life of having few material possessions. Jesus perhaps articulated a point-of-view with which the others could agree:

> Do not store up for yourselves treasures on earth, where moth and rust consume and where thieves break in and steal; but store up for yourselves treasures in heaven, where neither moth nor rust consumes and where thieves do not break in and steal. For where your treasure is, there your heart will be also.[2]

It would not be difficult to find comparable statements in the teachings of Confucius, the Buddha, and Muhammad. Each of the four embraced that principle and lived by it. None of them believed that there was something intrinsically wrong with wealth and possessions. Muhammad, for instance, led raids to recover the property some of the Muslims lost to the Makkans and transmitted revelations concerning the appropriate division of inheritances. Yet all four considered material belongings as being a great distraction to living the noble life. Possessions could easily become the objects of attachment, to use the language of the Buddha, or idols, to use the vocabulary of Jesus and Muhammad.

Simplicity not only cleared their lives of potential diversions and much anxiety; it also helped free up the time they required to devote to their spiritual discipline. Like the simple manner in which they lived, all four were committed to practices whose purpose was to bring them closer to their vision of ultimate reality and perfect humanity. None of them thought that the spiritual life was merely a matter of getting their beliefs and doctrines figured out; rather, they all thought that becoming a certain kind of person by

---

2. Matt 6:19–21, NRSV.

means of deliberate activities was essential. As we have observed, they each practiced different disciplines to facilitate their development. Confucius, you will recall, loved listening to and performing music, reciting poetry, and observing dances. He undertook these activities not for entertainment but for moral edification. The Buddha advocated and practiced exercises to awaken the latent compassion we have for all beings. Jesus loved to eat and elevated the sharing of food to a sacramental level. Muhammad found deep significance in circumambulating the Kaaba and instituted a carefully planned pilgrimage for all Muslims to undertake. These are all just mundane, ordinary activities—listening to music, sitting and thinking, eating, and walking—but with a particular kind of mindful attention, they became the avenues to human fulfillment.

But amid these diverse practices, one form of discipline is common to all four of these sages. Its commonality and centrality in their lives makes it tempting to suggest that perhaps this exercise was the secret of their success, but we should hesitate to reduce the richness of their experiences and insights to just one thing. Yet, if I *had* to name one thing, this would be it. Confucius, the Buddha, Jesus, and Muhammad *all took time to be quiet.* Confucius called it abiding in reverence and rectifying the mind; the Buddha called it *bhavana*, or mental cultivation; Jesus and Muhammad called it praying. In practice, each of these activities was slightly different from one another. Muhammad liked to retreat to a cave or stay up half the night; the Buddha preferred to sit at the base of a tree; Jesus liked the hills and gardens; Confucius sat on a mat in his room. But their disciplines shared common, basic features: they each involved making time to be alone, to focus on interior experience, and to allow the mind to settle and become receptive to what the world had to teach them.

Earlier in the discussion on Muhammad, we mentioned Bernard Shaw's play about Joan of Arc, in which she claims to hear voices from god. Later in the play, as Joan is being interrogated for suspicion of heresy, she is asked by King Charles, "Why don't the voices come to me? I am king, not you." Joan tells him:

> They do come to you; but you do not hear them. You have not sat in the field in the evening listening for them. When the angelus rings you cross yourself and have done with it; but if you prayed from your heart, and listened to the thrilling of the bells in the air *after* they stop ringing, you would hear the voices as well as I do.[3]

3. Shaw, *Saint Joan*, Scene 5, http://faculty.smu.edu/bwheeler/joan_of_arc/olr/07_saintjoan_gbshaw.pdf/, 66.

As Joan suggests, there is nothing extraordinary about hearing the voice of god, but one needs to make the effort to listen.

Whether we call what we hear the voice of god or of conscience, the sound of silence or the rhythms of the breath, the lives of our four sages remind us of the necessity to stop and pay attention to *our* lives. Taking time to be quiet and attending to our lives need not result in some intense, enlightening religious experience. Indeed, such intense moments are rare. But it must be a regular practice, just as Muhammad stopped to pray five times a day and the Buddha meditated in the quiet of each night. It is simply a way to remind ourselves of what is *really* important, because we forget.

Confucius, the Buddha, Jesus, and Muhammad were four lives separated by culture and time, each nurtured in different ways, each brought up with different educations and in different religious traditions, yet connected by a desire to live life to its fullest extent, to understand it at its deepest levels, and to face its truths with courage.

Their Teachings Compared

I confess to being a big fan of *The Simpsons*. I'm especially amused by the way the series exposes and gently spoofs the foibles of religion. One of the recurring objects of its religious satire is a character named Ned Flanders, the hyperpious goody-goody Christian who vexes Homer with his saintly ways. Ned's piety even gets on the nerves of Rev. Lovejoy, his minister. At one point, Rev. Lovejoy gets so put out with Ned's sanctity that he invites Ned to convert to another religion: "Have you considered one of the *other* world religions, Ned? They're all pretty much the same."

Rev. Lovejoy's belief that the religions of the world are "pretty much the same" voices a modern liberal sentiment held by many today. Interestingly, among those who first began to suggest that religions were "pretty much the same" were the critics of religion, those who thought humanity would be better off without it. Today, many religious folk themselves advocate this perspective, not to put an end to religion, of course, but to see the great divisions and rancor among religions diminished and perhaps eliminated.

One of the ways we can begin to assess the validity of this claim is to compare the teachings of our four sages. Comparing religious teachers is not, however, the same thing as comparing religions, which are far more complex realities than the philosophies of individuals. As I emphasized earlier, we cannot simply equate the teachings of Confucius with Confucianism or the teachings of Jesus with Christianity. But it is much easier to compare specific teachings than to compare whole religions, and doing so might offer some insight into the problems facing a religiously plural world. So let us turn now to reviewing the perspectives of our sages in relationship to one another. I think it should be apparent that the four teachers did in fact view the world in ways different from one another, and in many cases these differences were substantial. Nonetheless, in some important areas, particularly on matters of spiritual and ethical practice, they are not that far apart. We'll structure our comparative analysis of their teachings with the categories we have used throughout the book: metaphysics, anthropology, and ethics.

Metaphysics

It is in the metaphysical arena that we see some of the greatest differences among Confucius, the Buddha, Jesus, and Muhammad. Not only did they think of the ultimate reality in different ways; they thought differently about the importance of thinking about it. We observed in Confucius and the Buddha a marked reluctance to engage in matters they considered speculative. The Buddha regarded certain specific issues such as the origin and limits of the universe and the relationship between body and soul as matters that lead to fruitless and divisive speculation and divert attention from the immediate concern of attaining the end of suffering. Confucius, as his protégés often noted, did not like to talk much about the gods or human nature. Jesus and Muhammad, on the other hand, spoke freely and openly about some of the subjects that Confucius and the Buddha preferred to exclude from discussion. For Jesus and Muhammad, these topics were central to their perspectives, and they were not matters of mere speculation, because they had been disclosed in personal experience and revelation.

Yet, it is important to note that there were some points at which the metaphysical teachings of all four converge. For instance, each regarded reality as comprising different realms and diverse sorts of beings. All four spoke of heaven and earth, although there were some significant differences in the ways they imagined these domains and the relationships between them. The Buddha actually thought there were more than thirty realms of reality, not just heaven and earth. But both he and Confucius understood these domains to be populated with a vast number of spiritual entities, such as gods, ancestors, ghosts, titans, and demons. They also conceived of these realms as permeable; Confucius thought that human beings could become ancestors at death, and the Buddha thought humans could be reborn as demons, and gods could be reborn as humans. Jesus and Muhammad also accepted the idea of beings such as angels, demons, jinn, and Satan, but these were just the classes of creatures; humans did not *become* angels—and certainly not gods. Yet, angels and the Satan might at times appear in human form. Christians, of course, would later claim that their god became human in the form of Jesus, an idea that Muhammad emphatically rejected. Since Jews did not accept the idea of divine incarnation, I suspect Jesus would have rejected the idea as well had the concept been presented to him in the way it was suggested to Muhammad.

However, the notion of diverse levels of reality such as heaven and earth, and qualitatively different kinds of beings, played different roles in the teachings of each sage. For Confucius and the Buddha, the various realms of the world and beings such as gods and spirits simply described the way reality was structured. These things had no ultimate significance when it came to the highest goods of human life: moral self-cultivation according to Confucius, and liberation from *dukkha* according to the Buddha. But for Jesus and Muhammad, deity was *essential* to understanding the human's place in the world and achieving salvation at the end of time. Muhammad even made belief in *angels* vital to Islamic belief.

This key difference might be better understood by observing another point on which our sages agree. They each posited an absolute or ultimate reality, and they all agreed that this absolute—whatever it is—is critical to human welfare. But here is how they contrast: Confucius and the Buddha did not identify god or the gods as the ultimate reality; for Jesus and Muhammad, however, god *was* the ultimate reality. To Confucius and the Buddha, the ultimate reality was beyond the gods. For Confucius, it was heaven, conceived not as a place or as an anthropomorphized being, but as a principle. For the Buddha, ultimate reality was nibbana, which he sometimes called the absolute and the unconditioned. Confucius and the Buddha conceived of ultimate reality in impersonal terms, when they conceived of it at all. Both spoke of it sparingly, as if speaking of it were to distort it. Jesus and Muhammad, on the other hand, generally thought of the absolute in personal terms, with metaphors that suggested humanlike qualities: god was lord, creator, king of the universe, father, protector, teacher, judge, and forgiver. Whether intended or not, these terms have a propensity to conjure a sense of the divine that brings it closer to the human world than terms such as *the absolute* and *the unconditioned*. To be sure, Muhammad took great pains to avoid any comparisons of Allah with anything humans were or could possibly imagine. In this sense, Muhammad was aware of the same problem that Confucius and the Buddha understood: to speak of the ultimate reality is to risk misrepresenting it because the human imagination is simply not up to the task of understanding mystery. Making *shirk* the unpardonable sin was a way to foil the human pretense that we might somehow be able to think and speak adequately about god.

With these differences and similarities before us, let us pose this question inspired by Rev. Lovejoy's comment to Ned Flanders: if Confucius, the Buddha, Jesus, and Muhammad agree that there is some absolute or unconditional reality, are they all talking about the same reality even though they conceptualize and speak of it differently? Is Confucius's heaven the same as the Buddha's nibbana? Did Jesus and Muhammad worship the same god, as Muhammad thought they did? Was Jesus's heavenly Father the same reality the Buddha intended when he spoke of nibbana? Theologians and philosophers in the modern age have offered conflicting answers to these questions. Some say yes: there is an absolute beyond words, as all four sages (and perhaps all major religions) attest. But because of cultural and linguistic differences, this ultimate reality is necessarily conceived and expressed in different terms and images. But those differences are merely incidental, dissimilar ways of packaging the same essential reality.[4] Father, Allah, heaven, the unconditioned—these are just metaphors for the mystery that eludes every effort to articulate it. And some say no: Father, Allah, the unconditioned, and heaven ultimately mean different things. To say the absolute is father is significantly, not just incidentally, different from calling it nibbana. Proponents of this view might point to the way that thinking of the ultimate reality as father yields a different way of living in the world than thinking of it as nibbana. Thus, *how* we think of the absolute is significant.

Those who see real differences among these metaphysical views might go on to make other claims. For example, one might say, indeed, Confucius's view of heaven is *not* the same as Muhammad's Allah, and both cannot be correct. One is the correct view, or more correct than the other, or another view all together is better than either. In short, acknowledging genuine differences between metaphysical teachings might lead to a quest to find the right or best teaching or to the popular practice of regarding one's own religion as the right one and all others as wrong or less than fully correct.

But one need not take that approach. It is possible to say that Confucius, the Buddha, Jesus, and Muhammad were teaching different visions of ultimate reality leading to different ways of being genuinely human. Seeking nibbana and living in the light of the kingdom of heaven are two ways of leading a noble life. This perspective need not result in a kind of easy relativism in which one maintains that "they're all pretty much the same." It is conceivable that ultimate reality is such that it can be interpreted in many valid ways, leading to different ways of living an authentically human

---

4. See, for example, Schuon, *Transcendent Unity*.

existence, but that does not mean that *any* interpretation is appropriate or that *every* style of life is equally suitable. Some ways are better than others. This is another point on which our sages are in accord. For each of them, some ways of living are clearly superior to others.

Anthropology

In a moment, we will begin to compare their views on the manner of life each thought most congruous with the nature of reality. Before we arrive at that point, however, it will be helpful to remind ourselves of their basic anthropological perspectives, the way each of them thought of human nature and destiny.

For the most part, Confucius, Jesus, and Muhammad did not devote a great deal of time to analyzing the basic makeup of persons or trying to offer a novel viewpoint on the self. All three worked within the frameworks of their cultures' basic understandings of what human beings were. In general terms, each of them considered the human to comprise spiritual and physical components. At death, spirit and body would separate. Confucius thought the spirit would then take up residence in heaven. Muhammad believed that the last day entailed a resurrection of the body, at which time it would be reunited with its soul. Jesus also believed in a day of resurrection but offered few details to explain his understanding it. Of the four, only the Buddha offered a comprehensive teaching on the nature of body and self. Like Confucius, Jesus, and Muhammad, the Buddha clearly affirmed the impermanence of the body. But he would not accept the idea that those selfsame bodies returned to their spirits at a particular point in time, as suggested in the concept of resurrection. For the Buddha, bodies were in constant flux. The components that presently make up the body at one time composed other bodies and will in the future be part of still other bodies. Furthermore, for the Buddha, the perceptions, sensations, mental formations, and consciousness—what we might call the spiritual dimension of the person—are also impermanent. The Buddha expressly denied the idea of an immortal or substantial soul or self. On this point the teaching of the Buddha appears distinctly at odds with the perspectives of Confucius, Jesus, and Muhammad.

But despite these differences, all four sages believed in what we might call the spiritual equality of all persons. Confucius asserted that human beings share a common nature that can be shaped in good or bad ways. The Buddha argued that all persons comprise the five aggregates of being, and that differences among people are due to the karmic baggage they carry from previous births. But he also contended that all persons, regardless of their station in life, their gender, or their past karmas, are capable of seeing nibbana and ending their suffering on the wheel of existence. Jesus and Muhammad regarded all persons as creatures of the one god and hence fundamentally of equal value. This basic conviction seems to have inspired Jesus's opposition to the social conventions that separated pure and impure, rich and poor, the sinners and the righteous. Muhammad also affirmed the equality of all souls before Allah. He did, however, allow for certain social distinctions, particularly between women and men, as did the Buddha and Confucius.

The chief differences in the anthropological views of our teachers come in the ways they interpret what we might call the human predicament—that is, their understanding of the fundamental problems besetting human beings. As axial and postaxial thinkers, Confucius, the Buddha, Jesus, and Muhammad all considered the present state of humanity to be undesirable. Prior to the Axial Age, persons were not likely to imagine a fundamental flaw or problem in human nature itself. The purpose of religion before the Axial Age was to help human beings obtain the essential goods for living life—food, health, children, and protection from enemies—by maintaining cordial or at least respectful relationships with the gods or whatever powers controlled these things. In the Axial Age, however, the very function of religion began to change, and that transformation is reflected in the teachings of Confucius and the Buddha, who were axial thinkers, and of Jesus and Muhammad, who were heirs of the axial revolution. During and after the axial era, the role of religion came to be associated less with sustaining life by performing rituals to make the crops grow or offering sacrifices to feed the gods, and more connected with effecting *personal transformation*. This new function of religion emerged as greater numbers of people came to believe that there was some defect in human beings that needed to be rectified. Religions, at this point, began to provide an explanation of this defect and then proceeded to explain its solution. We see that dynamic at work in the teachings of all four of our sages.

For Confucius, humans were simply unable to live in harmony with one another because they had neglected the ancient ways of virtue taught by the sages of the golden past. The solution to that problem was to instill moral virtue by means of education, example, and self-cultivation. For the Buddha, beings suffered because of their fundamental ignorance about the true nature of reality and themselves. They wrongly believed in a permanent and substantial self, which led them to crave and become attached to a world in constant flux. The proper objective for human beings was to practice the manifold path that fostered insight into the world as it is and eased the desperate attempts to grasp and cling to what is impermanent. For both Jesus and Muhammad, human beings have departed from the way established for them by god. Jesus was especially concerned with the social distinctions imposed on the culture in which he lived. He envisioned a day in which those distinctions would be shown to be meaningless, and he urged his followers to join him in living as if the kingdom of heaven were a present reality. Muhammad shared Jesus's concerns about social distinctions and regulations that harmed human well-being, but he viewed these concerns in light of the human tendency to forget Allah and put other realities in the place where god should be: at the center of all we do and think. The Prophet revealed specific ways for people to remember their god and submit their wills to Allah.

The final destinies envisioned by the four sages are as different as their estimations of the human predicament. For Confucius, the goal of human life was perfect goodness, bringing to full manifestation our potential for being humane. Confucius promised no blissful afterlife for the hard work of moral cultivation. Goodness, or genuineness, to use Mencius's term, is its own reward; there is no greater joy. The Buddha promised liberation from the cycle of birth, death, and rebirth and hence the end of suffering. For Jesus, the reward for living a life centered in the divine being was eternal life, participating in the kingdom established by god, when the values of the current world would be turned on their head. To Muhammad, those who have submitted themselves to Allah will enjoy paradise, the place from which Adam and Eve were exiled, and those who have given their allegiance to any other so-called god are destined for hell. Although they imagine it in different ways, all four sages indicate that satisfaction or happiness lies at the end of the path for those who practice the way of the noble life. There is an optimistic tenor to each of their teachings.

Ethics

There is no doubt that all four teachers saw the ethical dimension of life as playing a key role in the meaning and purpose of existence and the ultimate human destiny. This characteristic was also a consequence of the religious and philosophical transformations wrought in the Axial Age. During that period, individual fulfillment became closely associated with the manner in which one treated and regarded other beings. Interestingly, Confucius, the Buddha, Jesus, and Muhammad seem to be closest to one another when we consider their ethical views, particularly when those views are abstracted from their metaphysics and anthropologies.

This fundamental convergence is most apparent when we examine their views on the role of the self in human life. All four sages thought that *self-centeredness is at the heart of human misery.* All four taught about the perils of self-centeredness, and all taught ways to diminish the deleterious effects of living selfishly.

Confucius, as we noted earlier, did not engage in much discussion about the nature of the self or the causes of self-centeredness; he simply offered practical advice for living with a greater concern for the well-being of others. He invited his followers to treat others in the manner they would treat themselves.

> The humane person, wanting to establish himself, helps others establish themselves, and wanting to be successful, helps others to be successful. Taking one's own feelings as a guide may be called the method of humaneness.[5]

He encouraged humility by example and precept. He told his protégés not to be concerned when others did not praise them: "not to be resentful at others' failure to appreciate one—surely that is to be a true gentleman."[6] Rather than responding to a petty person with judgment, Confucius invited his students to view the moment as an occasion for seeing the imperfections in oneself: "when you see an unworthy person, examine yourself inwardly"[7]

The Buddha not only offered practical advice for living selflessly; he went even further to argue that the self, as that concept is ordinarily understood, is a complete fiction, an illusion, with no basis in reality. When the selfless nature of human existence becomes apparent, persons cannot but help live compassionate lives, taking the suffering of others as seriously as one's own suffering. At the same time, engaging in compassionate practices—refusing to inflict harm and wishing for the well-being of all living beings—enables one to see more clearly the selfless and impermanent nature of reality.

Like Confucius, Muhammad and Jesus did not offer detailed analyses of self-centeredness, but they taught practical wisdom for living life in a more wholesome and liberating way. For Jesus and Muhammad, self-centered living was at the root of the injustices they observed in their societies. The rich and powerful had become so self-absorbed and concerned with their own pleasures that they neglected the well-being of everyone else. Confucius, too, saw this problem in the rulers of ancient China and

5. *Analects* 6.30, my rendering.
6. Dawson, trans., *Analects* 1.1 (p. 3).
7. *Analects* 4.17, my rendering.

urged them to return to the old rituals to remind them of their responsibility to ensure that virtue flourished in their kingdoms. In Jesus's day, even the righteous ones had become self-consumed. In the parable of the Good Samaritan, Jesus criticized the religious authorities and those aspiring to sanctity because they were more concerned about their own holiness than compassionately assisting a fellow human being. In the teachings of Muhammad, we see how self-centeredness need not be a phenomenon solely of the individual. Corporate bodies can act selfishly as well. Muhammad was critical of the way the self-interests of the tribe or clan came to override the basic demands of justice.

Both Muhammad and Jesus contended that the antidote to self-centeredness—whether individual or corporate—lay in recentering life in god, the absolute, ultimate reality. Indeed, they were so convinced of the priority of god over the self that they were prepared to sacrifice themselves to enable others to grasp to its importance. The Buddha and Confucius saw the situation differently. While they would have agreed with Jesus and Muhammad that living the self-centered life was fundamentally problematic, they did not envision the solution as putting a god in the place of self. The Buddha urged his listeners to recognize the illusory nature of the self and to cling to no beliefs about the self *or* about the nature of ultimate reality. For the Buddha, attachment to ideas about god was just as hazardous as clutching onto ideas about the self. (In his own way, Muhammad made a similar point by insisting on the inscrutability of Allah.) Confucius, on the other hand, imagined that the solution to self-centeredness lay in the practices established by the sages of old, activities that would remind the individual that he or she was part of a larger web of relationships.

While Confucius, the Buddha, Jesus, and Muhammad appear to teach very different things about the structure of the world and the nature of human beings, on this simple point they seem to be of one mind: *the self-centered life is fraught with suffering for individuals, communities, and the world as a whole.* The way out of our misery is via the path of kindness, compassion, and humility. Writing during a time much closer to our own, Albert Einstein seems to have captured this fundamental conviction shared by our ancient sages. Einstein writes:

> A human being is a part of the whole, called by us "Universe", [*sic*] a part limited in time and space. He experiences himself, his thoughts and feelings as something separated from the rest—a kind of optical delusion of his consciousness. The striving to free oneself from this delusion is the one issue in true religion. Not

to nourish this delusion but to try to overcome it is the way to reach the attainable measure of peace of mind.[8]

Their Enduring Significance: Some Personal Reflections

When we began this study, I acknowledged that my interest in Confucius, the Buddha, Jesus, and Muhammad is not merely academic but also existential. These teachers attract my attention not only because they are fascinating as historical figures but because they enrich my life, and the lives of countless others, with their words and examples. Now that we have come to the end of our studies of these individuals, and have spent time comparing and contrasting them, let us take a moment to reflect on the enduring significance of their legacies. Much of what I will say, I freely admit, derives from my personal experiences. I do not pretend to be able to separate my interpretations of these individuals from the rest of my life. My own history as a human being necessarily shapes how I see these four teachers.

Living Nobly

Living during times when nobility was understood as a quality of those who were born into a certain social rank, our four teachers sought to redefine that characteristic in ways that made it accessible to anyone, regardless of heritage or social position. By their very lives they exemplified ways for human beings to live noble lives and invited the rest of us to aspire to do the same. Their teachings and examples tell us that we are capable of much more than we think. Yet they are equally clear in telling us that the way to the noble life is no easy path. While we are all capable of being noble persons, the demands are heavy, and few will actually choose that road. But for those who do, the satisfactions are great, and there is no higher calling in life.

I am not sure where we as a culture stand on the concept of nobility. It was not an idea that I heard much while growing up, except with respect to the old-world aristocracies, precisely the association that our four sages sought to disrupt. I remember being encouraged to work hard and excel, but I don't recall being encouraged to live nobly. Still today, we are more likely to hear about the ideal of excellence rather than nobility. Excellence is a fine virtue, of course, but it not the same as nobility. Ordinarily, the virtue of excellence is used in the context of performance. When people or businesses

8. Einstein, from a letter to Robert S. Marcus, February 12, 1950, http://www.lettersofnote.com/2011/11/delusion.html/.

say they are committed to excellence, they are indicating that they wish to do an outstanding job or produce a fine product. Nobility involves doing well, to be sure, but it is doing well at *the things that really matter*. Nobility involves discerning what things are truly worth the pursuit of excellence.

The requirements of the noble life are not difficult to understand, but they are hard to implement. The first requisite is commitment to truth and understanding. Human beings are so adept at self-deception that this intention is essential, probably much more than we ordinarily think. Committing oneself to truth and understanding is not simply a single step on the noble path but an act that must be renewed continually. I am deeply impressed and inspired by Confucius's practice of rigorous self-examination, his willingness to look within himself and dispassionately observe his own shortcomings. We see the same devotion in the Buddha's quest to see the world "as it is" and not as we want it to be. What I struggle with in maintaining a commitment to truth is the fear of discovering something painful or unpleasant, something I believe I will be unable to endure. I am fully aware that I often I prefer my pleasant illusions to the realities that might interrupt my sense of who I *think* I am or who I think I ought to be, or (to be even more truthful) who I want *others* to think I am. What all of our four teachers tell us is that *truth is nothing to fear*. Seeing the world and ourselves as we really are is liberating; indeed, it is the only path to freedom. The Buddha sent a grieving mother on a quest for a mustard seed from a home that had never experienced death. She returned empty-handed but awakened to the impermanence of life and relieved of the great burden she carried. Jesus stated the point in his characteristically pithy way: "the truth shall make you free."[9]

The corollary to a commitment to truth is humility. Humility is not self-abasement; it does not mean thinking poorly of oneself. It simply means honesty in recognizing one's capacities and qualities; humility is merely self-knowledge. It is acknowledging one's limitations in the face of the mighty mystery that confronts us daily. The wiser they became, the more the four sages became humble. The Prophet Muhammad continued to wear the common garb and to cook and sew. The Buddha continued on his daily rounds to beg for food. Confucius refused to accept the title of sage and was engaged in self-cultivation to the end of his life. Jesus's humility took him to the cross, where he quietly accepted the fate that he believed his mission in life required. It is a bit ironic that those whom many have judged as humanity's most influential persons have led lives of such simplicity and modesty.

9. John 8:32, KJV.

The commitment to truth and the quality of humility are components of another virtue shared by these teachers: *they were willing to learn*. It takes both love for the truth and the awareness of one's limitations to be able to learn. The most difficult students to teach, in my experience, are the ones who think they already know. In Zen Buddhism, one of the first steps on the path to enlightenment is to disabuse the student that he or she understands anything. Only after the novice realizes the limitations and distortions of the conditioned mind is he or she able to see the world afresh, with the pristine openness necessary for learning. Zen master Shunryu Suzuki says, "In the beginner's mind there are many possibilities, but in the expert's there are few."[10] Each of our sages understood this principle in seeking wisdom. Confucius believed that everyone, regardless of their status in life, had something to teach him. Muhammad constantly consulted his wives and companions for their advice and was willing to be persuaded and corrected by them. The Buddha taught the importance of avoiding attachment to what he called "views," our everyday beliefs and judgments about the way things are. Nonattachment to views means acknowledging the possibility of being mistaken and maintaining openness to being corrected. Although later Christian tradition tended to downplay this aspect of Jesus's life for fear it might compromise claims about his divinity, he too must have been intensely dedicated to learning. I suspect his thirst for understanding led him to seek out John the Baptizer as a mentor and to the wilderness where he spent forty days and nights on a quest for clarity about his mission in life. Jesus's wisdom came not because he was omniscient but because he was observant and learned from his experiences.

Attentiveness

Humility and the love for truth are augmented by another quality shared by the four sages: attentiveness. We have already spoken of the way each teacher set aside time for regular periods of stillness and quietude. I even suggested that this practice comes close to being the single most important factor in the development of their spiritual depths. So significant was this discipline that they deliberately cultivated lives of great simplicity to devote time and energy to its exercise. In those moments of quiet, they gave attention to their inner life. The Buddha used this time to explore the nature of his own mind and to examine the characteristics of reality. Confucius took time to determine the congruence of his ideals and his behavior. Jesus and Muhammad spent their quiet moments articulating their private thoughts

10. Suzuki, *Zen Mind, Beginner's Mind*, 21.

and anxieties and repeating the truths of their traditions. Then they listened in silence.

I fear that our culture has almost completely lost sight of the importance of this discipline. We have become so conditioned to the constant distractions of television, the Internet, sports, movies, and other amusements and activities that many of us feel empty and even frightened without them. With the advent of these technologies and entertainments, there is little wonder that the average attention span, according to many estimates, has declined so significantly in the last century. We have become accustomed to seeking ever-new sources of stimulation, and we exercise little control over the things we allow to shape our minds. The Buddha taught that concentration is a skill that can be developed and refined, but it must be nurtured in the context of silence. Somehow, I believe, our world needs to rediscover the importance of being quiet and paying attention, and must make a place for it in our daily lives.

As the lives of Confucius, the Buddha, Jesus, and Muhammad exemplify, the noble life entails sensitivity to suffering—both to our own and to that of others. A keen awareness of the massive suffering in existence seems abundantly evident in the lives of all four. Confucius seemed especially attuned to those in grief and who were suffering bereavement. Jesus and Muhammad were particularly moved by the plight of the poor, the widowed, the sick, and outcastes. The Buddha made awareness of suffering the fundamental premise of his Four Noble Truths and taught ways to help cultivate a greater consciousness of it. He was convinced that the more we recognized and understood the nature and cause of suffering, the more motivated we would be to bring it to an end. The great emphasis placed on awareness of suffering by these teachers invites us to examine our lives as individuals and cultures to determine the ways in which we desensitize ourselves to this fundamental dimension of experience.

We have already spoken at length about the final attribute of nobility as understood by these sages: overcoming self-centeredness. We have remarked how each of them understood the genesis of self-centeredness in different ways and consequently offered different techniques for surmounting it. In large measure, their understanding of this fundamental human predicament was determined by their metaphysical and anthropological perspectives. For the Buddha, self-centeredness was grounded in a misapprehension of the true nature of reality; for Jesus and Muhammad, it was based in the failure to orient our lives toward god and instead place our faith in less-than-ultimate realities unworthy of our devotion; for Confucius, self-centeredness arose from the neglect of the way of virtue, the path initially described by the sages of old. Furthermore, the four sages recognized that self-centeredness was manifested in many ways, not simply in the tendency of the individual to act selfishly. Muhammad saw it in the ways that ethnic groups are inclined to pursue their own interests and enhance their own well-being at the expense of others. Confucius and Jesus observed the ways that the wealthy and powerful became so obsessed with their own comforts that they completely ignored the consequences of their actions on the lives in the rest of society. The Buddha even saw self-centeredness in the way human beings neglect the lives of other creatures, thoughtlessly destroying animal life to provide for our pleasures. In short, the propensity to regard the self as the center of reality resonates throughout our experience in both individual and corporate ways.

Although explained and presented in different ways, the solution to the predicament of self-centeredness lay in transforming our conditioned ways of thinking and acting. For each of the four teachers, transformation began with waking up to reality and gaining a clear apprehension of the "optical delusion," as Einstein puts it, that we are separated from all else.

Lessons from Each Sage

While on certain aspects of the noble life the four sages appear to come close to one another, in other areas each has something special or unique to offer. Perhaps *unique* is too strong a term. What I mean simply is that it was through a particular teacher than *I* gained an important insight. That is not to say, necessarily, that the same insight could not be learned from one of the others.

Three things in particular intrigue me about Confucius. Perhaps the most interesting is his belief in the near-magical power of virtue. Confucius thought that virtuous persons, those who practiced the way of moral self-cultivation, would effortlessly inspire others to act morally. We actually see that phenomenon displayed in the lives of our four teachers. Each of them evoked compassion and humaneness in others by their own acts of compassion. Perhaps it was the powerful response to their virtuous lives that led many of their followers to attribute superlative qualities to these sages, even to the point of elevating some of them to the divine level and beyond. In any event, this Confucian idea reminds us of the importance of keeping before us—as individuals and as cultures—models of virtuous behavior.

I confess that I do not know what happens to us when we die. Perhaps we are reborn; perhaps we wake up in some postmortem existence; perhaps we dissolve into a state of nothingness. I do not know. In view of my ignorance, I am attracted to Confucius's belief that goodness is its own reward.

I have never been really comfortable with the idea that we must act morally because we are commanded to do so or because we wish to be rewarded and avoid punishment. Confucius tells us that goodness is what fulfills our human nature. Perhaps virtuous behavior will pay dividends in some future existence; I do not know. But it is reassuring to think there is simple satisfaction in goodness, whether or not that is recognized by a god, rewarded in an afterlife, or even acknowledged by another human being. I urge my students to practice secret acts of goodness and never tell anyone about them.

Finally, I appreciate Confucius's teachings about attention to the mundane details of life and his conviction that our every word, act, and gesture is significant. Everything we do and say reflects our character and in turn shapes it. That attention to detail highlights the importance of living in the here and now with mindful awareness. It is what transforms an ordinary existence into a sacred one. Who knows? This may be the only existence there is. What a shame it would be to squander it.

The Buddha has taught me many things as well, but two now come to mind as more significant than all others. The first is the value of nonattachment. The Buddha's teachings offer a clear and compelling analysis of the dangers of holding on too tightly to anything. Before I studied the Buddha, I was certainly aware of the general principle of how attachment to things could lead to suffering. What transformed my thinking was the Buddha's inclusion of *everything* when he discussed attachments to things. It was easy enough to see that clinging to material possessions or even another person could certainly render us vulnerable to suffering. But the Buddha made it clear that attachment to ideas, beliefs, and values—what I call spiritual attachments—is also prone to cause us suffering. In fact, these spiritual attachments are the most intractable.

Closely connected to the virtue of nonattachment is the Buddha's criterion for accepting anything as true. He urged us to be rigorously critical in accepting any claim, belief, or value as valid, including his own teachings. In effect, the Buddha returns to us the responsibility for our own lives. We cannot take the easy way of claiming that our values and beliefs are correct merely because they are handed down by tradition, accepted authorities, or respected teachers. The Buddha insists that our practices and convictions be rooted in our own experience of what is wholesome and beneficial to life.

My appreciation of Jesus is complicated by a long history of trying to understand him and his significance for my life. I have distinct recollections of being absolutely perplexed by the man. I remember my deep confusion at age five trying to reconcile two things I was told in Sunday school. First, I was told that I should be good like Jesus, or else bad things would happen to me; and second, I was told that Jesus was god. That struck me as absolutely unjust: I was expected to live up to the standards set by Jesus, yet he had the great advantage of being divine. How on earth could I possibly be expected to be good like Jesus when I was just a kid and he was the king of the universe! At some point along the way, I settled into the traditional Christian belief that I could *not* live up to the standards of Jesus and therefore had to rely on him to save me. When that happened, Jesus lost his humanity for me and was no longer someone to follow.

Since that time it has been important for me to see Jesus as a real human being facing some of the same struggles we all face in life: self-doubt, limitations of understanding, the fear of dying. Only after recovering for myself the sense of Jesus's humanity have I been able to learn from him again. What now impresses me about his life and teachings is his courage to affirm life in the face of death and the forces that threaten to diminish life's richness and abundance. I see that affirmation symbolized in the Christian belief in his resurrection but also in the manner in which he lived. He envisioned life in the kingdom of heaven as a joyful celebration devoid of the artificial divisions we impose to separate us from one another. And he lived his life in accordance with this conviction, disregarding the complaints and ridicule of those who thought otherwise.

With Muhammad, two things stand out for me. The first is his teaching that one of the sources of human misery is the tendency to forget. Perhaps I appreciate that more today because as I age, I increasingly experience moments of forgetfulness. But of course, Muhammad was speaking of something deeper than our occasional lapses of memory. He was speaking of our existential condition, our forgetfulness of the things in life that are of ultimate significance. But Muhammad also taught ways to remember to remember. The practice of praying five times a day was one way. Fasting was another. As individuals, I think we are well advised by Muhammad to seek ways of habituating ourselves to remembrance, regardless of whether that consists of offering prayer to a god or simply recalling the things that are most meaningful to us. I cannot imagine anything that should stand in the way of a Christian or a Jew or a Hindu praying five times a day.

The second aspect of Muhammad's teaching that I find compelling is his insistence that the ultimate reality is inscrutable, utterly beyond our comprehension, completely mysterious. Of course, that conviction is kept in tension with the human need to speak of that reality by means of attributes, but Islam is careful to remind us that the absolute is beyond whatever we might attribute to it. The insistence on mystery ultimately prompts us to remember our limitations and finitude and encourages the sense of humility essential to the noble life.

At the mention of finitude and human limitation, I become aware that it is now time to draw these reflections to a close. As always, I am deeply cognizant of what I have not been able to articulate, whether due to the restrictions of space, the richness of my subject matter, or the paucity of my own knowledge and understanding. At this moment, I am mindful of each of these things.

GLOSSARY

abba: an Aramaic word translated as "father"; one of Jesus's names for god.

Abd al-Muttalib: Muhammad's grandfather.

Abdallah: Muhammad's father.

Abhidhamma: a systematic philosophical and psychological presentation of the Buddha's teachings; the third "basket" of the Pali canon.

Abraham: spiritual ancestor of Jews, Christians, and Muslims.

Abu Bakr: one of Muhammad's close friends, father of Muhammad's wife Aishah, and the first successor to the Prophet according to the Sunni faction of Islam.

Abu Talib: one of Muhammad's paternal uncles and his chief protector.

aggregates of being: the five processes the Buddha considered to be the only components of human existence: materiality, sensation, perception and apperception, conceptual constructs, and consciousness.

ahimsa (*ahimsā*): the practice of doing no harm to living beings, according to Hinduism, Buddhism, and Jainism.

Aishah: one of Muhammad's later wives.

al-Jahiliyyah (*al-Jāhiliyyah*): literally, "the days of ignorance"; the Muslim term for the period that began when the Arabs turned away from the religion of Abraham toward polytheism and that ended with the founding of Islam.

Ali: Muhammad's cousin, adopted son, and son-in-law; according to the Shi'a, Ali was the first successor of the Prophet.

Allah (al-Lah): Arabic term for god; literally, "the god."

Aminah: Muhammad's mother.

Analects: the collection of sayings and dialogues of Confucius, compiled (and at least partially composed) by his students after his death; known in Chinese as the *Lunyu* ("Conversations").

Ananda (Ānanda): the Buddha's personal attendant who memorized the Buddha's discourses and recited them at the First Buddhist Council; his recollections became the Suttas of the Pali Canon.

anatta: insubstantiality, the second of the Buddha's three marks of existence; literally, "no self" or "no soul"; known in Sanskrit as *anatman*, or no-atman.

ancestor reverence: treating one's forebears as living spirits whom one should honor, worship, and consult on important family decisions.

Angulimala: mass murderer who was confronted by the Buddha and ultimately became an arahant.

anicca: Pali word for "impermanence."

anthropology: the philosophical or theological study of the nature and purpose of humanity.

apophasis: saying by way of negation.

arahant: an awakened living being in Buddhism.

Aramaic: the family of languages often spoken in the ancient Middle East. Jesus spoke a dialect of Aramaic.

Aryans (Āryans): the central Asian pastoral nomads who migrated into Iran and India prior to the Axial Age.

ascetic: one who practices forms of self-denial (e.g., fasting, celibacy, abstaining from luxury and comforts) in order to attain higher spiritual goals.

Ashoka (Aśoka): 304–232 BCE, ruler of the Mauryan Empire in India who was responsible for the spread of Buddhism throughout India and other parts of Asia.

atman (*ātman*): Hindu term for the self or soul. Initially understood as the breath in the early Vedic era, the atman is later regarded by Hindus as immortal and transmigratory.

avijja (*avijjā*): Pali word for ignorance or misknowing.

Avyakata: the metaphysical matters that the Buddha refused to discuss; the word may be translated as "things that are not revealed" or "things that create unnecessary speech."

awakening: traditional metaphor for the experience of realizing the highest spiritual wisdom in Buddhism.

Axial Age: term coined by philosopher Karl Jaspers to denote the era of exceptional religious and philosophical creativity between 800 and 200 BCE that gave rise to the major world religions.

Babylonian captivity (the exile): the deportation of a large segment of the population of Judah to Babylon by King Nebuchadnezzar (586–536 BCE); this event marked the start of the Jewish diaspora.

bao: Chinese word for the desire to repay kindness with a similar act of kindness.

basileia tōn ouranōn: A Greek phrase from the Gospel of Matthew usually translated "kingdom of heaven."

basileia tou theou: Greek phrase for "kingdom of god" or "reign of god."

Beatitudes: A passage found in similar forms in the Gospels of Matthew (5:3–12) and Luke (6:20–23) wherein Jesus describes how people will live in the kingdom of heaven.

Benares (Banāras): the holiest city in India, situated on the Ganges River in the present state of Uttar Pradesh.

Bethlehem: village a few miles from Jerusalem reputed to be the birthplace of Jesus of Nazareth.

bhikkhu/bhikkhuni: Buddhist monk/nun.

bismillah: the words that begin all but one of the Qur'an's suras: "In the name of God, the all-compassionate, the all-merciful."

Bodh Gaya: northeastern Indian town, location of the Buddha's awakening.

Bodhi Tree ("Bo" tree): common term for the tree (*ficus religiosa*) under which Siddhattha Gotama realized awakening and became the Buddha.

brahman: the absolute, ultimate reality in Hindu theology.

Brahmin (Brāhmin): the caste of priests and intellectuals in Vedic religion and Hinduism.

Buddha: "the Awakened One"; one who grasps the causes of suffering and puts an end to it. In the Theravada Buddhist tradition, "the Buddha" is a title reserved for one who realizes awakening on his or her own; those who see nibbana through the teaching of a Buddha are called arahants.

caste: the stratification of society based on occupation, wealth, and/or purity. In India the term usually refers to the varna system, the fourfold classification of Brahmins, Kshatriyas, Vaishyas, and Shudras.

christology: the branch of Christian thought that seeks to understand the nature and significance of Jesus of Nazareth.

christos: the Greek translation of the Hebrew term *messiah*, meaning "anointed one."

contemplative prayer: a Christian practice of prayer in solitude and silence.

cosmic maintenance: the preaxial function of religion in which the processes of the world are supported or controlled by human activity.

cosmogony: creation story.

crucifixion: execution on a cross; in the Roman Empire, this form of punishment was reserved for crimes of sedition and insurrection.

Dan, Duke of Zhou: the brother of King Wu, founder of the Zhou Dynasty, who ruled as regent for his nephew following King Wu's death; the Duke of Zhou embodied many of the highest virtues, according to Confucius.

dana (*dāna*): in Buddhism, "generosity."

dao: the Chinese term for "path" or "way," as in a spiritual discipline; also, the reality underlying and governing the universe.

Daodejing: the Chinese classic (*jing*) of the way (*dao*) and the power (*de*); the basis of philosophical Daoism.

Daoism: an ancient Chinese school of thought that stressed the naturalness of virtue and the value of living simply.

Daughters of Allah: the three goddesses prominently worshiped in pre-Islamic Arabia: al-Lat, al-Uzza, and Manat.

day of requital (or day of judgment): the end of the world as we know it according to Zoroastrianism, Judaism, Christianity, and Islam.

de: Chinese term for "virtue" and "moral charisma."

Deer Park: the site of the Buddha's first discourse; located in present-day Sarnath, near Benares, India.

deva: Sanskrit term for "god."

Devadatta: a cousin of Siddhattha Gotama and Buddhist monk who attempted to kill the Buddha.

devi (*devī*): Sanskrit term for "goddess."

dhamma: the teaching of the Buddha.

dharma: Sanskrit word meaning "truth"; sacred duty according to caste; and the principle of cosmic order.

di: in Chinese religion, earth; the material realm.

Di: shortened form of Shang Di, the early Chinese high god.

divination: the practice of communicating with the spirits through the interpretation of tangible elements.

dragon bones: nickname for the inscribed cattle bones used for divination in the Shang Dynasty.

dukkha: Pali term usually translated as "suffering," "disappointment," "unsatisfactoriness," and "insatiability"; one of three marks of existence according to the Buddha.

Easter: the day celebrated by Christians to commemorate the resurrection of Jesus.

Eastern Zhou: see Zhou Dynasty.

epistemology: the philosophical study of knowledge.

equanimity: the attitude of calmness and serenity.

eschatological: pertaining to the end of days or the ultimate destiny of humankind.

eschaton: the end of time.

Essenes: a Jewish sect, active between the second century BCE and first century CE whose members lived in quasi-monastic communities and were concerned with maintaining ritual purity.

ethicization: the interpretation of events or practices in ethical terms; one of the characteristic processes of Axial Age religions.

ethics: the study of morality and proper human behavior.

Eucharist: the Christian sacrament that commemorates the Passover meal Jesus shared with his followers in the Gospels (Matt 26:17–29; Mark 14:12–25; Luke 22:7–38) shortly before his execution.

evil, problem of: the dilemma posed by the belief in a god who is considered both all-good and all-powerful in a world in which evil exists; logically, according the traditional formulation of the problem, if evil exists, then god must be either not all good or not all powerful.

ficus religiosa: scientific name for the Bodhi tree.

filial piety: the practice of reverencing and honoring one's parents both during their lives and after their deaths.

First Great Awakening: Siddhattha Gotama's rejection of his privileged life for a life of seeking nibbana; also called the Great Renunciation.

Five Precepts: the vows taken by Buddhists to guide wholesome action. They include the promise to abstain from harming sentient beings, from false speech, from misusing sexuality, from taking what is not offered, and from taking intoxicating substances.

Four Noble Truths: the core formulation of the Buddha's dhamma—namely, that *dukkha* is a fact of unenlightened existence, suffering comes from attachment, beings can escape from *dukkha*, and cultivating compassion and wisdom leads to freedom from *dukkha*.

Four Sights: according to later Buddhist tradition, the experience that prompted Siddhattha Gotama to renounce his home life to seek an end to suffering. According to this tradition, Gotama saw a sick person, an old person, a corpse, and a samana in an excursion outside the palace precincts.

Gabriel (*Jibrīl*): the angel who revealed the Qur'an to the Prophet Muhammad.

ghosts: in Chinese religion, the spirits of the unburied.

Gotama, Siddhattha: given name of the Sakyan noble who became the Buddha. Sanskrit spelling: Siddhārtha Gautama.

guru: teacher.

hadith: quotations and vignettes of Muhammad's life written after his death. Different branches of Islam accept different groups of hadith as authentic and give different levels of importance to them.

Hagar (Hajar): mother of Abraham's son Ishmael.

Hajj: the obligatory greater pilgrimage to Makkah.

Han Dynasty: the family who ruled China, 206 BCE–220 CE, one of most prosperous and stable periods in Chinese history.

hanif: pre-Islamic Arabian monotheist.

Herod the Great: 74/73–4 BCE, half-Jewish client king of Judea.

hijab: the veil worn by many Muslim women as a gesture of modesty.

hijrah: the flight of Muhammad and the fledgling Muslim community from Makkah to Madinah in 621 CE.

Hinduism: the Western term for the Indian religions that regard the Vedas as the highest authority.

householder: the stage of life for men and women in India in which they marry, raise children, work, and contribute to the good of family and society.

huaxia (*huáxià*): literally, "grand florescence" or "illustrious blossoming"; one of ancient Chinese culture's names for itself.

Iblis (Iblīs): the Arabic name for Satan; in Islam, a jinni who was cast out of heaven by Allah for refusing to bow to Adam.

Ibn Ishaq: the individual who wrote the earliest known biography of Muhammad.

idolatry: confusing the ultimate reality with what is less than ultimate.

impending model: the belief of early Christians (and probably Jesus himself) that the coming of the kingdom of heaven was imminent.

Indus Valley Civilization: one of the great cultures of the ancient world; flourished 3000–1600 BCE in northwestern India along the Indus River system; also known as the Harappan (Harappān) civilization.

involvement model: the belief of later generations of Christians that the coming of the kingdom of heaven was not a scheduled event but depended on human action to bring it about.

Isa (Īsa): the Arabic name for Jesus, who is an important prophet and messenger in Islam.

Isaac: son of Abraham and Sarah.

Ishmael (Isma'il): son of Abraham and Hagar.

isnad: chain of transmission to confirm the authenticity of a *hadith*.

Jainism: religious tradition whose origins date to the ferment that initiated Buddhism and classical Hinduism.

Jambudvipa (Jambudvīpa): "the island of the rose-apple tree"; ancient mythic term for India used by Jains, Buddhists, and Hindus.

Jaspers, Karl: 1883–1969, German philosopher who coined the term *die Achsenzeit*, or Axial Age, to designate the period 800–200 BCE.

jihad (jihād): literally, "struggle."

John the Baptizer: first-century Palestinian prophet and mentor of Jesus.

Joseph: according to some sources, the earthly father of Jesus.

Judas: the follower whom the New Testament considers the one who betrayed Jesus to the temple authorities.

junzi (*jūnzi*): the gentleman or noble man in Confucianism; the most important ideal type for Confucius.

Kaaba: literally, "the house of god"; the shrine at the center of the Great Mosque of Makkah, the holiest site in the Muslim faith.

kahin: in pre-Islamic Arabia, an oracle or shaman. (Plural: *kahanah*)

karma: in Indian thought, an action and its consequences.

karuna: the Pali word for compassion.

keen discernment: the Confucian term for forestalling reflexive actions to obtain a clearer understanding of one's limitations and abilities.

Khadija bint Khuwaylid: Muhammad's first wife.

khalif: successor to the Prophet in Islam.

Kisagotami: a young woman who begs the Buddha to bring her dead son back to life; the Buddha instructs her to find a mustard seed from a home that has never been touched by death.

Kongqiū: Confucius's given name. *Kong* translates loosely to "gratitude for an answered prayer" and *qiū* translates to "hill."

Kongzi: "Master Kong"; traditional Chinese title for Confucius.

Kshatriyas (**Kṣatriyas**): the Indian caste of warriors and administrators.

K'ung-fu-tzu: literally, "Mister K'ung"; the honorific that was Latinized into "Confucius."

Kushinagara: northeastern Indian village near the site of the Buddha's parinibbana, or final liberation.

Laozi: the legendary founder of Daoism and the traditional author of the *Daodejing*.

Legalism: an ancient Chinese philosophical school opposed to Confucianism; embraced by the Qin Dynasty, Legalism favored absolutism and the welfare of the state above the welfare of the people.

li: originally, the Chinese term for religious rituals and ceremonies. Confucius broadened the term to include everyday behavior and manners.

LORD: English translation for the Jewish god Yahweh.

Lu: home province of Confucius.

Lumbini: legendary birthplace of the Buddha.

Lunyu: the Chinese name for Confucius's *Analects*.

Madinah: the adopted home and burial place of the Prophet Muhammad.

magi: word for priests in Zoroastrianism.

Mahamaya, Queen: according to Buddhist tradition, the wife of King Suddhodhana and mother of Siddhattha Gotama. Queen Mahamaya died seven days after the birth of Siddhattha, who was then raised by Queen Mahaprajapati, Mahamaya's sister.

Mahaprajapati, Queen: Siddhattha Gotama's foster mother and aunt, she became the first Buddhist nun.

Mahavira (Mahāvīra): the "Great Hero"; a traditional title for Vardhamāna, the twenty-fourth Tirthankara of Jainism.

Mahayana (Mahāyāna): Sanskrit term for the "Great Vehicle"; a branch of Buddhism that developed in the early centuries CE and that brought a new understanding of the Buddha and the nature of liberation.

Makkah: the birthplace of the Prophet Muhammad and the holiest city in Islam.

mandate of heaven: in Chinese thought, the moral authority by which the ruler rules. The concept—believed to have been first articulated by the Dan, the Duke of Zhou—was used to justify the Zhou overthrow of the Shang Dynasty; Chinese: *tiānming*.

mantra: a sound or phrase embodying sacred power, often repeated for spiritual benefits.

Mara: the tempter, in Buddhism.

Mencius (Mengzi): 372-289 BCE, early Confucian philosopher who argued for the innate goodness of human beings.

metaphysics: the study of the fundamental character and qualities of reality, including the origin of the universe and the nature of the divine.

metta: Pali term for lovingkindness.

Middle Way: the course of life promoted by the Buddha in which one avoids the extremes of indulgence and deprivation.

Miriam of Magdala (Mary Magdalene): one of Jesus's most important followers, sometimes associated with him in a romantic sense.

Mohism: school of Chinese philosophy developed by Mozi. In contrast to Confucianism, Mohism advocated the universal love of humanity.

moksha (*mokśa*): release or liberation from the wheel of samsara in Hinduism.

Moses: legendary hero who led the ancient Israelites out Egyptian slavery under the auspices of the god Yahweh.

Mozi: Chinese philosopher who advocated "impartial caring" or "universal love" and criticized Confucius's belief that one should love others in proportion to the benefit one receives from them.

muruwah (*murūwah*): often translated as "manliness"; the Arabic cultural virtue encompassing courage, resilience, a willingness to avenge wrongdoing, and the defense of the weak.

mushaf: the printed form of the Qur'an.

Nazareth: village in Galilee and hometown of Jesus.

nibbana (*nibbāna*): Pali term for the end of suffering and rebirth; Sanskrit: nirvāna.

Night Journey: one of the Prophet Muhammad's spiritual experiences, in which he visited Jerusalem and spoke with Allah's previous prophets, including Abraham, Moses, and Jesus.

no-self, not-self: the Buddha's denial of a permanent, substantial self or soul; Pali: *anatta*, Sanskrit: *anātman*.

Noble Eightfold Path: the Buddha's prescription for realizing nibbana, includes right understanding, right intentions, right speech, right action, right livelihood, right effort, right concentration, and right mindfulness.

One Hundred Schools of Thought: Chinese era during the late Spring and Autumn and Warring States periods in which many schools of philosophy were established, including Confucianism and Daoism.

oracle: a communication from the spirit world, or the medium of that communication.

Pali (**Pāli**): a simplified vernacular form of Sanskrit in which the discourses of the Buddha were first written.

Pali Canon: the earliest collection of Buddhist scriptures, comprising the Suttas (discourses) the Vinaya (monastic rules), and Abhidhamma (the codification of the Dhamma).

parinibbana (*parinibbāna*): the final liberation of a fully realized person.

Passover: The Jewish festival commemorating the escape from Egyptian domination.

Pharisees: Jewish sect that arose in the second century BCE and is the ancestor of modern rabbinic Judaism. Its members believed in the importance of the Oral Torah (later written down as the *Mishnah*), the primacy of scriptural study over temple sacrifice, and the resurrection of the dead.

polygyny: the marriage of one man to more than one woman.

Presley, Elvis: the undisputed king of rock and roll.

prophet: one who speaks for the god, often urging people back to an authentic form of religious practice at a time when religion has become corrupt.

Q (*Quelle*): lost source text used by the authors of the Gospels of Matthew and Luke.

Qin Dynasty: the period of Chinese history between the Zhou and Han Dynasties; from to 221 to 206 BCE; during the Qin, China was unified and Legalism was the dominant philosophy.

quiet sitting: the Confucian term for introspection or meditative practice.

Qur'an: the central sacred text of Islam, accepted by all its traditions as the revealed word of Allah to Muhammad.

Quraysh: prominent Makkan tribe and the custodians of the Kaaba.

rabbi: teacher in Judaism.

Rahula (Rāhula): the son of Siddhattha Gotama; later a Buddhist monk.

rakaʻah: in Islam, a formal unit of prayer that begins with the first sura of the Qur'an.

Ramadan (Ramadān): the Muslim holy month of fasting; the ninth month of the Muslim calendar.

rasul: the Arabic word for "messenger"; in the context of Islam, a prophet who is given a major revelation through the angel Gabriel.

ren: humanity or humaneness; in Confucianism, the chief virtue of the morally perfect individual.

renunciation: to relinquish; in the South Asian context, renunciation is giving up home, possessions, social standing, and family ties to "go forth" into the world to seek liberation from samsara.

ritual purity: the state of cleanliness that is necessary for being in the presence of the sacred.

rose-apple tree: a south and southeast Asian tree with small, edible fruits. It was under this variety of tree that Siddhattha Gotama had his first meditation experience as a boy.

Rumi, Jalal ad-Din Muhammad (Rūmī, Jalāl ad-Dīn Muhammad): 1207–1273, Muslim mystic and poet.

Sadducees: Jewish sect that arose in the second century BCE and promoted traditional temple-centered worship and the authority of the priestly class over the scholarly (rabbinic) class.

sage (*sheng ren*): in Confucian philosophy, an individual of great compassion and wisdom.

Sahih Bukhari: compiled by Muhammad al-Bukhari, the collection of *hadith* considered most authoritative by Sunni Muslims.

Sakya (*Sākya*): the clan of Siddhattha Gotama.

samana: Pali term for a wandering ascetic. Sanskrit: *shramana*.

***samsara* (*samsāra*)**: the term for rebirth; literally, "meandering," suggesting an aimless, meaningless process.

sangha: the Buddhist community of monks and nuns.

Sarah: according to the book of Genesis, the chief wife of Abraham.

Second Great Awakening: Siddhattha Gotama's enlightenment, the moment he earned the title of Buddha.

Shabbat: the Jewish sabbath day, celebrated from sundown Friday to sundown Saturday.

shahadah: the Muslim profession of faith: "I bear witness that there is no god but Allah and that Muhammad is his messenger."

shalom: Hebrew term for the condition of peace, plenty, and well-being.

Shang Di: name for the high god of early Chinese religion; also known as Di.

Shang Dynasty: ca. 1500-1045 BCE; the earliest Chinese dynasty for which there is historical evidence.

shen: spirits, the minor deities of ancient Chinese religion.

Shi'a: Muslims who consider Ali, Muhammad's cousin, his first official successor, rather than Abu Bakr. They constitute 15 to 20 percent of the present Muslim population.

shirk: connecting with Allah something that is less than ultimate, or giving to something less than ultimate what belongs to Allah alone. According to Islam, persisting in *shirk* is the only unpardonable sin.

shu: Chinese word for "reciprocity."

Shudras (Śudras): the lowest of the four varnas in India; the caste of peasants and servants.

Sicarii: violent anti-Roman Jewish sect of the first century CE believed to be named for the daggers (*sica*) they carried.

Siddhattha: the given name of the one who became the Buddha; "Siddhattha" means "he who attains the goal."

Sima Qian: ca. 145-185 BCE, a court historian of the Han Dynasty who wrote the first biography of Confucius.

son of man: Jewish concept of the individual who appears at the apocalypse as a divine judge; the title Jesus most often applied to himself in the Gospel of Mark.

spiritual discipline: set of practices designed as a part of the means of attaining full humanity and relating to the ultimate reality.

Spring and Autumn Period: the first of two eras of the Eastern Zhou Dynasty in China, ca. 722-481 BCE.

stupa (stūpa): a Buddhist reliquary.

Suddhodhana, King: legendary ruler of the Sakya Kingdom; husband of Queen Mahamaya and Queen Mahaprajapati and father of Siddhattha Gotama.

Sunni: Muslims who consider Abu Bakr to be Muhammad's first official successor. They constitute 80–85 percent of the present Muslim population.

sura: a chapter of the Qur'an.

Suttas: the discourses of Buddha; the first "basket" of the Pali Canon.

synoptic gospels: the collective name for the Gospels of Matthew, Mark, and Luke.

Tanakh: the Hebrew Bible; acronym of the first Hebrew letter of each of three traditional subdivisions of the scripture: Torah ("Teaching"), Nevi'im ("Prophets"), and Ketuvim ("Writings").

tanha: Pali term for craving; literally, "thirst."

tawaf: circumambulations of the Kaaba.

tawhid: often translated as "unity"; the Muslim doctrine that Allah is not simply one but is unique and incomparable.

Theravada (Theravāda): the "way of the elders"; the oldest extant variety of Buddhism; also called "Southern Buddhism" because of its prominence in South and Southeast Asia.

three marks of existence: in Buddha's teaching, the three basic qualities of the world: impermanence, insubstantiality, and insatiability.

tian (*tiān*): Chinese for "heaven," the spiritual realm. It was sometimes conceived of as a force and sometimes as a being.

transmigration of the soul: reincarnation as understood in Hinduism.

Trinity: the orthodox Christian doctrine that god is three "persons": Father, Son, and Holy Spirit.

Triple Refuge: a statement of Buddhist identity: "I take refuge in the Buddha; I take refuge in the Dhamma; and I take refuge in the Sangha."

Ubbiri: one of several grieving mothers whom the Buddha helped to cope with the death of her child.

ummah: the Muslim community of the faithful.

'umrah: the "lesser pilgrimage"; a pilgrimage to Makkah that contains fewer ritual elements than the Hajj and may be performed at any time of the year.

Upali: the Buddhist arahant who recited the Vinaya at the first Buddhist council following the Buddha's death.

Upanishads (Upaniṣads): a collection of early Hindu writings in which the ideas of transmigration of the soul and the identity of Brahman and atman are first proposed.

Vaishyas (Vaiśyas): the caste of farmers, cattle herders, artisans, and businesspeople.

Vajrayana (Vajrayāna): a form of Buddhism practiced mainly in Tibet and Mongolia; literally, the "diamond" or "thunderbolt" vehicle.

Veda: sacred wisdom believed to have been revealed to ancient rishis. The Veda is now regarded as the most sacred of Hindu scriptures.

Vesak: annual festival that celebrates the birth, awakening, and parinibbana of the Buddha.

via negativa: the way of negation; a theological technique of referring to ultimate reality by saying what it is not.

Vinaya: the Buddhist monastic rule; the second "basket" of the Pali Canon.

Warring States Period: the second of the two eras of the Eastern Zhou Dynasty in China, 475 or 403 until 221 BCE; a time in which the warlords of small feudal kingdoms sought to annex other states to extend and consolidate their power.

Wen, King: the "Cultured King," symbolic first ruler of the Zhou Dynasty.

Western Zhou: see Zhou Dynasty.

wisdom: in Buddhism, to see the world as it is.

Wu, King: "Martial King," the ruler who led the overthrow of Shang rulers and established the Zhou Dynasty of China; son of King Wen.

Wu Jing: the "Five Classics"; used by Confucianism as a basis for study; includes the *Book of Songs* (*Shī Jīng*), the *Book of Changes* (*Yì Jīng*), the *Book of Rites* (*Lî Jīng*), the *Book of History* (*Shū Jīng*), and the *Spring and Autumn Annals* (*Lín Jīng*).

Xia Dynasty: legendary first dynasty of ancient China.

Xunzi: ca. 310—ca. 235 BCE, early Confucian philosopher who argued against the innate goodness of humanity.

Yashodhara (**Yaśodhara**): wife of Siddhattha Gotama; mother of Rahula; later a Buddhist nun.

Yijing (*Yì Jīng*): the *Classic of Changes*, the ancient Chinese book of divination.

yoga: a discipline for the purposes of enlightenment and liberation. Yoga literally means "yoke."

Zealots: an aggressively anti-Roman Jewish political sect active between the first century BCE and the first century CE.

zhongguo (*zhōngguó*): literally, "central kingdom"; a name for the ancient Chinese kingdom in the Yellow River Valley.

Zhou (Zhōu) Dynasty: the period of Chinese history between the Shang and the Qin Dynasties; 1045–221 BCE; divided into the Western and Eastern Zhou in 771 BCE when invaders forced the move of the capital eastward.

Zoroaster: ancient Iranian prophet who maintained that the cosmos was the battleground of the powers of good and evil. Modern scholarship suggests he might have lived any time between 1700 and 600 BCE.

BIBLIOGRAPHY

Works Cited

Abdel Haleem, M. A., trans. *The Qur'an*. Oxford: Oxford University Press. 2004.

Adler, Joseph Alan. *Chinese Religious Traditions*. Upper Saddle River, NJ: Prentice Hall, 2002.

Ahmad, Mirza Tahir. *Revelation, Rationality, Knowledge, and Truth*. Surrey, UK: Islam International, 1998.

Ahmed, Leila. *Women and Gender in Islam: Historical Roots of a Modern Debate*. New Haven: Yale University Press, 1993.

Al-Gailani, Noorah, and Chris Smith. *The Islamic Year: Surahs, Stories, and Celebrations*. Stroud, UK: Hawthorn, 2003.

Ali, Abdullah Yusuf, trans. *The Holy Qur'an*. Hertfordshire, UK: Wordsworth, 2000.

Al-Oadah, Salman Bin Fahad. *Alleviating the Difficulties of the Hajj*. Riyadh, Saudi Arabia: Islam Today Foundation, 2006.

Alsop, Stewart. *Stay of Execution: A Sort of Memoir*. Philadelphia: Lippincott, 1973.

Andrae, Tor. *Mohammed, the Man and His Faith*. Translated by Theophil Menzel. London: Allen & Unwin, 1936.

Armstrong, Karen. *Muhammad: A Biography of the Prophet*. New York: HarperOne, 1993.

Bartlett, Robert C., and Susan D. Collins, trans. *Aristotle's Nicomachean Ethics*, by Aristotle. Chicago: University of Chicago Press, 2012.

Bodhi, Bhikkhu, trans. *The Connected Discourses of the Buddha: A Translation of the Saṃyutta Nikāya*. Boston: Wisdom, 2000.

———, trans. *In the Buddha's Words: An Anthology of Discourses from the Pali Canon*. Boston: Wisdom, 2005.

Bly, Robert, trans. *The Kabir Book: Forty-four of the Ecstatic Poems of Kabir*. Boston: Beacon, 1977.

Brooks, E. Bruce, and A. Taeko Brooks, trans. *The Original Analects: Sayings of Confucius and His Successors*. Translations from the Asian Classics. New York: Columbia University Press, 1998.

Bryant, Edwin. *The Quest for the Origins of Vedic Culture: The Indo-Aryan Migration Debate*. Oxford: Oxford University Press, 2001.

Buyukcelebi, Ismail. *Living in the Shade of Islam*. Translated by Ali Unal. Rutherford, NJ: The Light, 2005.

Cage, John. *Silence: Lectures and Writings*. Middletown, CT: Wesleyan University Press, 1961.

Chin, Annping. *The Authentic Confucius: A Life of Thought and Politics*. New York: Scribner, 2007.

Cleary, Thomas, trans. *The Qur'an: A New Translation*. Chicago: Starlatch, 2004.

Conze, Edward, trans. *Buddhist Scriptures*. Penguin Classics. Harmondsworth, UK: Penguin, 1959.

Colledge, Edmund, and Bernard McGinn, trans. *The Essential Sermons, Commentaries, Treatises and Defense*, by Meister Eckhart. Classics of Western Spirituality 28. New York: Paulist, 1981.

Cook, David. *Understanding Jihad*. Berkeley: University of California Press, 2005.

Dawson, Raymond, trans. *The Analects*. World's Classics. Oxford: Oxford University Press, 1993.

De Bary, William Theodore, and Irene Bloom, comps. *Sources of Chinese Tradition*. 2 vols. 2nd ed. Introduction to Asian Civilization. New York: Columbia University Press, 1999.

Durant, Will. *The Story of Philosophy: The Lives and Opinions of the Greater Philosophers*. New York: Simon & Schuster, 1926.

Einstein, Albert. Letter to Robert S. Marcus, 12 February 1950. http://www.lettersofnote.com/2011/11/delusion.html.

Eisenman, Robert H. *James, the Brother of Jesus: The Key to Unlocking the Secrets of Early Christianity and the Dead Sea Scrolls*. New York: Viking, 1997.

Epstein, Mark. *Open to Desire: The Truth about What the Buddha Taught*. New York: Gotham Books, 2006.

Esposito, John. *Islam: The Straight Path*. 3rd ed. New York: Oxford University Press, 2004.

Feldman, Christina, and Jack Kornfield. *Stories of the Spirit, Stories of the Heart: Parables of the Spiritual Path from around the World*. San Francisco: HarperSanFrancisco, 1991.

Fingarette, Herbert. *The Secular as Sacred*. Long Grove, IL: Waveland, 1998.

Glassé, Cyril. *The Concise Encyclopedia of Islam*. San Francisco: Harper & Row, 1989.

Graham, A. C. *Disputers of the Dao: Philosophical Argument in Ancient China*. Chicago: Open Court, 1989.

Guillaume, A., trans. *The Life of Muhammad: A Translation of Ibn Ishaq's Sirat Rasul Allah*, by Abd Al-Malik Ibn Hisham. Oxford: Oxford University Press, 1955. Reprinted, 2002.

Hart, Michael H. *The 100: A Ranking of the Most Influential Persons in History*. Rev. ed. New York: Citadel, 1992.

Hick, John. *An Interpretation of Religion: Human Responses to the Transcendent*. New Haven: Yale University Press, 1989.

Hoffer, Eric. *The True Believer: Thoughts on the Nature of Mass Movements*. New York: Harper, 1951.

Huang, Chichung, trans. *The Analects of Confucius*. New ed. New York: Oxford University Press, 1997.

Ivanhoe, Philip J., trans. *The Daodejing of Laozi*. New York: Seven Bridges, 2002.

Izutsu, Toshihiko. *Ethico-religious Concepts in the Qur'an*. McGill Islamic Studies 1. Montreal: McGill University Institute of Islamic Studies, McGill University Press, 1966.

Jensen, Lionel. *Manufacturing Confucianism: Chinese Traditions and Universal Civilization.* Durham, NC: Duke University Press, 1997.

Khattab, Nasiruddin, trans. *English Translation of Musnad Imam Ahmad Bin Hanbal.* Riyadh, Saudi Arabia: Darussalam, 2012.

Kierkegaard, Søren. *Concluding Unscientific Postscript to Philosophical Fragments.* Translated by David F. Swensen. Princeton: Princeton University Press, 1941, 1968.

Kurzweil, Arthur, *On the Road with Rabbi Steinsaltz: 25 Years of Pre-Dawn Car Trips, Mind-Blowing Encounters, and Inspiring Conversations with a Man of Wisdom.* San Francisco: Jossey-Bass, 2006.

Lau, D. C., trans. *The Analects,* by Confucius. Penguin Classics. London: Penguin, 1979.

————, trans. *Mencius.* London: Penguin, 1970.

Lawrence, Bruce B. *The Qur'an: A Biography.* New York: Atlantic Monthly Press, 2006.

Legge, James, trans. *The Chinese Classics.* Vol. 4, *The She king.* Hong Kong: Hong Kong University Press, 1960.

Legge, James, and James H. Ford, trans. *The Teachings of Confucius: The Analects, the Great Learning, the Doctrine of the Mean.* El Paso: El Paso Norte, 2005.

Lewis, Bernard. *What Went Wrong? The Clash between Islam and Modernity in the Middle East.* New York: Harper Perennial, 2003.

————. *The Political Language of Islam.* Chicago: University of Chicago Press, 1988.

Lings, Martin. *Muhammad: His Life Based on the Earliest Sources.* 2nd ed. Rochester, VT: Inner Traditions, 2006.

Locke, John. *The Reasonableness of Christianity, and A Discourse on Miracles, and part of A Third Letter concerning Toleration.* Library of Modern Religious Thought. Stanford: Stanford University Press, 1958.

Mascaró, Juan, trans. *The Upanishads.* Penguin Classics. Harmondsworth, UK: Penguin, 1965.

Maugham, W. Somerset. *The Razor's Edge: A Novel.* Garden City, NY: Doubleday, Doran, 1944.

McCracken, Peggy, trans. *Barlaam & Josaphat: A Medieval Christian Tale of the Buddha,* by Gui de Cambrai. Penguin Classics. New York: Penguin, 2014.

McLuhan, Marshall. *Understanding Media: The Extensions of Man.* New York: Signet Books, 1964.

Miller, Robert J., ed. *The Complete Gospels: Annotated Scholars Version.* Rev. ed. New York: HarperOne, 1994.

Muesse, Mark W. "Crossing Boundaries: When Founders of Faith Appear in Other Traditions," in Patrick Gray, ed., *Varieties of Religious Invention: Founders and Their Functions in History.* New York: Oxford University Press, 2015, 175-192.

Ñāṇamoli, Bhikkhu. *The Life of the Buddha according to the Pali Canon.* Onalaska, WA: BPS Pariyatti, 2001.

Ñāṇamoli, Bhikkhu, and Bhikkhu Bodhi, trans. *The Middle Length Discourses of the Buddha.* Boston: Wisdom, 1995.

Ñāṇamoli, Bhikkhu, and Bhikkhu Bodhi, trans. *Numerical Discourses of the Buddha.* International Sacred Literature Trust Series. Walnut Creek, CA: AltaMira, 1999.

Phipps, William E. *Muhammad and Jesus: A Comparison of the Prophets and Their Teachings.* New York: Paragon, 1995.

————. *Was Jesus Married?* New York: Harper & Row, 1970.

Pseudo-Dionysius. "The Mystical Theology." In *The Complete Works*, 135–41. Translated by Colm Luibheid and Paul Rorem. Classics of Western Spirituality. New York: Paulist, 1988.

Ramadan, Tariq. *In the Footsteps of the Prophet: Lessons from the Life of Muhammad.* Oxford: Oxford University Press, 2007.

Rodinson, Maxime. *Muhammad: Prophet of Islam.* New York: Pantheon, 1980.

Santayana, George. *The Life of Reason, or, The Phases of Human Progress.* New York: Scribner, 1954.

Schuon, Frithjof. *The Transcendent Unity of Religions.* Wheaton, IL: Quest, 1984.

Schwartz, Benjamin I. *The World of Thought in Ancient China.* Cambridge, MA: Belknap, 1985.

Shaw, George Bernard. *Saint Joan: A Chronicle Play in Six Scenes and an Epilogue* (1924). http://faculty.smu.edu/bwheeler/joan_of_arc/olr/07_saintjoan_gbshaw.pdf.

Slingerland, Edward, trans. *Analects: With Selections from Traditional Commentaries,* by Confucius. Indianapolis: Hackett, 2003.

Smith, Jane Idleman. *Islamic Understanding of Death and Resurrection.* Oxford: Oxford University Press, 2002.

Starr, Kenneth. *Communication from Kenneth W. Starr, Independent Counsel, Transmitting a Referral to the United States House of Representatives Filed in Conformity with the Requirements of Title 28, United States Code, Section 595(c)* (Washington, DC: U.S. Government Printing Office, 1998), 125n1091.

Steinberg, Michael. *The Symphony: A Listener's Guide.* New York: Oxford University Press, 1995.

Sultan, Sohaib N. *The Qur'an and Sayings of Prophet Muhammad: Selections Annotated and Explained.* Woodstock, VT: SkyLight Paths, 2007.

Suzuki, Shunryu, and Trudy Dixon. *Zen Mind, Beginner's Mind.* New York: Weatherhill, 1970.

Tillich, Paul. *Systematic Theology.* Vol. 1, *Reason and Revelation. Being and God.* Chicago: University of Chicago Press, 1973.

United Nations Office of Public Information. *The Universal Declaration of Human Rights.* New York: 1958, http://www.un.org/en/universal-declaration-human-rights/.

Van Norden, Bryan W., trans. *Mengzi, with Selections from Traditional Commentaries,* by Mencius. Indianapolis: Hackett, 2008.

Vermès, Géza. *Jesus the Jew: A Historian's Reading of the Gospels.* Philadelphia: Fortress, 1981.

Waley, Arthur, trans. *The Book of Songs.* New York: Grove Press, 1960.

Wallis, Glenn, trans. *Basic Teachings of the Buddha.* Modern Library Classics. New York: Modern Library, 2007.

Walshe, Maurice, trans. *The Long Discourses of the Buddha: A Translation of the Dīgha Nikāya.* Boston: Wisdom, 1995.

Wang, Xianqian, and Xunzi. *Xunzi Jijie.* Beijing: Zhonghua Shuju, 1954.

Watt, W. Montgomery. *Muhammad: Prophet and Statesman.* London: Oxford University Press, 1961.

Wrede, William. *The Messianic Secret.* Translated by J. C. G. Greig. Library of Theological Translations. Greenwood, SC: Attic, 1971.

Watson, Burton, trans. *Xunzi: Basic Writings.* Translations from Asian Classics. New York: Columbia University Press, 2003.

X, Malcolm. *The Autobiography of Malcolm X: As Told to Alex Haley*. New York: Ballantine, 1992.

Yu-lan, Fung. *A History of Chinese Philosophy*. Vol. 1, *The Period of the Philosophers*. Translated by Derk Bodde. Princeton: Princeton University Press, 1952.

For Further Study

Confucius

Ames, Roger T., and Henry Rosemont Jr., trans. *The Analects of Confucius: A Philosophical Translation*. Classics of Ancient China. New York: Ballantine, 1998.

Berthrong, John H., and Evelyn Nagai Berthrong. *Confucianism: A Short Introduction*. Oxford: Oneworld, 2000.

Hall, David L., and Roger T. Ames. *Thinking through Confucius*. SUNY Series in Systematic Philosophy. Albany: State University of New York Press, 1987.

Ivanhoe, Philip J. *Confucian Moral Self Cultivation*. 2nd ed. Indianapolis: Hackett, 2000.

Ivanhoe, Philip J., and Bryan W. Van Norden. *Readings in Classical Chinese Philosophy*. New York: Seven Bridges, 2001.

Poo, Mu-Chou. *In Search of Personal Welfare: A View of Ancient Chinese Religion*. SUNY Series in Chinese Philosophy and Culture. Albany: State University of New York Press, 1998.

Tu, Weiming, and Mary Evelyn Tucker, eds. *Confucian Spirituality*, Vol. 1. World Spirituality 11-A. New York: Crossroad, 2003.

Van Norden, Bryan W., ed. *Confucius and the Analects: New Essays*. Oxford: Oxford University Press, 2002.

The Buddha

Access to Insight. http://www.accesstoinsight.org/.

Armstrong, Karen. *Buddha*. New York: Penguin, 2001.

Bodhi, Bhikkhu. *The Noble Eightfold Path: The Way to the End of Suffering*. Kandy, Sri Lanka: Buddhist Publication Society, 1994, http://www.vipassana.com/resources/8fpo.php/.

Carrithers, Michael. *The Buddha: A Very Short Introduction*. Very Short Introductions 41. Oxford: Oxford University Press, 1996.

Collins, Steven. *Selfless Persons: Imagery and Thought in Theravada Buddhism*. Cambridge: Cambridge University Press, 1982.

Dhamma, Rewata. *The First Discourse of the Buddha*. Boston: Wisdom, 1997.

Fronsdal, Gil, trans. *Dhammapada: A New Translation of the Buddhist Classic with Annotations*. Boston: Shambhala, 2005.

Gethin, Rupert, ed. and trans. *Sayings of the Buddha: New Translations from the Pali Nikayas*. Oxford World's Classics. Oxford: Oxford University Press, 2008.

Harvey, Peter. *An Introduction to Buddhism: Teachings, History, and Practices*. Cambridge: Cambridge University Press, 1990.

Holder, John J., ed. and trans. *Early Buddhist Discourses*. Cambridge: Hackett, 2006.

Mitchell, Robert Allen. *The Buddha: His Life Retold*. New York: Paragon, 1989.

Nelson, Walter Henry. *Buddha: His Life and His Teachings*. New York: Putnam, 1996.
Rahula, Walpola. *What the Buddha Taught*. New York: Grove Press, 1959.

Jesus

Borg, Marcus. *Jesus: Uncovering the Life, Teachings, and Relevance of a Religious Revolutionary*. New York: HarperCollins, 2006.
Borg, Marcus, and John Dominic Crossan. *The Last Week: What the Gospels Really Teach about Jesus's Final Days in Jerusalem*. New York: HarperOne, 2007.
Borg, Marcus, and N. T. Wright. *The Meaning of Jesus: Two Visions*. 2nd ed. New York: HarperOne, 2007.
Craffert, Pieter. *The Life of a Galilean Shaman: Jesus of Nazareth in Anthropological-Historical Perspective*. Matrix 3. Eugene, OR: Cascade Books, 2008.
Crossan, John Dominic. *The Historical Jesus: The Life of a Mediterranean Jewish Peasant*. San Francisco: Harper, 1993.
Early Christian Writings. Historical Jesus Theories. http://www.earlychristianwritings. com/theories.html.
Ehrman, Bart D. *Jesus: Apocalyptic Prophet of the New Millennium*. New York: Oxford University Press, 2001.
Fredriksen, Paula. *Jesus of Nazareth, King of the Jews: A Jewish Life and the Emergence of Christianity*. New York: Vintage, 2000.
Frontline. *From Jesus to Christ*. http://www.pbs.org/wgbh/pages/frontline/shows/religion/.
Johnson, Luke Timothy. *The Real Jesus: The Misguided Quest for the Historical Jesus and the Truth of the Traditional Gospels*. New York: HarperOne, 1997.
Kloppenborg, John S. *Q, the Earliest Gospel: An Introduction to the Original Stories and Sayings of Jesus*. Louisville: Westminster John Knox, 2008.
Miles, Jack. *Christ: A Crisis in the Life of God*. New York: Vintage, 2002.
Oakman, Douglas E. *The Political Aims of Jesus*. Minneapolis: Fortress, 2012.
Pelikan, Jaroslav. *Jesus through the Centuries: His Place in the History of Culture*. New Haven: Yale University Press, 1999.
Sanders, E. P. *The Historical Figure of Jesus*. New York: Penguin, 1996.
Schweitzer, Albert. *The Quest of the Historical Jesus*. New York: Macmillan, 1968.
Vermes, Geza. *Jesus in His Jewish Context*. Minneapolis: Fortress, 2003.
———. *The Religion of Jesus the Jew*. Minneapolis: Fortress, 1993.

Muhammad

Bennett, Clinton. *In Search of Muhammad*. London: Continuum, 1998.
Cleary, Thomas, trans. *The Wisdom of the Prophet: Sayings of Muhammad, Selections from the Hadith*. Shambhala Pocket Classics. Boston: Shambhala, 2001.
Emerick, Yahiya. *The Life and Work of Muhammad*. Indianapolis: Alpha, 2002.
Ibrahaim, Ezzeddin, and Denys Johnson-Davies, trans. *An-Nawawi's Forty Hadith: An Anthology of the Sayings of the Prophet Muhammad*. Cambridge: The Islamic Texts Society, 1997.